Intellectua

This book addresses several aspects of the law and economics of ... ...ual property rights (IPRs) that have been underanalyzed in the existing literature. It begins with a brief overview of patents, trade secrets, copyrights, and trademarks, and the enforcement and licensing of IPRs, focusing on the remedies available for infringement (injunctions, various forms of damages, and damages calculation issues); the standard of care (strict liability versus an intent- or negligence-based standard); and the rules for determining standing to sue and joinder of defendant for IPR violations. The authors demonstrate that the core assumption of IPR regimes – that IPRs maximize certain social benefits over social costs by providing a necessary inducement for the production and distribution of intellectual property – have several important implications for the optimal design of remedies, the standard of care, and the law of standing and joinder. They also demonstrate that many, though not all, of the variations in the ways that different bodies of IPR law handle these problems are consistent with a social value maximization approach that is tailored to the specific problems addressed by these different bodies of law.

Roger D. Blair is Huber Hurst Professor of Economics at the University of Florida, which he joined in 1970. He teaches courses in antitrust economics, law and economics, and the economics of sports. He has published extensively, including books, chapters in books, and articles in economic journals and law reviews. Among the books that he has coauthored are *Antitrust Economics, Law and Economics of Vertical Integration and Control* and *Monopsony: Antitrust Law and Economics*. Professor Blair has served as an antitrust consultant to the U.S. Department of Justice; the Federal Trade Commission; the Attorneys General of California, Arizona, Missouri, Oregon, Washington, and Florida; and numerous corporations.

Thomas F. Cotter is a Professor of Law, University of Florida Research Foundation Professor, and the Director of the Intellectual Property Program at the University of Florida Frederic G. Levin College of Law. He served as Senior Articles Editor of the *Wisconsin Law Review* and clerked for the Honorable Lawrence W. Pierce on the United States Court of Appeals for the Second Circuit. Before joining the faculty of the University of Florida in 1994, Professor Cotter practiced law at Cravath, Swaine & Moore and at Jenner & Block. He has published scholarly articles in the *California Law Review, Georgetown Law Journal, Minnesota Law Review, North Carolina Law Review,* and *William & Mary Law Review*, among others, and was the recipient of the 1996 Ladas Memorial Award for writing excellence on the subject of trademarks. Professor Cotter's current research interests center on intellectual property, international intellectual property, and law and economics.

Intellectual Property

Economic and Legal Dimensions of Rights and Remedies

ROGER D. BLAIR
University of Florida

THOMAS F. COTTER
University of Florida

CAMBRIDGE
UNIVERSITY PRESS

CAMBRIDGE UNIVERSITY PRESS
Cambridge, New York, Melbourne, Madrid, Cape Town, Singapore, São Paulo

Cambridge University Press
40 West 20th Street, New York, NY 10011-4211, USA

www.cambridge.org
Information on this title: www.cambridge.org/9780521833165

First published 2005

Printed in the United States of America

A catalog record for this publication is available from the British Library.

Library of Congress Cataloging in Publication Data
Blair, Roger D.
Intellectual property : economic and legal dimensions of rights and remedies / Roger D. Blair,
Thomas F. Cotter.
p. cm.
Includes bibliographical references and index.
ISBN 0-521-83316-7 (hardback) – ISBN 0-521-54067-4 (pbk.)
1. Intellectual property – United States. 2. Intellectual property – Economic aspects.
I. Cotter, Thomas F., 1961– II. Title.
KF2979.B55 2005
346.7304′8 – dc22 2004020379

ISBN-13 978-0-521-83316-5 hardback
ISBN-10 0-521-83316-7 hardback

ISBN-13 978-0-521-54067-4 paperback
ISBN-10 0-521-54067-4 paperback

For those who matter most in my life – my wife, Chau, my sons, Don and Dave, and their lovely families —

RDB

For my son, Alec —

TFC

Contents

Acknowledgments   *page* ix

1. Introduction   1
2. The Law and Economics of IPRs   7
3. A General Theory of Damages Rules   42
4. Departures from the General Theory   70
5. Liability Standards for IPRs   96
6. Who Is an Infringer?   132
7. Who Should Be Entitled to Sue for Infringement?   160
8. Calculating Monetary Damages   208
9. Concluding Remarks   263

Bibliography   267
Index   285

Acknowledgments

This book is the culmination of our research on the protection of intellectual property rights embodied in patent, trade secret, copyright, and trademark law. The book relies to some extent on earlier publications in the *William and Mary Law Review*, the *University of Cincinnati Law Review*, the *Tulane Law Review*, the *Texas Intellectual Property Law Journal*, and the *Berkeley Technology Law Journal*. We greatly appreciate the permissions we have received to draw upon our prior publications in writing the present book.

We also owe a debt of gratitude to many colleagues for extremely useful suggestions and for their encouragement. In particular, we want to thank, for their comments and criticism, Daralyn Durie, Jeffrey L. Harrison, Paul J. Heald, Michael Jacobs, Karl Kramer, Sumner LaCroix, Mark A. Lemley, Douglas Lichtman, Howard Lidsky, Lyrissa Barnett Lidsky, Stephen Maurer, Robert P. Merges, Gene Quinn, Margaret Radin, and John Schlicher, as well as the faculty and participants at workshops and conferences held at the University of Arizona James E. Rogers College of Law, the University of California at Berkeley School of Law (Boalt Hall), Case Western Reserve University Law School, George Mason University School of Law, and the University of Florida Fredric G. Levin College of Law. We also want to thank our research assistants over the years, in particular Jeff Boyles, Kenneth Eckstein, Bryan Gowdy, Kendra Hinton, and Craig Popalis. In addition, we received useful guidance from anonymous reviewers. Of course, these scholars must be held blameless for what follows. We retain responsibility for any remaining errors.

We received generous financial support from the Warrington College of Business Administration and the Fredric G. Levin College of Law at the University of Florida.

Finally, we would like to express our deep appreciation to our editor at Cambridge University Press, Scott Parris, who kept us going with his enthusiasm and encouragement.

ONE

Introduction

Until fairly recently, the law of intellectual property – a term that encompasses patents, trade secrets, copyrights, and trademarks, among other things – was something of a backwater. Of interest mostly to specialists within these fields, it garnered little attention from the broader legal community. Most economists manifested a similar indifference to these issues. Only a few gave serious consideration to the design of patent rights and even fewer paid much attention to trademarks or copyrights. Indeed, some law-and-economics scholars doubted that economics had much to say about any of these bodies of law.[1] Roughly within the last ten years, due in large part to the expanding role of high technology in our everyday lives, all of that has changed. The law of intellectual property – particularly patents and copyrights, but also trademarks and trade secrets and other related fields – has become a topic of major interest to lawyers, judges, and law professors. Many high-profile cases are making their way through the courts; new legislation is being introduced in many countries and international treaties are attempting to properly balance the incentives for investment against the need for access to the products of that investment, such as essential medicines. Economists have also taken up the challenge of modeling the consequences of high and low levels of protection and, to some extent, of testing these models against the empirical evidence. It is now common for leading law reviews and economics journals to publish articles on these issues – to say nothing of the popular press, with its endless fascination for such items as the attempt to patent the human genome, the ongoing controversy over the digital distribution of sound recordings and other copyrighted works,

---

[1] For example, in 1986, Yale law professor George Priest wrote that "economists can tell lawyers ultimately very little about how to enforce or interpret the law of intellectual property." See Priest (1986; 21).

and cases that push the envelope of trademark protection for remote source signifiers such as product design and color.

However, even within the burgeoning literature on the law and economics of intellectual property rights (IPRs), there is still relatively little discussion of the appropriate remedies for the infringement of patents, copyrights, trademarks, and trade secrets. There is, to be sure, a fairly widespread consensus that an injunction – an order to cease infringing – is the appropriate remedy in most cases in which the plaintiff proves that the defendant has trespassed the plaintiff's rights. But there is relatively little discussion of the law of damages, and this gap is curious. Even in a system that routinely grants injunctive relief, damages are a necessary remedy for the time period running from the beginning of the infringement to the entry of the injunction. And this may be quite a long time, depending on how difficult it is to detect infringement; the ease with which litigants may obtain preliminary injunctive relief; and the substantial time it takes for a case to go through the legal system. A system that awards very substantial damages in effect strengthens the owner's IPR, whereas a system that awards minimal or no damages, or that imposes insuperable difficulties to the proof of damages, necessarily weakens those rights. More generally, the remedies that are available for infringement in some respects drive the entire IPR system. Without effective remedies for the enforcement of these rights, the rights are worthless; on the other hand, if remedies and other enforcement mechanisms are too generous, they may cause the cost of protection to be raised to a point that outweighs the potential benefits. Inattention to remedies, in other words, can undermine the whole system, no matter how much careful thought and analysis have gone into devising the rules of substantive law.

WHERE THIS BOOK WILL TAKE US

This is the first book-length treatment of which we are aware of the law and economics of remedies and other closely-related issues in intellectual property (IP) law.[2] We begin in Chapter 2 with an overview of the law of patents, trade secrets, copyright, and trademarks, and of the economic rationales for (and critiques of) the principal features of these bodies of law. As this discussion will show, all of the various bodies of IP law ideally strike a balance between incentives (to create, to publish, to invest in product

---

[2] A just-published book by Landes and Posner presents a detailed economic analysis of many issues of IP law, but specifically disclaims a systematic analysis of the law of remedies. See Landes & Posner (2003; 7).

quality), on the one hand, and public access to the work product that results from these incentives on the other. Just where that ideal balance lies remains a matter of disagreement. Scholars are divided on the issue of how strong IPRs should be, particularly in the digital environment and with respect to new technologies. But our goal in this book is not to resolve these issues. Instead, we will assume that the policymaker has chosen a particular scope and duration for the IPR at issue, and that this choice reflects some reasoned consideration about the proper balance of social benefits and costs. We then offer some insights as to the advantages and disadvantages of different possible rules for the private enforcement of these rights in court. As we will see, some of these enforcement rules may function better than others at preserving the incentive structure embedded in the substantive law; others may be less costly to apply, but may not function as effectively at preserving that structure.

More specifically, we want to be able to answer the following sorts of questions. First, with respect to remedies, as we noted earlier, IP law evidences a marked preference for injunctive relief. Rules relating to damages and other forms of monetary relief are nevertheless also a necessary supplement, if only for those cases in which injunctive relief cannot be obtained immediately (or at all). But what sort of monetary relief should courts provide in order to preserve the incentive structure upon which the system is premised while at the same time avoiding the overdeterrence of lawful conduct? Is a lost profits or lost royalty remedy sufficient or should courts in some cases award relief in the amount of the defendant's gain instead of in the amount of the plaintiff's loss? How can one measure the amount of the plaintiff's loss (or defendant's gain) that was attributable to the act of infringement and not to other factors? If neither form of monetary relief can be calculated with confidence, should courts opt for some form of fixed or presumed damages, as in defamation cases? Is there a role for punitive or other super-compensatory relief? We address questions of this nature in Chapters 3 and 4, and then return to some measurement problems in Chapter 8.

A second set of issues with respect to enforcement relates to the proof of infringing conduct. Even if the defendant's invention, work of authorship, or trademark falls within the scope of the plaintiff's rights, should the defendant's liability be conditioned upon proof of a particular mental state (such as intent or negligence)? Or should liability in these cases be strict? U.S. IP law is often referred to as a body of strict liability law, but as we will show what we really have is a *sui generis* system in which the defendant's ability and effort to discover the plaintiff's entitlement *ex ante* has some bearing on the relief to which the plaintiff is entitled. Although the rules vary from one body of law to another, the remedies afforded for the infringement of IPRs are often conditioned upon proof of some sort of knowledge or notice or other mental state on the part of the defendant. This insight is trivially true with respect to injunctive relief. No court will enter a preliminary or permanent injunction, prospectively enjoining the defendant from infringing, unless and until the defendant has been served and has had an opportunity to be heard. But it is also, less obviously, often true with respect to damages remedies as well. Patent law, for example, conditions awards of damages upon proof of at least constructive notice (most of the time, at any rate) and copyright conditions all relief upon proof of copying (albeit sometimes unconscious copying is sufficient). Along the way, we discuss the merits and demerits of different possible liability regimes, including a "pure" strict liability regime, a negligence regime, and an intent-based regime.

A third set of issues relates to the identity of the proper parties to an infringement suit. U.S. patent law, for example, extends liability all the way down the chain of distribution by rendering manufacturers, sellers, and users jointly and severally liable, subject to the first-sale doctrine. Copyright and trademark law traditionally have limited liability to a greater extent, although some recent developments tend to move these bodies of law in the direction of the patent model. Is there any logic to the way in which these bodies of law have decided who should be responsible for the act of infringement and who should not? Similarly, is there any logic to the various ways in which IP law allocates the right to sue for infringement? Here, patent law is the most restrictive in allocating the right to sue; it essentially restricts suits to patent owners and their exclusive licensees who must join the owner as a party. Copyright law is the least restrictive and permits suits by any "beneficial owner" of a copyright interest, including owners and exclusive licensees of individual copyright rights falling short of the entire "bundle of sticks." The trademark rules are less easy to describe in a sentence or two but might be viewed as falling somewhere in between the rigorous patent and less rigorous copyright rules. Are there good reasons for these differences? Should the rules be modified? As we shall see, the answers to these questions depend in part upon the various ways in which rights may be licensed and in part on the likelihood of a right being invalidated in court, which varies from one body of law to another.

We anticipate two possible critiques of our analytical framework. One critique is that our analysis, which takes the existing scope and duration of IPRs as a given, cannot improve social welfare because the existing scope and duration of IPRs are suboptimal. To cite just a few problems, the duration of copyright is probably much longer than it needs to be under the incentive model; the optimal breadth of patents and copyrights is uncertain;

and the one-size-fits-all nature of much of patent and copyright law may be unfortunate as well, because equal terms are conferred on both high- and low-value products. To the extent that the current system is suboptimal, our suggested rules for preserving the incentive structure embedded in that system will only exacerbate the problems or not go far enough toward correcting market failures. A second critique is that, even if our task is worthwhile, it is impossible, because matters of enforcement and procedure cannot be sharply contrasted with matters of substance. This is perhaps most evident in connection with our discussion of liability standards: if a particular mental state is required (or not) for an act to be deemed infringing, then the scope of the IPR owner's rights is narrower (or broader) than if the rule were otherwise. But the point can be made in connection with the other chapters as well. A rule that awards the patent owner her lost profit confers a broader scope than does one that awards only a fraction of that lost profit, because in the latter instance some acts of infringement may be profitable to the infringer, and therefore will occur even though illegal; in effect, patent scope has been diminished under the latter rule for good or ill.

We recognize the force of these critiques, but nevertheless adhere to our basic framework for two reasons. First, while our analysis assumes the optimality of a given system of IPRs, it does not depend upon any *particular* system being optimal. In other words, even if the copyright term was shorter, the patent term was longer, and the scope of both bodies of law was more precisely calibrated with the maximization of social benefits, one would still need to confront the issues we discuss in this book. Moreover, one would – we think – still reach the same basic conclusions. Therefore, our analysis is, to borrow a metaphor from computer technology, platform-independent. As long as IP law is viewed as embodying certain incentives designed to maximize social welfare, one will need to craft enforcement rules so as not to undermine those incentives. Our analysis suggests a variety of ways of doing this, even if the current mix of incentives can itself be improved upon.[3]

---

[3] Another way of articulating our project would involve the positive/normative distinction that is commonly found in discussions of law and economics. In one sense, our analysis is largely positive, because it asks whether current enforcement and procedural rules are consistent with or help us to better understand the incentive structure that in theory is embedded in existing substantive law. Whether the existing substantive law is itself optimal is another matter. From another angle, our analysis might seem more normative, because it asks what the enforcement and procedural rules *should* look like, assuming the existence of a proper incentive structure is embedded in the substantive law. We think that the previous description of our project conveys what we intend to do and why we intend to do it, regardless of the label one chooses.

Our second response is jurisprudential. The current system may be sub-optimal and by various maneuvers one could manipulate the rules relating to enforcement to better align costs and benefits. For example, if one thinks that the patent system in its current state confers too many costs and too few benefits, one might try to remedy the situation in part by making it extremely difficult for patent owners to recover their lost profits from infringers. By tightening up judge-made rules relating to proximate cause and the like, judges could achieve precisely this end. While this step may not go very far toward improving the system, it would encourage some acts of infringement that, under this hypothesis, would be socially beneficial. As a general matter, however, we think that this sort of approach would be a bad way of attempting to correct a flawed system. For one thing, the perceived merits or demerits of the present system are likely to vary substantially from one observer to another. Any suggestion that courts should manipulate the rules of enforcement and procedure to attain desired substantive goals ultimately will be futile, if courts themselves are divided on the issue of whether IPRs are already too strong or too weak. More fundamentally, however, this view threatens to undermine the rule of law by substituting judges' idiosyncratic views of the merits of (say) the patent system for the view expressed by Congress in enacting the Patent Act. To be sure, we are not so naive as to believe that the only thing judges do is to follow the rules laid down or that Congress in enacting the Patent Act and its many amendments has been motivated exclusively by concern for the public interest. Judges are policymakers and Congress often responds more to interest-group pressure than to considerations of the public good (to say nothing of the difficulty of ascribing a motive to a collective body, such as Congress, at all). But there is an institutional concern in operation here. Warts and all, legislative bodies are probably the best place for the fundamental decisions about the scope and duration of IPRs to be debated and resolved (barring some constitutional constraint upon legislative power, as may occur when IPRs come up against principles such as freedom of speech). We believe that, as a general matter, courts *ought* to operate as if the intellectual property laws embody the proper balance when deciding how to best calculate damages or craft standing and joinder rules, or the like, and leave it to other branches of government to decide whether the underlying assumption is true or false. That is the premise, at least, upon which this book is based.

TWO

The Law and Economics of IPRs

In this chapter, we provide an overview of basic patent, trade secret, copyright, and trademark law, and a general sense of the ways in which courts enforce these rights. Our principal focus will be on U.S. law, although from time to time we will examine other countries' laws and how they sometimes differ from U.S. law. With respect to each of these four bodies of law, we first provide a brief description of the legal rights at issue, and then follow with a discussion of the standard economic justifications for, and challenges to, these rights. Finally, we review the debate over whether intellectual property rights (IPRs) are better protected by property or liability rules.

PATENTS AND TRADE SECRETS

Inventions and other industrial know-how sometimes may be subject to ownership under patent or trade secret law.[1] Because the same invention may not be protected by both patent and trade secret law, and because patents usually confer a more robust form of protection, an inventor will usually choose patent over trade secret protection when either is available. In this section, we examine the scope of these bodies of law and their suggested economic underpinnings.

---

[1] To be precise, inventions are protectable under the law of utility patents. Novel and distinct plant varieties are patentable in the United States for the same twenty-year period applicable to utility patents, under the Plant Patent Act, 35 U.S.C. §§ 161–4, and the Plant Variety Protection Act, 7 U.S.C. §§ 2321–2582. Plants also may be protected under utility patent law. See *J.E.M. AG Supply, Inc. v. Pioneer Hi-Bred Int'l, Inc.*, 534 U.S. 124 (2001). Designs that satisfy the three conditions of novelty, ornamentality, and nonobviousness are protectable for a fourteen-year period under the law of design patents, see 35 U.S.C. §§ 171–3. Other countries have analogous laws extending patent-like or *sui generis* protection to plant varieties and designs. Our discussion in this section centers upon the law of utility patents.

PATENT LAW

To qualify for patent protection, an invention must fall within the scope of patentable subject matter (a machine, process, manufacture, or composition of matter) and must meet the three statutory criteria of novelty, utility, and nonobviousness.[2] In the United States, the *novelty* requirement is normally satisfied as long as the patent applicant was the first to invent the claimed invention. For example, suppose that you file an application for a U.S. patent on a composition of matter comprising four elements: (A) water, (B) sugar, (C) electrolytes, and (D) glycerol in a concentration of approximately 0.5% to 5.0%. If, prior to the date on which you are deemed to have invented this composition, someone else already had invented and publicly disclosed in the United States a composition comprising these four elements, your invention would lack novelty.[3] The *utility* condition requires only that the invention work and that it serve some minimal human need. Although utility is a minimal criterion, it does manage to weed out a few purported inventions, including those that cannot work (such as perpetual motion machines) and those that do not have a sufficiently specific known

---

[2] See 35 U.S.C. §§ 101, 103. Patent protection is not available for laws of nature, natural phenomena, and abstract ideas. See *Diamond v. Diehr,* 450 U.S. 175, 185 (1981). In practice, the scope of patentable subject matter has expanded in recent years, as U.S. courts have concluded that genetically engineered life forms, refined or isolated versions of naturally occurring physical substances, computer software-related inventions, and even business methods are all potentially patentable.

[3] To be more precise, a claimed invention lacks novelty if another invention contains all of the "elements" or "limitations" of the claimed invention that are arranged in the same order and, prior to the date on which the applicant invented the claimed invention, the other invention was, *inter alia,* already known or used by others in the United States, or patented or described in a printed publication in the United States or abroad, or described in a pending and subsequently granted U.S. patent application, or was made and used in the United States by another who had not abandoned, suppressed, or concealed it, see 35 U.S.C. § 102(a), (e), (g). See also *id.* § 102(b), which denies patentability where the invention was patented or described in a printed publication, or in public use or on sale in the United States, more than one year prior to the date on which the applicant filed its U.S. patent application. Note that the invention lacks novelty (is anticipated) only if a *single* piece of qualifying prior art contains all of elements found in the invention. If you would have to put two or more pieces of prior art together to create an invention containing all of the elements, your invention might (or might not) fail the nonobviousness hurdle, but it would be novel.

Most other countries award the patent to the first to file a patent application, rather than the first to invent. In addition, many impose an absolute novely rule under which an inventor is not entitled to a patent if the invention disclosed in the application was publicly disclosed anywhere in the world prior to the date of his application. The merits of a first-to-file or first-to-invent system, and of an absolute novelty rule, are beyond the scope of this chapter.

use; a possible example of the latter are intermediate research tools such as expressed sequence tags used in biotechnological research.[4] The *nonobviousness* requirement denies patentability if the differences between the claimed invention and the relevant prior art are such that the claimed invention would have been "obvious at the time the invention was made to a person having ordinary skill in the art to which the subject matter pertains."[5] Nonobviousness is often the most difficult of the three conditions to satisfy. It is also the most difficult to describe or quantify, though in a rough sense it means that an invention is not patentable if it is an insubstantial improvement over the existing state of the art. In comparison with our previous example, a piece of prior art comprising (α) water, (β) sugar, (γ) electrolytes, and (δ) glycerol in a concentration of approximately 6.0% to 8.0% would not anticipate your invention – element D and element δ are not identical. Given the proximity of the range of glycerol concentrations, however, the prior art might render your invention obvious, unless (for example) the prior art "teaches away" (i.e., would lead the ordinary researcher to a different solution to the problem) from a lower glycerol concentration or the use of a lower concentration has unexpected properties.

Patent laws also impose upon the patent applicant a variety of disclosure requirements. Under U.S. law, the specification portion of the patent must include a written description of the invention "in such full, clear, concise, and exact terms as to enable any person skilled in the art to which it pertains . . . to make and use the same,"[6] and also must disclose the inventor's own "best mode" or preferred embodiment of the invention as of the time the application is filed.[7] It must "conclude with one or more claims particularly pointing out and distinctly claiming the subject matter that the applicant regards as his invention."[8] Other countries' laws have similar, though not necessarily identical, requirements.

---

[4] For more detailed discussions of utility, see *Brenner v. Manson*, 383 U.S. 519 (1966); 1 Chisum (2002; § 4.01, at 4–2.1); Schlicher (2002; § 3.02[1]); and see also Holman & Munzer (2000; 757–60). Most other countries have an analogous requirement, namely that inventions be "capable of industrial application."

[5] 35 U.S.C. § 103(a). Most other countries state that the invention must demonstrate an "inventive step." The precise application of this third requirement varies somewhat from one patent system to another.

[6] See 35 U.S.C. § 112. The portion of the statute just quoted actually contains two separate requirements: the written description requirement, which means that the description portion of the patent must conform to the claims and the enablement requirement, which means that the description must enable the hypothetical person of ordinary skill in the art to make and use the invention.

[7] See 35 U.S.C. § 112.

[8] *Id.*

Once the patent is granted, the U.S. patentee may exclude others from, among other things, making, using, or selling the invention in the United States for a term ending twenty years from the date on which the application was filed.[9] If the patent owner suspects that someone is making, using, or selling without her permission, she can file suit for patent infringement. Infringement itself comes in two forms. First, the patent owner may claim that the defendant has *literally infringed*, by making, using, or selling an invention that contains all of the elements of the patented invention. In our previously mentioned hypothetical, where we used the letters A, B, C, and D to denote the elements of a patented invention, the defendant would literally infringe if he made, used, or sold a composition containing those same four elements (alone, or in combination with another element or elements). Alternatively, the patent owner may assert that the defendant's product (sometimes called the *accused device*) infringes under the *doctrine of equivalents*, which is substantially though not literally the equivalent of the patented invention. In our hypothetical, an accused device comprising elements A, B, C, and E would not literally infringe but might infringe by equivalents if the substitution of element E for element D is an insubstantial or trivial variation over the patented invention. Not surprisingly, applying the doctrine of equivalents can be quite complicated. Interpreted too broadly, the doctrine could have a chilling effect on follow-up inventors; interpreted too narrowly, it could render patents virtually worthless to the extent that almost any knowledgeable researcher could avoid literal infringement by making some minor modification to the patented invention.[10]

---

[9] See 35 U.S.C. § § 154(a), 271(a). For example, if you file your patent application on May 1, 1999, and the application is granted on May 1, 2001, the patent term begins on the latter date and ends twenty years from the former date (i.e., on May 1, 2019). *Effective* patent life may be shorter than the eighteen-year period in this hypothetical case, however. Patent owners often fail to pay modest maintenance fees, thus allowing their patents to lapse prematurely. And some products (such as pharmaceuticals) cannot be marketed until other government agencies, such as the Food and Drug Administration, approve them, and this process sometimes takes several years. In such cases, though, it is sometimes possible to obtain an extension of the patent term.

Note that patent ownership is defined in terms of the right to exclude others from making, using, or selling and not in terms of an affirmative right to make, use, or sell an invention. As noted in the preceding paragraph, other laws (such as food and drug laws) may preclude the patentee from practicing her own invention for a period of time. Or the patentee may have obtained a patent on an improvement to another's patented invention. For example, suppose that you have a patent on A, B, C, and D and that we obtain a patent on an improvement comprising A, B, C, D, and E. Neither we nor you would be entitled to practice the improvement without obtaining the other's permission. This phenomenon is referred to as the "blocking patents" problem.

[10] For discussions of the U.S. law on the doctrine of equivalents, see *Festo Corp. v. Shoketsu Kinzoku Kogyo Kabushiki Co.*, 535 U.S. 722 (2002); *Warner-Jenkinson Co. v. Hilton Davis*

The defendant in a patent infringement action usually offers two defenses: roughly, "I didn't do it" and "It doesn't matter." The defendant asserts that he didn't do it by denying that his conduct infringes, either literally or by equivalents. Second, the defendant is likely to argue that, even if his product comes within the scope of the patent claims, it doesn't matter because the patent is invalid. A patent might be invalid for failing to satisfy any of the criteria of patentability, including novelty, utility, nonobviousness, and compliance with the relevant disclosure obligations; for example, the Patent Office might have overlooked, or misinterpreted the relevance of, some prior art that renders the invention obvious. The invalidity argument is successful in a substantial plurality of the litigated U.S. cases,[11] which suggests that the U.S. Patent and Trademark Office grants a large number of invalid patents. We return to this point in Chapter 7. A third possible defense is the *exhaustion* or *first-sale* doctrine. Once the patent owner releases into the stream of commerce a product that incorporates her patent, she cannot prevent the owner of that lawfully made product from using or reselling it, although she can prevent him from re-making it. As one would imagine, there is a fine line between lawful repair (a type of use) and unlawful re-making.[12]

If none of these defenses is successful, the defendant usually loses, because there are very few other exceptions to liability for patent infringement.[13] Indeed, people usually describe patent infringement as a strict liability offense, and this description is more or less correct, though subject to a few caveats we raise in Chapter 5. To illustrate, suppose again that you own a patent on an invention comprising elements A, B, C, and D, and you discover that

Chem. Co., 520 U.S. 17 (1997); Conigliaro et al. (2001); and Wagner (2002). For discussions of the doctrine of equivalents in other countries, see, e.g., Weston (1998) and Yamamoto & Tessensohn (1999).

[11] Allison & Lemley (1998; 205–7) found 46% of the patents were invalidated in a population that consisted of all final written decisions on validity from 1989 to 1996; Moore (2000; 391) found invalidation rates of 29% and 36% in a sample that consisted of all the U.S. trial court decisions from 1983 to 1999 with, respectively, juries and judges deciding the issue of validity. Invalidity is raised as a defense in most patent cases.

[12] For an overview of U.S. law, see Chisum (2002; § 16.03[3]).

[13] There is, for example, nothing as expansive as the copyright doctrine of fair use, which we discuss subsequently. In the United States, there is a very limited experimental use defense. Another exception exempts some conduct undertaken in connection with the submission of information to the Food & Drug Administration. See 35 U.S.C. § 271(e). Some countries recognize other limited exceptions, such as exceptions for private noncommercial use. This defense is not recognized in the U.S., as we discuss in Chapter 6. And in some rare instances a court may excuse literal infringement under the so-called *reverse doctrine of equivalents*. Under this doctrine, a court will permit the defendant to market an invention that literally infringes, but that is a radical improvement over the patented device. See Dam (1994; 266–7) and Lemley (1997; 1042–72).

we are making, using, or selling an invention comprising those same four elements without your permission. You sue us for patent infringement, but we assert that we did not copy from you; rather, we independently invented the same invention that is covered by your patent. Our assertion may be factually true – independent discovery does happen – but it is no defense to a charge of patent infringement. The laws of the United States and most other countries reduce the incidence of independent discovery to some extent by publishing most pending patent applications eighteen months after the date of filing; they also publish all issued patents, once the decision to grant the patent has been made. Patents therefore are public records, and so in theory the potential infringer could have discovered the patent in time to avoid the infringement. Again, we discuss the relevance of this observation in Chapter 5.

In a suit for patent infringement, the U.S. Patent Act (§§ 283–4) authorizes the court to award the prevailing plaintiff injunctive relief, as well as

damages adequate to compensate for the infringement, but in no event less than a reasonable royalty for the use made of the invention by the infringer, together with interest and costs as fixed by the court.

"Damages adequate to compensate for the infringement" may include an award of the plaintiff's lost profits attributable to the infringement; the amount of an established royalty; or a reasonable royalty. Significantly, U.S. courts do not interpret the Patent Act to provide for an award of the defendant's profits attributable to the infringement, although patent law once permitted these restitutionary awards.[14] A few other countries, including Canada and the United Kingdom, do permit restitutionary recoveries in patent law, but such recoveries appear to be rare.[15] In addition, U.S. courts may award multiple damages up to three times the plaintiff's actual damages, but courts generally exercise this discretion only in cases of willful infringement or bad faith litigation.[16] The statute also permits the court to award attorney's fees to the prevailing party in exceptional cases, which usually means those in which either the defendant is found to have willfully

---

[14] As far as we can discern, when the U.S. Congress changed the law in 1947 to foreclose restitutionary awards, it was acting upon the perception that the cost of calculating these awards (in terms of complexity, cost, and delay) outweighed their benefits and that sometimes smaller competitors simply gave in rather than incur the cost of litigating. Given the high cost of patent litigation even without these awards, and given the need to perform a similar calculation in order to determine the amount of a reasonable royalty, we doubt whether this rationale makes much sense.

[15] See generally Coury (2003).

[16] See 35 U.S.C. § 284; 7 Chisum (2002; § 20.03[4], at 20–300).

infringed or the plaintiff obtained the patent by fraud or brought the action in bad faith.[17] Prejudgment interest is usually awarded to the prevailing plaintiff as a matter of course.[18]

PATENT POLICY

The fundamental premise of the patent system is that society benefits when people conceive of new inventions; develop and commercialize new products incorporating those inventions (a process referred to as innovation, as distinct from invention); and publicly disclose information about their inventions, so that others may learn from and improve upon those inventions. Most people probably agree with this premise, and we will not bother to defend it. The difficult question is how to maximize these social benefits – or, more precisely, the surplus of social benefits over social costs. The patent system can be thought of as one way of attempting to achieve this goal.

To understand how the patent system may work to attain this end, it is important to recognize that one of the great things about information is that it is (or at least tends to be), in the language of economics, both *nonrival* and *nonexcludable*. Most tangible things are rivalrous, meaning that only one person or a small number of people can use or consume a particular good at any one time; while you use your computer or drive your car, for example, no one else can use that same computer or drive that same car. By contrast, a silicon chip located within your computer or your car may embody an invention that is simultaneously being used by thousands or even millions of people, and yet despite their simultaneous use the invention itself is never depleted (worn out). To put it another way, a nonrivalrous invention may be embodied in a rivalrous physical good. Only one person may be able to use that precise physical good at any one time and his or her use eventually may deplete that physical good. But the invention itself is an intangible thing, which is not depleted by use. The invention can be embodied in any number of physical goods.

Similarly, most goods are excludable, in the sense that you can take precautions – locks, guards, fences – to prevent other people from having access to them. But the only way to exclude others from having access to your idea for a new invention is to keep the idea to yourself. Once you disclose the idea to someone else, there may be no way to prevent that person

---

[17] See 35 U.S.C. § 285; 7 Chisum (2002; § 20.03[4], at 20–384 to –385).
[18] See 7 Chisum (2002; § 20.03[4][a], at 20–274 to –275). In the United States, there is no criminal penalty for patent infringement. There is in some countries.

from using it, assuming that he has the technical skill to do so. Of course, you could disclose your idea only to people you trust – or who are willing to sign nondisclosure agreements – and use locks and fences to keep everyone else from learning about it. But these measures are not foolproof. Once you embody your idea in a tangible object (say, a computer chip) and make copies of that object available to others (for example, by selling to them), the cat may be out of the bag. If the invention is valuable enough, someone will try to reverse-engineer it.[19] In this way, knowledge of useful information tends to spread. In general, this dissemination of knowledge is desirable, because it enables others to use the invention and to improve upon it.

We said previously that one of the great things about inventions is that they are nonrivalrous and nonexcludable, but nonrivalrousness and nonexcludability present a double-edged sword. Precisely because other people may be able to use your invention without your consent; once you have publicly disclosed it, your *ex ante* incentive to invest in creating or publicizing the invention is lower than it otherwise would be. Inventing something new often requires a substantial investment of time, money, and other resources. In the case of new drugs, for example, it may take hundreds of millions of dollars to come up with a safe, effective, and marketable drug; along the way, many promising candidates will be weeded out because of side effects or other problems. To copy someone else's new invention often costs considerably less, even if we factor in the cost of reverse-engineering. Thus, there may be a substantial incentive to take a free (or at least less costly) ride on someone else's investment. This potential for free-riding reduces the incentive to invent something new, because the inventor may be unable to recoup her sunk costs of invention. Competition from free-riders may reduce prices such that the cost of discovery and commercialization cannot be recovered. Moreover, to make optimal use of an invention, the inventor may need to disclose it to someone else who is better positioned to manufacture or market a tangible product that embodies the invention. But once she does so, the other party need not compensate her for the information; ideas, as we have said, tend to be nonexcludable. Of course, the parties could try to contract around this problem, but the potential recipient of the information may be unwilling to commit to not using the information until he knows what it is. After all, the information could turn out to be something in

---

[19] Some things are easier to reverse-engineer than others. The formula for Coca-Cola has proven notoriously difficult to reverse-engineer. Decompiling computer source code from the underlying object code is difficult, though it can be done by skilled computer engineers. Other products, however, may be relatively easy, even obvious, for a person of average skill to unravel.

the public domain. But once the recipient knows what the information is, the disclosure already will have taken place. Nobel laureate Kenneth Arrow noted this "information paradox" in a famous essay some forty years ago.[20]

The preceding analysis suggests that inventions are what economists refer to as a public good, similar to such things as parks, roads, national defense, and education. Almost everyone benefits from these sorts of things, either directly or indirectly. Even so, it can be difficult to limit access to public goods only to those who are willing to pay their fair share, whatever that means. Every beneficiary would be financially better off if he were to take a free ride, that is, to enjoy the benefits while others paid. If everyone acted this way, however, the good would not exist and everyone would lose out. In the case of parks, roads, national defense, and education, governments often try to solve this collective action problem by providing the public good and imposing taxes (a sort of user fee) upon the beneficiaries (in theory, everyone), to pay for it.[21]

For similar reasons, the free-rider problem may undermine the incentive to create, disclose, and commercialize new inventions, absent some corrective measure. Needless to say, the possibility of free-riding will not *always* have this effect; people were coming up with new inventions long before patent law ever came into existence, for a variety of reasons. Some inventions may not entail substantial sunk costs. Some inventors may be able to make up those costs merely by being the first on the market with a new product (the so-called first-mover advantage), particularly if the product is difficult to reverse-engineer or the cost of copying otherwise remains high. (It is no coincidence that intellectual property laws made little headway until the cost of copying started to come down, in the seventeenth and eighteenth centuries, due to the printing press and other innovations.) In other cases,

---

[20] Arrow (1962; 615).

[21] Attempting to solve the public goods problem through taxation gives rise to its own set of familiar problems. Some people will try to avoid paying their fair share; there will be debates over what a fair share is; interest groups will lobby government for special favors or exemptions; and so on. Ideally, a policymaker would consider the costs and benefits of other options for solving the free rider problem, as Coase and others remind us. See Coase (1974). Indeed, the law of intellectual property generally does not follow the taxation solution, for reasons we discuss in the text previously, although government does provide direct financing and tax benefits for some scientific research. In addition, some commentators have recently argued that a system under which government sometimes conferred prizes, or effected buyouts of patents, might be superior to the patent system alone as a way of addressing the public goods problem. See Abramowicz (2003), who reviewed the literature and proposed his own solution. For now this remains an interesting theoretical alternative, but it is not directly relevant to our exploration of optimal remedies under the current system.

self-help measures such as locks, fences, or nondisclosure agreements may be sufficient to deter copying until the sunk costs have been recouped. In yet other cases, private investors, philanthropists, or potential beneficiaries could promise *ex ante* to pay inventors for developing new inventions or could offer the inducement of *ex post* rewards and prizes. Nevertheless, the intuition remains that, absent further measures, some inventions that would benefit society would not be invented or would not be optimally disclosed or commercialized. The patent system is premised on the reasonable assumption that the public will enjoy additional benefits when the government takes additional steps to encourage the creation, commercialization, and disclosure or new inventions. More things will be created, commercialized, and disclosed. Also, some of the costs of self-help measures, such as locks and fences, can be avoided.

As we noted earlier, the way the law handles many other public good problems is through taxation: that is, the government provides the good and pays for it from tax revenues. Sometimes governments employ this method or analogous methods to finance the production of new inventions as well. Governments use tax revenues to fund some scientific research, and they also grant some tax benefits to private firms that engage in R & D. One problem, however, with relying exclusively or predominantly on these methods is that governments, unlike the decentralized marketplace, may lack the knowledge of what needs to be invented or how to value new inventions. And unlike most private actors, governments may not have to submit to the discipline of the marketplace. Incorrect decisions on the part of government decisionmakers could result in insufficient investment in invention, or investing in the wrong types of invention, or under- or overvaluation of that which has been invented. Competition for government funding also could lead to familiar rent-seeking[22] problems on the part of private actors or agency capture by the affected industries.

All of these considerations lead most theorists to conclude that a different method for encouraging invention – namely, the one a patent system provides – is preferable to relying predominantly upon direct funding. Under a patent system, society "funds" invention by allowing private actors to

---

[22] "Rent-seeking" behavior occurs when people seek economic "rent," that is, value in excess of that which they could obtain from their next-best investment. (More technically, economic rent is the value derived from an investment in excess of one's opportunity cost.) Some rent-seeking behavior may be socially inefficient (e.g., competition to obtain privately valuable, but socially wasteful, government benefits). In other instances, competition to obtain economic rents – such as the potential profits to be derived from a valuable patent – may dissipate the value of those rents. See *infra* pages 18, 20.

decide what to invent and then conferring exclusive rights upon them for a limited time. These exclusive rights are worthless if the invention turns out to be a dud, but ultimately the market decides what is valuable and what is not. If the inventor (or her licensee) can come up with a marketable embodiment of the invention, the exclusive rights will provide the inventor with an opportunity to recover her sunk costs. Correcting for the free-rider problem in this manner is the genius of the patent system.[23]

Critics nevertheless note that patents come with some substantial social costs and sometimes charge that the benefits may be overstated as well. As for the benefits, the empirical evidence that patents provide a necessary incentive to inventive activity is hardly overwhelming. Survey evidence suggests that many firms rely more heavily upon other incentives to invent (such as first-mover advantages and trade secrecy) and also that firms often patent for strategic reasons, such as preventing others from gaining a competitive advantage.[24] Patents nevertheless may provide a substantial incentive to invent in certain industries, such as pharmaceuticals, where sunk costs are particularly high. Their assumed role in inducing disclosure and commercialization might be important even if the incentive to invent is of lesser magnitude.

Patent systems do give rise to a variety of social costs, however, which policymakers must consider and which an ideal patent system would try to minimize. One is the systemic cost of processing, enforcing, and maintaining patent rights, which requires at a minimum a patent office and courts to resolve patent infringement claims. This cost is not terribly significant in the industrialized nations, but may prove burdensome for some less developed countries. Second is the potential for the patent system to inhibit future invention or innovation that is based upon existing patented inventions. Invention tends to be cumulative and thus one consequence of a patent system is to raise the cost of creating follow-up inventions based upon an earlier technology.[25] This could prove problematic, even if the follow-up inventor is willing and able to pay for permission to use the patent (which may not always be the case, due to budget constraints, the uncertainty of the future payoff, and so on). If the follow-up inventor must negotiate

---

[23] For further discussion of the traditional arguments that patents induce invention and disclosure, see, e.g., Dam (1994; 247) and Scotchmer (1991; 31); see also *Aronson v. Quick Point Pencil Co.*, 440 U.S. 257, 262 (1979). For a focus on the incentive to commercialize, see Kieff (2000) and Turner (1998; 186–93).

[24] See Cohen et al. (2000; 9–11 & Figures 1–4); Levin et al. (1987; 794–5); Mansfield et al. (1981; 915); Scherer et al. (1959; 118); and Taylor & Silbertson (1973; Chapter 9).

[25] See Merges & Nelson (1990) and Scotchmer (1991).

with a multiplicity of previous researchers, the mere cost of transacting could be enormous; critics argue that this problem is becoming acute in fields such as biotechnology,[26] although this critique is hotly disputed.[27] A third social cost is the cost associated with duplicative effort: the potential availability of a patent may induce a "race" to become the first to invent. At worst, such attempts to obtain patent "rents" can result in substantial wasted effort, because only one firm can win the race, and the expected benefits of obtaining the patent may be dissipated in the effort to win the race. On the other hand, patent races may speed up the development of new technology and may have unintended, but beneficial, spillover effects: on the way to discovering one thing, a researcher may discover something else that was unforeseen.[28] In light of these conflicting effects, the theoretical literature on patent races remains equivocal.

A fourth cost is the potential cost associated with monopoly rights. Monopolies can be troubling for two different reasons. First, monopolies transfer wealth from consumers to monopolists and depending on the circumstances and on one's theory of distributive justice, this outcome may be undesirable. Second, a monopoly is, in economic terms, allocatively inefficient, because it reduces social welfare. In other words, it is not just that the monopolist gets one more slice of the pie and consumers one less slice; the size of the pie is smaller. A monopolist maximizes profit by producing where marginal cost equals marginal revenue – we depict this phenomenon graphically in Chapter 3 – with the result that (compared to the outcome under perfect competition) price increases while both output and social welfare decrease. The monopolist is better off, but consumers are worse off and consumers' losses outweigh the monopolist's gains. Economists refer to this decrease in social wealth as a "deadweight social welfare loss."

Although the deadweight loss is a potential cost of any system of exclusive rights, it is important to bear in mind that most patents do *not* confer monopoly rights in any economically meaningful sense (despite the fact

---

[26] See Heller & Eisenberg (1998).

[27] See Wagner (2003; 12–13) for a review of empirical and theoretical challenges to the Heller-Eisenberg thesis.

[28] For discussion of some of the relevant literature, see Abramowicz (2003; 183–8); see also Scotchmer (1998; 275), who noted "two views on patent races: that they inefficiently duplicate costs and that they efficiently encourage higher aggregate investment"; see also Tirole (1988; 400), who noted that the loser in a patent race may benefit from positive spillovers, may develop another product, and may gain experience for future races. Merges & Nelson (1990; 870–9) argued that empirical evidence is more consistent with the theory that competition in the market for improvements spurs innovation, despite possible efficiency losses attributable to rivalrous invention. See also Reinganum (1989; 853–68).

that people often carelessly refer to patents, and sometimes other IPRs as well, as monopoly rights). For one thing, most patented inventions "read on" (that is, cover or render infringing) components of larger products and not on discrete products themselves. Often the market for the discrete product will be competitive, even if only one producer has the right to manufacture a particular component. A related point is that for most patented inventions (whether components or discrete products) there is a range of acceptable, nonpatented substitutes, which limit the patent owner's ability to obtain a monopoly profit. Indeed, a majority of patents are never commercialized at all, much less meet with commercial success. Of course, a few patents *do* result in the lucky patent owner obtaining a temporary monopoly or at least some competitive advantage even if it falls short of full-blown monopoly power. Indeed, the whole point of patent rights as we have outlined them is the potential they hold for the inventor to price above marginal cost for at least as long as is necessary to recoup the sunk costs of invention. Certainly patents do fulfill this promise sometimes. When they do, however, one must reckon with the corresponding deadweight loss. Even in this instance, however, one must consider how the world would have looked in the absence of the patent system. Even if the invention leads to temporary monopoly power, consumers might be better off than if the invention had not been invented at all or had been invented much later in time.[29]

There are some additional theories of patent rights that complement the standard incentive theory.[30] Of these, the most well known is Edmund Kitch's "prospect" theory. As developed by Kitch, this theory holds that patent rights enable inventors to efficiently coordinate investments by others in second-generation improvements.[31] Kitch argues that "pioneering" inventions in particular – meaning those that are likely to have a large number of follow-up applications – merit a broader patent "scope" than do more pedestrian inventions, because the pioneer patent owner can reduce the amount of rent-seeking by potential improvers. Kitch's theory remains influential but has been critiqued on several grounds. For one thing, the strong patent rights that the prospect theory appears to contemplate may weaken the incentive to create follow-up improvements, because the improver will

---

[29] See Arrow (1962; 619–20); Dam (1994; 251).

[30] In addition to the literature on the prospect theory discussed subsequently, the interested reader is advised to consult Kieff (2003), who argued that a number of patent doctrines function to reduce administrative costs; Long (2002) developed a theory that patents signal positive firm attributes.

[31] See Kitch (1977; 267–71).

capture only a portion of the gains from improvement. (On the other hand, allowing the follow-up improver to patent his invention provides him with some leverage, as does the possibility that the improvement will be held noninfringing under the reverse doctrine of equivalents.[32]) The prospect of obtaining broad patent rights also may stimulate races to obtain the pioneering patent with the potential negative consequences described earlier.[33] The prospect theory remains empirically suspect as well. One historical study argues that the development of follow-up improvements in fact has often had little connection with the existence or nonexistence of patent rights in the original discovery; another argues that patents owners often have not used broad patent rights to coordinate follow-up innovation, but rather have engaged in satisficing behavior.[34] Nevertheless, the prospect function remains a prominent theoretical justification for the patent system, even if only in conjunction with the more mainstream incentive theory.

In summary, the previous arguments posit that the ideal patent system would maximize the surplus of social benefits over social costs. The benefits include the development of new inventions, as well as their disclosure and commercialization (and, possibly, the prospect function described earlier); the costs include the various administrative, transaction, monopoly, and rent-seeking costs we have discussed. How close any patent system comes to satisfying this ideal, in comparison with alternative methods, remains a matter of speculation and will depend in part upon how "strong" or "weak" the patent rights under consideration are. Patent strength is a function of both duration and scope. Stronger rights – rights that have longer duration or broader scope – may increase the incentive to create, disclose, innovate, and coordinate investment in follow-up improvements, but they also may increase the attendant social costs.

The effect of patent duration upon patent strength is easy to understand: the longer the patent lasts, the more potential value it has and vice versa

---

[32] See Footnotes 9 and 13 in this chapter.

[33] See McFetridge & Smith (1980). Grady and Alexander argue, however, that the patent system limits rent-seeking in various ways. For example, it does so by foreclosing patent protection for pioneering discoveries that cannot be improved upon, such as laws of nature. See Grady & Alexander (1992). For a critique of the Grady & Alexander thesis, see Merges (1992).

[34] See Beck (1983) and Merges & Nelson (1990; 871–8). The term "satisficing" was coined by Nobel laureate Herbert Simon. Simon posited that firms sometimes seek not to maximize profits, but rather to attain a certain level of satiation: "a certain level or rate of profit . . . a certain share of the market or a certain level of sales. Firms would try to 'satisfice' rather than to maximize." Simon (1959; 263).

(although in practice most patents are obsolete long before their expiration dates).[35] As we noted, the patent term for all inventions is more or less standard and runs from the date of grant until twenty years after the date of filing. In theory, there is no reason why this must be so. One could, for example, award longer patents for inventions that are the result of large investments in research and development, or that confer substantial social benefits, and shorter patents for other inventions. Modern patent systems nevertheless shun this approach in favor of a "one-size-fits-all" patent term.[36] Arguably, this approach is justified in light of the difficulty of properly (and neutrally) determining the appropriate duration of patent rights; in any event, the worldwide standard today is a patent term ending twenty years from the date of the patent application with few exceptions.[37] Some inventions, therefore, may receive much more of a stimulus than is necessary, while others not enough.

Patent scope can refer both to patentable subject matter (and related issues) and to patent breadth. Patent scope in the sense of subject matter can be either broad or narrow. As discussed earlier, in the United States patent scope in this sense is quite broad, although even here it does not extend to the discovery of abstract ideas, laws of nature, and naturally occurring physical phenomena.[38] More generally, one might use the term patent scope to

---

[35] See Lemley (2001; 1503–4) who showed that more than 2/3 of U.S. patents lapse prematurely due to the owners' failure to pay modest maintenance fees. In the United States, maintenance fees are due at the end of $3\frac{1}{2}$ years, $7\frac{1}{2}$ years, and $11\frac{1}{2}$ years from the date of the grant in amounts that range from $910 to $3,220.

[36] Some countries, however, also award protection for minor innovations under a system of protection known as "utility models," "petty patents," or other names. (Australia, for example, recently revised and renamed its petty patent system to a system of "innovation patents.") In general, countries with utility model protection make this protection available to inventions that otherwise might not qualify for patent protection (because they are insufficiently nonobvious, for example). These petty patents typically confer exclusive rights for a short period of time, such as five or ten years. The United States does not award utility model protection.

[37] The international treaty known as the TRIPs Agreement, to which all member nations of the World Trade Organization (WTO) are parties, requires a minimum patent term ending twenty years from the date of application. It also generally forbids member nations from discriminating with respect to fields of technology, such as from awarding different patent terms for different types of inventions. Thus, whatever the theoretical merits may be of a more perfectly calibrated system, such a system does not appear to be a realistic possibility anytime soon.

[38] A system that awarded patents to the first person to discover a new law of nature would marginally increase the incentive to be such a discoverer. But the additional incentive may be unnecessary, in light of existing incentives such as research grants, prizes, and fame, and in light of the high social cost of conferring exclusive rights in such cases. See also Grady & Alexander (1992), who argued that conferring patent protection

delineate the class of inventions that fall within the definition of patentable subject matter *and* that satisfy the other requirements of patentability. For example, every patent system must decide what the terms novelty, utility, and nonobviousness mean within that system. In addition, every system will exclude from patent protection inventions that do not satisfy these requirements.[39] More commonly, however, when people use the term patent scope they mean patent breadth; a patent is broad if it reads on many possible embodiments. Patent breadth, in turn, is a function of several patent doctrines. Patent attorneys can draft individual patent claims broadly or narrowly. Drafting them too broadly, however, risks invalidation on a number of grounds, including enablement or anticipation by the prior art. In this sense, substantive patent law, by defining what an enabling disclosure is or what "counts" as prior art, indirectly controls patent scope. The law of infringement is yet another mechanism by which patent scope can be regulated. As we have seen, a patent confers the right to exclude others not only from literally infringing, but also from infringing by equivalents. A broad interpretation of the term "equivalent" expands patent breadth, whereas a narrow interpretation reduces it.

Patent scope is not quite as "one-size-fits-all" as is patent duration. In applying the doctrine of equivalents, for example, U.S. courts are directed to confer broader scope upon pioneering inventions.[40] Dan Burk and Mark Lemley also have argued that U.S. courts appear to have certain preconceptions – some of which may be incorrect – about various fields of technology, such as what sorts of inventions within those fields are obvious applications of the prior art, what type of information must be disclosed to enable a person of ordinary skill to practice the invention, and so on.[41] To the extent this observation is true, it suggests that patent scope, in a broad sense, will vary to some extent from one field to another. This type of variation, however, arises from the courts' and patent offices' application of general rules designed for all patentable subject matter and not from industry-specific statutory provisions.

upon discoveries which cannot be improved upon, such as laws of nature, would result in patent-race rent dissipation with no offsetting benefits in terms of follow-up invention.

[39] Kieff argues that many of the relevant rules can be explained as an attempt to minimize the administrative costs of the patent system. See Kieff (2003).

[40] See, e.g., *Augustine Med., Inc. v. Gaymar Indus.*, 181 F.3d 1291, 1301 (Fed. Cir. 1999) where this dictum was noted, although it was tempered with the observation that pioneering inventions typically have broader scope even without benefit of the doctrine of equivalents because claims to such inventions are less constrained by the prior art.

[41] See Burk & Lemley (2002).

Scholars, therefore, recognize that patent rights can be strengthened (or diminished) by expanding (or reducing) scope, duration, or both. Two points nevertheless remain problematic. First, there is little theoretical and no empirical evidence addressing the issue of what the optimal scope or duration of patent rights should be in the real world. Indeed, it is not clear how such empirical evidence ever could be produced; controlled experiments do not appear feasible. A second problem is that no one knows much about the tradeoff between scope and duration (e.g., how much scope could be reduced if the duration were extended without affecting patent strength). Some theoretical literature *does* address this issue, however, as well as the related issues of whether it is less socially costly to confer patents of broader scope and short duration or of narrow scope and long duration.[42] But no consensus has yet emerged as to which, if any, departures from the present system would increase social welfare.

TRADE SECRETS

Trade secret law differs from the law of patents in several crucial respects. One is that trade secret law is less uniform than patent law. In the United States, trade secret protection is based primarily on common law and state statutory law. Thus, unlike patent law that is based on a federal statute, trade secret protection can vary to some extent from one state to another. These differences have been reduced in recent years, however, by most states' passage of the Uniform Trade Secret Act (UTSA). Other countries' trade secret laws, nevertheless, may vary widely and there is very little international law addressing the topic.[43] When we discuss trade secrets in this book, our principal focus will be upon U.S. law as embodied in the UTSA.

A second difference is that trade secret protection is much easier to obtain than is patent protection. Under the UTSA, any information that provides a person with a competitive advantage as long as it remains secret is potentially protectable as a trade secret. The stringent novelty and nonobviousness conditions of patent law do not apply. Thus, even such unpatentable items as customer and supplier lists, recipes, and the amount of a secret bid can qualify as trade secrets; although potentially patentable, unpatented inventions

---

[42] See Gallini (1992) who advocated shorter, but broader patents, and took issue with other theorists who have advocated longer and narrower patents; see also Ayres & Klemperer (1999; 987 Footnote 2).

[43] TRIPs and NAFTA each contain one article dealing with trade secrets, but neither provides anywhere near as much specificity as the UTSA. Countries, therefore, retain considerable leeway to craft their trade secret laws as they see fit.

can qualify as trade secrets, too. Moreover, whereas patent law requires the patentee to disclose certain information to the public as a precondition of obtaining a patent, trade secret law affirmatively discourages the owner from making any public disclosure, because any such disclosure of trade secret information may result in the information losing its protectable status. Indeed, there is no government body, analogous to the patent office, that affirmatively bestows trade secret protection. Any information that qualifies as a trade secret under the definition above *is* a trade secret; no registration or other formalities are required.

From the standpoint of the inventor, the upside of trade secret protection is that it is much easier to obtain than patent protection; the downside is that it is also less robust and often more vulnerable to forfeiture. The owner of a trade secret may exclude another from, among other things, acquiring the secret by "improper means" such as theft or espionage or from using or disclosing the secret if the other knew (or had reason to know) at the time of disclosure or use that the secret was derived from a person who (1) had used improper means to acquire it, or (2) had acquired it under circumstances giving rise to a duty to maintain secrecy, or (3) owed a duty of secrecy to another.[44] To illustrate, suppose that your secret cookie recipe qualifies as a trade secret. Under the UTSA, you would have legal recourse against someone who breaks into your headquarters and steals the recipe. (Of course, you would also have recourse under other civil and criminal laws; occasionally, though, trade secret law penalizes an acquisition that would not violate any other body of law.[45]) You also would have a claim against someone (for example, a current or former employee) who discloses the recipe to a recipient in violation of a duty of secrecy imposed by contract or by the common law of agency. (Again, you might have other causes of action as well for breach of contract or breach of fiduciary duty.) Finally, you might have recourse against the recipient, if for example the recipient uses the recipe despite the fact that she knows, or should know, that the disclosing party violated a duty of secrecy. Often, a trade secret claim will be the only recourse against the recipient who in our hypothetical does not appear to be in privity of contract with the owner and may not owe him any common law fiduciary duty.

Unlike a patentee, the trade secret owner has *no* recourse against independent discovery or reverse engineering. Moreover, trade secret protection

---

[44] See UTSA §§ 1(2)(i), (ii); Restatement (Third) of Unfair Competition § 40.
[45] See *E. I. du Pont de Nemours & Co. v. Christopher,* 431 F.2d 1012 (5th Cir. 1970).

lasts only for as long as the information remains secret and valuable. Unfortunately, the information may become widely known despite the trade secret owner's best efforts to maintain secrecy and thus no longer be a secret; or it may become obsolete and, therefore, lose value. In these respects, trade secret protection is more tenuous and less valuable than patent protection, though one must take this observation with a grain of salt. On the positive side, trade secret protection may subsist in some subject matter – for example, customer lists and insufficiently nonobvious inventions – that would never qualify for a patent. In addition, because the duration of trade secret protection is indefinite, in some rare instances protection may persist for much longer than the term of a patent. Good examples include the formula for Coca-Cola and the recipe for Kentucky Fried Chicken. A related point is that obtaining a patent destroys the secrecy of the information, whereas trade secret protection does not. So, if the information is particularly difficult for others to reverse-engineer, trade secret protection can be more valuable than patent protection.

If the trade secret owner is able to prove the actual or threatened misappropriation of a trade secret, the court may award injunctive relief. The UTSA qualifies this right to an injunction, however, by providing that:

In exceptional circumstances, an injunction may condition future use upon payment of a reasonable royalty for no longer than the period of time for which use could have been prohibited. Exceptional circumstances include, but are not limited to, a material and prejudicial change of position prior to acquiring knowledge or reason to know of misappropriation that renders a prohibitive injunction inequitable.[46]

The plaintiff is also entitled to recover damages, which may include "both the actual loss caused by misappropriation and the unjust enrichment caused by misappropriation that is not taken into account in computing actual loss"; in the alternative, the court may award a reasonable royalty for a misappropriator's unauthorized disclosure or use of the secret.[47] Finally, in the event of a "willful and malicious" misappropriation, the UTSA permits

---

[46] UTSA § 2(b); see also Restatement (Third) of Unfair Ccmpetition, § 44 cmt. c.

[47] See UTSA §§ 3(a), (b); see also Restatement (Third) of Unfair Competition § 45 (similar). A damages recovery may be conditioned, however, on the defendant's not having incurred "a material and prejudicial change of position prior to acquiring knowledge or reason to know of misappropriation." UTSA § 3(a); *cf.* Restatement § 45 cmts. b and g, suggesting that the court may award a reasonable royalty for use made after the user is put on notice that the information is secret and an injunction conditioning further use upon payment of a royalty.

punitive damages in an amount not exceeding twice the amount of actual damages, as well as attorney's fees.[48]

Commentators have suggested that trade secret law supplements the patent system by providing an incentive to develop information that has some social value, though not enough to warrant a patent.[49] Perhaps more importantly, trade secret law arguably discourages socially wasteful measures to protect the secrecy of one's invention. A trade secret owner is required to take reasonable precautions (such as building a fence) in order to maintain trade secret protection, but the law may make it unnecessary for him to build a one-hundred-foot-high fence.[50] Trade secret law departs from patent law, however, insofar as it discourages the public dissemination of information. To critics, this aspect of trade secret law is sufficiently problematic to call the entire body of law into question.[51] The secrecy-enhancing character of trade secret law is nevertheless constrained to some degree by the rule permitting others to independently discover or reverse-engineer the secret, a point to which we return in Chapter 5.

COPYRIGHT

In 1710, the British Parliament enacted the first modern copyright law, the Statute of Anne, which thereafter became the model for the first U.S. Copyright Act and influenced early copyright legislation in other countries as well. As originally conceived, copyright in the United States and the United Kingdom subsisted only in "books, maps, and charts" and protected the author (or his assignee) only against unauthorized "printing, publishing, republishing, and vending."[52] Protection lasted for fourteen years (the same as the original patent term) and was measured from the date of first publication, although it could be renewed for an additional fourteen years. In addition, courts granted protection only against the literal or near-literal copying of a work in substantially its entirety, thus permitting the publication of unauthorized abridgements, sequels, and even translations until well

---

[48] See UTSA §§ 3(b), 4; Restatement (Third) of Unfair Competition § 45 cmt. i, which permits "punitive damages under the rules generally applicable in the jurisdiction to the award of punitive damages in tort actions."

[49] See Friedman et al. (1990; 63–4).

[50] See Burk (1999; 173) and Note (1992).

[51] Bone, for example, argues that the social benefits of trade secret law are modest, because much activity that trade secret condemns would violate other laws and that imposing trade secret liability upon other forms of conduct raises social costs without sufficient countervailing benefits. See Bone (1998).

[52] See Act of May 31, 1790, Chapter 15, § 1, 1 Stat. 124, 124 (repealed 1802).

into the nineteenth century. Over time, however, copyright protection has expanded to include many other works of authorship and additional rights have been added.

Today, copyright laws in the United States and elsewhere protect virtually all "original works of authorship," including literary,[53] musical, dramatic, and choreographic works; pictorial, graphic, and sculptural works; motion pictures and other audiovisual works; architectural works; and, in the United States and some other countries, sound recordings.[54] Originality is usually an easy condition to satisfy; in the United States, it means only that the work exhibit independent creation and some minimal degree of creativity either in the expression of underlying facts or ideas or in the selection or arrangement of those facts.[55] Significantly, ideas and facts themselves are not subject to copyright protection. For example, the date on which the Red Baron died (a fact), as well as the various ideas scholars have proffered concerning who shot him down, must remain in the public domain no matter how much work went into discovering or formulating them. Not surprisingly, the line between protectable expression, selection, or arrangement, on the one hand, and unprotectable ideas or facts, on the other, is often difficult to discern; the issue often comes to a head in cases involving labor-intensive, but unoriginal, presentations of facts. When copyright exists, it subsists from the moment of creation[56] and vests in the author of the work.[57] The standard copyright

---

[53] "Literary works are works, other than audiovisual works, expressed in words, numbers, or other verbal or numerical symbols or indicia. . . . " 17 U.S.C. § 101. They include both the source code and the object code of computer programs.

[54] A musical work would include such things as songs, symphonies, and concertos. A sound recording is a work that results "from the fixation of a series of musical, spoken, or other sounds," such as might be embodied in a compact disk or cassette tape.

[55] See *Feist Publications, Inc. v. Rural Tel. Serv.*, 499 U.S. 340, 344–51 (1991).

[56] This means that copyright protection, like trade secret protection but unlike patent protection, exists without the need for any government agency to first pass judgment on whether the work qualifies for protection. This is a relatively new development in the United States. Prior to 1978, state common-law copyright existed from the moment of creation, but it terminated upon publication at which point federal copyright protection sprung into existence, but only if all published copies of the work bore the appropriate notice of copyright. Failure to comply with the notice requirement resulted in the forfeiture of copyright. Registration of copyright is still required as a precondition to filing a copyright infringement action in the United States, subject to certain exceptions. Usually, though, registration is a mere formality, unlike the process of obtaining a patent.

[57] Oddly enough, there is no definition of the term "author" in the U.S. Copyright Act. In most countries, only the human being or beings who created the work can be authors, although exceptions are sometimes made in the case of motion pictures, computer software, and newspaper articles (in which instances employers sometimes are viewed as the owners of the work). In the United States, works created by an employee within the scope of his employment, as well as some specially commissioned works, are defined as "works made

term in the United States and most other industrialized nations now consists of the life of the author plus seventy years.[58]

Although they now encompass much more than the rights of "printing, publishing, republishing, and vending," the rights of a copyright owner remain somewhat less expansive than the corresponding patent owner's rights. Of paramount importance is the reproduction right, that is, the right to reproduce protectable expression, selection, or arrangement in tangible copies.[59] This right protects not only against literal copying but, in appropriate cases, against copying such aspects of a work as its plot and its fictional characters – though deciding at precisely what point these aspects of the work fall on the "expression," as opposed to the "idea," side of the line can be quite difficult.[60] The copyright owner also has the exclusive right to prepare derivative works, that is, works that are based upon the copyrighted work (such as a translation or a motion picture version of a novel).[61] This right, sometimes known as the adaptation right, is largely, though not entirely, coextensive with the modern reproduction right. In addition, the owner has the exclusive right to distribute copies of the work to the public; to perform and display the work publicly; and to import the work into the United States.[62] Each of these terms is a term of art; although we will not

for hire," copyright to which subsists *ab initio* in the employer or hiring party. See 17 U.S.C. §§ 101 that defines work made for hire, 201(b). Most countries, including the United States, also permit the author to freely assign or license most of the rights comprising copyright protection, subject to certain exceptions. In a few countries, however, authors can only license, but never assign, their copyrights.

[58] The U.S. Supreme Court recently upheld the life-plus-seventy term, which was adopted only in 1998, against constitutional challenge. See *Eldred v. Ashcroft*, 537 U.S. 186 (2003). The copyright term for works for hire and certain other works consists of ninety-five years from the date of publication or 120 years from the date of creation, whichever is shorter. Works published prior to January 1, 1978, but still under copyright protection in the United States as of January 1, 1999, enjoy a ninety-five-year term.

[59] See 17 U.S.C. § 106(1).

[60] See *Nichols v. Universal Pictures Corp.*, 45 F.2d 119, 121 (2d Cir. 1930) (Hand, J.) for details regarding the formulation of the famous "abstractions" test.

[61] See 17 U.S.C. § 101 that contains the definition of derivative work, § 106(2).

[62] See 17 U.S.C. §§ 106(4), 106(5), 106(6), 602. The performance right applies to literary, musical, dramatic, and choreographic works, pantomimes, motion pictures and other audiovisual works, and to digital sound recordings. See 17 U.S.C. §§ 106(4), 106(6). The display right applies to "literary, musical, dramatic, and choreographic works, pantomimes, and pictorial, graphic, or sculptural works, including the individual images of a motion picture or other audiovisual work." *Id.* § 106(5).

Many countries also confer upon authors or other entities additional rights known as *moral* rights and *neighboring* rights. Moral rights laws typically entitle the author to claim authorship of his work and to prevent certain distortions and mutilations of the work, even after the title to the work and its copyright have passed to another. U.S. law incorporates

dwell upon it here, there is considerable case law addressing such knotty issues as whether a particular performance is "public," whether a particular act qualifies as a "distribution," and so on.

As in patent cases, defendants in copyright cases often argue that their conduct does not infringe or that the plaintiff's IPR is invalid (for example, because the plaintiff's work lacks originality). Courts have developed a variety of tests, all of them rather vague, for determining whether an accused work is "substantially similar" to the complainant's work; we briefly refer to some of these in Chapter 5. In addition, copyright law admits many more exceptions than patent law. There is, first, a *first-sale* or *exhaustion* doctrine, similar to what we find in patent law, which permits the owner of a lawfully made copy to distribute and display that copy without permission of the copyright owner.[63] Second, a variety of limited exceptions apply only to certain works or certain uses; many of these provisions of the U.S. Copyright Act tend to be highly technical.[64] Third, the United States recognizes the *fair use* defense, an open-ended exception that, when successful, can exempt the defendant from liability in a number of different situations. Courts generally consider four factors in deciding whether a use is fair, and thus exempt; we briefly discuss this issue in Chapter 6. (Other countries generally eschew fair use in favor of more specific, less open-ended exceptions. Even the analogous "fair dealing" exception found in some countries of the British Commonwealth is considerably narrower than the fair use doctrine.) Finally, *independent discovery* is not actionable in copyright; absent the copying of another's work, there can be no liability. We discuss some reasons why this rule makes sense in Chapter 5.

Most of the time, the prevailing plaintiff in a copyright infringement action obtains an injunction – although the U.S. Supreme Court has recently

some limited moral rights protection under the Visual Artists Rights Act and some other bodies of law. See Cotter (1997). Neighboring rights often confer a degree of protection, falling short of a full-blown copyright, upon performers and other entities not covered by copyright law. In the United States, § 1101 of the Copyright Act confers neighboring rights protection upon musical performers only.

[63] See 17 U.S.C. §§ 109(a), (c). The first-sale doctrine does not apply to computer programs and sound recordings, however, see *id.* § 109(b), because, as one commentator has noted with respect to these works, "the dangers of renter copying are particularly apparent." Netanel (1996; 300). Moreover, the owner retains a right to prohibit the display of the work by projection of more than one image at a time or to viewers not present at the place where the copy is located. See 17 U.S.C. § 109(c).

[64] See 17 U.S.C. §§ 108, 110–22. For example, § 114 provides some exceptions to the copyright owner's exclusive rights in sound recordings in connection with, *inter alia*, webcasting. In a standard edition of the U.S. Copyright Act, this section takes up nearly twenty pages of text and is virtually incomprehensible to nonspecialists.

cautioned that injunctions are not automatic.[65] In addition, there are a few discrete situations in which copyright law mandates compulsory licensing instead of an injunction.[66] Under U.S. law the victorious copyright owner is entitled to his "actual damages and any additional profits of the infringer that are attributable to the infringement and are not taken into account in computing the actual damages."[67] Normally, this means that the plaintiff is entitled to the larger of either (1) his own lost profits or (2) the defendant's profits attributable to the infringement. As we shall see, these numbers need not be identical. To recover the defendant's profits, once the copyright owner presents proof of the infringer's gross revenue, the burden shifts to the defendant "to prove his or her deductible expenses and the elements of profits attributable to factors other than the copyrighted work."[68] In the alternative, and at the election of the copyright owner, the court may award "statutory damages for all infringements involved in the action with respect to any one work . . . in a sum of not less than $750 or more than $30,000 as the court considers just."[69] In cases of willful infringement, the court may increase statutory damages to a sum of not more than $150,000; in cases of innocent infringement, the court may reduce them to a sum of not less than $200.[70] The court in its discretion also may award the prevailing party costs and attorney's fees and (arguably) prejudgment interest, but not punitive damages.[71]

Like patent law, copyright can be viewed as performing both an incentive and a prospect-like function. The incentive theory suggests that, in the absence of copyright protection, the number of works created and published would be less than optimal due to the ability of others to free-ride upon the efforts of creators and publishers and thereby prevent them from recouping their investments in creation and publication. At the same time, theorists recognize that too strong a system of copyright protection may

---

[65] See *New York Times Co. v. Tasini*, 533 U.S. 483, 505 (2001) and *Campbell v. Acuff-Rose Music, Inc.*, 510 U.S. 569, 578 n.10 (1994).

[66] For examples under U.S. law, see 17 U.S.C. § 104A(d)(3) that authorizes owners of derivative works based on "restored works," as defined by *id.* § 104A(h)(6), to continue using derivative works upon payment of reasonable compensation; *id.* U.S.C. § 111(c) that provides compulsory licensing for secondary transmissions by cable systems; and *id.* § 114(d)(2), (f) that provides compulsory licensing of copyrights in sound recordings for use in digital transmission subscription services.

[67] 17 U.S.C. § 504(a).

[68] *Id.* § 504(b).

[69] *Id.* § 504(c)(2).

[70] See *id.*

[71] See *id.* § 505; 3 Nimmer (2002; § 14.02[B], at 14–24 to –28).

deter the creation of new works that build upon earlier ones due to the presence of transaction costs and other bargaining obstacles that may restrict access to these earlier works.[72] The prospect theory suggests that according ownership rights in all of the various uses for any given copyrighted work will maximize social welfare by encouraging the efficient development of markets for those uses.[73] Both theories are subject to the same general critiques discussed previously, as well as some new ones.[74] Moreover, in some cases, the two theories can produce conflicting policy recommendations. Providing the copyright owner with an exclusive right to prepare derivative works, for example, may be difficult to justify on the basis of an incentive theory alone, because in most cases the additional incentive to creativity attributable to this right will be small.[75] From the standpoint of prospect

---

[72] See Landes & Posner (1989); Sterk (1996; 1204–5). The administrative costs of the copyright system are probably lower than the corresponding costs of the patent system, however, due to the low level of scrutiny that the Copyright Office employs before registering a work. In addition, monopoly costs are in general probably lower as well, due to the presence of substitutes for many copyrighted works and to a variety of copyright doctrines, such as merger and scenes à faire. Under the merger doctrine, when there are only a small number of ways of expressing a given idea, the idea "merges" with the expression and no copyright may subsist in the expression. The scenes à faire doctrine prohibits copyright protection for standard characters or plot devices or for standard computer programming techniques.

[73] See Goldstein (1994; 178–9) ("The logic of property rights dictates their extension into every corner in which people derive enjoyment and value from literary and artistic works. To stop short of these ends would deprive producers of the signals of consumer preference that trigger and direct their investments."); see also Netanel (1996; 308–36) who critiqued this theory.

[74] Some recent work purports to show, for example, that under certain conditions, content providers may be *better* off if (1) they charge a higher price to the initial purchasers of copyrighted works, and (2) then permit the purchasers to make unlimited copies. See Boldrin & Levine (2002); Watt (2000; 24–70); and *cf.* Klein et al. (2002). Others argue that in the digital environment, the production and dissemination of works of authorship can be underwritten by content *users'* investment in computer hardware and software. See Ku (2002). Alternatively, one could attempt to reimburse content providers by imposing a tax upon copying equipment and then directing some portion of the tax revenues to content providers rather than by imposing copying restrictions. This approach has made limited headway in the United States but has been used to a greater extent elsewhere. See Watt (2000; 132–4). In addition, when network effects are present, copyright protection can result in very strong rights to control the direction of an industry. See Lemley & McGowan (1998). In these instances, the monopoly costs of protection may be very high. Finally, the cost and efficacy of self-help measures such as encryption may be different in the digital environment than in the nonvirtual world. Whether this phenomenon renders copyright unnecessary, or calls for ever more vigilance to protect some of the values (such as fair use) embodied in traditional copyright law, remains a matter of intense debate.

[75] See Sterk (1996; 1215–17). Sterk recognizes, however, that under some circumstances, the expectation of derivative revenues may be a motivating factor in creating the original work, but he argues that these circumstances are atypical. And there are other possible utilitarian

theory, on the other hand, the adaptation right may seem desirable because it facilitates the copyright owner's ability to efficiently coordinate investment in specific derivative works for which consumers are willing to pay and reduces the probability that overuse will cause the value of a copyrighted work to fall.[76]

TRADEMARKS

Yet another source of intellectual property law, in addition to patents and copyrights, is the law of unfair competition. In one sense, classifying this body of law under the same general heading as patents and copyrights is problematic, because in many respects the rationale for its existence is quite different from the rationales that underlie the other two. Moreover, the term "unfair competition" itself encompasses many bodies of law, including the law of trade secrets, as well as trademarks, false advertising, product disparagement, and the right of publicity. For present purposes, we limit our focus to trademarks, that is, words and other symbols that signify a unique source or sponsor of a product or service.[77]

Under the expansive view that prevails in most industrialized countries today, a trademark can be *any* symbol that identifies a unique product or service. The most obvious examples are words, such as COCA-COLA or MICROSOFT, but trademark rights can subsist in other distinctive symbols as well, such as pictures (the MICHELIN man for tires), numbers (NO. 1 ouzo), and letters (ABC, for a variety of products and services including the television network). Even attributes such as colors (the color pink for fiberglass), fragrances (the scent of plumeria blossoms applied to yarn),

---

justifications for the adaptation right. In the absence of such a right, the first person to make a particular adaptation may effectively preempt the field, discouraging anyone else from adapting the same work. This outcome is undesirable if the first adaptor is not as talented as another adaptor would have been. Alternatively, perhaps no one would bother to create a resource-intensive derivative work, if others were free to create competing derivative works based upon the same underlying work. See Netanel (1996; 379).

[76] See 2 Goldstein (2002; § 5.3, at 5:81); Landes & Posner (2002; 13–15); and Landes & Posner (1989; 354–5). See Lemley (1997; 1044–77) where a critique of prospect-theoretical justification for the current scope of adaptation rights is provided. These differences of opinion concerning the appropriate scope of copyright law tend to divide law and economics scholars who write in this field into two camps, which Neil Netanel refers to as the "minimalist" and "neoclassical" schools. Netanel (1996; 309–11).

[77] Virtually any symbol, including colors, sounds, fragrances, product packaging, and product configuration can serve as trademarks, as long as they are sufficiently distinctive and nonfunctional. See *Wal-Mart Stores, Inc. v. Samara Bros.*, 529 U.S. 205 (2000) and *Qualitex Co. v. Jacobson Prods.*, 514 U.S. 159 (1995).

sounds (the NBC chimes), and "trade dress" – a term that can refer to product packaging, product shape, and even restaurant decor – can serve as source signifiers, subject to the qualifications that they be distinctive (meaning that consumers are believed to perceive them as source signifiers) and nonfunctional (meaning, roughly, that the attribute does not significantly affect the cost or quality of the article of which it is a part or place nonusing competitors at a significant nonreputation-related disadvantage).[78]

In most countries other than the United States, a person acquires trademark rights through registration, although subsequent use of the mark within a specified period of time is usually necessary to keep the registration in force. In the United States, by contrast, use is generally a prerequisite to protection: the first person to make a lawful, commercial use of a symbol to identify her product or service acquires a trademark right by operation of law, although this right may be enforceable only within the geographic area in which the product or service has been sold or advertised.[79] Since 1947, however, the United States has eased the common-law rule by permitting the federal registration of marks used in interstate commerce. Registration under the federal Lanham Act creates a presumption of nationwide rights, generally enforceable even in areas outside of the trademark owner's actual market.[80] Since 1989, firms also may effectively reserve some marks for a period of time prior to actual use by filing an intent-to-use (ITU) application, although no actual trademark rights spring into existence unless and until the owner begins actual use.[81] Subject to some exceptions – including a first-sale or exhaustion doctrine, similar to the one we have encountered in patent and copyright law[82] – trademark rights may persist for as long as

---

[78] Some symbols – for example, "fanciful" words such as KODAK – are viewed as being inherently distinctive, meaning that consumer identification of the symbol with a unique source is presumed. Trademark protection springs into existence upon first use (or first filing, in most countries), without the need to prove that consumers actually identify the word with a single source. On the other hand, if a symbol is noninherently distinctive – for example, a descriptive term (TASTY salad dressing) or product design trade dress – the person claiming trademark rights must be prepared to demonstrate that the symbol has acquired distinctiveness (in trademark parlance, "secondary meaning") – that is, that a substantial portion of the relevant class of consumers has come to identify the symbol with a unique source. Finally, if a word is the generic term for a class of products, it cannot serve as a trademark. Because competitors need to use generic terms to market their products without fear of liability, there can be no SOAP brand soap or CAR brand automobiles. For more detailed discussions of functionality, see Barrett (2004); Thurmon (2004).

[79] See Cotter (1995).

[80] See *id.* at 492 n.24, 536–37.

[81] See 15 U.S.C. § 1051(b).

[82] See Restatement (Third) of Unfair Competition § 24 cmt. b, which stated that "the rights of the trademark owner are exhausted once the owner authorize[s] the initial sale of the

consumers continue to identify the mark with a unique source. To maintain the additional benefits flowing from federal registration, however, the owner must periodically renew her registration.

Ownership of a trademark entails two principal rights. First, and more importantly, the owner has a right to exclude others from the commercial use of a mark that is likely to cause confusion with the owner's mark as to the source or sponsorship of the parties' goods or services.[83] For example, if you started selling a soft drink and called it COCA-COLA – or something similar to COCA-COLA – there is a good chance that some nontrivial percentage of consumers coming into contact with your product would mistakenly assume some connection between that product and genuine COCA-COLA products. In this example, your unauthorized use of the words COCA-COLA to sell a soft drink is close to counterfeiting, which itself is a variety of trademark infringement. But trademark infringement goes beyond such obvious examples. Consumers may think, for example, that the words ORLANDO MAGIC on a tee shirt imply that the basketball team has endorsed or authorized the shirt, even though the team's principal business is entertainment and few people would expect the team itself to have manufactured the shirt. In this example, the unauthorized use of a mark to convey a false message of sponsorship is another variety of infringement. Similarly, a small company known as DREAMWERKS that sponsored Star Trek conventions successfully asserted a claim against the Spielberg/Katzenberg/Geffen media giant on a theory of "reverse confusion." Here, the parties were not marketing competitive products or services, and there was little chance that consumers would be confused into thinking that the small company was the source of DREAMWORKS-produced films. The claim was, in fact, the opposite – that consumers would believe the small company was using the name with permission of the giant. Although it is possible that the small firm would benefit from such false association, it is also possible that it could be harmed (through loss of control over its mark, consumer disappointment upon discovering the limited nature of DREAMWERKS's services, and so on); therefore, this possibility is sufficient to state a claim under a theory

product under that trademark"; see also *Champion Spark Plug Co. v. Sanders,* 331 U.S. 125 (1947), that held that the use of the original trademark on reconditioned spark plugs did not infringe, where accompanied by an appropriate disclaimer. As with patents and copyrights, the issue sometimes arises whether the first sale that "counts" for purposes of exhaustion is the first sale within the country in which protection is sought or the first sale anywhere. U.S. law adds to the confusion over this issue by introducing a partially overlapping body of customs law to the equation. But these are issues we do not take up in this work.
[83] See 15 U.S.C. §§ 1051, 1072, 1115.

of "reverse confusion."[84] Under modern law, the gist of the infringement cause of action is that a *substantial* portion of the likely purchasers of the products or services at issue is *likely* to be confused as to the source or sponsorship of *either* party's goods or services. Courts consider a variety of factors in determining whether confusion is likely.[85] Significantly, there is no requirement that consumers know the identity of the unique source the mark signifies (how many people know, for example, that COCA-COLA is the ultimate parent company of SPRITE?); or that the products be competitive (e.g., DREAMWERKS); or that any consumers have been *actually* confused; or that the plaintiff prove that the expected confusion will be material to consumers' purchasing decisions. There are, however, a variety of defenses and doctrines that confine the trademark owner's rights in certain discrete cases.[86]

A second right, applicable only to famous, highly distinctive marks,[87] is the right to prevent trademark dilution. Dilution is the lessening of the capacity of a mark to identify a unique product or service.[88] For example, when you hear the word KODAK, you immediately think of film, but if the word KODAK appeared (even nonconfusingly) on other products (e.g., KODAK tires, KODAK cola, and so on), it would no longer call to mind a single product or product source. The principal theory behind antidilution laws is that such uses diminish the value of the mark; the benefit of these laws to consumers is more difficult to discern, although there may be some benefit in,

---

[84] See *Dreamwerks Production Group, Inc. v. SKG Studio*, 142 F.3d 1127 (9th Cir. 1998).

[85] Most are variations on the factors set forth in the Restatement (Third) of Unfair Competition § 29. They include, *inter alia*, the similarity of the marks; the inherent and acquired distinctiveness of the plaintiff's mark; the proximity of the plaintiff's and defendant's goods; the degree of purchaser sophistication; the manner in which the goods are marketed; any evidence of actual confusion; and the defendant's intent. See also Cotter (1995; 530).

[86] For example, the nonconfusing use of another's mark either to describe one's own products or to refer truthfully to the owner's products for purposes of comparative advertising can be a lawful use. Similarly, the plaintiff's mark can be invalidated on a number of grounds, including genericness. Many once-trademarked words have become the generic terms for a class of products. Examples include aspirin, trampoline, yo-yo, and Murphy bed.

[87] The federal antidilution law limits its protection to marks that are famous and highly distinctive. It lists a variety of factors that are relevant to the issue of whether a mark is famous, and courts have come up with additional factors. See 15 U.S.C. § 1125(c)(1). There is, at present, a split of authority on the issue of whether marks must be not only famous but also inherently distinctive to merit protection under the federal law. Courts also differ as to whether fame must be nationwide and pervasive, or whether geographic or niche fame is sufficient. In addition, some states also have antidilution laws that differ in some respects from the federal act.

[88] See 15 U.S.C. § 1127 (definition of dilution) and Restatement (Third) of Unfair Competition § 25 cmt. e (1995).

for example, preserving against dilution the value of marks that consumers view as status symbols.[89] Courts further distinguish dilution by blurring, which is at issue in the KODAK example, from dilution by tarnishment, in which the defendant uses the mark in connection with an unwholesome product (for example, ADULTS-R-US for a pornographic website).[90] In the United States, federal antidilution protection has existed only since 1996, although about half of the states already had parallel antidilution laws as of that date and have retained these laws. A recent Supreme Court decision holds that the federal act provides a remedy only against *actual*, not likely, dilution,[91] but this limitation may not be as significant as it seems given that the definition of actual dilution as a "lessening of capacity" itself seems to contemplate some degree of potential harm. In any event, most of the state laws that address dilution use a "likelihood of dilution" standard and there is a good chance that the language in the federal act that the Court interpreted as requiring a showing of actual dilution was a result of poor drafting that Congress will eventually repair.

The prevailing plaintiff in a federal trademark infringement action is entitled to injunctive relief and, like her counterpart in a copyright case, also may recover the defendant's profits attributable to the infringement and any damages sustained by the plaintiff as long as the court avoids double counting.[92] (The Federal Trademark Dilution Act authorizes courts to

---

[89] See Kozinski (1993; 969–70) who argues that, to some extent, modern trademark law protects the value of marks as status symbols.

[90] See *Toys "R" Us, Inc. v. Akkaoui*, 40 U.S.P.Q.2d 1836 (N.D. Cal. 1996).

[91] See *Moseley v. V Secret Catalogue, Inc.* 537 U.S. 418 (2003).

[92] See *id.* §§ 1116(a), 1117(a). Certain exceptions to damages liability apply, however, with respect to defendants whose only involvement in an infringement is the printing or advertising of an infringing mark. See *id.* § 1114(2). In cases involving counterfeit marks, however – defined as the use of a "counterfeit of a mark that is registered on the principal register of the United States Patent and Trademark Office for such goods or services sold, offered for sale, or distributed and that is in use, whether or not the person against whom relief is sought knew such mark was so registered," 15 U.S.C. § 1116(d)(1)(B) – the plaintiff may recover treble his actual damages or the defendant's profits, whichever is greater, see *id.* § 1117(a), (b), or he may elect to recover statutory damages in the amount of "not less than $500 or more than $100,000 per counterfeit mark per type of goods or services sold, offered for sale, or distributed, as the court considers just," 15 U.S.C. §§ 1117(c)(1). If the court finds that the counterfeiting was willful, it may assess statutory damages of "not more than $1,000,000 per counterfeit mark per type of goods or services sold, offered for sale, or distributed, as the court considers just." *Id.* § 1117(c)(2). The court is also authorized to order the seizure, upon *ex parte* application, of goods bearing counterfeit marks, 15 U.S.C. § 1116(d), and in cases involving either infringement or counterfeiting to order the destruction of any goods found to bear an infringing or counterfeiting mark, *id.* § 1118. See also 18 U.S.C. § 2320 regarding imposing criminal penalties for trafficking in counterfeit goods or services.

enjoin the dilution of famous marks and, in cases of willful dilution only, to apply the same set of damages remedies that are available for trademark infringement.[93]) Historically, however, courts have been reluctant to award the defendant's profits, unless the infringement implies "some connotation of "intent" or a knowing act denoting an intent to infringe or reap the harvest of another's mark and advertising."[94] As in the copyright context, the plaintiff satisfies her burden of production on this issue by providing evidence of the defendant's sales, at which point the burden shifts to the defendant to prove which costs should be deducted to arrive at the correct profit amount.[95] With respect to actual damages, the court may award (1) the plaintiff's lost profits attributable to the infringement, (2) the amount necessary to undertake a corrective advertising campaign, or (3) a reasonable royalty for use of the mark.[96]

The Lanham Act also authorizes the enhancement of damages awards in appropriate cases. First, the court may enhance the amount of actual damages by entering a judgment "according to the circumstances of the case, for any sum above the amount found as actual damages, not exceeding three times such amount."[97] Second:

[i]f the court shall find that the amount of recovery based on profits is either inadequate or excessive the court may in its discretion enter judgment for such sum as the court shall find to be just, according to the circumstances of the case.[98]

In effect, this latter provision enables the court to "[i]ncrease or decrease an award of profits by any amount if the court finds the profit recovery is "either inadequate or excessive."[99] In general, however, courts usually enhance damages only when the defendant is found to have willfully infringed the plaintiff's mark. The court may award reasonable attorney's

---

[93] See 15 U.S.C. § 1125(c)(1), (2).

[94] See 4 McCarthy (2002; § 30:62, at 30–101) and Restatement (Third) of Unfair Competition, § 36 cmts. b, c, § 37 & cmt. e.

[95] See 15 U.S.C. § 1117(a).

[96] See 4 McCarthy (2002; §§ 30:79–87) and Restatement (Third) of Unfair Competition § 36, which states that the plaintiff's actual damages may include (1) losses resulting from sales or other revenues lost because of defendant's conduct; (2) sales made by plaintiff at prices that have been reasonably reduced because of such conduct; (3) harm to market reputation of plaintiff's goods, services, business, or trademark; and (4) reasonable expenditures made by plaintiff to prevent, correct, or mitigate confusion.

[97] 15 U.S.C. § 1115(a).

[98] *Id.* The statute goes on to state that "[s]uch sum in either of the above circumstances shall constitute compensation and not a penalty." *Id.* The precise meaning of this sentence is unclear. See 4 McCarthy (2002; § 30:91).

[99] 4 McCarthy (2002; § 30:90, at 30–146).

fees to the prevailing party in exceptional cases; whether it should ordinarily award her prejudgment interest as well or whether such relief should be
limited to exceptional cases is an issue on which the U.S. courts currently are
divided.[100]

Trademarks serve several economic functions. First, they lower search
costs by allowing consumers to distinguish between products that differ in
quality but that, in the absence of differing brand names, would be difficult or
impossible to distinguish at the point of purchase.[101] In order for trademarks
to fulfill this function, however, the goods or services they identify must be
of more or less uniform quality. Therefore, a second function of trademarks
is to encourage producers to invest in quality control or, more broadly,
the development of the consumer goodwill that trademarks symbolize. Put
another way, trademarks encourage firms to invest in creating goodwill
by conferring a legal right against some, though not all, free-riding upon
that goodwill.[102] A third, more controversial, quality of trademarks that
may be more relevant to the antidilution cause of action is the ability of
trademarks to serve as vehicles for persuasive advertising, which is a function
that may be undermined by another's use of a similar mark (even if that use
is unlikely to cause confusion) that threatens to "blur" the distinctive nature
of the mark or to "tarnish" its image. A fourth, even more controversial,
function of trademarks may be to promote monopolistic competition by
encouraging consumers to perceive differences among products that are
not, in any meaningful sense, distinct. This argument – really more of a
critique than an argument in favor of trademark protection – is no longer
very popular, but occasionally surfaces in the critical literature.[103]

PROPERTY RULES AND LIABILITY RULES

One issue of considerable importance to the design of intellectual property
laws is whether it is preferable to protect IPRs by means of "property rules"

---

[100] See 15 U.S.C. § 1115(a); 4 McCarthy (2002; §§ 30:91, 30:93).

[101] These would be so-called *experience* goods, which must be consumed in order for the
purchaser to evaluate their quality. The rationale would not apply to *inspection* goods,
which can be examined prior to consumption and evaluated for quality differences.

[102] The anti-free-riding theory does not explain reverse confusion, however, which as discussed earlier is actionable more because of its potential impact upon the small senior
user's ability to control the mark. In a reverse confusion case, the defendant's use threatens
to destroy the value of the plaintiff's investment but does not constitute free-riding. For
further discussion of the law and economics of reverse confusion, see Feldman (2003).

[103] See Carter (1990; 768), who discusses, but does not endorse this view.

or "liability rules." In a famous article, Guido Calabresi and Douglas Melamed (1972; 1092) distinguished these rules in the following manner:

An entitlement is protected by a property rule to the extent that someone who wishes to remove the entitlement from its holder must buy it from him in a voluntary transaction in which the value of the entitlement is agreed upon by the seller. It is the form of entitlement which gives rise to the least amount of state intervention: once the original entitlement is decided upon, the state does not try to decide its value. It lets each of the parties say how much the entitlement is worth to him, and gives the seller a veto if the buyer does not offer enough. . . .

Whenever someone may destroy the initial entitlement if he is willing to pay an objectively determined value for it, an entitlement is protected by a liability rule. . . . Obviously, liability rules involve an additional stage of state intervention: not only are entitlements protected, but their transfer or destruction is allowed on the basis of a value determined by some organ of the state rather than by the parties themselves.

As our previous discussion shows, the law generally entitles the owner of an IPR to obtain an injunction against the unauthorized use of his patent, copyright, trademark, or trade secret; in so doing, the law encourages the owner and the would-be user to bargain for a transfer of rights at a mutually agreed-upon price. In these respects, IPRs are a paradigmatic example of entitlements protected by property rules, although there are some instances in which the would-be infringer is entitled, as under a liability-rule system, simply to "breach and pay damages" whenever he wishes to use another's intellectual property.[104]

---

[104] For examples in copyright law, see *supra* note 66. In the law of trade secrets, as we have seen, in exceptional cases a court may permit the defendant to continue using the secret upon payment of a reasonable royalty. In addition, an employee who is deemed to own an invention or other valuable information created during the period of his employment may be required to provide his employer with a "shop right" – an irrevocable, nonexclusive, royalty-free license to use the invention in its own business. See Cotter (1996; 594). There are a few situations in which the U.S. government has required the compulsory licensing of patents, such as as a remedy for patent misuse or other anticompetitive conduct, and in certain other discrete settings. Other countries may impose compulsory licensing for other reasons, such as to combat national health emergencies. See Cotter (2004). The U.S. government also may effect a taking of intellectual property for a public purpose, subject to the Fifth Amendment's requirement of just compensation. See, e.g., *Jacobs Wind Elec. Co. v. Department of Transportation*, 626 So. 2d 1333 (Fla. 1993). In fact, the federal government licenses many patents to itself, largely for military purposes. See Cotter (1998).

In a provocative article, Nance (1997; 853) challenges the conventional understanding of Calabresi and Melamed's distinction between property rules and liability rules, arguing that "property, liability, and inalienability rules should be considered prescriptions concerning what people should do, not descriptions of what they can or must do." In other words, Nance views the distinction as incorporating a normative aspect. On this understanding, a property entitlement means that others *should not* encroach (but not

Many law and economics scholars have argued that it is generally prefer-able to protect IPRs through the use of property, as opposed to liability, rules. As Robert Merges has explained, in the context of patents:

[A] property rule makes sense . . . because: (1) there are only two parties to the trans-action, and they can easily identify each other; (2) the costs of a transaction between the parties are otherwise low; and (3) a court setting the terms of the exchange would have a difficult time doing so quickly and cheaply, given the specialized nature of the assets and the varied and complex business environments in which the assets are deployed. Hence the parties are left to make their own deal.[105]

For these reasons, Merges and other scholars contend that compulsory li-censing schemes, under which the owner of an intellectual property right is required to license users at some statutorily fixed or judicially fixed rate, are often less efficient than is a system of property-like protection.[106]

To say that property rules are generally preferable is not to say that they are necessarily desirable under all circumstances. As we noted earlier, IPRs sometimes are protected by liability rules instead, whereas in other settings alternative compensation schemes (such as taxes on copying equipment) are in place. These alternatives might make sense if, for example, the transac-tion costs of bargaining are unusually high and the likelihood of voluntary solution to this problem unusually low. This could occur, for example, if one would need to bargain with many rightholders in order to improve upon a technology and other obstacles block the implementation of vol-untary solutions to the transaction cost problem, such as patent pools.[107]

---

necessarily that encroachments will be enjoined), whereas a liability rule means that others *may* encroach (but will be required to pay for doing so). Even under Nance's interpre-tation, however, IPRs are protected (most of the time) by property rules, insofar as the law prescribes that one should not infringe another's IPR. The damages to which one would be entitled for the period of time preceding the entry of an injunction would be, under Nance's terminology, protected under a "remedial compensation rule." See *id.* at 873, 902–5; see also Coleman & Kraus (1986) (similar).

[105] See Merges (1994; 78) and Merges (1996) where an argument is made that compulsory licensing schemes are suboptimal because they are subject to "legislative lock-in."

[106] See, e.g., Adelstein & Peretz (1985); Gordon (1982; 1613); and Kitch (1977; 286–7). But see Ayres & Talley (1995; 1092–4) for an argument that, under some circumstances, a compulsory licensing system will induce the owner and user to reveal their true valuation of the subject property, and therefore may help to overcome bargaining obstacles arising out of strategic behavior. See also Lemley & Volokh (1998), who argue against the routine granting of preliminary injunctions in copyright infringement cases on First Amendment grounds.

[107] But even then, scholars like Merges have argued that it may be preferable to foster the development of private solutions to transaction-cost problems rather than to impose compulsory licensing. On the other hand, Ayres and Talley have argued that, in some set-tings, liability rules may induce the owner and would-be user to disclose more information

Alternatively, there may be cases in which policymakers opt for a liability rule in order to implement a particular vision of social justice. An example might be the recent controversy over the use of compulsory patent licensing to enable greater access to AIDS drugs and other essential medicines in developing countries. Some scholars also are concerned about the overuse of injunctions in copyright and trade secrets cases to the extent that these applications can affect freedom of speech or other constitutional rights.[108] We do not resolve these controversies here. We think it is fair to state, however, that intellectual property law in general prefers property rules to liability rules and that – if the premises upon which the intellectual property system is based are sound – a rebuttable presumption in favor of property rules probably makes more sense than would a presumption favoring liability rules. Deviations from the norm may be justified in some cases, but we will assume that the norm is a property rule.

concerning their subjective valuation of property. See Ayres & Talley (1995; 1092–4). The applicability of this insight to IPRs outside the bilateral monopoly setting has been challenged, however. See Merges (1996; 1304–5); see also Burk (1999; 142).

[108] See Lemley & Volokh (1998).

THREE

A General Theory of Damages Rules

As we have seen, the standard justification for patents and copyrights is that they provide a necessary incentive to create, disseminate, and commercialize inventions and works of authorship. They also may serve other functions, such as enabling the rights holder to coordinate investment in follow-up improvements. Trade secret law may supplement patent protection and conserve on some social costs, whereas trademark law reduces consumer search costs and provides an incentive to invest in quality control. A general preference for injunctions as a means for enforcing these rights would tend to preserve these incentive structures, but injunctive relief alone may be incomplete due to time lags, the cost of enforcement, and other real-world problems. Detecting and proving infringement is rarely instantaneous, for example, and thus some time will elapse from the moment the infringement begins until a court can enter an injunction. Damages rules, therefore, may be necessary to preserve the incentive structure, both by deterring infringement and by appropriately compensating the rights holder when infringement does occur. In this chapter, we construct a simple model of optimal damages rules for patent cases. In the following chapter, we compare our simple model with the actual rules that prevail in patent, trade secret, copyright, and trademark law.

THE PATENT INCENTIVE

We begin by presenting a stylized model of a firm's decision to invest in creating and marketing a new invention. At the initial stage, nearly all of the variables that are likely to affect this decision are uncertain. The costs that will be necessary to produce the invention cannot be known with certainty until they are actually incurred. These costs will be incurred before (sometimes long before) the first dime of revenue is realized. The firm can subjectively assess the likelihood that a particular research agenda will be successful, but at the outset the probability of success cannot be known with any certainty either. Assuming that the inventive effort is successful, the economic worth of the resulting invention also cannot be known with certainty before the invention is brought to market. Granted, the decision to invest will not be made in the dark – at least, not entirely. A rational investor will try to estimate the relevant variables before making an investment decision. But substantial uncertainty nevertheless surrounds the entire process.

The first thing a rational investor will try to estimate is the cost of research. We can model these costs algebraically: at time t, the research costs c_{it} may assume n different values with (subjective) probabilities p_i.[1] The expected value of the research cost at time t can be written as

$$C_{rt} = \sum_{i=1}^{n} p_i c_{it} \qquad (3.1)$$

where $\sum_{i=1}^{n} p_i = 1$; in other words, the sum of the probabilities is one.

Once the firm has produced an invention, it must incur development costs k_{jt} to turn the invention into a marketable product. These costs also are unknown until they are actually incurred, but their expected value can similarly be estimated for each time period during the development stage. These expected development costs can be written as C_{dt}:

$$C_{dt} = \sum_{j=1}^{m} q_j k_{jt}$$

where q_j is the probability that the development cost will equal k_j at time t. Again, the probabilities sum to one: $\sum_{j=1}^{m} q_j = 1$.

If the expected costs of research and development are the only costs that we consider, then the present value of the R&D costs at the investment decision point is given by

$$PV(R\&D) = \sum_{t=1}^{R} \frac{C_{rt}}{(1+i)^t} + \sum_{t=R+1}^{D} \frac{C_{dt}}{(1+i)^t}$$

where R is the number of periods that it takes to conduct the research, D is the length of the development period, and i is the discount rate.

---

[1] The expected value is a probability weighted average of the possible outcomes. Suppose, for example, that the research cost in year 1 could take on one of three values: $1.0 million, $2.0 million, and $4.0 million. If the respective probabilities are 0.2, 0.3, and 0.5, then the expected value is $C_r = (0.2)(\$1.0 \text{ million}) + (0.3)(\$2.0 \text{ million}) + (0.5)(\$4.0 \text{ million}) = \$2.8$ million. Similar computations must be done for other years.

Second, the rational investor may try to estimate the potential profits to be earned from the venture – although at the beginning this may amount to little more than guesswork. If the R&D effort is successful, a patented product will be sold and profits will be earned. The future profit at each point in time is also stochastic (probabilistic). The expected profit at time t can be written as π_t. The present value of the expected future profit flow is

$$PV(\pi) = \sum_{t=D+1}^{T} \frac{\pi_t}{(1+i)^t}$$

where T is the end of the product's life. The summation starts at $D+1$ because the R&D must be completed before any profits can be earned.

Next, we assume that a rational investor will invest only when the net present value (NPV) of doing so is positive. In our simple model, the R&D expenditures are incurred over the first D periods and the profits are earned over the $D+1$ to T time frame. As a result, the NPV of the prospective project is

$$NPV = \sum_{t=D+1}^{T} \frac{\pi_t}{(1+i)^t} - \sum_{t=1}^{R} \frac{C_{rt}}{(1+i)^t} - \sum_{t=R+1}^{D} \frac{C_{dt}}{(1+i)^t}.$$

If the present value of the future expected profit flow exceeds the present value of the expected R&D costs, then the NPV will be positive, which means that the investment is expected to be profitable and will be undertaken. Thus, the NPV constitutes the incentive to invest in a risky R&D project.[2]

As we discussed in Chapter 2, the possibility that someone may free-ride upon the originator's R&D reduces her expected future profit, and this reduction in expected profit in turn reduces the incentive to invent, disclose, and commercialize. In the *NPV* equation, the first term on the right-hand side is reduced by infringement, whereas the second and third terms are unchanged. As a result, one would predict that some socially valuable projects would not be undertaken. The existence of a patent right

---

[2] As an illustration, suppose that the expected research costs are $2.8 million for three years, the expected development costs are $2.0 million for two years, and the expected operating profit is $4.5 million for five years. Assuming a 10% discount rate, the present value of the research costs is $6.96 million. The present value of the development costs is $2.61 million. The present value of the expected operating profit is $10.59 million. Thus, the NPV is

$$NPV = \$10.59 - 6.96 - 2.61 = \$1.02 \text{ million.}$$

Even though the annual operating profit appears to be substantial relative to the annual R&D costs, these profits are received well into the future and the investment is not excessively profitable. If the annual operating profits were $4.0 million per year, the NPV would have been negative.

backed up by a right to injunctive relief helps but, as we noted earlier, may be incomplete. To preserve the original incentive structure, we must devise damages rules that leave the NPV unchanged. One way to accomplish this is to compensate the innovator so that she is no worse off as a result of any infringement. Another way is to deter infringement, thereby preventing any deterioration in the NPV in the first place.

Again, we hasten to add that there is no guarantee that any particular incentive structure is optimal. Perhaps patent rights last too long, or not long enough, or are too broad or too narrow. Perhaps a set of rules that encourage some limited infringement would provide more social benefits than costs. We are not attempting to resolve these issues. What we are trying to determine is how to preserve the incentive system that is embedded in the patent laws, *whatever that incentive system is.* In other words, we start from the assumption that we want to maintain the right-hand side of the equation at whatever level it would be, but for the infringement. At the outset, the legislature will have to decide what that level should be; once that decision has been made, the relevant policymaker must craft appropriate damages rules to prevent that decision from being undermined.

DETERRING INFRINGEMENT

As a first approximation, deterring infringement requires a set of rules that render infringement unprofitable. The guidance that this observation provides can be developed in a simple analysis.

If one person infringes another's intellectual property, the infringer will increase his profits by an amount that we denote as π_i. Suppose that the probability of detecting the infringement is P and that the probability of undetected infringement is $(1 - P)$. The return to the infringer is uncertain. The actual return will be either π_i or π_i less the sanction for infringing, which we will denote as F. Accordingly, the expected return to infringing can be written as:

$$E[\pi] = P(\pi_i - F) + (1 - P)\pi_i,$$

where E is the expectations operator and π is the uncertain return to the infringer.

In a stochastic world, we can make this risky venture unprofitable in an expectations sense.[3] That is, we can make the expected return less than or

---

[3] In other words, infringing is profitable to the infringer if he gets away with it and it is unprofitable to him if he does not. By making the expected value of infringement less than

equal to zero by operating on the penalty for infringing (F). Algebraically rearranging $E[\pi]$ yields:

$$E[\pi] = P\pi_i + (1 - P)\pi_i - PF = \pi_i - PF.$$

Thus, an expected sanction (PF) equal to the profit due to infringement makes the expected return equal to zero. This will leave a potential infringer indifferent between infringing and not infringing. If PF exceeds π_i, the potential infringer will be deterred because on average he will earn less profit by infringing than by not infringing. This means that the sanction must be a multiple of the profit due to infringing:

$$F \geq \pi_i/P.$$

Since P is necessarily a fraction in the unit interval, $0 \leq P \leq 1$, the sanction will always exceed π_i except when the probability of detection equals one. In all other cases, F will be a multiple of π_i. For example, if the probability of catching an infringer is one in four (0.25), the sanction will be $4\pi_i$.

This analysis is subject to some important qualifications – both of which derive from the fact that if the infringement is detected, the infringer will be enjoined from further unauthorized use of the property. The first is that the cost of complying with the injunction probably should be subtracted from the calculation of π_i in the event that the defendant is enjoined.[4] Second, there may be some cases in which *no* penalty other than an injunction would be necessary to deter infringement. To illustrate, suppose that the would-be intellectual property user plans to produce goods having a market value of $1,000,000; that the expected production costs are $800,000; and that expected marketing and distribution costs are $100,000. If the user decides to negotiate *ex ante* with the intellectual property owner, he will agree to pay no more than his expected profit of $100,000 in exchange for a license. Now suppose that the user decides instead to infringe, but that he is enjoined immediately after having expended the $800,000 in production costs. Once the injunction is entered, the infringer has two choices: he can

or equal to zero, the policymaker can render infringement unprofitable in an expectations sense. Thus, any infringement that is not detected will be profitable, but on average infringement will not be profitable. See Blair & Kenny (1982; 161).

Richard Craswell (1999) notes that the analysis of multipliers of which ours is an example may not always hold. If, for example, under a system of no multipliers the potential defendant can substantially reduce his chances of getting caught by violating the rule only to a small extent, the multiplier necessary to induce perfect compliance will not have to be as high as the conventional analysis suggests.

[4]   These compliance costs act as a further sanction, i.e., they supplement F. See Heald (1988; 644–5).

either abandon his use of the property or he can agree to a license. Under these circumstances, however, the infringer would be rational to pay up to $900,000 for the license, because in its absence the already-produced goods will be worthless. In this example, the $800,000 production costs are sunk and do not influence subsequent decisions. In the intermediate case in which the infringer is enjoined after having produced only a portion of the expected output, the *ex post* value of the license will fall somewhere in between $100,000 and $900,000. A rational would-be user will factor these potential losses into his expected revenue function. Thus, under a system in which only injunctive relief is available, a more complete description of that function would be:

$$E[\pi] = (1 - P)\pi_i + P(\beta\pi_i - (1 - \beta)C),$$

where β is a measure of the infringer's bargaining strength vis-à-vis the owner, such that $0 < \beta < 1$, and C is the sunk cost the infringer expects to have incurred by the time, if ever, the injunction issues. Assuming that the user and infringer are equally good bargainers, such that $\beta = .5$; that the probability of detection is .25; and that C = $800,000, the user's expected revenue equals $(.75)(100,000) + (.25)(50,000 - 400,000) = -12,500$. On these assumptions, a rational user would choose to negotiate a license *ex ante* rather than to infringe, even in the absence of a damages remedy.[5] The analysis, therefore, suggests that, in cases in which both owner and infringer have an interest in allowing the infringer to continue using the property – i.e., in cases in which the infringer is a more efficient user of the property than is the owner – the minimum sanction necessary to deter may be less than our simple model suggests.

IMPLICATIONS OF THE SIMPLE MODEL

There are three aspects of our simple model that may lead to extraordinary complexity. First, the decision maker must be able to measure π_i accurately. Second, the appropriate multiplier $(1/P)$ will vary from case to case. Third, the potential infringer may be risk-averse. Each of these problems can lead to further refinements of the model.

The first problem is how to measure correctly the infringer's profit attributable to the infringement. This measurement is complicated, because the infringer may have earned some profit without infringing; our model

---

[5] If the values of P, C, or ß change, however, the results may change. For example, if C < $700,000, all else being equal, some damages award will be necessary to deter infringement.

seeks to capture only the incremental profit, π_i, that would not have existed but for the infringement. One way of trying to handle the inherent complexity of this calculation – the way favored by U.S. copyright and trademark law, which both authorize awards of the defendant's profits – is for the infringer to bear the brunt of this uncertainty. That is, the plaintiff has the burden of proving the total profit earned by the infringer; at that point, the burden shifts to the defendant to prove how much of its total profit would have been earned absent the infringement. If the defendant is a firm that produces many different products, this may involve a substantial effort. There also may be complicated questions of allocating common costs to various lines of business, but the defendant is responsible for that problem.

A second problem involves how to compute the optimal multiplier. We suggested previously that the optimal multiplier is the reciprocal of the probability of catching the infringer, but this probability will vary from case to case. Even in one specific case, it is not obvious how one would assess (or estimate) the probability of detecting an infringer. In its classic form, probability is a relative frequency; thus, the probability of detection is the number of instances in which an infringer is detected, divided by the total number of infringements. The problem is that if some infringement is undetected, one cannot know the total number of infringements; as a result, one can never accurately calculate the probability of detection.

A third problem involves risk aversion. In our analysis, we have assumed that the parties are risk-neutral, which means that they compare risky alternatives solely on the basis of expected outcome.[6] A risk-neutral individual, for example, will be indifferent between betting $10 and betting $1,000 on the flip of a fair coin, because the expected outcomes are the same. The reason such indifference strikes most of us as peculiar is that we all tend to be risk-averse, meaning that we take into account the variance in the possible outcomes.[7] Faced with a choice between a $10 bet and a $1,000 bet on the flip of a coin, the risk averter will prefer the $10 bet because that bet has a smaller variance, even though the expected outcomes of the two bets are the same.

If the sanction for infringing is $F = \pi/P$, the risk-neutral potential infringer will be indifferent between infringing and not infringing, because the expected return on infringing is zero. The risk averter, however, will

---

[6] See Blair & Kenny (1982; 161–9).

[7] See Nicholson (1992; 250): "[I]ndividuals, when faced with a choice between two gambles with the same expected value, usually will choose the one with a smaller variability of return."

look at the variance in returns as well and infringing introduces a substantial variance. Although the expected return for the risk averter is, of course, zero, the possible outcomes are π_i with probability $(1 - P)$ and $\pi_i - F$ with probability P. To get a sense of what this means, suppose that π_i, the profit on infringing, is \$1 million and P = 0.25. The range of outcomes then is \$1 million and −\$3 million, because F = \$4 million. This variation in outcomes can be avoided by not infringing and, therefore, the risk-averse potential infringer will be deterred. The important point, however, is that an expected sanction that leaves a risk-neutral decision maker indifferent definitely will deter a risk averter. In most instances, however, there may be no way of estimating the degree to which the decision maker is risk-averse.[8]

IDENTIFYING THE PATENTEE'S INJURY

We have suggested that the expected profits of a potential investor in the creative enterprise must be protected if the incentive structure embodied in the patent system is to be maintained. We have also seen that infringement

---

[8] Scherer speculates that some *patentees* may be less risk-averse than most people. He notes that the return on most patents is small or nonexistent, but that the return on a few of them is very large. This skewed distribution of returns might provide an additional motivation for investment, for much the same reason that people who are otherwise risk-averse may play the lottery. See Scherer (2000). Scherer's analysis suggests that preserving the patent incentive might remain important even if other reasons to invent, such as first-mover advantages and trade secret protection, coexist.

    If, on the other hand, the patentee is also risk-averse, an additional complication arises. Suppose, for example, that a patentee suspects that her patent has been infringed. Suing to recover the damages due to the infringement is a risky proposition, because there is a chance of losing even a meritorious suit. If we let D represent the damage suffered by the patentee and C denote the cost of litigation, the expected value of litigation is:

$$E[V] = PD + (1 - P)(0) - C$$

where P is the probability of winning and $(1 - P)$ is the probability of losing. This expression simplifies to:

$$E[V] = PD - C.$$

Litigation will not have a positive expected value unless PD > C. The smaller the probability of winning, the less likely that E[V] will be positive. Moreover, the greater the cost of litigation, the less likely that E[V] will be positive. It is important to remember that the actual result of the litigation will be an award of D or a loss of C. Thus, there is a possible loss as well as a possible gain. This uncertainty can be avoided by not filing suit. If the patentee is risk-averse, she avoids fair bets; consequently, the expected value of litigation must be decidedly positive for her to file suit. Thus, if we want to encourage private suits to protect intellectual property rights, the expected damages award (D) should be enhanced. This consequence of the patentee's assumed desire to avoid risk, however, would have to be set off against the effect of the infringer's risk aversion.

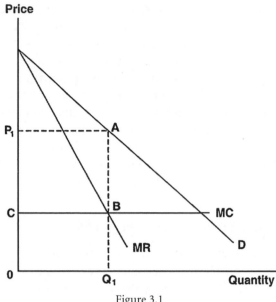

Figure 3.1

can be deterred by making infringement unprofitable, which involves ex-pected sanctions that are at least as large as the profits from infringing. In some instances, these sums are equal, but there are times when they diverge. In the next few paragraphs, we model the various possible outcomes of competition between a patentee and an infringer, when the infringer is (1) equally efficient, (2) less efficient, and (3) more efficient than the patentee. On the basis of this analysis, we will then be better able to de-vise rules to prevent this competition from occurring (that is, to deter the infringement from taking place) and to restore the patentee's *ex ante* incentives.

Schlicher (1996; § 9.05) develops some simple economic models that il-luminate these concepts and assist in constructing optimal damages rules. Following Schlicher, we first consider the situation in which a patent owner directly sells a product embodying the patented invention to consumers within a given geographic market. For simplicity, we also assume that the patentee does not engage in price discrimination and that there are no close substitutes for the patented invention. In order to maximize her profits, the patentee will produce that output where marginal cost equals marginal rev-enue. In Figure 3.1, demand is denoted by D, the corresponding marginal revenue is MR, and marginal cost is MC. The optimal (i.e., profit maximiz-ing) output is found where marginal cost equals marginal revenue: Q_1. The patentee will charge a price of P_1, which is the price on the demand curve that corresponds to an output of Q_1. The profit that results from this process is $(P_1 - MC)Q_1$, which is area P_1ABC in Figure 3.1.

Now consider the effect upon the patentee's profit of a rival's decision to infringe the patent. Initially, we concentrate on the situation in which the infringer and the patentee are equally efficient producers of the relevant product. (By "equally efficient," we mean that they can produce the product at the same marginal cost.) In this case, the infringer's best strategy is to match the price of the patentee and produce one-half of the patentee's former output level.[9] The patentee's best response to the infringer's entry is to reduce its output to one-half of its former quantity and continue to charge P_1. In this way, the maximum profit possible will be earned and it will be split between the patentee and the infringer. Each producer will earn a profit of $(P_1 - MC)Q_2$, where Q_2 is one-half of Q_1. The loss to the patentee is one-half of her former profit, which is precisely equal to the profit of the infringer. In this case, a restitutionary sanction equal to the infringer's gain will make infringing unprofitable and will restore the incentive for investing in the creative effort. Alternatively, a sanction equal to the patentee's lost profit will also make infringement unprofitable.

These results are shown in Figure 3.2. In this graph, MC represents the marginal cost of both the patentee and the infringer. The patentee's new output level will be Q_2, which is one-half of Q_1. Since the infringer also produces Q_2, the total output remains the same as before the infringement, Q_1. As a result, the price remains at P_1 and the total profit is again equal to area P_1ABC. This profit is divided equally between the two parties. The patentee now earns a profit equal to area P_1EFC and the infringer earns an equal profit represented by area EABF.

Matters worsen if the infringer tries to gain an even bigger market share by cutting price below P_1. This could lead to a complete deterioration of price. In this event, price could fall to the competitive level, which is marginal cost.[10] This outcome yields no profits to either party. The patentee's loss would be equal to its former profit, which was area P_1ABC in Figure 3.1.

---

[9] This insight can be traced to Chamberlin (1962; 46–51). See also *infra* pp. 241–2, where we return to the Chamberlinian model.

[10] This is the result of Bertrand price competition with homogeneous products. Even though there are only two rivals, the competitive price and quantity result. This analysis can be traced to Bertrand (1883). See also *infra* pp. 239–41, where we return to the Bertrand model. We discuss competition on the basis of quantity (the Cournot model) *infra* pp. 188–9, 236–9.

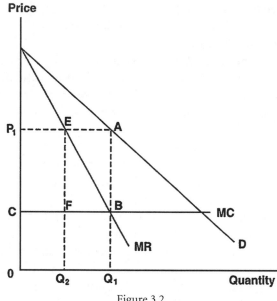

Figure 3.2

Here, of course, the loss to the patentee far exceeds the gain to the infringer, which is zero.

A second possibility is that the infringer will be a less efficient producer than the patentee, meaning that his marginal cost curve (MC_i) will be higher than the patentee's marginal cost curve (MC_p).[11] When this is the case, the infringer maximizes his profit by matching the patentee's selling price. Until the patentee can enjoin the infringer, the patentee can respond in either of two ways or by some combination of the two.

First, the patentee may decide to maintain her selling price at P_1. Under this strategy, total output will remain the same, but the patentee's profit ($\pi^*_{p,2}$) once again will decrease from P_1ABC to P_1EFC. Because the infringer's profit ($\pi^*_{i,2}$) equals only EAGH, aggregate profits have diminished in the amount of HGBF. Note that, under this scenario, the lost aggregate profits HGBF constitute a deadweight loss, because more resources are being used to produce Q_1 than when the patentee served as the exclusive producer.[12]

---

[11] See Schlicher (1996; § 9.05).

[12] Under some circumstances, this outcome could be avoided even in the absence of enforceable intellectual property rights. In a two-person economy with low bargaining costs, for example, one would not expect this inefficiency to persist; the party we have been referring to as the patentee would find it sensible to pay the party we have been referring to as the infringer up to EABF to refrain from producing, and the infringer would be better off if

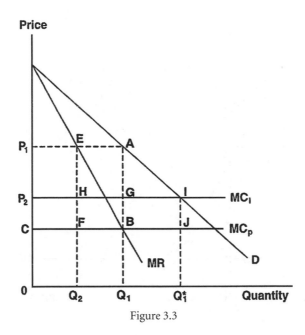

Figure 3.3

In the alternative, the patentee can lower its price to $P_2 = MC_i$ and increase its output to Q_1^*. This strategy eliminates the infringer's share of the monopoly profit and the incentive to infringe; it also increases consumer surplus in the amount bounded by the region P_1AIP_2. At the same time, however, the patentee's profit falls to $(P_2 - MC_p)Q_1^*$, which is represented by area P_2IJC in Figure 3.3. The decrease in profit attributable to infringement is the difference between areas P_1AGC and P_2IJC. Alternatively, the loss can be expressed as $P_1AGP_2 - GIJB$. Note that this loss of profit must be positive. When the patentee sells Q_1 at a price of P_1, she maximizes her profit. If the patentee could have earned more by selling Q_1^*, at a price of P_2, she would have done so. Therefore, this change must lead to lower profit.[13] Although this outcome increases aggregate wealth in the short term, the attendant

---

it received any amount larger than EAGH. Thus, a mutually beneficial bargain should be struck in which the patentee does all the producing and the infringer gets paid something between EAGH and EABF. As the number of potential infringers increases, however, this strategy becomes untenable, unless the patentee has some method for distinguishing the bona fide would-be infringers from those who would only threaten to infringe in the hope of extorting a payment. See Merges (1996; 1304–5).

[13] As the patentee expands output beyond Q_1, the increase in revenue (measured by marginal revenue) is less than the increase in total cost (measured by marginal cost). As a result, the net effect is to reduce profit.

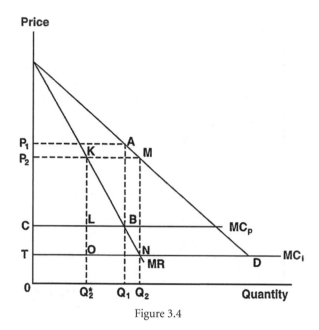

Figure 3.4

transfer of wealth from patentee to consumers may undermine long-run efficiency by weakening the incentive to invest in creative activity; that is the premise of the patent system.

The third possibility is that the infringer will be a more efficient producer than the patentee.[14] Under these circumstances, the infringer maximizes his profit by producing output at the point where the infringer's (lower) marginal cost equals marginal revenue. The infringer will attempt to sell Q_2 at price P_2, but the patentee can respond by lowering her price from P_1 to P_2. Because both firms are selling the same product, they will presumably split the demand at a price of P_2. The patentee will sell Q_2^*, which is one-half of Q_2 in Figure 3.4. The patentee's profit falls from her pre-infringement level of P_1ABC to P_2KLC. The infringer's profit is equal to area KMNO. Because of the infringer's superior efficiency, total profits, which are equal to the sum of P_2KLC and KMNO, are lower than the maximum possible profits of P_2MNT. This difference is equal to area CLOT and is due to the higher production costs of the patentee. It would be more efficient and more profitable for the infringer to do all of the production. In such a case, if the patentee is able to enjoin the infringement before the infringer can earn any profit, it will be in both parties' interests to negotiate a license under which the infringer

[14] See Schlicher (1996; § 9.05).

will be granted the right to use the patent in exchange for a royalty. In other words, under these circumstances, it is less efficient for the patentee to sell directly to consumers than it is for the patentee to license the would-be user to sell instead; private efficiency and social efficiency operate in the same direction. On a per-unit basis, the amount of the royalty is indeterminate, but it must provide revenues at least equal to the profit that the patentee can earn on its own. These revenues cannot exceed $(P_2 - MC_i)Q_2$, as this is the maximum profit obtainable by the more efficient producer.

IMPLICATIONS OF THE BASIC MODEL FOR PATENT DAMAGES

The table below summarizes the various possible outcomes described in the preceding section.

		Patentee and infringer are equally efficient	Patentee is more efficient	Infringer is more efficient
Would-be infringer avoids use	Patentee profit	π_p	π_p	π_p
	Infringer profit	0	0	0
	Aggregate profit	π_p	π_p	π_p
Infringer infringes	Patentee profit	$\pi^*_{p,1}$	$\pi^*_{p,2}$	$\pi^*_{p,3}$
	Infringer profit	$\pi^*_{i,1}$	$\pi^*_{i,2}$	$\pi^*_{i,3}$
	Aggregate profit	π_p	$\pi^*_{p,2} + \pi^*_{i,2}$ $(<\pi_p)$	$\pi^*_{p,3} + \pi^*_{i,3}$ $(>\pi_p)$
Would-be infringer acquires license	Patentee profit	–	–	$R(>\pi_p)$
	Infringer profit	–	–	$\pi^*_{i,3} - R(>0)$
	Aggregate profit	–	–	$\pi^*_{i,3}(>\pi_p)$

As the table shows, if the infringer is a more efficient producer than the patentee, the short-term optimal result is for the infringer to use the patent, either with or without the patentee's permission. The premise of the patent system, however, is that permitting infringers to use patents without authorization will reduce the incentive to invest in the creation, dissemination, and commercialization of inventions. On this reasoning, the better result is to require the infringer to pay for a license.[15] In the alternative, if the

---

[15] As we noted in Chapter 2, there are circumstances in which one may use another's intellectual property without permission (though relatively few in patent law). Some of these

patentee is the more efficient user of the invention, the optimal result is for the infringer to avoid using the patent altogether. This result will follow automatically because the potential infringer will find it unprofitable to obtain a license from the patentee. Furthermore, if transaction costs are positive (which they always will be in the real world), conferring a right to enjoin the infringer when both patentee and infringer are equally efficient should be optimal as well, because this result economizes on the cost of negotiating a license. In the absence of enforceable patent rights, however, the infringer's incentive in either case would be to use the patent without compensation (assuming that the infringer's cost of unauthorized use is less than or equal to the cost of negotiating for and purchasing a license). Therefore, the question arises regarding how to craft a set of damages rules that will encourage the would-be infringer to purchase a license in the first instance and to avoid use altogether in the second.

Our previous analysis suggests that the answer to this question will vary, depending upon whether the would-be infringer is a more or less efficient user of the patented invention than is the patentee. If the would-be infringer is less efficient than or as efficient as the patentee, the minimal sanction necessary to induce the would-be infringer to refrain is the profit attributable to the infringement.[16] Requiring the less-efficient infringer to disgorge its profit, in other words, renders it no better off as a result of the infringement and should deter its unauthorized use.[17] Alternatively, if the infringer is the more efficient user, the minimal sanction necessary to deter infringement (and, concomitantly, to induce the user to seek a license) is not the entire profit attributable to the infringement, but rather only the amount of the royalty the parties would have agreed upon *ex ante* as a condition of the more efficient party's use. As noted, this amount will be less than or equal to the profit attributable to the infringement. An award of the forgone royalty, like

---

exceptions apply in instances in which it may be appropriate to assume that the market for licensing fails. Our discussion assumes that the infringer's use of the patentee's property is not subject to any such exception and, therefore, constitutes an infringement.

[16] More precisely, an award of profits will render the would-be infringer indifferent between infringing and avoiding use. If we relax the assumption that the risk or litigation costs incurred by the would-be infringer are zero, then, given our other assumptions, a rule requiring the infringer to disgorge its profit will induce it to avoid using the patented invention.

[17] In the event that an infringement actually occurs, of course, an award of the defendant's profit will not be sufficient to compensate the patentee, inasmuch as the patentee's lost profit must be greater than (or, at best, equal to) the defendant's profit. In the present model, however, in which information and litigation costs are zero, the prospect of a restitutionary award should be sufficient to head off the infringement in the first instance. Our analysis of the optimal remedy changes somewhat when these assumptions are relaxed.

an award of restitution in the preceding case, renders the would-be infringer no better off as a result of the infringement and should be sufficient to deter unauthorized use.

To summarize, the preceding analysis suggests that, when there are no substitutes for the patented product and all information, litigation, risk, and transaction costs are zero, the optimal damages rules are as follows. First, when the infringer's use of the patent is no more efficient than the patentee's, the minimum sanction should be the restitution of the profit attributable to the infringement. Second, when the infringer is the more efficient user, the minimum sanction should be the amount of the royalty the patentee and infringer would have agreed to *ex ante*.[18] In the following section, we consider the effect upon these conclusions of relaxing both the nonsubstitutability and zero-cost assumptions.

FURTHER REFINEMENTS TO THE MODEL

For ease of exposition, the model described in the preceding sections was based upon some fairly unrealistic assumptions, among them that the patented product had no close substitutes – thereby promising to reward its owner with a monopoly profit – and that information, litigation, risk, and transaction costs were zero. Relaxing the nonsubstitutability assumption, however, should not materially alter the conclusions set forth earlier. As we noted in Chapter 2, few patents result in economic monopolies due to the existence of substitutes. But most commercially successful patents probably do confer some profit above that which could be earned under perfect competition.[19] Awarding the patentee anything less than the profit attributable to the infringement or the patentee's forgone royalty would render the infringer better off as a result of the infringement and thereby encourage him to use the intellectual property without permission in contravention of the statutory incentive scheme. For purposes of assessing damages, the only real difference between the monopoly and the imperfect competition scenarios resides in the application of the optimal rule. In the arguably rare case in

---

[18] A mixed recovery might be appropriate, however, in a case in which the infringer competes directly with the patentee in one market and also serves another market in which the patentee does not compete. In such a case, it is conceivable that the patentee might be the more efficient user in the market in which the two compete and if so she would be entitled to an award of restitution for that market. With respect to the market in which only the defendant competes, the patentee presumably would be entitled to recover only the forgone royalty.

[19] See, e.g., Dam (1994; 249–51).

which a patent confers pure monopoly power, the profit attributable to the patent will be, by definition, the entire profit derived from the sale of the product. When instead there are imperfect substitutes, the profit attributable to the patent will be something less than this amount because the defendant could have lured away some of the plaintiff's customers by offering to sell them lawful substitutes for the plaintiff's product.[20] Not surprisingly, determining the correct amount of the profit attributable to an act of infringement in the latter situation can present very difficult factual issues, which we take up in Chapter 8, but in theory the basic analysis is no different from the one developed previously under the assumption of pure monopoly.

Relaxing the assumption of zero information, litigation, and transaction costs, on the other hand, suggests the need for a substantial modification of the optimal rule, both for cases in which the infringer is the less efficient user of the patent and for cases in which he is the more efficient user. Consider first the case of the less efficient infringer. If information or litigation costs are greater than zero, a restitutionary remedy may fail to deter some inefficient would-be users from infringing, either due to ignorance or to the expectation that their conduct will go undetected. One could impose a multiplier, but calculating the appropriate amount of the multiplier may be impossible, as we have seen. An alternative would be to require the less efficient infringer to compensate the patentee for the patentee's lost profit (which in this situation will exceed the amount of the infringer's profits). This rule has the advantage of providing some additional deterrence; it also guarantees that, in cases where (for whatever reason) the would-be infringer is not deterred from infringing, the patentee will be no worse off as a result of the unauthorized use (putting aside, for the time being, the issue of whether the patentee is entitled to prejudgment interest, attorney's fees, and so on).[21]

---

[20] See Schlicher (1996; §§ 9.05[2][a], 9.05[2][d]).

[21] *A contrario*, Elkin-Koren and Salzberger argue that a court should award the defendant's profit in this instance – though perhaps defined as only that amount of the profit that reflects "the relative share of the investment in R&D made by the patentee, which was appropriated by the infringer" – because otherwise the award "may not provide enough incentives to break the monopoly." Their point appears to be that the policymaker should encourage the patent owner to bargain with potential licensees and that a rule awarding the owner its lost profit will not have this effect. See Elkin-Koren & Salzberger (1999; 569). In our view, however, the law of damages should not encourage "break[ing] the monopoly"; it should instead be consistent with the premise that the patent "monopoly" promises greater long-term benefits. Moreover, it is not clear to us why licensing would be desirable when the defendant is less efficient, because the defendant will produce the product at higher marginal cost than the patent owner. One would not expect the parties to voluntarily bargain to this outcome.

Similar considerations require a modification of the rule when the infringer is the more efficient user of the patent. As discussed earlier, when this condition holds and other relevant costs are zero, awarding the patentee the amount of her forgone royalty should be sufficient both to compensate the patentee and to deter the infringer from engaging in unauthorized use. We noted in Chapter 2, however, that one of the claimed advantages of protecting IPRs by means of property rules is that the owner and would-be user may be capable of accurately assessing the value of these rights at lower cost than are courts and other governmental agencies. A rule that requires the more efficient infringer to forfeit *all* of his profit attributable to the infringement, therefore, might be preferable to one that requires him only to pay a reasonable royalty to the extent that a forfeiture rule avoids saddling the court with the difficult task of determining whether a license would have been forthcoming and, if so, on what terms. This rule also tends to reinforce the property-like nature of patent rights by discouraging would-be infringers from opting out of the licensing market. If the would-be user is more efficient than the patentee, the user should negotiate for permission to use the invention and a forfeiture rule discourages the user from opting out of negotiations.[22]

One possible objection to the preceding framework – which argues for awarding the patentee's lost profit in a case in which the patentee is equally

---

[22] This view is consistent with Judge Posner's discussion of the analogous issue in *Taylor v. Meirick*, 712 F.2d 1112, 1120 (7th Cir. 1983), a copyright case:

> It is true that if the infringer makes greater profits than the copyright owner lost, because the infringer is a more efficient producer than the owner or sells in a different market, the owner is allowed to capture the additional profit even though it does not represent a loss to him. It may seem wrong to penalize the infringer for his superior efficiency and give the owner a windfall. But it discourages infringement. By preventing infringers from obtaining any net profit it makes any would-be infringer negotiate directly with the owner of a copyright that he wants to use, rather than bypass the market by stealing the copyright and forcing the owner to seek compensation from the courts for his loss. Since the infringer's gain might exceed the owner's loss, especially as loss is measured by a court, limiting damages to that loss would not effectively deter this kind of forced exchange. This analysis also implies that some of the "windfall" may actually be profit that the owner would have obtained from licensing his copyright to the infringer had the infringer sought a license.

See also Posner (1985), who argued that much of criminal law can be explained as a means of discouraging market bypassing.

A contrario, Elkin-Koren and Salzberger argue that a liability rule will preserve the patentee's incentive to invest in innovation – which is the point we made in our first approximation – but they do not address our further point that a property rule may be preferable because it will induce the parties to negotiate a voluntary license. See Elkin-Koren & Salzberger (1999; 568).

or more efficient than the infringer and the defendant's profit attributable to the infringement when the defendant is more efficient – is that courts are not well-placed to determine which party is the more efficient user of the patent. Marginal cost curves are notoriously difficult to estimate in real life. But this objection falls away when we restate our proposed rule to be that the patentee obtains the larger of her own lost profit or the defendant's profit attributable to the infringement. The two rules are identical, because in a case in which the patentee is more efficient her lost profit will exceed the defendant's profit; in a case in which the patentee is less efficient, the defendant's profit will be higher. Providing the patentee with the option of recovering either actual damages (her lost profit) or restitution (the defendant's profit) enforces our proposed rule without requiring the court to make difficult determinations of relative efficiency.

A second objection, also based upon the assumption of positive information and litigation costs, is that awarding a compensatory recovery when the infringer is less efficient and a restitutionary recovery when he is more efficient might induce overdeterrence; that is, would-be users will over-comply with their legal obligations out of fear that borderline cases will be decided against them. Overdeterrence provides the patent owner with a greater reward than she is entitled to under the patent laws[23] (and may have other perverse consequences),[24] which could be a real problem if the laws are imperfectly enforced. As we saw in Chapter 2, the substantive legal standards that courts apply in actions for infringement are often vague and difficult to articulate. (Consider, for example, the concepts of *nonobviousness* in patent law, of *substantial similarity* in copyright law, and of *likelihood of confusion* in trademark law.) Uncertainty over potential liability may deter some would-be users from making, using, or selling products that are only marginally beyond the patent's scope.[25] The problem will be compounded

---

[23] See Craswell & Calfee (1986; 280–9), who make this point about overdeterrence generally.

[24] Landes (1983; 655, n.4) notes two possible problems arising from the overdeterrence of inefficient conduct: (1) that "if all fines are large and differences between them are small relative to differences in harm, offenders tend to commit the most harmful offenses" and (2) "legal error . . . combined with large fines can deter socially valuable business behavior." We discuss the second problem in the previous text. The first problem is the problem of marginal deterrence; we do not want sanctions for pickpockets to be so severe that we encourage them to kill their victims. This problem could arise in the present context, but its impact is probably fairly minimal. The more the defendant infringes, the greater his profits attributable to infringement are likely to be; more harmful offenses, therefore, should lead to distinctly harsher sanctions.

[25] One of the authors of this book has argued elsewhere that, in the presence of uncertainty, the risk of incurring an award of enhanced damages may deter some potential defendants

if we drop our assumption that users are risk-neutral or if the user is likely to have incurred substantial sunk costs prior to detection. Especially in the latter situation, the *ex ante* probability of having to negotiate *ex post* from a position of extreme disadvantage may well prompt the user to overcomply with the law.

In summary, our analysis has suggested that when various market imperfections are taken into account, the optimal rules stated in the preceding section should be modified in three respects. First, when the infringer is the less efficient user of the patent, the base-level recovery should be the patentee's own lost profits rather than the infringer's profits attributable to the infringement. Second, when the infringer is the more efficient user, the base-level recovery should be the defendant's profit attributable to the infringement rather than the amount of the forgone royalty. Third, in some cases it may be appropriate to further modify the patentee's damages by some amount in order to correct for the distortions otherwise arising from the presence of information and litigation costs. Therefore, the general baseline rule suggested by our analysis is that the courts should award the prevailing patentee either her own lost profits attributable to the infringement or the defendant's profits attributable thereto, whichever is greater. In an appropriate case, a court may enhance or diminish these baseline damages for the purpose of optimally deterring unlawful but otherwise undetectable acts of infringement. However, whether over- or underdeterrence presents the greater risk, either as a general matter or in a specific case, may be difficult to discern.

CHALLENGING THE BUT-FOR CAUSATION STANDARD

In a recent article, Ian Ayres and Paul Klemperer argued that, contrary to our conclusions, social welfare would increase if patent owners were

from lawfully "coming close" or designing around a patented invention. See Cotter (2004). To the extent this overdeterrent effect exists, it deprives the public of some of the benefits of lawful competition. Building upon the law-and-economics literature on punitive damages, Cotter suggests limiting enhanced damages to cases in which the probability of evading detection is substantial, or the defendant's conduct is particularly egregious (so that overdeterrence is not a concern). In the present context, the previous text suggests that even restitutionary awards, without any damages multiplier, could have an overdeterrent effect when uncertainty is present. This insight might imply that, if restitutionary awards were to be reintroduced into patent law, they should be limited to cases involving deliberate or "willful" infringement, as they are in trademark cases. See *infra* Chapter 4. However, some of the reasons we suggest for so limiting these awards in trademark law – in particular, the apportionment problem – may not be quite so difficult to overcome in patent cases.

entitled to recover only some portion of the losses they incur as a result of infringement.[26] Although we agree that, as in other tort-law contexts, principles of proximate causation should at some point limit the patent owner's right to recover for "remote" harms (such as loss of profits on goods that are only weakly complementary to the patented product, which we discuss in Chapter 8), Ayres and Klemperer advance the more sweeping proposition that courts should compensate patent owners for only a portion of their direct, proximately caused injury. There are some serious theoretical and practical problems with this suggestion.

Ayres and Klemperer present their partial damages thesis in connection with the broader argument that some degree of delay and uncertainty in the enforcement of patents would increase social welfare.[27] Specifically, Ayres and Klemperer observe that a small reduction from a monopolist's profit-maximizing price will cause a disproportionately large reduction in the attendant deadweight social welfare loss; thus, they argue, measures that limit the patent owner's ability to exploit her market power to the maximum would be justified by the resulting increase in consumer welfare.[28] To illustrate, suppose that the patentee/monopolist faces demand, marginal revenue (MR), and marginal cost (MC) curves identical to those depicted above in Figure 3.1. To quantify these amounts, suppose that MC = \$40 and that the demand for the product at issue (call them widgets) can be expressed as

$$P = 100 - 0.1Q \tag{1}$$

where P denotes price and Q represents the number of widgets. The negative coefficient on Q means that the demand curve has the customary negative slope indicating that larger quantities will be demanded at lower prices. Assuming that the patentee has a legal monopoly of the production and sale of widgets, the patentee will maximize its profit (π), which is the difference between total revenue and total costs

$$\pi = (100 - 0.1Q)Q - 40Q, \tag{2}$$

by producing where marginal revenue and marginal cost are equal. In this case, the patentee will produce where

$$100 - 0.2Q = 40. \tag{3}$$

[26] See Ayres & Klemperer (1999; 1028–31).
[27] See *id.* at 987.
[28] See *id.* at 994–1001.

Solving this equation for Q yields the optimal (i.e., profit maximizing) quantity, which is 300. Substituting this quantity into the demand function (Equation (1)) provides the profit maximizing price, which is 70. The patentee's maximum profit is then

$$\pi = 70(300) - 40(300)$$

or \$9,000. Monopoly causes an allocative welfare loss (or "deadweight loss") resulting from the monopolistic restriction of the quantity produced. In our example, the deadweight loss is equal to $\frac{1}{2}(70 - 40)(300)$ or \$4,500. Now assume that the monopolist reduces her price by 1% to \$69.30. The corresponding quantity sold is 307 and the patentee's profit falls to $(\$69.30 - 40)(307) = \$8,995.10$ – a reduction of only \$4.90 or five one-hundredths of one percent (0.05%). The impact on social welfare, however, is quite substantial: the deadweight loss is now only $\frac{1}{2}(\$69.30 - 40)(293) = \$4,292.45$, which amounts to a welfare gain of \$207.55 (4.6%). Thus, a minute reduction of the patentee's profit (0.05%) leads to a disproportionately large increase in social welfare (4.6%). Based on a similar analysis, Ayres and Klemperer argue that constraining patent owners from charging the full monopoly price may substantially reduce the deadweight loss attributable to the exercise of patent rights, while at the same time having relatively little effect on the patent owner's incentive to invent and disclose.[29] They further argue that awarding the patent owner less than 100% of her but-for profit may have a similar effect of constraining her from charging the full monopoly price, without materially affecting her *ex ante* incentive to invent.[30]

To illustrate this latter point, suppose that the patentee and infringer face identical marginal cost curves and that they compete on the basis of quantity as depicted in Figure 3.2. Assume further that the patent owner is entitled to recover as damages 75% of her lost profit of \$5,000, that is, \$3,750. On these facts, and ignoring for the moment the cost of litigation, the infringer makes a profit net of damages of \$250 (that is, \$4,000 − \$3,750), before being enjoined from further infringement. As Ayres and Klemperer note, under such a system "interim producers would be certain to pay damages, but because the damages would not increase the patentee's payoffs to the monopoly level, limited amounts of infringement would occur."[31] Moreover, during this period of interim infringement, the deadweight loss in our

[29] See *id.* at 994–1001.
[30] See *id.* at 1028–31.
[31] See *id.* at 1029.

example decreases by over 55% from \$4,500 to \$2,000.[32] If the additional \$1,250 the patent owner would have recovered under a make-whole regime is not material to her *ex ante* incentive to invent, this result is efficient in that consumers obtain the benefits of the invention at a lower social welfare cost. Ayres and Klemperer therefore argue that rules resulting in awards of "partial damages . . . on the order of say 70–90% . . . of the losses relative to full monopoly profit" might "induc[e] limited amounts of infringement without unduly lessening innovation incentives," and thus would be "generally socially beneficial."[33]

We nevertheless remain skeptical of the Ayres-Klemperer proposition for several reasons. First, for a partial damages rule to work as intended, the proportion of damages awarded to the patent owner must be calculated with sufficient precision to induce only limited infringement, on the one hand, and to avoid deterring inventive activity, on the other. In our previous hypothetical example, setting the percentage of damages recoverable at 80% or higher would not induce limited infringement, because it would leave the infringer with zero (or negative) profits net of damages.[34] (Indeed, even if damages were set at a percentage below 80%, the infringer might retain no net profit after litigation expenses, which we ignored in our previous example.) Setting damages at some lower percentage, on the other hand, would at some point induce limited infringement and thereby reduce the deadweight loss (in the amount of about 55% in our example). But it would do so only at the cost of reducing the patent owner's expected payoff from inventing and we are not as sanguine as Ayres and Klemperer that this reduction in incentive would be *de minimis*. In our example, it takes at least a 20% reduction in damages (and probably more, once litigation costs are factored in) to induce any welfare-enhancing limited infringement. Of course, one might

---

[32] Absent infringement, the social welfare loss is \$4,500 ($= \frac{1}{2}(70 - 40)(300)$). If the infringement results in the Cournot price and output, the social welfare loss falls to $\frac{1}{2}(60 - 40)(200) = \$2,000$. Thus, infringement reduces the welfare loss by \$2,500.

[33] Ayres & Klemperer (1999; 1029, 1030, 1031). The problem with this analysis is fairly obvious. The authors *assume* that the adverse effect on the incentive to invent is immaterial and, therefore, the gain in social welfare is essentially free, but the adverse effect may not actually be immaterial.

[34] If we let f represent the fraction of the lost profit that is recoverable by the patentee, the value of f that leaves a would-be infringer indifferent between infringing or not is that value that makes the damages award just equal to the profit from infringing:

$$f\pi_L = \pi_I,$$

where π_L is profit lost by the patentee and π_I is the infringer's profit. Solving the equation for f yields $f = \pi_I/\pi_L$. In our example, $\pi_I = \$4,000$ and π_L is \$5,000; thus, the critical value for f is 0.80. If f exceeds 0.80, infringement will not occur.

construct other models in which a lesser reduction will still induce some limited infringement,[35] but this observation only underscores the point that the real world presents a variety of possible cost curves, each having its own unique characteristics.[36] Crafting a partial damages rule that applies across-the-board to all cases of patent infringement and that on balance both induces limited infringement and preserves the *ex ante* incentive to invent would raise some daunting empirical questions to say the least. In a world in which no one really knows the effect of the patent incentive upon behavior, it is not at all clear that the reductions necessary to induce limited infringement would have the benign effect envisioned by Ayres and Klemperer.

Several other objections relate to both practical and theoretical problems with implementing the Ayres-Klemperer thesis. First, even if it were possible to calculate the optimal amount of partial damages (70%? 80%?), it is not clear that any existing patent rule achieves the desired target. Of course, one could recommend in the place of the existing rules an explicit command to award patent owners (say) 75% of their provable loss, and not more, but absent compelling proof that 75% is the "right" figure any such recommendation would be rash, as well as politically infeasible. A second problem is that many, perhaps most, patent owners do not charge the full monopoly price to begin with, in light of actual and potential competition from noninfringing alternatives. As Ayres and Klemperer themselves recognize, this fact may suggest that deadweight loss is not as severe as the model assumes.[37] At the same time, if the patentee's expected payoff is already a

---

[35] *Cf.* Ayres & Klemperer (1999; 998) present a heuristic example in which a 25% reduction from the monopoly price reduces the patent owner's payout by only 16%.

[36] A producer who is less efficient than the patentee, for example, in the sense that his marginal cost curves lies above that of the patentee, may not have an incentive to infringe and pay damages unless the damages are considerably lower than 100%. On the other hand, when an infringing producer is more efficient than the patentee, the latter is better off seeking a reasonable royalty, which should exceed the amount the patentee could have earned by manufacturing the product herself. To induce limited infringement in this context would require setting the reasonable royalty at some percentage of the amount the parties would have agreed to *ex ante*; given the difficulty of accurately estimating this amount to begin with. an award of some hypothetical optimal percentage of the full royalty only compounds the uncertainty.

[37] See Ayres & Klemperer (1999; 1016–19). Ayres and Klemperer nevertheless argue that their basic observation – that small reductions in price cause disproportionately large gains in social welfare – holds, even when market forces constrain the patent owner from earning a full-blown monopoly profit. See *id.* Whether a substantial (20% or more) decrease in potential damages, however, would have an effect upon an oligoplistic patent owner's *ex ante* incentives is less clear.

substantial discount from the monopoly price, any further reduction due to a partial damages rule will only further reduce the incentive to invent. Finally, the fact that litigation expenses typically are not recoverable unless the defendant acted in bad faith further reduces the amount ultimately recovered by victorious patent owners, perhaps substantially in light of the expense of patent litigation.

For these reasons, we remain skeptical about proposals to consciously reduce the patent owner's damages to some amount below her actual loss. Ayres and Klemperer may be correct that *small* decreases would have no effect upon incentives, but the magnitude of reductions necessary to induce limited infringement may be more significant than Ayres and Klemperer assume.

EXTENDING THE MODEL TO TRADE SECRETS, COPYRIGHTS, AND TRADEMARKS

Extending our model to the law of trade secrets and copyrights seems like a logical step, given the broadly similar policies underlying patent, trade secret, and copyright law. Like patent law, the law of trade secrets induces desired behavior by providing information producers with a (limited) right to exclude others from copying or using their innovations. Copyright law also rewards creators and publishers by providing them with a set of exclusive rights enforceable against the world. Moreover, the arguments in favor of protecting patent rights under the umbrella of a property rule, due largely to valuation problems, would seem to apply with more or less equal force to trade secrets and copyrights. Applying the same general remedial framework to all three bodies of law, therefore, seems reasonable as a first approximation.

Trademarks, on the other hand, may seem more difficult to fit within the general model, because the standard rationale for their existence differs from the rationale that underlies the law of patents, trade secrets, and copyrights. Trademark law does not exist to encourage the production of catchy names for goods and services. Trademark law nevertheless does serve something of an incentive function, insofar as it encourages the trademark owner to invest in maintaining a consistent level of quality in its products and services. Trademarks also serve a signaling function which helps both to lower consumer search costs and (arguably) to facilitate the trademark owner's ability to coordinate investment in a powerful selling tool. Damages rules, therefore, may also help to preserve the incentive structure of trademark law, although the precise manner in which trademarks fit within this general framework merits further consideration.[38]

The paradigmatic example of trademark infringement is the practice known as "passing off" or "palming off" under which a competitor uses the owner's mark to identify the competitor's (typically lower quality) goods or services. (In Chapter 2, we suggested as an example the hypothetical use of the words COCA-COLA on a non-genuine soft drink.) From the standpoint of consumers, this situation (initially) will *appear* to resemble what was depicted in Figure 3.4. The infringer seems to be producing the same good or service as the trademark owner but – because the infringer takes a free ride upon the owner's investment in quality control – at a lower cost. The previous analysis, therefore, suggests that the trademark owner's typical damages remedy in cases of passing off lower-quality goods probably should be the restitution of the infringer's profits. The *actual* effect, however, of passing off goes well beyond what is depicted in Figure 3.4. The reality is that the infringer is selling a lower-quality product rather than the same product at a lower price. When passing off his goods as those of another, the infringer harms two different sets of victims. First, the infringer harms the owner by threatening the owner's reputation as a purveyor of high-quality goods; second, the infringer perpetrates a fraud upon consumers who pay more than they knowingly would have paid for the quality of goods offered by the infringer. In turn, consumers who are unable to determine whether the goods they are buying are genuine may adapt by reducing the amount they are willing to pay for the trademarked product, which is to the owner's further detriment.[39] The infringer will internalize these costs only if, in addition to being required to disgorge any profits attributable to the infringement, he also is liable for any actual damages resulting from injury to the owner's reputation and from the deception of consumers. In theory,

---

[38] In a recent paper, Parchomovsky and Siegelman argue that trademark law complements patent law in a manner that is welfare-enhancing by providing an incentive for a patent owner to lower price during the patent term in order to develop a base of consumers who will continue to buy the brand-name product from the patent owner after the patent expires. This strategy reduces the deadweight loss during the patent term. After the patent term, it results in a transfer of income from the brand-name-preferring consumers to the patent owner but permits competition between the brand-name and generic substitutes with respect to those consumers who are price-sensitive. In this sense, trademark law working in conjunction with patent law provides an incentive to invent, disclose, and commercialize. See Parchomovsky & Siegelman (2002). If Parchomovsky and Siegelman are correct, our argument that damages rules ought to preserve the incentive structure embedded in trademark law is all the stronger.

[39] See Akerlof (1970) for a demonstration that bad products can drive out good products.

this latter interest could be vindicated either by a direct action on the part of those consumers or by allowing the trademark owner to recover enhanced damages.[40]

Of course, not every act of trademark infringement fits within this paradigm. Even in some cases of genuine passing off, the infringer may operate on a higher marginal cost curve than does the owner, despite the cost advantage accruing from not having to develop his own goodwill. When this occurs, the analysis we presented earlier suggests that the trademark owner's lost profits attributable to the infringement will exceed the infringer's profits. Allowing the owner to recover her lost profits in such a case ensures that the trademark owner will be no worse off as a result of the infringement, which arguably preserves the incentive to invest in quality control. In other instances, the infringer may be genuinely operating on a lower marginal cost curve than the owner in the sense that its costs are lower even apart from any advantage conferred by the infringement. Alternatively, the infringer may be selling in a product or geographic market in which the trademark owner does not engage in direct sales. In either of these cases, the infringer's profit will be greater than or equal to the owner's lost profit. Following the earlier analysis, we again conclude that the principal damages remedy should be either the owner's forgone royalty or – if we doubt the courts' ability to accurately estimate the value of such a royalty – the restitution of all of the defendant's profits attributable to use of the mark. Note, however, that in the case of trademarks, it may be even more difficult than in the case of patents to determine exactly how much of one's profit derived from the unauthorized use of the relevant intellectual property, which is a point that we return to in the next chapter.

CONCLUSION

In summary, a simple model of IPRs suggests that the prevailing plaintiff in a patent, trade secret, copyright, or trademark infringement action should be able to recover the greater of her lost profits attributable to the infringement or the defendant's profits so attributable. In some cases the award should be further modified for optimal deterrent effect. As our discussion in this chapter shows, trade secret law conforms to this model quite closely,

---

[40] A similar analysis would apply to the case of "reverse passing off," under which the infringer places his own name on the goods of another. The effect of both passing off and reverse passing off, of course, is that the infringer takes a free ride upon the trademark owner's efforts. See McCarthy (1997; § 25:6); Restatement (Third) of Unfair Competition (1995; § 5), Borchard (1977; 1–5, 16–18).

because the UTSA authorizes courts to award either actual damages or the infringer's profits – whichever is greater – and to enhance the plaintiff's damages for "willful and malicious" appropriation. In many respects, the damages rules that govern in patent, copyright, and trademark law also mirror the results predicted by our model. In all three bodies of law, the prevailing plaintiff is generally entitled to recover actual damages; the court is authorized, under some circumstances, to award damages enhancements. When someone infringes on a copyright, and in some cases, a trademark, the court is authorized to award restitution. In other material respects, however, the rules under U.S. patent, copyright, and trademark law differ both from our model and from one another. Most importantly, the United States Patent Act does not permit the prevailing plaintiff to recover restitution; the U.S. Copyright Act entitles the plaintiff to choose, as an alternative to actual damages or profits, so-called "statutory" damages. In trademark law, most American courts hold that the plaintiff is entitled to restitution only in cases of willful infringement. In the following chapter, we consider whether further inquiry into the scope and nature of these three bodies of intellectual property law suggests an efficiency rationale for these or similar departures from the model.

FOUR

Departures from the General Theory

In Chapter 2, we discussed the principal economic justifications for IPRs. In Chapter 3, we proposed a damages rule, consistent with these justifications, under which the IPR owner would recover the larger of her own lost profit or the defendant's profit attributable to the infringement. Ideally, this would be subject to appropriate modifications when necessary to prevent either overdeterrence or underdeterrence. The rules that U.S. courts actually apply in patent, copyright, and trademark law, however, depart from our proposed rule in some important ways.[1] In this chapter, we consider in some detail these departures and begin with the absence of a restitutionary remedy in U.S. patent infringement cases. As we shall see, this rule – which is at odds with our recommendation that the prevailing patent owner be entitled to the greater of her own lost profit *or* the defendant's profit attributable to the infringement (i.e., restitution) – may be justified by the difficulty (high private and social cost) of properly calculating the portion of the defendant's profit attributable to the infringement, but we remain skeptical. Awarding the prevailing patent owner the amount of the royalty the parties would have agreed to *ex ante* hardly appears to be a simpler task.

Second, we analyze the availability of statutory damages under U.S. copyright law. On its face, this rule also, violates our precept by permitting the court to award an arbitrary sum, unrelated to either the plaintiff's loss or the defendant's gain. We will demonstrate, however, that statutory damages provide an adequate second-best solution to a problem that may be more

---

[1] Interestingly, trade secret law is almost entirely consistent with our proposed rule, departing only insofar as the UTSA limits upward modifications of damages awards to twice the amount of actual damages.

pronounced in copyright than in the other bodies of IP law. This problem is the pervasiveness of small-scale infringements that (1) in the aggregate, significantly undermine the copyright owner's statutory entitlement, but (2) taken singly, and in the absence of an appropriate damages multiplier, would often not be worth the cost of fighting over. Statutory damages, in other words, function more or less like a damages multiplier. As we shall see, courts appear to have been reasonably sensitive to the need to relate the amount of statutory damages to some estimate of actual harm or gain. Third, we examine the rule limiting restitution in trademark cases to those involving so-called willful infringement. We argue that this rule too may serve a valid purpose, because (1) accurately apportioning profits in cases involving nonwillful trademark infringement may be nearly impossible and (2) the prospect of awarding suprarestitutionary damages in cases involving nonwillful infringement may have a substantial overdeterrent effect.

Our analysis in this chapter has both a positive and a normative side. On the positive side, we will attempt to discover whether there is any plausible economic reason for the departures we observe: is there something peculiar to patents, copyrights, or trademarks that demands further refinements to our model? On the normative side, we will argue that patent law's departure is difficult to rationalize and probably should be abandoned. The departure we observe in copyright law, on the other hand, may be roughly consistent with what a more refined version of our theory would propose. Trademark law's departure is perhaps the most interesting, because it highlights some ways in which the purpose and structure of trademark law differs greatly from the purpose and structure of patent, copyright, and trade secret law. The limitation on restitution is arguably consistent with these differences; no firmer conclusion is warranted.

RESTITUTION IN PATENT LAW

Prior to 1946, the U.S. Patent Act explicitly authorized courts to award the defendant's profits in an appropriate case. A 1946 amendment deleted this provision and the deletion was retained when the next major revision of the U.S. Patent Act took place in 1952. An award of the defendant's profit still remains possible (though infrequently used) in design patent cases. Some other countries permit these awards in utility patent cases, too. In 1998, for example, a British court in *Celanese International Corp. v. BP Chemicals Ltd* awarded the plaintiff the defendant's profits in the amount of £567,000, less taxes.[2] But even in Britain, restitution in patent cases is rare; *Celanese* was the first British case to award these damages in over 100 years.

The deletion of restitutionary awards from the Patent Act was not inadvertent. In a report on the 1946 amendments to the Patent Act, the House of Representatives Committee on Patents pointed to the difficulty of accurately determining the amount of profits attributable to an infringement, as well as the attendant cost and delay, as reasons for limiting the prevailing plaintiff to an award of compensatory damages.[3] Our analysis in the preceding chapter suggests that this reasoning is not altogether implausible. If these costs are high enough, they may outweigh any efficiency gains derived from permitting such a recovery. Moreover, restitutionary awards may overdeter potential users from making, using, or selling inventions that are lawful but only slightly beyond the scope of the patent's claims.

We nevertheless are inclined to agree with Kenneth Dam (1994; 256–7) that restitution should still be an available remedy in patent cases. First, it is not clear to us that the risk of overdeterrence is systemic or omnipresent in this context. Again, we must make clear that we are taking the substantive law of patents as a given. It may be that patent scope is broader than it ought to be – perhaps the doctrine of equivalents should be further curtailed or eliminated, for example – but this is not our concern in this book and we do not think it would be appropriate in any event to premise narrow damages rules on the theory that these rules will compensate for defects in the substantive law. Having said that, we are not aware of any evidence that the risk of overdeterring conduct that is lawful under the substantive law would be significantly greater under a regime that permitted restitutionary awards. Moreover, the flipside risk under the current system is one of underdeterrence, because a reasonable royalty theoretically leaves the defendant no worse off than it would have been had it sought a license at the beginning. This latter risk is diminished, however, by the general noncompensability of attorneys' fees and by the possibility that the royalty will tilt in favor of the patentee.[4]

---

[2] [1999] R.P.C. 203. For an overview of the availability of this remedy in Canada and a few other countries, see Coury (2003).

[3] H.R. REP. NO. 79-1587 (1946); S. REP. NO. 79-1503 (1946), *reprinted in* 2 U.S.C.C.A.N. 1387 (1946). Donald Chisum (2002; § 20.02[4][a]) suggests that an alternative reading might be that Congress only intended "to eliminate a *mandatory* accounting of profits where the patent owner is willing to have recovery based on a reasonable royalty." The courts, however, have rejected any such narrower reading of the statutory text and legislative history.

[4] An intriguing alternative, suggested by an anonymous reviewer, is to limit restitutionary awards to cases involving willful patent infringement, in much the same way and for much

We find the argument that the cost of calculating restitutionary damages is too high similarly unpersuasive. As noted previously, restitutionary awards remain available under some circumstances in design patent, trade secret, copyright, and trademark law. It is not apparent why the calculation of these damages should be appreciably more difficult in utility patent cases than in these other types of cases.[5] Furthermore, when the infringer is more efficient than the patentee, the alternative to awarding restitution is to award a reasonable royalty, i.e., "a hypothetical royalty resulting from arm's length negotiations between a willing licensor and a willing licensee."[6] But a reasonable royalty so defined may not be any easier to calculate than the defendant's profit attributable to the infringement. We suggested in Chapter 3 that restitution is preferable precisely *because* courts are not likely to be very good at estimating the hypothetical terms of hypothetical licenses. Our economic analysis also shows that in the typical case the upper limit of the hypothetical royalty will be the profit the defendant expected to earn from the use of the patented invention.[7] Calculating the actual profit earned

---

the same reasons, that restitution is generally available in trademark cases only when the infringement is willful. We argue later in this chapter that the trademark rule probably makes sense, but we are less sure about imposing such a limitation in patent law. For one thing, the distinction between willful and nonwillful infringement is, arguably, more clear in trademark than in patent law. A discussion of the meaning of willfulness in patent law would, however, take us well beyond the scope of the present discussion. For another, in cases involving willful trademark infringement, it may be that all or most of the defendant's profit is attributable to the unlawful use of the mark, for the reasons we discuss later in this chapter. Whether that is true with respect to patents is not so clear. In other words, the potential error costs are not necessarily smaller in cases involving willful patent infringement, in which case the need for drawing that particular distinction is less clear.

[5] Perhaps one could argue that the problem of apportionment is more acute in patent cases, because patented inventions frequently are used only as components in other products and often could be substituted for nonpatented components, whereas in many trademark and copyright cases one might assume that the defendant would not have sold *any* products absent the infringement. This argument is problematic. Copyrights and trademarks also sometimes serve as components – or are analogous to components – of larger products in which case apportionment can be quite difficult. Consider, for example, the difficulty of calculating the amount of profit attributable to the defendant's use of an infringing slogan to advertise its product or to the unauthorized inclusion, in a motion picture, of a copy of a copyrighted drawing. (At least with patents, it may be possible to identify the defendant's next-best design choice and to estimate what the consequences would have been of adopting that choice.) Moreover, it is hardly clear that calculating the amount of the defendant's profit attributable to the infringement is more difficult than calculating the plaintiff's lost profit or a reasonable royalty for reasons we discuss in Chapter 8.

[6] *Hanson v. Alpine Valley Ski Area, Inc.*, 718 F.2d 1075, 1078–9 (Fed. Cir. 1983).

[7] As Donald Chisum observes, "[c]ourts give considerable weight to the anticipated profits or cost savings that the infringer would derive from use of the patented product or process. The theory is that a willing licensor and willing licensee would divide between them the

cannot be more difficult than calculating an expected profit (absent a smoking gun, such as a memo stating "We expect to earn $x from infringing this patent"). However, the law trusts the courts to perform the latter, but not the former, calculation. This does not appear to make a great deal of sense. (We will return to the problem of calculating the hypothetical license fee in Chapter 8.)

Interestingly, the rule against awarding defendant's profits may have less of an impact upon the courts' behavior than one might have thought. Although it is usually considered erroneous to award the prevailing plaintiff 100% of the profit attributable to the infringement, commentators sometimes accuse courts of doing so anyway *sub silentio*.[8] The availability of enhanced damages for willful infringement also dulls the impact of the no-restitution rule, insofar as the plaintiff's actual damages, suitably enhanced, may exceed the amount of the defendant's profit.[9] The no-restitution rule nevertheless remains something of a theoretical curiosity, difficult to justify absent firm evidence of overdeterrence.

STATUTORY DAMAGES IN COPYRIGHT LAW

A second set of puzzles surrounds the institution of statutory damages in copyright law. As long as the prevailing plaintiff in a copyright infringement action has registered his copyright prior to infringement (or within three months of the work's publication), he may choose at any time prior to the entry of judgment[10] to forgo recovering actual damages or the defendant's profits and may opt instead for an award of statutory damages. In other words, the plaintiff may elect to recover statutory damages even after the

---

predicted economic benefits to be realized by the licensor's adoption of the product or process." Chisum (2002; § 20.03[3][iv]). Chisum also notes one exception to the principle that the defendant's expected profit forms the upper boundary of a reasonable royalty: "In some circumstances, indirect benefits of the invention to the infringer may have induced him to agree to a royalty equal to or even in excess of the direct profits to be derived from adopting it." As an empirical matter, we do not know how commonly this occurs.

[8] Conley (1987; 376) argues that, in practice, judicially determined royalties often "equal or exceed the entire benefit resulting from the use of the invention, notwithstanding the fact that courts give lip service to the setting of a royalty at a level that would have been reached by negotiation between the parties"; and that courts "often just subtract the infringer's usual profit from the profit earned by the infringement, and award the entire difference to the patent owner." Pincus (1991; 124) points out that "triers of fact theorize that it would be inequitable to charge the wrongdoer/infringer only that amount that a lawful negotiation would have brought."

[9] Dam (1994; 256) makes this point.

[10] See 17 U.S.C. § 504(c)(1).

jury returns a verdict as long as a judgment has not yet been entered. (Alternatively, after the Supreme Court's 1998 decision in *Feltner v. Columbia Pictures Television, Inc.*,[11] the plaintiff may request a jury determination of statutory damages. Our review of post-*Feltner* decisions, however, indicates that in most of the reported cases so far, plaintiffs still prefer to have judges set the amount of statutory damages.) This is most apt to occur in a case in which the jury returns a verdict in the plaintiff's favor but in an amount that he finds disappointing. In general, the judge or jury has discretion to award statutory damages ranging from $750 to $30,000 per work infringed, but may reduce that amount to $200 in the case of an innocent infringement or increase it to as much as $150,000 in cases at the other end of the spectrum.[12]

As Paul Goldstein (2002; § 12.2) explains, the traditional justification for statutory damages is that "because actual damages are so often difficult to prove, only the promise of a statutory award will induce copyright owners to invest in and enforce their copyrights and only the threat of a statutory award will deter infringers by preventing their unjust enrichment." But this rationale begs the question of why it is desirable to deter unauthorized use, when the use does not result in any provable harm to the copyright owner or provable gain to the infringer or why the prospect of a damages award in excess of those provable damages is necessary to induce investment. Perhaps the answer lies in the fact that every act of infringement provides some gain to the infringer (otherwise she would not have infringed) and causes some harm to the copyright owner (because in the absence of infringement, the user would have agreed to purchase the right to use the work or else the owner would have forbidden the use).[13] Proving the amount of that harm nevertheless may be quite difficult, particularly in light of the apportionment problem, which is the problem of determining how much of the plaintiff's loss or the defendant's gain was attributable to the infringement.[14]

Consider, for example, the facts of *Woods v. Universal City Studios*.[15] Lebbeus Woods is the author of several copyrighted books of fantasy architecture. One of Woods's drawings is of a high-ceilinged room containing

---

[11] 523 U.S. 340 (1998).

[12] See 17 U.S.C. § 504(c)(1), (2).

[13] In cases in which the parties would not have reached agreement, due to transaction costs or other bargaining obstacles, or due to the owner's desire to censor critical commentary, the fair use doctrine may absolve the defendant's unauthorized use. See Gordon (2002; 154–7).

[14] One of the advantages of statutory damages, from the standpoint of the copyright owner, is that it becomes unnecessary to apportion the defendant's profit attributable to the infringement. See *Twin Peaks Productions, Inc. v. Publications Int'l, Ltd.*, 996 F.2d 1366, 1382 (2d Cir. 1993).

[15] 920 F. Supp. 62 (S.D.N.Y. 1996).

a chair attached to a wall and a sphere suspended in front of the chair. The director Terry Gilliam saw a copy of this drawing and used it as his inspiration for a handful of scenes that lasted less than five minutes in the movie *12 Monkeys*. In these scenes, the Bruce Willis character is strapped to a similar chair attached to a wall in a room resembling the one depicted in Woods's drawing. After Universal City Studios released the movie, Woods sued for copyright infringement and the court entered a preliminary injunction against the public performance or distribution of the film; the defendants, after all, had copied Woods's drawing, albeit into a different medium and only for use in a few brief scenes of a two-hour movie. The case then settled – presumably on terms quite favorable to Woods – but it is interesting to speculate on what the appropriate measure of damages would have been had there been no settlement. On the one hand, it is difficult to imagine that Woods suffered any lost profits; it also would seem virtually impossible to ascertain what portion of the film's profit was attributable to the infringement. Estimating an appropriate royalty might have been nothing short of arbitrary.[16] It is perhaps not surprising that Learned Hand once described the apportionment problem in copyright law as "strictly speaking . . . insoluble."[17]

In most other bodies of law, the plaintiff who can prove neither actual harm nor unjust enrichment either loses on the issue of liability or recovers only nominal damages.[18] There are a few, however, in addition to copyright law, that do not always follow this principle, so perhaps some clue can be found in these other bodies of law. The most familiar example comes from the law of defamation.[19] At common law, the prevailing plaintiff in an action for libel or slander is sometimes entitled to "recover presumed damages," which means that the trier of fact may award damages as compensation

---

[16] Or, to use a more familiar example, consider the case of a local bar that provides live or prerecorded music for its patrons and earns an annual profit of $100,000. What part of that profit is due to the music and what part is due to its favorable location, its service, its world-class chicken wings, and so on?

[17] *Sheldon v. Metro-Goldwyn Pictures Corp.*, 106 F.2d 45, 48 (2d Cir. 1939).

[18] See, e.g., *United States Football League v. National Football League*, 644 F. Supp. 1040, 1042, 1053–56 (S.D.N.Y. 1987), in which the prevailing antitrust plaintiff was awarded nominal treble damages of $3, *aff'd*, 842 F.2d 1335 (2d Cir. 1988). The plaintiff's ability to recover punitive damages also may be constrained by his inability to prove any actual damages. See Dobbs (1993; § 3.11(11)).

[19] In 1996, the U.S. Congress made statutory damages available for trademark counterfeiting as well. See 17 U.S.C. § 1117(c). In addition, there is also a line of cases dating back to the eighteenth century, which hold that a plaintiff may recover presumed damages for a violation of the right to vote. See *Memphis Community School Dist. v. Stachura*, 477 U.S. 299, 311 n.14 (1986), which collects the cases.

for the harm to the plaintiff's reputation, even though the plaintiff neither pleads nor proves any quantifiable injury. The rationale for presumed damages is that defamation causes real harm but that this harm is difficult to quantify; hence, in the absence of presumed damages, defendants will not be sufficiently deterred and plaintiffs will not be sufficiently compensated. But the availability of presumed damages in defamation law hardly constitutes a ringing endorsement for applying a similar rule in copyright. In recent years, judges and scholars have advocated restricting or eliminating presumed damages on the grounds, among others, that in practice the rule provides juries with an almost unfettered discretion to award damages far in excess of the value of the plaintiff's injury (or even when there is no injury) in order to punish the defendant or to censor unpopular views.[20] Similar concerns might be raised with respect to statutory damages in copyright law, particularly when the jury sets the amount; wrongly applied, copyright doctrine can impinge upon freedom of speech.[21] Even in the absence of such concerns, it remains unclear why statutory damages should be permitted in copyright and not in other bodies of IP law, such as patents, trade secrets, and (except in cases involving counterfeiting) trademarks, in which the calculation and apportionment of damages or profits also might prove difficult. Is there something different about copyright that merits a different rule?

We think a reasonably strong argument *can* be made for permitting statutory damages in copyright, even if the rule is not followed in the other branches of IP law. The argument rests upon the observation that the cost of detecting the vast number of more or less private acts of copyright infringement that occur every day – ranging from the casual reproduction of newspaper and magazine articles and cartoons on office photocopy machines to the videotaping of television programs for the purpose of building

---

[20] For example, the United States Supreme Court has stated that "[t]he largely uncontrolled discretion of juries to award damages where there is no loss unnecessarily compounds the potential of any system of liability for defamatory falsehood to inhibit the vigorous exercise of First Amendment freedoms" and that "the doctrine of presumed damages invites juries to punish unpopular opinion rather than to compensate individuals for injury sustained by the publication of a false fact." *Gertz v. Robert Welch, Inc.*, 418 U.S. 323, 349 (1974). Commentators as well have been unfavorable. See, e.g., Anderson (1984; 749–56) (arguing that "presumed damages may be more pernicious than punitive damages" because "punishment in the guise of presumed compensatory damages is entirely subterranean and, therefore, difficult to identify and control"); Lidsky (1996; 44–5) noted that abolition of presumed damages rule would force courts to rely upon objective criteria in determining the amount of damages awards.

[21] Several copyright doctrines, including fair use and the merger doctrine, are intended to prevent copyright from interfering with free speech, but the proper application of these doctrines is necessary to prevent this interference. For discussions, see, e.g., Cotter (2003).

a home videotape library[22] to the unauthorized copying of software into one's home computer – would be enormous. The cost of detecting a host of somewhat more "public" uses – ranging from the unauthorized performance of a musical composition in a nightclub to the posting of copyrighted materials on the internet to the manufacture and sale of bootleg compact discs – is probably somewhat lower. Even so, the actual damages or profits attributable to any single act of infringement often may not be high enough to justify incurring this cost: a single unauthorized performance or reproduction is likely to have little impact on the owner's financial well-being (although a large number of infringements very well may).

Therefore, the statutory damages rule can be seen as a response to the potential underenforcement problem arising from this set of (assumed) facts. By offering the copyright owner the possibility of recovering damages in excess of his actual loss or the defendant's gain – and by providing a minimum damages "floor" below which the recovery may not fall – the rule provides the owner with a greater incentive to detect violations and to enforce his rights than would otherwise exist. Of course, a rule authorizing an award of multiple damages, like the rules in place in patent, trade secret, and trademark law, also would serve to increase that incentive. If we are correct in supposing, however, that a single act of copyright infringement often causes only minimal harm, then even a treble damages rule might provide too weak an incentive for effective detection and enforcement, even when the aggregate harm caused by many such individual acts of infringement is great.[23] Because a statutory damages award may be *many* times greater than the actual harm or benefit derived from the defendant's unauthorized use, the threat of such an award may be sufficient to prevent the value of the owner's copyright from being dissipated by a multitude of small-scale infringing acts.[24]

---

[22] Home videotaping for the purpose of viewing a free network-broadcast program at a more convenient time is deemed to be a noninfringing fair use of the work. See *Sony Corp. of Am. v. Universal City Studios, Inc.*, 464 U.S. 417 (1984). Home videotaping of cable or pay-TV programs, however, or of free television programs for archival purposes (that is, for the purpose of building a home videotape library) may not constitute fair use. See Patry (1985; 413–14).

[23] Suppose, for example, that the profit derived from an infringement is $5, but that the probability of detection is very small – say, .01. Our earlier analysis suggests that the minimum sanction needed to deter the infringement is that which reduces the infringer's *expected* profit to zero. On these assumed facts, that sanction is $500 (= $5/.01), which is 100 times the infringer's profit.

[24] One might argue that a rule authorizing the court to award punitive damages would have a similar effect. According to some courts, however, the value of a punitive award must

The preceding analysis still does not answer the question of why there is no corresponding damages rule in the law of patents, trade secrets, and (except for counterfeiting) trademarks. One plausible hypothesis, which further empirical research may be able to shed some light upon, is a lower average cost of detection and a greater average magnitude of harm attributable to a single act of infringement in these other bodies of law. Consider first the law of trademarks. To prevail on a claim of trademark infringement, the owner must prove that a *substantial* number of consumers are likely to be confused by the infringer's unauthorized use. By definition, the infringer's use must be sufficiently public and notorious to reach these consumers or else there can be no liability. (Like "jumbo shrimp," a private act of trademark infringement would be something of an oxymoron.) This insight suggests that the average cost of detecting trademark infringement might be lower than the corresponding average cost of detecting copyright infringement; only *some* copyright infringements occur before a large public audience. At the same time, the average harm flowing from a single act of trademark infringement may be greater than the average harm attributable to a single act of copyright infringement. Again, this may be true because the former act (by definition) must have a likely impact a substantial number of consumers. (This point is more open to question, however, for reasons we discuss later in the chapter.) Copyright infringements may add up in the aggregate, but each act individually may be insignificant.[25]

A similar analysis can be applied to patents and trade secrets to the extent that a public sale of a product embodying a patented invention or trade secret necessarily risks disclosing the infringer's activities to the IPR owner. The analysis is complicated, however, because some acts of patent infringement or trade secret misappropriation can be done in private and these acts may be difficult to detect. This is particularly true when the patent or trade secret covers a process rather than a product. Most processes can be used behind

---

bear some relationship to the value of the plaintiff's actual damages. Moreover, unless the traditional standard for awarding punitive damages were revised, it is likely that the conduct of many copyright defendants would be insufficiently egregious to merit the imposition of a punitive award.

[25] Why then did Congress go to the trouble of adding a provision to the Lanham Act allowing victims of trademark counterfeiting to obtain statutory damages? The legislative history suggests (not surprisingly) that trademark owners pushed for this amendment because they wanted an effective, low-cost remedy against counterfeiters. H. Rep. No. 104-556, *reprinted in* 1996 U.S.C.C.A.N. 1074. Dispensing with the need to prove actual harm satisfies these conditions, and counterfeiters have few friends on Capitol Hill. Our previous analysis suggests that it might be unwise, however, to extend this remedy to run-of-the-mill, noncounterfeiting trademark cases.

closed doors. On the other hand, one might speculate that the majority of patent infringements and trade secret misappropriations involve inventions or other information having substantial commercial value; there would seem to be little point in infringing a patent or trade secret *without* such value. But if the subject information has substantial value to the infringer in its business, the actual harm resulting from a single act of infringement also may be high, at least in comparison with the harm resulting from the typical copyright infringement. Consequently, even with a statutory damages rule, the corresponding incentive to detect and enforce should be greater for patents and trade secrets than for copyrights.

STATUTORY DAMAGES IN PRACTICE

Our analysis *does* appear to be largely consistent with the ways in which U.S. courts actually apply the statutory damages rule. Among the factors courts consider in determining the amount of statutory damages are "the expenses saved and profits reaped by the defendants in connection with the infringements, the revenues lost by the plaintiff as a result of the defendant's conduct, and the infringer's state of mind – whether willful, knowing, or merely innocent"; the fair market value of the rights infringed; "whether each party has complied with its contractual obligations to the other"; the interests in adequately compensating the plaintiff, preventing the defendant's unjust enrichment, and deterring future infringements; and the interest in punishing the infringer.[26] Courts have substantial leeway in deciding precisely how to weigh these factors and there are no rules accurately predicting the amount of a statutory award. (Predictions could become even more indeterminate if more litigants opt for jury determinations of statutory damages in the future.) A review we conducted of every reported decision from 1992 to 1997, and again from 2000 to 2002, in which a court awarded statutory damages nevertheless suggests some general trends or patterns. Three observations based upon this analysis, as well as upon some earlier case law, are of particular interest.

Our first observation concerns the statutory language that limits the plaintiff to one award of statutory damages "for all infringements involved

---

[26] The previous text quotes from several sources, including *N.A.S. Import Corp. v. Chenson Enters.*, 968 F.2d 250, 252 (2d Cir. 1992); *Chi-Boy Music v. Charlie Club, Inc.*, 930 F.2d 1224, 1229–30 (7th Cir. 1991); *Walt Disney Co. v. Video 47, Inc.*, 40 U.S.P.Q. 2d (BNA) 1747, 1753 (S.D. Fla. 1996); *Branch v. Ogilvy & Mather, Inc.*, 772 F. Supp. 1359, 1365 (S.D.N.Y. 1991); *Songmaker v. Forward of Kansas, Inc.*, No. 90–4156-SAC, 1993 WL 484210, at *4 (D. Kan. Sept. 13, 1993); and Nimmer & Nimmer (2002; § 14.04[B][1][a]).

in the action, with respect to any one work," as opposed to one award for every act of infringement.[27] At first blush, this language appears to create a pair of perverse incentives: first, for the defendant to infringe a single work many times rather than just once, because the defendant can be liable for only one set of damages in any one action; and second, for the plaintiff to file successive lawsuits in order to recover multiple awards. But recall the substantial range within which a statutory award may lie. In general, the court may award anywhere from $750 to $30,000 for each work infringed. It may also reduce the award to as little as $200 for an innocent infringement or increase it to as much as $150,000 for a willful infringement. Given this range, one might expect courts to minimize the potential undesirable effects of the rule limiting the plaintiff to one award for every work infringed by awarding damages at the higher end of the spectrum in cases involving multiple infringements of a single work. Although the data provided by the reported decisions are not sufficient to permit a rigorous test of this hypothesis, the case law appears to be roughly consistent with it. Awards tend to be relatively high in cases in which the defendant has infringed a single work over a long period of time or on many occasions.[28] We shall refer to decisions adhering to this pattern as "Category 1" cases.

A second observation is that, when sufficient evidence is presented for the court to estimate the value of the plaintiff's actual damages (or the amount the defendant saved in licensing fees), but the plaintiff requests an award of statutory damages instead, courts tend to award statutory damages ranging from approximately the same amount as those actual damages or fees[29]

---

[27] 17 U.S.C. § 504(c)(1).

[28] For examples, see *Wildlife Express Corp. v. Carol Wright Sales, Inc.*, 18 F.3d 502, 511–13 (7th Cir. 1994), which affirms a statutory award of $50,000 for each of three sculptural works infringed, where the defendant (a major mail order company) sold infringing items for over two years; *Video Aided Instruction, Inc. v. Y & S Express, Inc.*, No. 96 CV 518 (CBA), 1996 WL 711513, at *4 (E.D.N.Y. Oct. 29, 1996), which recommends, a statutory award of $40,000 for each of four copyrighted books, where the defendants aggressively marketed and advertised counterfeits; *Central Point Software, Inc. v. Nugent*, 903 F. Supp. 1057, 1060–1 (E.D. Tex. 1995), where $10,000 was awarded for each of three software works infringed, where the defendant, operator of a for-profit computer bulletin board, encouraged subscribers to download infringing software; *Peer Int'l Corp. v. Luna Records, Inc.*, 887 F. Supp. 560, 568–9 (S.D.N.Y. 1995), where $15,000 and $25,000 was awarded for infringement of two musical compositions, where the defendant knowingly made and distributed infringing phonorecords of these compositions for at least three years.

[29] See, e.g., *Jordan v. Time, Inc.*, 111 F.3d 102, 103–4 (11th Cir. 1997), which affirmed a statutory award of $5,500, where the plaintiff's actual damages totaled $5,000.

or (more commonly) roughly double[30] or triple[31] that amount. In most of the cases falling within this category (Category 2), the defendant made a commercial use of a popular copyrighted work that was subject to a standard licensing agreement, with the result that the amount of lost profits, or at least lost licensing revenue, was largely quantifiable. Sometimes the defendant's activity appears to have been reasonably susceptible of detection,[32] but in many of these cases detection would have been difficult due to the small scale or evanescent nature of the infringement. As our theory predicts, in these latter cases courts often award statutory damages in excess of the plaintiff's provable loss. Therefore, our review of the cases suggests that when (1) there is some basis upon which to quantify the plaintiff's loss and (2) detection costs are high, courts tend to award statutory damages roughly equal to double or treble damages.

Third, when the plaintiff either presents no evidence (or insufficient evidence) of its actual damages or the defendant's profits, courts tend to award low statutory damages unless the defendant infringes the work often enough or for a long enough period of time for its conduct to fall into Category 1 instead.[33] Unfortunately, there is no hard and fast rule (e.g., the defendant must infringe a single work x times or for x days) for distinguishing Category 3 from Category 1 cases; at some point, the distinction will be arbitrary. The statutory scheme, therefore, may yet provide some incentive to infringe a single work more than once. On the other hand, the minimum $750 award for noninnocent infringement probably far exceeds the actual gain or loss at issue in most of the cases we view as falling into Category 3, even if multiple infringements were involved. Many of these cases appear to have involved the offering for rental of bootleg videocassettes, legitimate

---

[30] See, e.g., *Broadcast Music, Inc. v. Star Amusement, Inc.,* 44 F.3d 485, 487–9 (7th Cir. 1994), which affirmed a statutory award of $140,000, where the defendant avoided paying license fees of approximately $75,000; *Canopy Music, Inc. v. Harbor Cities Broadcasting, Inc.,* 950 F. Supp. 913, 916–17 (E.D. Wis. 1997), where statutory damages of $40,000 were awarded and forgone license fees totaled approximately $23,000.

[31] See, e.g., *Chi-Boy Music v. Charlie Club, Inc.,* 930 F.2d 1224, 1227, 1229–30 (7th Cir. 1991), which affirmed a statutory award approximately three times the amount of forgone license fees; *Broadcast Music, Inc. v. Entertainment Complex, Inc.,* 198 F. Supp. 2d 1291 (N.D. Ala. 2002), where statutory damages of $43,000 were awarded and forgone license fees totaled $14,361.

[32] See, e.g., *Knitwaves Inc. v. Lollytogs Ltd.,* 71 F.3d 996 (2d Cir. 1996), which involved infringement of sweater design by a large manufacturer of children's clothing; *Twin Peaks Prods. v. Publications Int'l Ltd.,* 996 F.2d 1366 (2d Cir. 1993), involving a book that was held to infringe television episodes by providing detailed summaries of their plots.

[33] See, e.g., *Florentine Art Studio, Inc. v. Vedet K. Corp.,* 891 F. Supp. 532, 540–1 (C.D. Cal. 1995), which awarded $200 for each of two innocent infringements of sculpture.

copies of which the defendants undoubtedly could have purchased for much less than $750 each. The patterns we detected therefore seem to make some rough economic sense: in awarding statutory damages, courts appear to have at least some general idea of the probable harm or gain involved and to be sensitive to the need to set an award high enough to encourage the detection and enforcement of small-scale infringements.

THE REGISTRATION REQUIREMENT

An additional question is whether conditioning statutory damages upon the timely registration of the copyright, as the U.S. Copyright Act does, makes economic sense. Specifically, the rule is that the copyright owner may not recover statutory damages or attorney's fees unless the work is registered prior to its infringement or within three months of its publication.[34] This rule may be consistent with an efficiency rationale, although the evidence is far from clear. It *is* clear that the rule encourages owners to register. Therefore, it advances whatever purposes are served by registration. Among the purposes that registration might serve are: (1) facilitating negotiations with the copyright owner, by putting the world on notice of the owner's identity and claim to copyright;[35] (2) reducing frivolous litigation, by allowing the Copyright Office to screen unmeritorious claims of copyright; and (3) maintaining the comprehensiveness of the Library of Congress's collection (registrants may satisfy the Copyright Office's deposit requirement by depositing two copies of their works with the Library of Congress). To the extent these purposes are desirable, one might favor conditioning an award of statutory damages upon registration. But none of these justifications for registration is directly related to any of the reasons we have identified as underlying the statutory damages rule itself.

Aside from the general purposes that registration may serve, however, there is another possible reason more directly related to the purpose of statutory damages: namely, that registration provides a signaling function. Although registration is usually simple and inexpensive and the Copyright Office denies very few registration applications, the fact that the copyright

---

[34] 17 U.S.C. § 412 .

[35] See, e.g., Koegel (1995; 537–9). But also see Perlmutter (1995; 583–7), who disputes the necessity of mandatory formalities for effecting this purpose. Note that there is no guarantee that the person who registers the copyright will be the copyright owner at the time the later user wishes to obtain permission to use the work. Transferees are encouraged to record their interests with the Copyright Office but are not required to do so. See 17 U.S.C. § 205.

owner takes even the minimal pains necessary to register the work suggests that the owner believes the work has some economic value in excess of these minor expenses. Our previous analysis suggests that permitting the recovery of statutory damages (potentially in excess of actual damages or illicit profits) when the work has some greater-than-de-minimis value may be warranted, because the infringement of such works in the aggregate could undermine the statutory incentive scheme. The infringement of works that do not motivate the owner to incur even a $30 filing fee, on the other hand, may not have much of an effect upon incentives; statutory damages in this instance would bestow a benefit upon the owner with no corresponding public benefit. In a rough sense, perhaps the registration requirement serves as a method for distinguishing between works whose infringement merits public concern and works whose infringement does not. Whether registration is a sufficiently accurate screening device to justify its costs – including not only the resulting administrative burden, but also the uncertainty generated by creating a trap for unwary copyright owners – nevertheless remains open to question.

LIMITATIONS UPON RESTITUTIONARY DAMAGES
IN TRADEMARK LAW

Three observations relevant to trademark law follow from the economic analysis in Chapter 3. First, if we follow the principle that damages rules should preserve the statutory incentive – in this instance, the incentive to invest in quality control that reduces consumer search costs – the successful plaintiff in a trademark infringement action should never recover less than her actual damages (i.e., its lost profit or licensing fee). Our model is consistent with the Lanham Act in that it authorizes the court to award the prevailing plaintiff her actual damages.[36] A second observation is that a court should enhance the plaintiff's damages in cases in which the infringement is of a type that is difficult to detect or that causes substantial injury to consumers as well as to the trademark owner. Awarding enhanced damages under other circumstances, however, threatens to expand the scope of the owner's rights beyond their optimal level by encouraging would-be users to overcomply with their legal obligations. Again, the Lanham Act is largely consistent with these observations. The Act authorizes courts to award treble damages or (theoretically) unlimited multiples of restitutionary

---

[36] See 15 U.S.C. § 1117(a).

damages.[37] Although the statute itself does not provide much guidance concerning the circumstances under which such awards are appropriate, in practice courts award enhanced damages only when the defendant is found to have "willfully" infringed.[38] The effect of this self-imposed limitation is that courts tend to award enhanced damages only when the defendant is found to have used the infringing mark as a means of diverting some portion of the plaintiff's goodwill to itself or otherwise has intentionally injured the plaintiff.

A third observation is that our model generally advises courts to award restitutionary damages whenever the defendant is (or appears to consumers to be) the more efficient (lower marginal cost) user, which is to say whenever the defendant's profit attributable to the infringement exceeds the plaintiff's lost profit. In this regard, trademark law appears to depart from the model. In trademark cases, U.S. courts do not award restitution as a matter of course, but rather only if the infringement implies "some connotation of 'intent,' or a knowing act denoting an intent, to infringe or reap the harvest of another's mark and advertising."[39] The issue we examine here is whether further inquiry into the economic function of trademarks renders this limitation more sensible than it otherwise may appear.

There are several unusual things about trademark law that might help to explain or justify this departure from our model.[40] One, which we noted in Chapter 2, is that the plaintiff can obtain an injunction upon a showing of *likelihood* of confusion. Proof that consumers have actually been confused, or that such confusion has affected their purchasing decisions, is not an element of the tort. Proof of actual, material confusion *is* required, however,

---

[37] See *id.* We are not aware, however, of any cases in which a court has awarded a multiple greater than three times the amount of the defendant's profits attributable to the infringement.

[38] Note the parallel to patent law, which follows a similar rule. Note also that, in cases involving the use of counterfeit marks, the court is *required* (absent extenuating circumstances) to award three times the plaintiff's actual damages or the defendant's profits – or the court may award statutory damages, as discussed earlier.

[39] McCarthy (2003; § 30:62). *Champion Spark Plug Co. v. Sanders*, 331 U.S. 125, 131 (1947), suggests that restitution is inappropriate in the absence of fraud or palming off.

[40] Note that, when we refer above to explanations and justifications, we are not talking about historical explanations or justifications. In its early days, trademark infringement was an intentional tort and so even injunctive relief was conditioned upon proof that the defendant intended to deceive consumers. Trademark law gradually abandoned this rule for the most part, but one remnant of it may be the limitation upon restitutionary recoveries. Our concern here is not with historical explanations of why trademark law is the way it is, however, but rather whether its features are consistent with the economic function of trademarks.

to recover lost profits, because in the absence of such proof the trademark owner cannot prove that it lost any sales, and hence profits.[41] The point is that lost profits are not a forgone conclusion in every trademark case, because liability can arise before any consumer has actually suffered confusion.

A second point is that, strictly speaking, the defendant's profit attributable to the infringement should be only the profit the defendant earned from using *this* mark, as opposed to the next-best alternative mark. In other words, if the defendant disgorges only its profit attributable to the infringement, the defendant should then occupy the same position it would have occupied without the infringement. Consider then a case in which the defendant adopts a mark – say, ZAZU for a hair coloring product – that a court believes is confusingly similar to the plaintiff's mark ZAZU for a hair salon.[42] Suppose further that there is no evidence that any consumers bought the defendant's product based upon the mistaken assumption that it shared a common source or sponsor with the hair salon, but that the defendant did earn $100,000 in profit from sales of its ZAZU products. The portion of its profit attributable to the infringement should be only the amount that it would not have earned if it had used a different mark. On these facts, this amount is probably zero, because there is no evidence that the defendant diverted any consumers from the plaintiff. Had the defendant chosen a different mark, it probably would have earned the same profit.[43]

At the other end of the spectrum, consider the case of a defendant who sells counterfeit GUCCI bags. Consumers who are deceived into thinking the bags are genuine may buy them because of their assumed quality or because of the cachet of the GUCCI mark; sporting a GUCCI bag is a way of signaling one's status within society. Consumers who are not deceived may buy the bags

---

[41] See, e.g., *International Star Class Yacht Racing Ass'n v. Tommy Hilfiger, U.S.A., Inc.*, 80 F.3d 749, 753 (2d Cir. 1996). There also are a few cases stating or implying that a court may choose not to award *any* damages – including the plaintiff's actual damages – when the defendant has not infringed "willfully" or in "bad faith," but this appears to be a minority view.

[42] The hypothetical is loosely based upon *Zazu Designs v. L'Oreal, S.A.*, 979 F.2d 499 (7th Cir. 1992). One of the authors (Cotter) served as counsel to L'Oreal in this case.

[43] Stephen Carter (1990; 759) posits that some marks may be "better" or "more efficient" than others, in the sense that they may allow the user to build goodwill more quickly than would other, less efficient marks. A catchy, easy-to-remember word – for example, EXXON – will be more efficient in this sense than an awkward, ugly, or difficult-to-pronounce word – for example, GRODROK. Carter's point is well taken, but we doubt that it has any application to the law of damages. In the previous hypothetical, the defendant might have earned some profit from using a catchy name like ZAZU as opposed to a mark possessing less inherent magnetism. But surely there were other, equally magnetic marks available and it is not clear to us how one could quantify a mark's marginal inherent selling power in any event.

because the bags enable these consumers to convey the same status message at a lower price. In either case, virtually every sale made by the defendant is attributable to the presence of the false GUCCI mark. The defendant might have sold some bags had it used a noninfringing mark, but the sales volume almost certainly would have been much lower. Therefore, in this case, nearly all of the defendant's profit is properly attributable to the infringement. In addition, as we noted in Chapter 3, in a case like this one the defendant may only *appear* to be operating at a lower marginal cost curve than the trademark owner. In fact, the plaintiff and defendant are selling different goods. (Even if the products' inherent quality is identical, a genuine product is a different commodity than a fake if consumers value the two differently and if the law backs up that expectation. Moreover, the counterfeiting defendant does not have to invest in quality control, so its marginal cost may well be less than the plaintiff's, but not because of greater efficiency.) Our model suggests that, if the defendant's profit attributable to the infringement exceeds the plaintiff's lost profit – as it might here, given the defendant's presumed lack of investment in quality control and the likelihood that some purchasers of the counterfeit goods would not have paid for the genuine item – the plaintiff should recover the fee it would have charged the defendant for a license (if we trust courts to calculate this amount correctly) or the defendant's profit from the infringement (if we don't, and if we want to encourage voluntary bargaining). In this hypothetical, though, it is extremely unlikely that the plaintiff would have agreed to license the defendant in any event, so even if we thought that courts could calculate license fees with precision the desired remedy here would be the disgorgement of the defendant's profit.

Other cases may fall between these two extremes. Most trademark infringement does not involve outright counterfeiting, but even so consumers sometimes are confused into buying products that they wrongly believe come from some other source. When the infringement is "willful" or in "bad faith," meaning that the defendant intended to divert goodwill from the plaintiff, it may be fair to assume that a substantial portion of the defendant's profit would not have been earned but for the infringement. Not surprisingly, trademark law permits the plaintiff in such a case to recover that profit in lieu of its own lost profit.[44] (More precisely, if the plaintiff

---

[44] Courts are reluctant to infer bad faith when the second user had what appears to be a reasonable belief that his use of a mark similar to one already in use would not constitute an infringement, either because of differences between the two marks or between the goods or services to which they are affixed. To the extent that the defendant reasonably believed that his use would not be infringing, a court is unlikely to assess a restitutionary or enhanced award – even if it concludes that the defendant was mistaken and that his use does, in fact,

invokes this option, the burden shifts to the defendant to prove what portion of its profit was *not* attributable to the infringement.) This option is entirely consistent with what our model would predict.

What happens when the infringement is not willful, but the defendant nevertheless has gained some advantage from the use of an infringing mark? Going back to our ZAZU hypothetical, suppose that the defendant is a nationwide corporation that neglected to perform a pre-use trademark search that would have disclosed the existence of the hair salon or that, having performed the search, it concluded that its use of the ZAZU mark on hair products would not infringe the salon's rights. Suppose further that the defendant does earn some profit from using the ZAZU mark that it would not have earned from the use of another mark. (Maybe a few consumers *do* buy the hair products on the mistaken assumption that they come from the salon, but they wouldn't have bought the products otherwise.) Finally, suppose that the defendant's product turns out to be junk, but that the hair salon cannot prove that it actually lost any customers as a result of the ensuing confusion over the source. What should the plaintiff's damages be?

One possibility would be to take a clue from copyright law – or more directly, from defamation – and award some type of statutory or presumed damages for the harm to the plaintiff's reputation. As we have seen, however, the use of presumed damages in defamation law is problematic because of its vagueness.[45] Also, the use of statutory damages in copyright appears to be justified principally because of the potential aggregate impact of acts that individually cause little harm. In any event, trademark law has avoided this approach, except in some recent cases involving counterfeiting. Alternatively, trademark law can (and does) permit the owner to recover its actual damages. However, in this hypothetical in which there are no provable lost profits, these actual damages would be limited to a reasonable royalty and an award for corrective advertising. Finally, the law could permit the owner to recover the defendant's profit attributable to the infringement, which in this case is assumed to be positive, although less extensive than in the cases

---

infringe. Of course, the plausibility of the defendant's claim that his knowing use was in "good faith" will depend in part on the strength of the evidence of likely (or actual) confusion.

[45] The vagueness is troubling because of its potential implications for freedom of speech. Defamatory speech itself enjoys no First Amendment protection, but the potential impact of the law of defamation upon protected speech – the so-called chilling effect – is a reason for cabining in the reach of defamation law, including the presumed damages rule. Trademarks are a form of commercial speech, entitled to some measure of First Amendment protection. A free-wheeling presumed damages doctrine in trademark law could have some impact upon this form of protected speech.

involving counterfeiting and other willful infringement. However, unless the court views this defendant's conduct as involving willfulness or bad faith, which does not appear likely on these facts unless those words take on a legal definition that goes far beyond their everyday meaning, this last option is not available. Our model would predict otherwise. Does the defect lie in our model or in the law?

It may be that the law's solution makes sense in this context for two reasons. The first is that the cost of determining the profit attributable to the infringement in a case in which only a relatively small portion of the defendant's profit is so attributable may outweigh the potential social benefit. That is, unless the defendant intended to, and did, deceive a substantial number of consumers, most of the defendant's profit probably is *not* attributable to the infringement. It would have been earned anyway using a different mark. This implies that (1) the profit attributable to the infringement may not be much more than the plaintiff's lost profit, if any, and (2) determining precisely how much of the profit was so attributable might be quite costly and time-consuming. The difficulty can be finessed to some extent by placing the burden upon the defendant to prove what portion of its profit is attributable to causes other than infringement, which is the procedure the law uses. But the defendant's cost is a cost nonetheless, and to the extent that the inquiry invites arbitrariness or error, overdeterrence remains a potential negative consequence. Perhaps then the rule that restitution is available only in cases of willful infringement is simply a shorthand way of expressing the idea that restitution should be an available remedy only when all or most of the defendant's profit can be attributed to its wrongful act; when it is likely that most of the profit is attributable to other sources, the social cost of engaging in such fine distinctions may outweigh the benefits.[46]

---

[46] Of course, even when the plaintiff is entitled to recover the defendant's profits, the defendant is, in general, allowed to deduct from its gross profits expenses not properly apportionable to the infringing goods, as well as sales revenue attributable to noninfringing merchandise. But as a practical matter, an award of defendant's profits in a trademark case is often going to be (largely) a matter of all-or-nothing – or else will rely on some arbitrary division – because it may be impossible to estimate how much of the profit on a given product line was earned as a result of the infringement *and would not have been earned otherwise.* The U.S. Supreme Court made this very observation many years ago. See *Hamilton-Brown Shoe Co. v. Wolf Bros. & Co.,* 240 U.S. 251, 261–2 (1916). If restitution were routinely granted, then, trademark defendants often would be overpenalized – assuming they had the burden of proving which portion of their profit was not attributable to the infringement. If the burden rested on the plaintiff, on the other hand, the apportionment problem would result in restitution rarely being awarded. Limiting restitution to cases in which the defendant probably would not have earned much, if any, profit absent the infringement may make some sense. Moreover, there is much less concern about overdeterrence in such cases.

Of course, the consequence of not awarding restitution in cases like our hypothetical ZAZU case is that the court may have to calculate a royalty or corrective advertising award. This calculation is also costly and time-consuming, if accurate estimation is a goal. Both royalties and corrective advertising awards are relatively new phenomena in the law of trademarks, however. These remedies are sparingly used and the case law remains largely undeveloped. Our sense from reading the relatively few cases on this point is that courts generally do not engage in scrutiny comparable to that which they employ in determining reasonable royalties in patent law; the analysis appears to be much more *ad hoc*.[47] Whether any of this has an impact upon the incentive system embedded in trademark law remains anyone's guess. Perhaps the fact that trademark law imposes liability before any actual and material confusion has occurred, coupled with the availability of preliminary injunctions and awards of the defendant's profits in cases of willful or bad faith infringement, does a serviceable enough job of preserving those incentives without the need for greater conformity with our model in ZAZU-like cases.

A second reason why trademark law's approach to restitution may be adequate is that the definition of willful or bad faith infringement *is* subject to some give-and-take in an appropriate case. In this regard, it may be useful to further consider the distinction between intentional and unintentional infringement; this discussion will also be relevant to our analysis in Chapter 5 of whether IP law really is a regime of strict liability or something different.

In a sense, all types of infringement – patent, copyright, and trademark, as well as trade secret misappropriation – can be viewed as intentional.[48] Patents are public documents, and thus in theory one could always avoid infringing a patent by conducting a thorough search beforehand. Many copyrights and trademarks also are registered. As we suggested previously, one of the possible justifications for retaining the copyright registration system is that registration facilitates negotiations between owners and users. Of

---

Counterfeiting and other similar examples of willful trademark infringement serve no valid social purpose and probably are not close enough to other potentially valid practices that there is much reason to be concerned about possible chilling effects.

[47] In cases involving holdover franchisees – that is, defendants who were previously licensed to use the mark and then terminated – courts tend to award as a reasonable royalty the amount the defendant paid during the franchise relationship. In other cases in which reasonable royalties have been awarded, courts have looked to the value of other comparable licenses. For general discussion of the case law, see 5 McCarthy (2002; §§ 30:85–6). Corrective advertising awards have been criticized for bearing little if any relation to the value of the mark. See *Zazu Designs v. L'Oreal, S.A.*, 979 F.2d 499 (7th Cir. 1992); Heald (1988).

[48] Posner (1992; § 6.15, at 206) makes this point with respect to torts.

course, many other copyrights and trademarks are not registered – and no trade secrets are – but this hardly means that it is *impossible* to discover that they exist. For example, you can use the Internet to conduct your own investigation of whether a trademark you would like to adopt is already in use or hire a professional trademark search firm to do a thorough search of not only the federal registry but also state registries and other relevant databases. (Searching for nonverbal source identifiers, however, such as sounds, fragrances, and trade dress, still remains pretty difficult.) As long as pre-use search is possible, the use of a particular work of authorship, trademark, or other information without full knowledge that no one else has a superior claim is in some sense always an intentional act.[49]

To illustrate, consider again our ZAZU hypothetical – or another real case, involving Coca-Cola's use of the mark SURGE for a soft drink. A small firm in Arkansas filed suit against Coca-Cola claiming that the latter's use of that mark violated the plaintiff's preexisting common-law right to use the name SURGE for a beverage product. It may well be that Coca-Cola adopted the name SURGE without knowledge of the small firm's alleged earlier use of the mark. If so, Coca-Cola's conduct was unintentional in the everyday sense of the word. But even if this is so, one could refer to Coca-Cola's conduct as intentional in a probabilistic sense, because there is always some risk that someone else has made a previous use of the desired mark. As noted, the would-be user can reduce this risk by retaining a search firm, but the cost of the search will always be positive and will depend in part upon its scope. It will seldom be optimal (or even possible) to acquire complete information concerning earlier use. Instead, a potential infringer should be expected to search efficiently, i.e., in a cost-effective fashion. This idea can be developed in a simple model of optimal search.

Suppose that the cost of searching records and registries is linear and takes the following form:

$$C = cS$$

---

[49] In addition, most acts of copyright infringement can be viewed as intentional for the simple reason that one of the elements of copyright infringement is *copying*. Independent discovery is not actionable in copyright – although *unconscious* copying can constitute copyright infringement – or in trade secret law. For example, *Bright Tunes Music Corp. v. Harrisongs Music, Ltd.*, 420 F. Supp. 177, 180–1 (S.D.N.Y. 1976), concluded that the defendant George Harrison had unconsciously infringed a popular song. Trade secret law also requires proof that the defendant acquired the information by improper means such as theft or espionage – acts that are hardly consistent with innocence – or that the defendant knew or should have known that the information it used or disclosed was another's trade secret.

where C denotes total search cost, c is the cost per unit of the search activity, and S represents the search activity. The benefit of searching is the reduction in the expected penalties for infringing the intellectual property rights of another. Let D represent the sanction for infringement and P be the probability of infringing. The potential infringer can reduce the probability of infringing through the search and thus the probability of infringing declines as the search continues. We may write:

$$P = P(S) \text{ and } dP/dS < 0.$$

The expected penalty for infringing an intellectual property right is then the probability of infringing times the sanction for infringing:

$$E\,[\text{Penalty}] = P(S)D.$$

For the potential infringer, the expected cost is the sum of the expected penalty, $P(S)D$, plus the cost of whatever search is done, cS:

$$E[TC] = P(S)D + cS.$$

The potential infringer will minimize the expected total cost by increasing its search activity until the marginal benefit of the additional search equals the marginal cost of the additional search. This occurs where

$$dE[TC]/dS = FdP(S)/dS + c = 0.$$

The marginal cost of the additional search is c, whereas the marginal benefit equals the penalty if one infringes (D) times the decrease in the probability of infringing resulting from the additional search ($dP(S)/dS$).

In Figure 4.1, the expected total cost to the potential infringer is the vertical sum of the expected penalty for infringing, $P(S)D$, and the cost of searching, cS. It is clear that the firm minimizes its total cost by engaging in S^* units of search. At this intensity level, the probability of infringing is $P(S^*)$, which is *not* zero. Consequently, a rational firm will incur expected infringement penalties equal to $P(S^*)D$, which is positive. In this sense, one can conclude that infringement is "intentional" because the firm did not search until the probability of infringing was zero. But to search this much would be economically irrational, because the private benefit of additional search beyond S^* is less than the added cost of searching.

Two additional matters of particular interest emerge from this model. First, the policymaker can induce the potential infringer to invest more heavily in searching by increasing the amount of the penalty D (although this would be inadvisable, because S^* is the socially optimal amount of search if D is equal to the amount of the harm caused by the infringement).

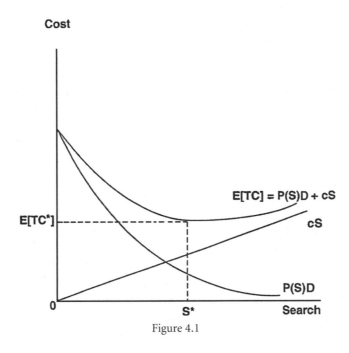

Figure 4.1

At the margin, the potential infringer will search more intensively as D is increased. But if the marginal cost of search (c) is high compared to the decrease in the probability of infringement attributable to an increase in search $(dP(S)/d(S))$, it may take a very large increase in the penalty to have a substantial effect upon the amount of search undertaken. Second, the same model can be used to illustrate a slightly different, although analogous, problem faced by some potential infringers. Suppose that a firm wishes to use a mark that it knows to be similar, but not identical, to a mark that is already in use by another or that it wants to use a mark that it knows to be similar or identical to a mark already in use, but for an entirely different type of good or service. Whether the contemplated use of the mark will be deemed an infringement can be very difficult to predict. To minimize its exposure, this second type of potential infringer can incur additional "search" costs in the sense of legal advice whether its projected use is likely to be found infringing. As before, however, a rational party will invest only so much in searching. Given the uncertainty involved in determining whether a given use infringes, it is conceivable that the potential user might decide that the minimal increase in certainty attributable to an additional "search" is not worth the expense.

We can now return to the question of whether a second user's failure to search prior to adopting what turns out to be an infringing mark, as in our ZAZU hypothetical, can ever constitute bad faith giving rise to an award of restitution. Most of the cases that have addressed the analogous issue of whether there is a duty to investigate prior uses before applying for a federal registration have concluded that there is not.[50] However, in one recent decision regarding *International Star Class Yacht Racing Association v. Tommy Hilfiger, U.S.A., Inc.,*[51] the Second Circuit suggested that a defendant's failure to conduct a full search prior to adopting a design that incorporated the plaintiff's mark was evidence of bad faith. (Ultimately, however, after two remands to the trial court, the litigation concluded with a finding that the defendant had not acted in bad faith by failing to conduct a full search.)[52] A few other courts have stated that a failure to search can be evidence of bad faith, but to our knowledge no post-*Hilfiger* court has yet concluded that a defendant breached a duty or actually acted in bad faith by not searching.[53] Our analysis nevertheless suggests that requiring *some* level of search activity prior to commencing use of a mark may make more sense than absolutely excusing second users from any investigation. Perhaps the *ex ante* prospect of incurring restitutionary liability will induce marginally more search, which may be justified if the search heads off an otherwise socially costly dispute. In other words, a court could characterize a defendant's failure to search as an act of bad faith in a case in which the additional, restitutionary sanction might be appropriate to adequate deterrence.

Balanced against the preceding analysis is the fact that restitution only marginally increases the second user's expected damages beyond the amount

---

[50] See *Money Store v. Harriscorp Fin., Inc.,* 689 F.2d 666, 671–2 (7th Cir. 1982), in which the defendant did not have a duty to further investigate whether the other companies revealed by its search had made a prior use of the mark in interstate commerce; Rosso & Mastracco, Inc. v. Giant Food, Inc., 720 F.2d 1263, 1266 (Fed. Cir. 1983); International House of Pancakes, Inc. v. Elca Corp. 216 U.S.P.Q. 521, 524–5 (T.T.A.B. 1982).

[51] 80 F.3d 749, 753–4 (2d Cir. 1996).

[52] On the first remand, the district judge adhered to his earlier decisions that the defendant had not adopted in bad faith. See 959 F.Supp. 623 (S.D.N.Y. 1997). The Second Circuit reversed, on the ground that the district judge had improperly relied upon findings of fact made in an earlier, unrelated case. See 146 F.3d 66, 70–1 (2d Cir. 1998). On the second remand, the district judge again concluded that the defendant had not acted in bad faith. See No. 94 CIV 2663 (RPP), 81980, 1999 WL 108739, at *1–3 (S.D.N.Y. Mar. 3, 1999). The third time up on appeal, the Court of Appeals affirmed, in an unpublished opinion. See 205 F.3d 1323 (2d Cir. 2000)(table).

[53] See *King of the Mountain Sports, Inc. v. Chrysler Corp.,* 185 F. 3d 1084, 1091–2 (10th Cir. 1999); SecuraComm Consulting, Inc. v. Securacom, Inc., 166 F.3d 182, 188–9 (3d Cir. 1999); First Jewellery Co. of Canada v. Internet Shopping Network, LLC, 53 U.S.P.Q. 2d 1838, 1843–4 (S.D.N.Y. 2000).

of the reasonable royalty or lost profits it otherwise risks incurring. If restitution is easier to calculate than a royalty, the wider availability of restitutionary liability is desirable, but we have already seen that trademark law (rightly or wrongly) rejects this theory in other contexts. Because there is no particular reason to expect *ex ante* that the failure to search will result in profits the bulk of which will be attributable to infringement, the facile equation of a failure to search with bad faith would be dubious. And if, in most instances, the prospect of restitutionary recovery is *not* likely to induce additional search, there may not be much point of awarding restitution in the typical case.

A final puzzle is why the federal trademark dilution statute limits the award of any damages recovery – even actual damages – to cases of willful dilution.[54] Because an action for dilution is available only with respect to "famous" marks, one would expect that in most cases the evidence will show that the defendant was aware of the plaintiff's mark before engaging in the conduct at issue. By restricting the availability of damages relief to acts of "willful" dilution, however, the act appears to contemplate that not all such acts of "knowing" dilution should be considered willful. Nothing in the case law thus far or in the legislative history suggests a reason for making actual damages unavailable in cases of nonwillful dilution.[55] However, one might speculate that this limitation is at least partially attributable to long-standing concerns over the potential for courts to use the dilution doctrine as a means of expanding trademark owners' rights beyond their optimal scope or of inhibiting free speech. In any event, given the vagueness of the dilution concept, it may be the rare case in which the plaintiff will be able to demonstrate any actual damages attributable to the dilution of her mark, whether the defendant's conduct is willful or not.

---

[54] 15 U.S.C. § 43(c)(2).
[55] See Bowen (1996; 84), who noted that neither language of act nor legislative history defines term "willfully intended."

FIVE

Liability Standards for IPRs

In this chapter, we take up the related issues of mental states and standards of liability in intellectual property law. For example, should liability depend upon proof of a proscribed act (such as reproduction) regardless of mental state (strict liability), or should it turn upon proof of intent, or negligence, or something else? Courts and commentators sometimes refer to infringement as a strict liability tort, but we will show that this description is not entirely accurate. Before stating our basic conclusions and proceeding with our analysis, however, it may be useful to explain how the issues we discuss in this chapter relate to the other topics in this book, which for the most part concern remedies and procedure.

As we stated in the introduction, our purpose in this book is not to prescribe the optimal design of *substantive* intellectual property law. That is, whether the incentive structure embedded in the patent laws, the UTSA, the copyright laws, or the Lanham Act is too generous to IPR owners, or not generous enough, or should admit more or fewer exceptions, is not our concern here. We take as our starting point the premise that the substantive laws embody some optimal tradeoff that, if properly applied and enforced, maximizes the surplus of social benefits over social costs. The question then becomes how to ensure proper application and enforcement so that infringers do not undermine the incentive structure. This is a question that policymakers must address under any system of IPRs, whether it be the current system or some future incarnation. In the preceding two chapters, we developed a model that attempts to ensure that the owner of the IPR is no worse off and the infringer no better off as a result of the infringement. We also compared this model against the existing law in an effort to discern departures from the model and whether these departures might be consistent with a more refined version of the model. We argued that the damages rules generated by our model, properly refined and applied, should deter infringement and preserve the incentive structures embedded in the intellectual property laws. The subsidiary question of how to properly calculate the damages arising from the application of these rules requires considerable additional analysis, to which we return in Chapter 8.

The question we wish to take up in these intervening chapters is what, exactly, it means to be an infringer. As a general matter, all of the various IP laws can be seen as attempts to curb free-riding of one sort or another, although clearly it would not be in society's interest to discourage all free riding. The exceptions and limitations upon the owner's rights all permit various types of free-riding, ideally under circumstances in which the social benefits outweigh the costs. For example, patent and copyright rights exist only for a limited time; are subject to various exceptions such as first-sale and, in copyright, fair use; and protect only certain subject matter, not including ideas and facts. Trademarks and trade secrets are more limited in scope, although theoretically unlimited in duration. But we still haven't defined precisely what we mean by free-riding – that is, *what* types of conduct by *whom* should fall within the statutory proscription, absent an exception.[1] One could, for example, decide that only intentional free riding can count as an infringement, or that all free-riding potentially counts, or only negligent free-riding. Second is the question of what acts constitute unlawful free-riding, given the requisite mental state, if any. Subject to the appropriate standard of liability (intent, strict liability, negligence), one might proscribe all duplication of the plaintiff's property, or only some duplications, and similarly for acts such as distribution, use, and so on. Deciding what acts to proscribe largely answers the "who is liable" question: whoever is a duplicator, or a distributor, or a user, or whatever. A related issue is what it means to "duplicate" (or distribute, or use, or do whatever the relevant conduct is with respect to) someone else's property. Here, one might ask whether the defendant is liable only if it reproduces the work exactly, or in substantial part or approximately; if the answer is "in substantial part or approximately," then one must attempt to specify how close is too close and how to prove that the defendant has transgressed the boundary. Finally, there is a question of who has the right to enforce the IPR, because many persons may claim some interest in it, including assignees, assignors, and various types of licensees.

---

[1] The *where* question is usually easy: because IPRs are territorial, they are enforceable only in the country that recognizes the right. *When* is a question of statutory or common-law duration.

In this chapter and Chapters 6 and 7, we address all of these issues *except*
the issue of what it means to "duplicate" someone else's property.[2] The
present chapter discusses the consequences and implications of the various possible liability standards, including strict liability, negligence, and
intent. As we shall see, the inclusion of this topic in a book that concentrates
on remedies makes sense, because mental state often has an impact upon
the type and amount of damages that the plaintiff may recover. Somewhat
surprisingly, none of the principal bodies of IP law embodies a true strict
liability standard, if we define that standard as one in which the defendant
is required to compensate the plaintiff for past injuries regardless of the
defendant's mental state at the time of the wrongful act.[3] In various ways,
U.S. patent, trade secret, and copyright law all place substantial limitations
upon damages recoveries, absent some other element such as actual or constructive notice (in patent law), negligence or intent (in trade secret law), or
copying (in copyright law). Also relevant to this discussion is the fact that
copyright and trade secret law recognize independent discovery as a defense,
whereas patent and trademark law do not. We discuss some reasons why this
distinction probably is correct. By contrast, the common law of trademark
infringement permits compensatory damages upon a showing of actual confusion, regardless of mental state, but it limits restitutionary awards to cases
of "willful" infringement. None of these bodies of law permits damages to

---

[2] A discussion of this last issue would entail, among other things, an examination of the all-
    elements rule, the doctrine of equivalents, and the reverse doctrine of equivalents, in patent
    law; of the various methods for determining substantial similarity in copyright law, which
    in the United States vary from one type of subject matter to another and from one circuit
    court to another; and of the vagaries of likelihood of confusion in trademarks. Discussion
    of these topics alone could easily take up an entire book. Moreover, many other scholars
    have already addressed them, although the topics are hardly exhausted. What we will focus
    on in this and the next two chapters are the remaining questions outlined previously, which
    have received relatively little scholarly treatment.

[3] Strict liability is typically defined as liability without fault, see Restatement (Second) of Torts
    (1959; § 504–24A). However, even in general tort law this description can be misleading,
    because many of the factors that are relevant to a determination of negligence are equally
    relevant to a determination of strict liability. See, e.g., *Flaminio v. Honda Motor Co.*, 733
    F.2d 463, 466–7 (7th Cir. 1984). Strict liability can arise in a variety of common-tort-law
    settings, such as when a person engages in unusually dangerous activity or a manufacturer
    distributes a defective product. In the latter instance, a court may require the defendant
    to pay damages in compensation for injuries caused by the defective product even if the
    defendant was unaware prior to the occurrence of the injury of the defect's existence. We
    suspect that, when people use the term "strict liability," they are thinking of fact patterns
    like these, in which the defendant is liable for past injuries bearing some causal relationship
    to her conduct, even though that conduct may not embody actionable negligence, much
    less an intentional tort.

be awarded across the board, in all cases, under a true strict liability standard. We will argue that these limitations, which we describe in more detail in the next section, are roughly consistent with the underlying purpose of these laws, although they could perhaps be improved upon in some respects. This is particularly true of patent law, in which damages are, in a substantial minority of cases, available *without* proof of actual or constructive notice – and in which the "constructive notice" standard, as currently applied, in some cases may approach a true strict liability standard.

PATENT LAW: REMEDIES ARE CONTINGENT UPON THE RECEIPT OF ACTUAL OR CONSTRUCTIVE NOTICE

Patent infringement is a strict liability tort in the sense that a defendant may be liable without having had any notice, prior to the filing of an infringement action, that her conduct was infringing. In other words, innocent (i.e., unintentional or inadvertent) infringement is not a defense to a patent infringement claim and a court will prospectively enjoin the defendant from infringing even though the defendant was put on notice only by the filing of the lawsuit. Patent law nevertheless departs from the "pure" strict liability model in two important respects. First, the defendant's state of mind can be relevant to a variety of substantive and procedural maters. Under U.S. law, for example, a defendant who "willfully" infringes may be liable for up to three times the amount of the plaintiff's damages and the most important factor in determining willfulness is whether the defendant knew of the plaintiff's patent before she started infringing.[4] Because patent plaintiffs frequently plead willful infringement, the defendant's state of mind is a common issue in patent litigation, notwithstanding the frequent characterization of patent infringement as a strict liability tort. The defendant's state of mind may be relevant to other issues as well, including nonobviousness and infringement under the doctrine of equivalents.[5] In these respects, however, patent infringement is not qualitatively different from other torts.

---

[4] See 35 U.S.C. § 284, which states that courts may award treble damages; *Read Corp. v. Portec, Inc.*, 970 F.2d 816, 826 (Fed. Cir. 1992), which sets forth factors relevant to willful infringement.

[5] A finding that the defendant copied the plaintiff's invention is evidence that the invention was nonobvious. See *Apple Computer, Inc. v. Articulate Sys.*, 234 F.3d 14, 26 (Fed. Cir. 2000). Similarly, in determining whether a device infringes under the doctrine of equivalents, evidence of independent discovery weighs against a finding that a person of ordinary skill in the art would have known that a particular element was interchangeable with an element of the patented invention. See *Warner-Jenkinson Co. v. Hilton-Davis Chem. Co.*, 520 U.S. 17, 35–6 (1997). Evidence of copying, therefore, can weigh in favor of infringement by

In a "strict" products liability action, for example, the defendant's state of mind may be relevant to a variety of issues including whether a product was defective or unreasonably dangerous, whether there was a duty to warn, and amenability to punitive damages.[6]

Our principal focus therefore will be upon another, more idiosyncratic way in which patent law departs from the strict liability model. In contrast to other alleged tortfeasors, the defendant in a patent infringement suit often is not liable for *damages* arising from her unlawful conduct until the plaintiff puts her on notice; at that point, she becomes liable only for damages arising from her subsequent conduct. Specifically, § 287(a) of the U.S. Patent Act states:

Patentees, and persons making, offering for sale, or selling within the United States any patented article for or under them, or importing any patented article into the United States, may give notice to the public that the same is patented, either by fixing thereon the word "patent" or the abbreviation "pat.", together with the number of the patent, or when, from the character of the article, this can not be done, by fixing to it, or to the package wherein one or more of them is contained, a label containing a like notice. In the event of failure so to mark, no damages shall be recovered by the patentee in any action for infringement, except on proof that the infringer was notified of the infringement and continued to infringe thereafter, in which event damages may be recovered only for infringement occurring after such notice. Filing of an action for infringement shall constitute such notice.

Thus, a patentee who markets products embodying his patent can recover damages only for infringing conduct that occurs after he has provided the requisite notice in one of the three ways described in § 287(a). First, the

equivalents. See *Advanced Display Sys. v. Kent State Univ.*, 212 F.3d 1272, 1287 (Fed. Cir. 2000).

[6] See Flaminio, 733 F.2d at 467; *Thomas v. American Cystoscope Makers, Inc.*, 414 F. Supp. 255 (E.D. Pa. 1976). Another analogous body of law in which it is sometimes claimed that strict liability applies is the law of trespass – and one might think that trespass, either to real or personal property, would provide a good analogy to the infringement of intellectual property rights. Some scholars have made this association, particularly as it relates to digital works, such as websites. See Hardy (1996). Others question the value of the real or personal property analogies because, as we have noted, intellectual property is nonrivalrous and nonexclusive and may incorporate content to which the public has or eventually will have lawful access. See Burk (2000); Burk (1999; 132–6); Cohen (1998). Another problem with the trespass analogy is that most personalty or realty belongs to *someone*, even if the trespasser does not know who that someone is (although personalty and realty can be abandoned or publicly owned). One of the dilemmas in intellectual property law is how to know whether the information you develop has already been developed independently, and is owned, by someone else. Finally, the characterization of traditional trespass as a strict liability tort is not entirely accurate. See Burk (2000; 28); Ciolino & Donelon (2002; 369–70).

patent owner may put the defendant on notice by commencing an infringe-ment action against the defendant.[7] Second, the patent owner may provide actual, specific notice of the infringement, prior to the filing of the lawsuit.[8] Third, the patent owner may provide constructive notice by affixation. In this regard, one might conclude that the Patent Act makes the recovery of damages contingent upon the defendant's *intentional* decision to infringe after having received notice and that this outcome is considerably different from the common meaning of strict liability. Indeed, the Federal Circuit has suggested as much, stating that § 287:

serves three related purposes: (1) helping to avoid innocent infringement; (2) en-couraging patentees to give notice to the public that the article is patented; and (3) aiding the public to identify whether an article is patented.[9]

The preceding discussion nevertheless overstates our case in at least two respects. First, a patent owner who does not market any products that em-body his patent may recover damages for infringing conduct that occurs prior to the defendant's receipt of notice. Thus, the owner of an infringed *process* patent may be able to recover damages accruing from the beginning of the infringement, regardless of whether the defendant is on notice or has knowledge of the patent prior to the service of the complaint.[10] Similarly, the

---

[7] There are two other circumstances in which the Patent Act departs from the strict liability model. See 35 U.S.C. § 287(b) that sets forth the conditions under which one may obtain a remedy for the unauthorized manufacture, sale, use, or importation of an unpatented product made by a patented process; *id.* § 154(d)(A), which sets forth the conditions under which one may obtain a remedy for the unauthorized manufacture, sale, use, or importation of an invention described in a published patent application that later results in the issuance of a patent. These provisions are of only limited importance, and we omit them from our earlier discussion.

[8] The case law provides some detail concerning what constitutes actual notice. See *Lans v. Digital Equip. Corp.*, 252 F.3d 1320, 1326–8 (Fed. Cir. 2001), where it was held that notification must come from and identify the patentee and that notice even from one "closely associated with the patentee" is therefore insufficient; *SRI Int'l, Inc. v. Advanced Tech. Labs., Inc.*, 127 F.3d 1462, 1470 (Fed. Cir. 1997), which states that "§ 287(a) is satisfied when the recipient is informed of the identity of the patent and the activity that is believed to be an infringement, accompanied by a proposal to abate the infringement, whether by license or otherwise"; *Amsted Indus. v. Buckeye Steel Castings Co.*, 24 F.3d 178, 187 (Fed. Cir. 1994), which holds that actual notice "requires the affirmative communication of a specific charge of infringement by a specific accused product," and that the defendant's actual knowledge of the patent or its own infringement is irrelevant.

[9] *Nike, Inc. v. Wal-Mart Stores, Inc.*, 138 F.3d 1437, 1443 (Fed. Cir. 1998).

[10] See, e.g., *Crystal Semiconductor Corp. v. Tritech Microelectronics Int'l, Inc.*, 246 F.3d 1336, 1353 (Fed. Cir. 2001). The rationale for not requiring marking in the case of process patents is that processes cannot be marked. See *American Med. Sys. v. Medical Eng'g Corp.*, 6 F.3d 1523, 1538 (Fed. Cir. 1993). Patent law nevertheless could restrict the process patent owner

owner of an idle patent may recover damages for conduct occurring prior to the receipt of notice, although typically these damages will take the form of a reasonable royalty rather than lost profits (see Chapter 8).[11] In these two instances, patent infringement is in all relevant respects a strict liability tort. Second, many patent owners who sell products that embody their patents make use of the marking provision, which means that in many cases defendants are on at least constructive notice from the date they begin to infringe; because constructive notice does not necessarily imply actual knowledge, an "innocent" defendant may still be liable for damages, as under a true strict liability regime. But not every manufacturing or selling owner does mark;[12] in cases in which they do not do so, damages liability accrues only from the date of actual notice. Therefore, in some instances, the use of the term "strict liability" in connection with patent law can be quite misleading.

COPYRIGHT LAW: LIABILITY IS CONTINGENT UPON PROOF OF COPYING

In copyright law, the departure from strict liability is even more pronounced. Unlike patent law, copyright law recognizes independent creation

from recovering damages attributable to "innocent" infringement – or else provide for some other form of constructive notice of a process patent – but at present it does not. Moreover, when the patent contains both product and process claims, the patent owner's failure to mark his patented products sometimes *may* prevent him from recovering damages attributable to the prenotice infringement of either type of claim. For a good discussion of the (highly complex) case law on this topic, see Voelzke (1995).

[11] See *Wine Ry. Appliance Co. v. Enterprise Ry. Equip. Co.*, 297 U.S. 387, 398 (1936); *Rite-Hite Corp. v. Kelley Co.*, 56 F.3d 1538, 1544–9 (Fed. Cir. 1995) (en banc).

[12] There are several reasons why patent owners sometimes fail to mark. First, in cases in which the patent owner licenses someone else to manufacture the patented article, the patent owner may encounter problems in monitoring the licensee's compliance with § 287. Second, in cases in which the patent owner begins marketing its product before the patent issues, it may be expensive to add the required notice to existing products after issuance. Although firms sometimes mark their products with the words "patent pending" prior to the issuance of an actual patent, the use of these words does not constitute sufficient notice for purposes of § 287. Third, even after the patent issues, it may be difficult or expensive to comply with § 287, for example, by correctly marking a product that embodies many discrete patents, especially if the product design changes over time. Fourth, it is not clear what constitutes sufficient marking under every conceivable fact pattern, thus leaving open the possibility that patent owners' good faith attempts to comply with § 287 will sometimes fail. Fifth, Robert Merges suggests that there may be strategic reasons not to mark in some cases. See Merges (1997), who stated that lawyers sometimes advise their clients not to mark, either "to plan a 'sneak attack' on competitors" against whom an injunction will be sought after the latter have invested in plants and equipment or to avoid calling attention to a patent that will be easy to invent around. For further discussions, see McKeon (1996); Moore & Nakamura (1994); Oppedahl (1995).

as a defense, which means that a copyright defendant is liable only if she engages in the unauthorized *copying* of another's work.[13] This distinction has led a few courts to break away from the herd and declare copyright infringement an intentional, rather than a strict liability, tort.[14]

As was the case with patent law, however, the departure from the strict liability standard is itself mitigated in several ways, so that in truth the end result is something that lies in between a strict liability and a fault-based regime. For one thing, unconscious copying is still copying. Thus, the defendant is liable even if the trier of fact concludes that she copied the plaintiff's work unintentionally. This was the outcome of a famous case brought against former Beatle George Harrison.[15] From this principle it follows that the plaintiff can prove copying by circumstantial evidence alone, and this evidence can take one of two forms. First, the trier of fact may infer copying if the works are similar and the defendant had a reasonable opportunity to copy the plaintiff's work.[16] Second, most courts follow the rule that if the works are "strikingly" similar, the trier of fact may infer access from this fact alone.[17] Another way in which copyright law stakes out a

---

[13] A more precise statement of the law is that one may be liable for violating any of the copyright owner's exclusive rights under §§ 106, 106A, 611, or 1101 of the Copyright Act. The point we make in the previous text nevertheless holds true, regardless of which section of the Copyright Act is at issue: independent creation is a defense to any claim for copyright infringement.

[14] See *Pritikin v. Liberation Publications, Inc.*, 83 F. Supp. 2d 920, 923 (N.D. Ill. 1999).

[15] See *Bright Tunes Music Corp. v. Harrisongs*, 420 F. Supp. 177 (S.D.N.Y. 1976). The issue in *Bright Tunes* was whether Harrison's song *My Sweet Lord* infringed the song *He's So Fine*. The court did not believe that Harrison intentionally copied the melody from *He's So Fine*, but did conclude that Harrison probably copied the tune without realizing it. *He's So Fine* was a big hit in the early 1960s, which meant that Harrison must have heard it on numerous occasions, and the melodies of the two songs are very similar.

[16] See *Bouchat v. Baltimore Ravens, Inc.*, 241 F.3d 350, 353–4 (4th Cir. 2001).

[17] See *id.* at 355–6. More precisely, if the works are strikingly similar, the burden shifts to the defendant to prove that similarity resulted from some innocent reason, such as both parties borrowing from a common, public-domain source, or the simplicity of the expression. See *Ty, Inc. v. GMA Accessories, Inc.*, 132 F.3d 1167, 1170–71 (7th Cir. 1997); *Selle v. Gibb*, 741 F.2d 896, 904 (7th Cir. 1984).

Given that copying can be inferred from similarity (or more commonly from evidence of similarity plus access), one might ask whether independent discovery really *is* a defense in a copyright case or, to be more precise, whether the plaintiff really does have to prove copying. The answer is yes: no copying, no liability. Absent *direct* evidence of copying, however – eyewitness testimony or an admission on the part of the defendant – one can *infer* copying from similarity. To put the matter in perspective, Learned Hand once correctly observed that if someone with no prior access to Keats's poetry were to independently write *Ode on a Grecian Urn*, he would not be liable for copyright infringement, even if Keats's poem was still subject to copyright protection. *Sheldon v. Metro-Goldwyn Pictures Corp.*, 81 F.2d 49, 54 (2d Cir. 1936). But of course this would never happen. Although an infinite

middle position is that the plaintiff does not need to show that the defendant *knew* the work she was copying was subject to copyright protection. Thus, the defendant may be liable if she copied, even if she had no reason to know that the specific work she was copying was protected.[18] Furthermore, once liability is established, a court may assess damages accruing from the beginning of the infringement. There is no provision in U.S. copyright law analogous to the patent marking statute, although the absence of a copyright notice can have some marginal effect upon the *amount* of damages awarded – specifically, by lowering the amount of statutory damages to \$200.[19]

TRADEMARK LAW

A court will almost always enjoin a defendant who uses a symbol that is likely to cause confusion with, or to dilute, the plaintiff's trademark, regardless of whether the defendant had any prior awareness of the plaintiff's mark. In this sense, trademark law, like patent and to a lesser extent copyright law, seems to follow a regime of strict liability. Like patent and copyright law, however, trademark law also qualifies this strict liability principle in some significant respects.

First, as we noted in Chapter 2, determining whether the use of a symbol is likely to cause confusion often depends upon consideration of a wide variety of factors, including the defendant's intent (or lack thereof) to trade on the plaintiff's reputation. In a marginal case, therefore, an "innocent" defendant is more likely than a knowing copier to prevail. There are several possible justifications for this rule. One is that the defendant's state of mind is a rough proxy for that of consumers, such that if the defendant is unaware of the plaintiff's mark, consumers also are unlikely to be aware of it and

---

number of monkeys tapping on typewriters will eventually reproduce the complete works of Shakespeare, once we move from the infinite to the finite the precise duplication of a complex work of literature cannot happen merely by chance. It *is* possible, however, for people to independently create works of authorship that (1) are relatively uncomplicated, but (2) nevertheless exhibit sufficient minimal creativity to merit copyright protection – for example, some simple designs, short melodies, simple plots, etc. The cases recognize this point.

[18] The Second Circuit recently reaffirmed the rule that one who "innocently" copies another's work, as embodied unlawfully in an intermediate product, is liable to the copyright holder. See *Lipton v. Nature Co.*, 71 F.3d 464, 471 (2d Cir. 1995). This rule greatly troubled Learned Hand. See *DeAcosta v. Brown*, 146 F.2d 408, 414 (2d Cir. 1944) (L. Hand, J., dissenting); see also Ciolino & Donelon (2002) who argue against finding the innocent infringer liable.

[19] See 17 U.S.C. §§ 401(d), 402(d), 504(c)(2); see also *Davis v. Gap, Inc.*, 246 F.3d 152 (2d Cir. 2001).

therefore are unlikely to be confused.[20] Now that consumer surveys are widely used in trademark litigation, however, this rationale no longer seems very persuasive. A better reason for considering the defendant's state of mind is that, if the defendant adopted the mark with the intent to free ride upon the plaintiff's reputation, confusion is more likely than it otherwise would be, because the defendant (presumably) was familiar with the relevant market and thus her expectations are likely to come true.[21] By contrast, when the defendant is unaware of the plaintiff's mark, perhaps the plaintiff's mark is not strong enough to warrant extensive protection from close, but not identical, marks. Even so, one can often prove the defendant's state of mind only by circumstantial evidence, and the facts that would tend to prove a guilty (or innocent) mind are often the very same facts that would tend to prove (or disprove) likelihood of confusion.[22] As in copyright law, state of mind is often difficult to separate from the ultimate question of liability.

Second, even if the defendant is liable for trademark infringement, her lack of knowledge can affect her damages liability. To recover damages under the federal Lanham Act, the owner of a federally registered mark must, like the patent owner, either mark his products or provide actual notice of the registration.[23] Few if any state trademark laws contain similar provisions, however. Thus, the owner of a mark (whether federally registered or not) who sues for infringement under state law typically has no obligation to mark; nor does one who sues for the infringement of a nonfederally registered mark under § 43(a) of the Lanham Act.[24] As we have seen, however, restitutionary damages are usually not recoverable unless the infringement was willful and most jurisdictions include a similar restriction on damages for dilution.

TRADE SECRETS

The only major body of intellectual property law that is almost never characterized as a strict liability regime is trade secret law. From a doctrinal perspective, this result follows directly from the definition of trade secret misappropriation. As we discussed in Chapter 2, a person may misappropriate a trade secret by acquiring secret information that he knows or should know was acquired by improper means.[25] Moreover, the term "improper

---

[20] See 4 McCarthy (2001; § 26:12, at 26–18 to –19).
[21] See Cotter (1995; 539–41).
[22] See McCarthy (2001; § 23:124, at 23–282).
[23] See 15 U.S.C. § 1111.
[24] See McCarthy (2001; § 19:144, at 19–346).
[25] See Unif. Trade Secrets Act § 1(2)(i).

means" itself invariably refers to acts that are almost always classified as intentional, such as theft or espionage.[26] Second, a person may misappropriate a secret by disclosing or using secret information that (1) she used improper means to acquire or (2) she knew or should have known (a) was derived from a person who used improper means to acquire it, or (b) acquired under circumstances giving rise to a duty of confidentiality, or (c) derived from a person who owed the plaintiff a duty of confidentiality.[27] Although it is conceivable that a person could be liable for accidentally disclosing or using secret information that she knew or should have known belonged to another – for example, by leaving an employer's trade secret formula in a place where another was able to find it – we are aware of no reported decisions in which liability has been imposed under this theory. Moreover, a person's use or further disclosure of a secret that another has accidentally disclosed to him is expressly *not* actionable as a misappropriation, unless the defendant is aware of the circumstances surrounding the disclosure and has not materially changed his position in reliance on his ability to use the information.[28] Thus, while in theory there may be cases in which one could be strictly liable for the accidental disclosure of a trade secret, in virtually every real-world instance trade secret liability appears to depend upon an intentional, knowing, or negligent act. This feature of trade secret law is consistent with the relative weakness of trade secret as opposed to patent protection, which we discuss later.

SHOULD INDEPENDENT DISCOVERY BE A DEFENSE TO AN INFRINGEMENT CLAIM?

At first blush, the thesis that independent discovery should be a defense to an infringement claim seems counterintuitive. As we have seen, the most common justification for patent and copyright systems is that the provision of exclusive rights in inventions and writings is necessary to induce people to create and to disclose the fruits of their efforts. An independent discovery defense threatens to reduce these benefits. The question therefore arises why copyright and trade secret law recognize independent discovery as a defense. Conversely, if there are good reasons for the defense in copyright and trade secret law, why do patent and trademark law reject the defense?

---

[26] See *id.* § 1(1).
[27] See *id.* § 1(2)(ii)(A), (B).
[28] See *id.* § 1(2)(ii)(C).

In fact, an independent discovery defense makes a great deal of sense in both copyright and trade secret law. As we noted earlier, copyright subsists in all original works of authorship that are fixed in a tangible medium of expression, from the moment of creation until seventy years after the author's death. The sheer ubiquity of copyrighted works means that it would be virtually impossible for an author to search for all copyrighted works that his own work might infringe, even if a method of conducting such a search were theoretically possible.[29] (It is not, because not all works are registered. Most countries do not register copyrights at all and even in the United States registration is not mandatory until the filing of litigation – and even then, there are some exceptions.) A true strict liability system therefore might have a chilling effect upon the publication of new works; and this result would be problematic not only from a purely "economic" perspective, but also because of its First Amendment implications. At the same time, although it is legal for someone to independently create a work of authorship that is substantially similar to an existing work, in practice the accidental authorship of a substantially similar work that would compete against the original is probably uncommon. The possibility that one might face such competition down the road is therefore unlikely to affect the incentive to produce copyrightable works.[30] Analogous considerations suggest that independent discovery is a good fit for trade secret law as well. Trade secret law protection is, by design, less powerful than patent protection. As a consequence, the trade secret owner's rights are not valid against the world, but rather only against persons who have acquired the secret in certain ways or who stand in a confidential relationship to the owner. And for obvious reasons, there is no central registry of other persons' trade secrets.

The situation in trademark and patent law is considerably different. In trademark law, the need to prevent consumer confusion over the source of goods suggests that the infringer's independent creation of a substantially similar mark should be of no concern, except in the very limited sense that the infringer's state of mind might in some respects serve as a proxy for those of consumers. Patent law presents a more complicated case, for two reasons. First, a pre-invention search of patented inventions is in theory feasible, because all patents are public records. Even so, the cost of conducting a patent search prior to engaging in the manufacture or sale of a new product

---

[29] See Blair & Cotter (1999; 31–2); Landes & Posner (1989; 345–6).

[30] See Blair & Cotter (2001; 69); Nimmer (2001; 38–9); Landes & Posner (1989; 345–6). This observation is reinforced by the fact that copyright does not subsist in things such as facts, ideas, short phrases, and scenes à faire, and by the merger doctrine. See Cotter (1999; 220–1).

is not trivial and, in some cases, can be quite high. Second, the probability of the independent development of an invention containing all the elements of a patented invention also may be relatively high – as witnessed by the fact that, at any given time, multiple researchers *are* working on similar engineering and scientific problems.[31] Having to distinguish whether such cases involve copying or independent discovery might impose more substantial costs and have a more serious effect upon incentives than is the case in the copyright system.

Although the preceding considerations suggest some reasons for rejecting an independent discovery defense in patent law, they are hardly dispositive. In a provocative paper, Stephen Maurer and Suzanne Scotchmer argue that an independent discovery defense in patent law would, in some cases, provide the patentee with a sufficient reward while also reducing the potential deadweight loss from the assertion of patent rights.[32] In the following paragraphs, we sketch out the intuition behind the Maurer-Scotchmer thesis. We then address some potential problems with the thesis.

THE MAURER-SCOTCHMER THESIS

Maurer and Scotchmer begin with a model in which the cost of research and development, as well as the cost of independent invention, are relatively low. On the basis of this assumption, they demonstrate that a patentee can deter entry on the part of an independent inventor (who would otherwise enter and compete as a Cournot duopolist)[33] by licensing his patent to n licensees for a royalty that is less than the cost each licensee would face if she were to independently invent. Using this strategy, the patentee can ensure that the licensees will be better off as licensees than they would have been as independent inventors/competitors. At the same time, the patentee is better off than he would be if the licensees were to independently invent and compete against him. Of course, the patentee earns a lower profit than he would have earned under a regime without an independent invention defense, but – significantly – his licensing revenue will exceed his own research and development costs. His reward therefore is sufficient to

---

[31] For some well-known historical examples, see Ogburn & Thomas (1922; 93–8), who list prominent inventions and discoveries that were independently made (cited in *Kewanee Oil Co. v. Bicron Corp.*, 416 U.S. 470, 490 (1974)).

[32] Maurer & Scotchmer (2002). For papers that foreshadow some aspects of the Maurer-Scotchmer analysis, see Leibovitz (2002); Lichtman (1997; 720–3).

[33] In a Cournot duopoly, firms compete by setting quantities. See Carlton & Perloff (2000; 153–93).

induce him to undertake R & D, but will result in a lower deadweight loss. Maurer and Scotchmer also show that, under these assumptions, the threat of *ex post* competition will deter some firms from entering the race to invent the patented item, thus potentially reducing wastefully duplicative research and development costs.[34]

The limitations imposed by the model's assumptions nevertheless suggest extreme caution in deriving any practical policy recommendations from it. First, as Maurer and Scotchmer recognize, their proposal does not improve social welfare if the patentee's cost of research and development is high relative to the cost of independent discovery, for example, when the *ex ante* probability of inventive success is low.[35] To make up for this potential defect, Maurer and Scotchmer suggest that Congress could enact a series of exemptions from the independent-discovery defense for certain classes of inventions.[36] One problem with this approach, however, is that it would encourage rent-seeking on the part of industries claiming an entitlement to the exemption. Moreover, those industries in which R & D costs are sufficiently high that they ought to be exempt from the independent discovery defense (Maurer and Scotchmer suggest that the pharmaceutical industry is one) may well be the same ones in which the deadweight

---

[34] *See* Maurer & Scotchmer (2002; 540–1).

[35] See *id.* at 543–4. Maurer and Scotchmer explain:

> There are two basic reasons why the costs of duplication can be lower. First, merely knowing that someone has invented a product can be important for expected costs of duplication in cases where significant *ex ante* doubts exist about whether the proposed product can be made at all. (The atomic bomb is a particularly notorious example.) Second, competitors can cheat by claiming that they independently invented what they surreptitiously copied.
>
> Pharmaceuticals are probably the best example of an industry with significant *ex ante* uncertainty about success. The probability of achieving a marketable, FDA-approved drug is about 1/5, conditional on having sunk the development costs. If the cost of every pharmaceutical that comes to market is $ 0.2 billion, firms must anticipate $ 1 billion in revenues in order to cover costs on average. The effective cost of each new drug is therefore $ 1 billion, since this is the minimum compensation needed to induce firms to invest. On the other hand, an independent invention defence could let imitators avoid 'dry holes' and cut their R & D costs by 80%. In such a case, the threat of duplication would undermine the patent-holder's profit to the point where he could no longer cover his costs.

> *Id.* at 543.

[36] Alternatively, Maurer and Scotchmer suggest that, "in cases with significant *ex ante* uncertainty of success (e.g., pharmaceuticals) judges would rule that independence is impossible" or that "courts should set patent breadth so that the costs of imitation approximate the original inventor's effective cost averaged over an appropriate number of dry holes." *Id.* at 543–4. Judges may be less susceptible to regulatory capture than legislators or administrative agencies, but we remain skeptical over courts' ability to pick the right industries or to set patent breadth with such precision.

loss attributable to patent protection is highest, because there are fewer nonpatented alternatives to their patented products. In other industries, by contrast, the probability that a patent will confer monopoly rights in an economically meaningful sense is probably much lower (or, to put it another way, designing around the patent to create a competing but non-infringing product is probably more feasible), which means that the dead-weight loss attributable to patent protection may be relatively low even in the absence of an independent discovery defense. If this is so, however, then under the Maurer-Scotchmer proposal the independent discovery defense would apply only in cases in which there is the least need for it. Such limited benefits must then be offset against the social cost of effecting the change.

A second problem with an independent discovery defense, which Maurer and Scotchmer also recognize, is that the patentee's competitors may have an incentive to copy and feign independent discovery and that the attendant cost of determining whether a competing product is the result of copying or independent discovery could be substantial.[37] In response, Maurer and Scotchmer suggest that competitors could borrow the practice of software companies, which use "clean room" procedures to isolate their code-writing engineers from contact with the code embedded in products with which the companies wish to compete;[38] presumably, firms that do not adopt clean room procedures would have a difficult time proving independent discovery. Once again, however, we question whether the proposed modification would be practical as applied to patentable inventions. In the software industry, an engineer may be relatively unlikely to accidentally come into contact with a competitor's code. Limiting exposure to a wide variety of patented inventions is not so easy, however, as other commentators have pointed out.[39] Creating an incentive to avoid contact with existing patents might also have perverse consequences, inasmuch as the information contained in existing patents might inspire researchers to discover new and better ways of achieving the same result, or new avenues of research altogether. Absent a

---

[37] See *id.* at 544.

[38] See *id.* Conceivably, the actual *use* of clean rooms would not be necessary if the Maurer-Scotchmer plan worked as intended. A would-be user could merely threaten to use a clean room to independently invent, in the event that the patentee refused to license her, thus inducing the licensing transaction that promises to make both parties better off. In addition, presumably a competitor would be able to take advantage of the clean room procedure only if it did not give the clean-room-sequestered employees "hints" about how the problem should be solved.

[39] See Adelman (1977; 984).

practical means of avoiding such contact, however, cheating may be rampant and the resulting administrative costs of detecting it must be weighed against any potential benefits of independent discovery.

A third problem is that, even if an independent discovery defense leaves intact the incentive to invent, it might undermine the inventor's incentive to disclose the fruits of his invention (or, to put it another way, might encourage him to rely upon trade secret protection). Thus, even if the reward to be earned under a regime that recognizes an independent-discovery defense is sufficient to cover the patentee's R & D costs, the inventor will opt for trade secrecy if the latter offers the prospect of a higher reward. Of course, independent discovery of a trade secret is lawful as well, but the inventor does not have to disclose his information to the world in exchange for trade secret protection.[40] In some cases, the existence of an independent discovery defense in patent law might encourage secrecy, and whether the expected reduction in the deadweight loss outweighs the social cost of secrecy is unclear. Alternatively, an independent discovery defense in patent law might undermine the rationale of the U.S. Supreme Court's decision in *Kewanee Oil Co. v. Bicron Corp.*[41] that federal patent law does not preempt state trade secret law. One of the factors the Court cited, in support of its conclusion that trade secret law is sufficiently weak in comparison with patent law to avoid preemption by the latter, is that trade secret law permits independent discovery.[42] An independent discovery defense to a patent infringement claim therefore might lead to the preemption of trade secret law, but it is far from clear that this would be a good result; many analysts believe that trade secret law provides a useful complement to patent protection.

A fourth problem is that the Maurer-Scotchmer thesis depends upon the patentee being able to license the invention, but in the real world licensing is not always a feasible choice. The transaction costs of, and other obstacles to, licensing can be burdensome for a number of reasons, including asymmetric information; the potential for competition from substitutes for the patented invention; the interdependence of potential licensees' demand curves; and

---

[40] If the invention is a product that the inventor sells to the public, it is likely that someone will discover the trade secret through reverse engineering sooner or later. See *id.* at 982. Reverse engineering or independent discovery may not be inevitable, however; witness the long-lasting trade secret on the recipe for Coca-Cola syrup. Moreover, if the invention is a process, reverse engineering of the resultant product does not necessarily reveal the nature of that process.

[41] 416 U.S. 470 (1974).

[42] See *id.* at 489–90.

the fact that licensees are free to challenge the patent's validity.[43] As a result, licensors typically receive only a portion of the total profit that is theoretically available from the exploitation of their inventions, with one study showing an average of just 40%.[44] Of course, licensing can nevertheless be a rational strategy when the licensees can produce or market the good at issue at lower cost than can the patentee, or have other advantages. To the extent, however, that Maurer and Scotchmer assume away the transaction costs of licensing, their proposal may overestimate the social benefits to be gained from an independent discovery defense.

Fifth, suppose that, in a system that recognizes the independent discovery defense, A patents an invention, B independently discovers the same invention, and C then markets yet another embodiment of the same invention. If B's invention is not patentable and C is therefore free to copy from B, the value of A's patent plummets further.[45] Of course, B will not independently invent and C, therefore, will not copy from B, if A follows the licensing strategy suggested by Maurer and Scotchmer. But if for some reason that strategy turns out to be impracticable, A risks having his patent become worthless. (C also would have an incentive to cheat by claiming to have copied from B and not A, even if he actually copied from A.) Alternatively, if B's independently discovered invention *were* patentable, this would create problems of its own. For one thing, this policy would prolong the eventual date on which the invention falls into the public domain, unless in cases such as this the law provided that all patent terms for the same invention must end on the same date. For another, it would complicate matters for potential users or licensees of the invention. Would potential licensees have to license from both A and B? If so, would this deter the optimal use of the invention? Or would it cut into the incentive to invent, by lowering both A's and B's expected reward? Who knows?[46]

Sixth, as Maurer and Scotchmer themselves recognize, there is considerable debate over whether patent races are, on balance, a bad thing.[47] Although patent races may give rise to wastefully duplicative research and development expenses, they also may accelerate the production of the invention

[43] We return to these points below in our discussion of standing. See *infra* Chapter 7. See also Lemley (1997; 1052–66), who argues that transaction costs may inhibit some otherwise beneficial licensing transactions from going forward.

[44] See Caves et al. (1983; 258).

[45] B's independently discovered invention would *not* be patentable, absent further modifications of the law. See 35 U.S.C. § 102(a).

[46] For a suggested way of dealing with the above problem, see Leibovitz (2002; 2280–1).

[47] See Maurer & Scotchmer (2002; 545).

or give rise to new insights along the way.[48] To the extent that patent races may confer benefits upon society, an independent discovery rule designed to reduce the incidence of these races may be counterproductive. Finally, recognition of an independent discovery defense in patent law, whatever its merits may be, would probably be unlawful under article 28 of the TRIPs Agreement.[49] While this is not an argument against the proposal on the merits, it does highlight the practical difficulty of implementing it.

NEGLIGENCE VERSUS STRICT LIABILITY

A second alternative to an intent-based standard would be a negligence standard, under which an infringer would be liable only if she did not conduct an efficient amount of searching. This might be less harmful to the IPR owner than would be an independent discovery rule, because some independent discovery would remain illegal. However, a negligence standard would also impose high administrative costs, because the standard of care would vary from one case to another. For this reason, we conclude that strict liability is superior to negligence in this context. For convenience, our focus will be on patents, although the analysis can be applied as well to copyrights and is similar to the analysis presented in Chapter 4 with respect to trademarks.

1. Strict Liability

A rule of strict liability for patent infringement means that no accommodation can be made for inadvertent or accidental infringement. Irrespective

---

[48] Scotchmer herself has written on the division of opinion regarding the desirability of patent races. See Scotchmer (1998; 275); see also *supra* Chapter 2, Footnote 26.

[49] Under article 28 of the TRIPs Agreement, member nations are obligated to confer upon patent owners the exclusive right to prevent others from making, using, offering for sale, selling, or importing the patented invention (Agreement on Trade-Related Aspects of Intellectual Property Rights, April 15, 1994, Marrakesh Agreement Establishing the World Trade Organization, Annex 1C, Article 28, Legal Instruments – Results of the Uruguay Round vol. 31, 33 I.L.M. 1197 (1994) [hereinafter TRIPs]). Nations may provide limited exceptions to these rights, "provided that such exceptions do not unreasonably conflict with a normal exploitation of the patent and do not unreasonably prejudice the legitimate interests of the patent owner, taking account of the legitimate interests of third parties." *Id.* Article 30. Although we are aware of no authority addressing the issue of whether an independent discovery defense would conflict with TRIPs, we also are not aware of any country that currently recognizes this defense. This fact by itself suggests that such an exception would "unreasonably conflict with the normal exploitation of the patent." See also Correa & Yusuf (1998; 207–8); Correa (2000; 240–1) (listing common exceptions contemplated by article 30); Nolff (2001; 19–21).

of the fact that the infringer took measures to avoid patent infringement, if she infringed a valid patent, the infringer will be liable for the full economic injuries that the infringement caused. In principle, the patentee will be fully compensated for any injury due to the infringement.

Presumably, if unintentional infringement occurs, the infringer is unaware that her "new" invention infringes a valid patent. A careful analysis of all existing patents would reduce, although not necessarily eliminate, the probability of inadvertent infringement.[50] But these search efforts are costly and, therefore, a complete search, i.e., perfect information, is not optimal. In this regard, the inventor's decision to search can be modeled in exactly the same way as the would-be trademark owner's decision to search, as presented earlier in Chapter 4.[51] We reproduce Figure 4.1 from that chapter as Figure 5.1. As before, the potential infringer will expand her search efforts to the point where the marginal cost equals the marginal benefit of further search (i.e., the marginal decrease in the expected damage award). In other words, she will minimize her expected total cost by engaging in S* units of search.

Since the total costs to the potential infringer are all of the costs borne by anyone, these are also the social costs associated with possible infringement. Thus, a rule of strict liability leads to the *socially* optimal amount of search (S*), i.e., the social cost minimizing quantity of search. Strict liability for patent infringement is allocatively efficient in the sense that the socially efficient quantity of resources is allocated to searching patent records and analyzing them for possible infringement. As a distributive matter, all of the risk associated with possible patent infringement falls on the potential infringer. No matter how extensive her search efforts, if infringement occurs, the infringer bears all of the costs. The patentee bears none of the risk of loss due to infringement.

At the cost minimizing search level (S*), the total cost is E[TC*], which is composed of the search costs (cS*) plus the expected infringement damages, P(S*)D. Since P(S*)D is positive, this means that the optimal amount of search does not reduce the probability of infringement to zero. There is, in other words, a socially (and privately) optimal amount of infringement, which is not zero. This makes sense because reducing the probability of infringing such that P(S)D is lower than P(S*)D is neither socially nor privately cost justified – it would cost more than it is worth. This, however, raises a question about what one means by *inadvertent* or *unintentional*

---

[50] See Shapiro (2001; 9) (describing patents as "*partial* or *probabilistic* property right[s]").
[51] What follows is an adaptation of the model of precaution presented in Cooter & Ulen (1988; 347–60).

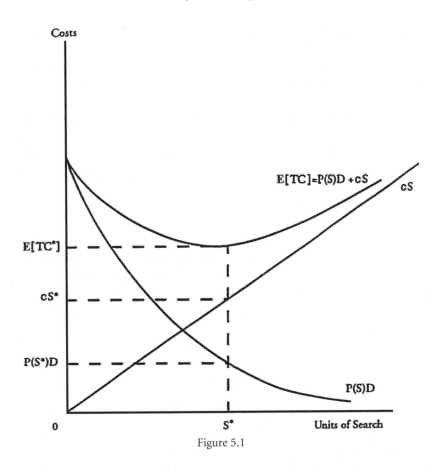

Figure 5.1

infringement. The potential infringer proceeds knowing full well that some stones were left unturned and that the probability her invention will infringe is not zero. While she does not proceed knowing for certain that infringement will occur, she surely knows that it is a possibility.

2. Simple Negligence

Under a simple negligence rule, a firm engaged in R&D could protect itself from a patent infringement suit by meeting some standard of care regarding search. That is, a potential infringer has a burden of taking care not to infringe. If we define this duty in terms of search, say, $S = S'$, then a potential infringer will not be liable for inadvertently infringing a valid patent if her actual search efforts are equal to or greater than S'. In that event, no matter how great the economic loss to the patentee, the infringer will not be liable for damages. In contrast, if the infringer has not met her burden, i.e., if S is less than S', then the inadvertent infringer will be fully liable for the actual damages suffered. In this case, a miss is as good as a mile. If S just falls short of S', the innovator will be liable if her product or process infringes a valid patent.

If precedent establishes a socially optimal duty of care (S' = S*), then we will have the same allocatively efficient result as under strict liability. The privately optimal amount of search will be S*, which we know to be socially efficient. The major difference is that the risk of injury is shifted to the patentee. No matter how extensive the economic harm associated with infringement, if S equals or exceeds S*, the burden of the loss falls on the patentee rather than on the infringer.

The optimality of simple negligence requires the equality of the judicially determined standard of precaution, S', and S*. Suppose, for example, that S' exceeds S* as shown in Figure 5.2. In that event, the potential infringer's cost coincides with E[TC] until S = S', at which point the infringer's cost drops to wS. The potential infringer will invest in search up to S', which is socially excessive albeit privately optimal. Although the additional search (S' − S*) is *privately* cost justified, it is not *socially* cost justified and, therefore, is excessive. There are, of course, limits on how far past S* the duty to search can be set. The critical value is at S'' where cS'' = E[TC(S*)]:

$$cS'' = cS^* + P(S^*)D.$$

When the duty of care is above S'', the private search cost will exceed the combination of search cost and expected damage payment at a search level of S*. Thus, if the standard of care exceeds S'', the potential infringer will behave as though there were a rule of strict liability. In that event, the potential infringer will invest in search at the socially optimal level: S = S*.

The practical problem is that under a negligence standard, courts must determine the optimal amount of search, which will vary from case to case. The socially optimal value of S depends upon the values of c and D. The more expensive the search (i.e., the higher the c), the lower the socially optimal value of S. Although some products or processes may have fairly low search costs, the costs for others may be quite substantial. For example, in the semiconductor industry, there are literally thousands of patents, which are often quite complex and, therefore, quite expensive to analyze; industry participants have responded by entering into broad cross-licensing agreements that protect them from patent infringement suits.[52]

---

[52] See Hall & Ziedonis (2001; 102, 109).

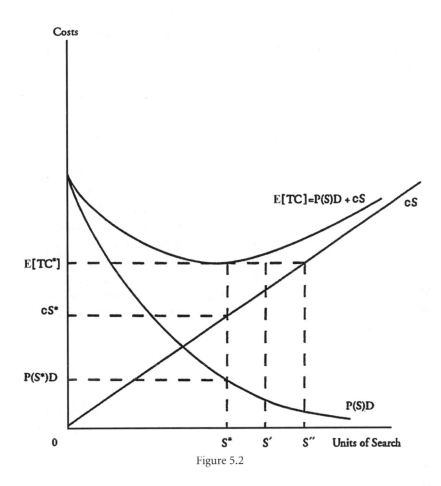

Figure 5.2

The damage due to infringement will vary from case to case as well. Obviously, the greater the value of D, the larger the socially optimal value of S will be. The more serious the possible injury, the greater the effort to avoid it will be.

In summary, a simple negligence approach to assigning fault is complicated because the cost of search will vary from case to case, as will the harm inflicted by patent infringement. This means that the socially optimal extent of search will vary from case to case. As a result, the jury would have to decide whether a specific case of inadvertent infringement should be excused because the defendant acted reasonably. This, of course, is difficult to do *ex post* because the defendant acted *ex ante*. If juries tend to impose too severe a standard of precaution ($S \geq S^*$), then some resources will be wasted on excessive search.[53] If the standard tends to be too low ($S < S^*$), then search will be inadequate and *permissible* patent infringement will be socially excessive.

3. Contributory Negligence

Strict liability and simple negligence impose no burden whatsoever on the patentee. If the patent is valid, the patentee's behavior does not affect liability (except in the rare case in which the patentee has engaged in conduct rising to the level of an antitrust violation or patent misuse).[54] In some circumstances, however, a burden can be put on the patentee. For example, if a patentee has a duty to provide notice and fails to do so, he will have contributed to the infringement problem and will not be able to recover losses due to infringement should that occur.

The notice requirement is a duty to inform potential infringers. Suppose the notice requirement, i.e., the adequacy of the notice, is N^*. Also, suppose that the standard for adequate search is S^*. Then the liability rules can be explained as follows:

1. If $S \geq S^*$, then the potential infringer is not negligent and cannot be liable for any harm no matter what the patentee does. Even if $N \geq N^*$, the infringer will not be liable.
2. If the patentee fails to meet his burden, i.e., if $N < N^*$, then the patentee cannot recover for infringement. Even if $S < S^*$, i.e., the potential infringer has not met his burden, the patentee cannot recover.

Imposing a notice requirement on the patentee can be seen as a means of reducing the search costs for a potential infringer. To the extent that it is relatively cheaper for the patentee to provide notice than it is for a potential

---

[53] For empirical evidence consistent with the common belief that juries are more pro-patent owner than are judges, see Moore (2001; 386–9). Another potential weakness of the negligence approach is that, as under the independent invention regime, the social cost of determining what the defendant knew and when she knew it will arise in at least some cases. To illustrate, suppose that the defendant (1) made, used, or sold the patented invention without permission, but (2) claims not to be liable because she only made, used, or sold after having conducted an adequate search that failed to turn up the patent. Once again, the court would have to determine whether the defendant independently invented or copied the invention.

[54] If the parties behave in a privately optimal fashion, there is no allocative significance, as either rule results in the socially optimal extent of search. The difference is that the risk of loss in instances in which infringement occurs anyway falls not on the infringer as with strict liability, but on the patentee.

infringer to search patent records, it is socially beneficial to impose notice requirements, as resources will be saved. If, however, it is relatively costly for the patentee to provide adequate notice, this may lead to a waste of resources. We should note, however, that a contributory negligence standard also poses administrative difficulties. For example, it would not seem to be easy to select the appropriate value of N, i.e., the value that will minimize social costs. This value is not unique as the cost of providing notice will vary from case to case, depending on the size of the article, its method of distribution, and other factors.[55] In addition, the contributory negligence approach also requires a determination of the search standard, which is complicated.

We can employ familiar principles to explore the optimal decision to provide notice. For simplicity, we shall assume that if a patentee sues for lost profits suffered as a result of patent infringement, he will win and will be awarded the full lost profits. This, of course, is somewhat unrealistic because the probability of prevailing in court is not one. Moreover, there is some chance that the jury will undercompensate him or that the defendant will

---

[55] In fact, the existing statutory scheme does require courts on occasion to consider whether the patentee has provided sufficient constructive notice under § 287. First, the notice itself must be legible. See, e.g., *Trussell Mfg. Co. v. Wilson-Jones Co.*, 50 F.2d 1027, 1030 (2d Cir. 1931), which held that marking must be legible without resort to a magnifying glass. Second, it must be sufficient to "notify the public concerning the patent status of items in commerce," *Amsted*, 24 F.3d at 185. For a sampling of cases discussing whether the patentee's marking was sufficient, see, e.g., *Douglas Press, Inc. v. Arrow Int'l, Inc.*, No. 95 C 3863, 1997 WL 441329, at *5–7 (N.D. Ill. July 30, 1997); *Shields-Jetco Inc. v. Torti*, 314 F. Supp. 1292, 1303–04 (D.R.I. 1970), *aff'd on other grounds*, 436 F.2d 1061 (1st Cir. 1971); Seberoff (1994; 799). Third, as noted earlier, the patentee must make reasonable efforts to ensure that its licensees comply with the marking requirement.

The interplay of these requirements can be complex. Consider, for example, the case of a patent on a component that is used in the interior of a common product, such as a television set. In light of the above authorities, does the patent owner have a duty to ensure that its licensee (the manufacturer of the completed television set) mark the outside of the set, so as to notify every potentially liable party in the chain of distribution (including not only the manufacturer of the television, but also distributors, retailers, and consumers)? Or is it sufficient for the patentee to mark the components themselves on the theory that potential copiers of the component will take the set apart to view the component? See also Meyer (2001; C5), who notes the difficulty that marking presents with respect to component manufacturers.

Finally, when marking the product itself is not feasible (for example, because of the product's size) the patentee may mark the product packaging instead. See 35 U.S.C. § 287(a). Courts, therefore, sometimes must determine whether marking the product is feasible and, if not, whether the marking on the package is sufficient. See, e.g., *Sessions v. Romadka*, 145 U.S. 29, 49–50 (1892); *Rutherford v. Trim-Tex Corp.*, 803 F. Supp. 158, 162–4 (N.D. Ill. 1992). For further discussion, see 7 Chisum (2001; § 20.03[7][c][iii], at 20–626 to 30); 1 Horwitz & Horwitz (2001; §§ 1.02[4][vi], [ix]); Meyer (2001; C5); Oppedahl (1995; at 213–15).

be unable to pay the damages award. Even under our assumptions, however, there will be the costs associated with the litigation.

We shall denote the litigation costs as L. These costs will only occur if infringement occurs and this, of course, is not certain. Let p represent the probability that a latecomer will independently discover and market the same invention. Because we are dealing with inadvertent infringement, we assume that the latecomer will not go to market, and thereby infringe a valid patent, if she knows that a valid patent already exists. The patentee can reduce the probability of inadvertent infringement by investing in notice (N) at a cost of C(N). From the patentee's perspective, the question is what value of N will minimize the costs of litigation and notice:

$$E[TC] = p(N)L + C(N).$$

The optimal value of N solves the first-order condition

$$dE[TC]/dN = Ldp(N)/dN + dC(N)/dN = 0.$$

The optimal value of N occurs where the marginal cost of additional notice $dC(N)/dN$ equals the marginal benefit of reducing the expected litigation costs, $Ldp(N)/dN$. This does not mean that N is necessarily positive. It can be optimal for the patentee to invest no resources in notice, i.e., it is possible for $N^* = 0$.[56]

STRICT LIABILITY WITH NOTICE OR KNOWLEDGE AS A PRECONDITION TO DAMAGES RECOVERY

Yet another variation would be to apply a strict liability standard, but to condition the IPR owner's ability to obtain a remedy upon the infringer's actual knowledge or receipt of notice that her conduct infringes the plaintiff's rights. This framework is similar to the contributory negligence standard discussed previously, except that the defendant would be liable for infringement regardless of how much (or how little) a search she engaged in, if she made, used, or sold an infringing product with knowledge or after receipt of notice. In the following sections, we provide some reasons why this type of system – a form of which is embodied in the Patent and Lanham Acts – may be superior to a "true" strict liability system. We also suggest, however, that

---

[56] This will occur if $p(N)L$ evaluated at $N = 0$ lies below $p(N)L + C(N)$ for all values of $N > 0$. What drives this outcome are large fixed costs of providing notice. That is, the cost of notice function is of the form $C(N) = a + \omega(N)$, where a is a fixed cost that can be avoided if no notice is given (i.e., if $N > 0$). If a is sufficiently large, it is possible for $p(N)L$ at $N = 0$ to be below $p(N)L + C(N)$ for all values of $N > 0$.

the optimal form of such a rule is elusive, thus leaving open the question whether applicable law should be amended in any significant way. As before, our analysis will focus on patents, although much of what we have to say might be applicable to copyrights and trademarks as well.

The Relevant Considerations

We begin our analysis of a "pure" versus modified strict liability regime by assuming that A is the leader in a patent race between A and B. A therefore must decide (1) at time t_1 whether to invest in creating a new invention which, if invented, will be patented and marketed at time t_2 and (2) at time t_2 whether to attempt to put B on notice of A's patent. Whether or not A is obligated to provide notice to potential infringers, A will choose to do so if the expected benefit – deterring infringement, which otherwise may cause A to incur uncompensated losses – outweighs the expected cost. Thus, A will invest in providing notice up to the point at which $dC(N)/dN = -Ldp(N)/dN$. We assume further that, if B receives actual notice of the patent at time t_2, B will decide not to invest in creating the same invention, and that her expected return will be zero. Unless B can be sure of receiving actual notice of every relevant patent, however, B must decide at time t_2, if she has not yet received any actual notice, whether to conduct her own independent search of the prior art before investing in the new invention. As discussed above, we would expect B to search up to the point at which $c = -(dP/dS)D$.

On these assumptions, the total social cost of infringement would include $p(N)L + C(N) + c(S)$. Ideally, a social planner would construct a rule that would minimize this cost, but this is easier said than done for several reasons. The first is that the values of $c(S)$ and $C(N)$ are likely to be related: the more that A invests in notice, the less that B will need to invest in search, and vice versa. Unless we know *how* these variables are related, however, any effort to reduce social cost will be at most an educated guess. A second problem is that these variables are likely to differ from one case to another, thus further complicating the task of crafting an optimal rule to cover all situations. Third, it is conceivable that in some cases the choice of the "wrong" rule could deter invention on the part of either A or B. A might be deterred if the cost of requiring A to notify potential infringers is so high as to make it pointless for A to seek any damages for conduct occurring prior to the commencement of litigation, that is, if the possibility of recovering such prenotice damages, in addition to (1) injunctive relief and (2) postnotice damages, is a necessary component of the patent incentive system. For analogous reasons, B might be deterred even though, if she had more complete information, she would know that in some cases there was no serious risk of infringement.

The following example shows how the choice of a pure strict liability rule might deter B from investing in invention in some cases. Under such a rule, B's expected return if he does not search is

$$E[R] = \pi_B - r(D + s + L_B),$$

where π_B is B's expected profit from marketing her invention; r is B's subjective probability that her invention will infringe a valid patent and that she will be sued successfully; D represents the expected damages award that B will incur if she infringes; s represents certain sunk costs; and L_B is B's litigation costs if she is sued. If B searches, her expected return is equal to the probability that her invention does not infringe a valid patent $(1 - r)$, times the profit that she could earn by marketing her invention minus the cost of the search. This can be written as

$$E[R] = (1 - r)\pi_B - c_B,$$

where c_B is B's cost of conducting a search (for example, by reviewing existing patents). B will search only if the expected return from doing so exceeds the expected return without a search:

$$(1 - r)\pi_B - c_B > \pi_B - r(D + s + L_B).$$

If A and B are equally efficient manufacturers of the product that embodies the patent, π_B will equal D, because π_B will equal A's lost profit. In that event, a search will occur provided that $c_B < r(s + L_B)$. If A is more efficient than B, the damages award (D) should exceed B's profit (π_B). In that event, a search will be optimal if $r(\pi_B - D) + c_B < r(s + L_B)$. Because $(\pi_B - D)$ is negative, $r(\pi_B - D) + c_B < c_B$ and a search is more likely than when B expects her potential competitor A to be only equally efficient.

Depending on the values of some of these variables, B may decide not to undertake investment in the new invention even though, if she had complete information, she could do so safely. For example, suppose that B expects a hypothetical competitor's profit on the sale of products embodying the contemplated invention to be high in comparison with B's own expected profit; that the probability of independent discovery is low; and that the probability of infringement, the cost of searching, and expected litigation costs are moderately high. For example, assume that π_B is $2,000; D is $10,000; r is .50; c_B is $1,000; L_B is $1,000; and, for simplicity, that B would incur no sunk costs prior to the entry of an injunction. Absent notice from A, B's expected payoff if she does not search is $(2,000) - (10,000 + 1,000)(.50) =$

−$3,500, whereas her expected payoff if she searches is $(2,000)(1 - .50) - 1,000 = \$0$. B therefore prefers not to invest in the invention at all, even though half the time she would create a marketable, noninfringing product.

What, then, can we say about the relative merits of a pure strict liability system versus a system that conditions the recovery of damages upon the provision of notice? Our intuition is that, in patent law at least, a rule requiring the patentee to provide *some* sort of notice is preferable to one that does not. First, we suspect that in many cases the cost of searching will be substantial, given both the length of the patent term and the number and complexity of patents that may be relevant to a given undertaking. Even if B has an incentive to conduct some search anyway – for example, to reduce the risk of a lawsuit that might lead only to injunctive relief – creating an incentive for more extensive searching may be socially wasteful, if A can reduce the likelihood of inadvertent infringement at lower cost. The second, and related, point is that A may be capable of doing precisely that, at least if some form of constructive notice is deemed sufficient.[57] Third, as long as the notice requirement is not too severe, it seems unlikely that some restriction upon A's ability to recover damages for prenotice conduct will have a substantial impact upon A's incentive to invent. The empirical evidence to date suggests that the patent incentive may be relatively important only in a minority of industries; even in these, the ability to recover *all* damages proximately caused by the infringement, including those that accrue prior to notice, may not be material. On the other hand, given the existing state of our knowledge and the possibility that the ability to recover damages for conduct occurring prior to the commencement of litigation *may* provide a significant incentive for inventive activity in some cases, we do not recommend doing away with such damages altogether. We do suspect, however, that the system may be able to accommodate the competing interests we have identified by requiring some form of notice as a condition for recovering prelitigation damages.[58] Although the precise form that a modified

---

[57] Of course, the question arises whether some form of constructive notice *ought* to be sufficient; maybe actual notice should be required in all cases. Balanced against this possibility, however, are the concerns that (1) at least in some cases the ability to recover full damages may be material to the patent owner's incentives and (2) the cost of detecting and pursuing infringers can further eat into that incentive. The problem is that both patentee and infringer face information costs if the law requires each to discover the other's existence. Although we can make an educated guess concerning the best way to resolve this problem while maintaining the proper incentives, ultimately the problem may not admit of any firm conclusions.

[58] One might speculate that a notice requirement would serve other purposes as well. Placing the burden on the patentee in effect allows patentees to signal whether they are interested

strict liability rule should take may elude precise analysis, we can point out some of the advantages and disadvantages of various types of notice rules under a modified strict liability standard.

Section 287 and Other Alternatives

If we wish to create a system in which patent owners are encouraged to invest, to some degree, in providing notice, there are still a variety of ways to implement such a system. At one extreme, one could argue that since patents are, by definition, public records, potential infringers are always on constructive notice and, therefore, the patent owner should always be entitled to recover damages attributable to infringing conduct. This was the perspective embodied in the earliest patent acts in the United States. It is not a trivial position; requiring the public disclosure of patented inventions surely reduces the cost of searching for those inventions. However, that cost may still be substantial given the sheer volume and complexity of existing patents. The question therefore arises whether conditioning an award of damages upon compliance with a more rigorous notice standard makes sense given that (1) the more costly the standard is to comply with, the greater the potential is for decreasing the patent owner's incentive to invent and (2) the less costly the notice is in comparison to the search, the greater is the potential for reducing social costs and the potential chilling effect upon the inventive efforts of latecomers.

Section 287 of the U.S. Patent Act attempts to resolve these issues by conditioning the patent owner's recovery of damages upon his providing actual or (by marking) constructive notice to the infringer, but the way in which the statute applies in several common situations is problematic. Despite the statute's intended purpose of "helping to avoid innocent infringement," it may sometimes leave "innocent" infringers vulnerable to substantial damages liability. At the same time, § 287 allows knowledgable (even willful) infringers to remain immune from damages liability, unless and until the

---

in maximizing their potential damages recovery. Those who choose not to put potential infringers on notice may, in some cases, induce some degree of preinjunction infringement; but if the losses attributable to this interim infringement have no effect on the patentee's *ex ante* incentives, this interim infringement benefits the public by reducing price and increasing output. In addition, the case for allowing nonmanufacturing patent owners to recover lost profits on sales of goods that compete with infringing products is, as we discuss in Chapter 8, a close one. To the extent there are good reasons to permit this recovery, however, those reasons are significantly weaker if the infringer is not aware that his product infringes (and the potential anticompetitive effect of this rule is more serious).

patentee provides them with actual notice of information already in their possession.

As for innocent infringers, as noted above, the statute does not apply unless the patentee or his licensee manufactures products covered by the patent. As a result, an infringer of a process patent – or of any patent that the owner holds idle – can be liable for all damages proximately caused by the infringement, even if she had no notice prior to the filing of the complaint that the invention was patented. Moreover, even as to nonidle, nonprocess patents, the mere fact that the patentee has marked its articles in conformity with § 287 is no guarantee that an innocent infringer will actually encounter the mark. This leaves open the possibility that an "innocent" defendant who independently discovers an invention already subject to patent protection can be liable for substantial damages, even if she ceases infringing immediately upon receipt of actual notice. Taken to its logical conclusion, this principle would suggest that a patent owner could comply with § 287 by making, marking, and marketing just a few "token" articles. In such a case, his lost profits probably would be minimal, but the infringer could be liable for a reasonable royalty, and in some cases, lost profits on the sales of other products marketed by the patentee (see Chapter 8). For that matter, a literal reading of the statute would allow a patent owner who uses the patented product solely in his own business, and does not sell it to third parties, to recover damages from the beginning of the infringement, as long as he properly marks – even though the product never makes its way to the marketplace and the infringer has no way of encountering it. In such a case, compliance with the marking requirement is an empty formality in light of the statutory policy, but could have serious consequences in terms of the appropriate remedy.

A second difficulty is that the statute partially immunizes from damages liability some persons who *knowingly* infringe patents, but who have not received actual or constructive notice prior to the filing of the complaint. This rule seems troubling for two reasons. First, requiring the patentee to provide actual notice to knowing infringers imposes an unnecessary cost, although we should not overemphasize this point. Providing actual notice to infringers of whom the patentee is aware is not costly, and (at least in some cases) neither is the provision of constructive notice by compliance with the marking statute. A second problem is that the rule provides knowing infringers with a perverse incentive to continue infringing up until the receipt of actual notice, but this point too should not be overstated. The cost of complying with an injunction forbidding future use of an invention can be high, particularly if the defendant has incurred significant sunk costs in connection with the use of the infringing product or process. Furthermore, any deliberate infringement that occurs after receipt of actual or constructive notice would risk incurring up to treble damages for the patentee's resulting injuries. Persons with knowledge of the patent therefore already have some incentive not to infringe, even in the absence of actual or constructive notice.

Moreover, one can imagine that holding knowing infringers liable for damages accruing prior to their receipt of actual or constructive notice could itself have undesirable consequences. First and foremost is the possibility that an "actual knowledge" standard might require courts and litigants to bear substantial administrative costs in determining whether the defendant in a particular case had the requisite state of mind.[59] Further, an actual knowledge rule might give some potential infringers an incentive to avoid searches that could lead to the acquisition of actual knowledge – unless the rule were further modified to penalize infringers who "know or should have known" of the patent's existence, which then would give rise to further administrative costs. But perhaps this incentive too is minimal, in light of the availability of injunctive relief. In addition, if an actual knowledge standard were coupled with the existing constructive notice rule, the task of determining whether the defendant had actual knowledge would arise only in cases in which the patent owner failed to mark (or in cases involving process and idle patents, if the rules relating to these patents were also amended), which may be a minority of cases. Under such a system, however, the incentive to mark would also be reduced, thus making the ultimate consequences even more difficult to predict.

Even if a rule exempting knowing infringers from damages liability until the receipt of actual or constructive notice is generally sound, the application of this rule in certain recurring situations is nonsensical. To illustrate, suppose that the patent owner proves that the infringer began infringing on January 1, 1998; that he provided actual or constructive notice to the infringer on January 1, 1999; and that the infringement was willful from the very beginning, i.e., from January 1, 1998. On these facts, the patent owner is entitled to damages for the period beginning January 1, 1999, and a court may increase these damages on account of the infringer's willfulness, but the patent owner is not entitled to damages for the year 1998, despite the fact that the evidence demonstrates the defendant's willfulness during that

---

[59] To the extent that the plaintiff seeks enhanced damages for willful infringement, however, some inquiry into the defendant's state of mind is likely to take place anyway; the incentive not to acquire actual knowledge may be a by-product of the willfulness rule as well. For discussion, see Cotter (2004).

period. (These are, in essence, the facts and outcome of *Amsted Industries v. Buckeye Steel Castings Co.*, a 1994 Federal Circuit decision.) Applying the actual and constructive notice rules in a case like this does not reduce administrative costs – proof of what the infringer knew and when she knew it is essential to a claim of willful infringement – and permits the knowing infringer to escape some damages liability, even though the purpose of the notice requirement is to protect innocent infringers. Or consider a case in which the patent owner sues the defendant for contributory infringement or actively inducing another person to infringe. In either case, in order to prove his substantive claim, the patent owner must prove that the defendant knew or should have known that his activity would cause another to infringe the patent,[60] but the patent owner may not recover damages for any period preceding the defendant's receipt of actual or constructive notice. Once again, this result is difficult to square with the purpose of § 287. If one reason for requiring actual or constructive notice is to avoid the expense of proving the defendant's state of mind, shouldn't this requirement be waived in cases in which the plaintiff must prove that state of mind in order to prevail on its substantive claim? In these cases, the evidence that the defendant had knowledge may be clear and yet a literal reading of the statute can result in avoiding damages liability.[61]

At the end of the day, just as we are reluctant in the absence of strong empirical evidence on the incentive effects on patents to advocate adopting of a full-blown strict liability system, we are hesitant to propose adopting *tout court* of an "actual knowledge" standard. We can nevertheless suggest

[60] Contributory infringement occurs when a person sells a material component of a patented invention, "knowing the same to be especially made or especially adapted for use in an infringement of such patent, and not a staple article or commodity of commerce suitable for substantial noninfringing use" (35 U.S.C. § 271(c)); see also *Hewlett-Packard Co. v. Bausch & Lomb Inc.*, 909 F.2d 1464, 1469 & n.4 (Fed. Cir. 1990), which states that § 271(c) makes "clear that ... proof of a defendant's *knowledge* ... that his activity cause infringement was necessary to establish contributory infringement" and that the plaintiff must prove that the defendant has "knowledge of the patent which proscribed that use." Active inducement, which in some cases may overlap with contributory infringement, occurs when a person intentionally causes another to infringe. See 35 U.S.C. § 271(b); *Hewlett-Packard*, 909 F.2d at 1469 that required "proof of actual intent to cause the acts which constitute the infringement." As in the former case, the plaintiff must prove that the defendant acted with knowledge. See *Manville Sales Corp. v. Paramount Sys.*, 917 F.2d 544, 553 (Fed. Cir. 1990), which states that "the alleged infringer must be shown to have *knowingly* induced infringement"; 4 Chisum (2001; § 17.04[2], at 17–70).

[61] Another possible consequence of the applicability of § 287 to products but not processes is that the statute may affect the way in which patent attorneys draft and prosecute patent applications and litigate patent cases. For discussions, see Markarian (1997); Moore & Nakamura (1994); Oppedahl (1995); Remus et al. (1995); Voelzke (1995).

some reforms that would make the current system more coherent. The first relates to some specific situations in which an actual knowledge standard would make sense. The second relates to process and idle patents, and the third to constructive notice.

A first set of reforms would entail adopting an actual knowledge standard in a few discrete situations in which the policies that otherwise may favor an actual or constructive notice standard do not apply. In light of our earlier discussion, we think it is relatively easy to justify a rule permitting the patent owner to recover damages from a knowing infringer in cases in which the infringer's state of mind is necessarily at issue in light of the nature of the claims (e.g., willful or contributory infringement).[62] In addition, one could probably specify certain other cases in which it might make sense to apply an actual knowledge standard, such as when the infringer is a former licensee under the patent at issue (and therefore *must* have had actual knowledge). More controversially, one might consider adopting an actual knowledge standard in still other cases in which the possibility of liability for "innocent" infringement seems particularly troubling. Perhaps one could argue that such a standard would make sense in cases in which patent owners seek damages against nonmanufacturing infringers, that is, against sellers and users who may lack knowledge that the manufacturer of the product they sell or use has infringed another's patent.[63]

A second set of reforms would center around patented processes and idle patents. Under the current system, there is some risk that strict liability will deter potential defendants from undertaking inventive activity (for example, in industries in which process patents predominate, such as biotechnology) or otherwise lead to socially wasteful searches. One possible response would be to condition damages liability in these cases upon the receipt of actual notice. Balanced against this recommendation, however, is the possibility (however slight) that the resultant reduction in the patent owner's expected return could have an impact upon his incentive to invent. In addition, if there is no tangible product to mark, constructive notice may not be an option

---

[62] Cases in which the defendant has deliberately infringed might also be promising candidates for restitutionary awards, if Congress were ever to revisit the issue of restitution in patent law. As we discussed in Chapters 3 and 4, restitutionary awards may be an effective means for deterring would-be users from deliberately bypassing the licensing market.

[63] As we argue in Chapter 6, the need to extend liability from infringing manufacturers to mere sellers and users in order to preserve the patentee's incentives is somewhat attenuated, even if sellers and users would have a right of indemnification from the manufacturer. If so, the adoption of an actual knowledge standard with regard to sellers and users may help to reduce the likelihood that the latter will be victimized by a fly-by-night manufacturer.

and the cost of providing actual preinfringement notice to all potential infringers is likely to be high. Perhaps no reform is necessary with respect to these cases, if they represent only a small fraction of all patent disputes or if, in the case of process patents, it is relatively uncommon for someone to infringe a process patent and *not* a related product patent as well. In this regard, further empirical research on the incidence and magnitude of damages awards in cases involving process-patent and idle-patent infringement might be a helpful addition to the literature.

A third set of reforms would target some of the inconsistencies in the current marking regime. One obvious change would be to amend § 287 to clarify that marking applies only when the patent owner *sells* a product embodying the patent and not when he only makes and uses the product for his own internal business. Even if one takes the view that an actual knowledge standard would be preferable to strict liability, there is no reason in this particular setting to condition the patent owner's damages on his having complied with a pointless formality.[64] In addition, two other more sweeping reforms may be worth considering, although these are likely to be more costly and, hence, controversial: the adoption of uniform federal regulations on marking and the adoption of a federal registry for commercialized inventions in lieu of a marking requirement.

In theory, the adoption of uniform regulations, dictating in advance where to mark a product, how large the marking must be, and so on, would not be difficult to achieve. The main problem would be the familiar ones: that regulators may not foresee all possible situations and may therefore opt for a standard that is suboptimal or that the regulatory process may become subject to industry capture. This possibility, however, must be evaluated in light of the uncertainty that currently exists regarding compliance with the statute in many other cases. U.S. regulations on the placement of copyright notice would be the obvious model to draw upon, and may not be difficult to modify for use in the present setting.[65]

---

[64] Alternatively, the rule could be that in a case of this nature the defendant is not liable for damages for conduct occurring prior to the receipt of actual notice or actual knowledge. The point is that requiring the patent owner to mark as a precondition to recovering damages is, in this instance, absurd.

[65] Although the Copyright Act does not require the inclusion of copyright notice on works published on or after March 1, 1989, it offers some benefits to authors who include the notice on published copies of their works. See 17 U.S.C. § 401(d), which states that the inclusion of copyright notice on published copies to which the defendant had access defeats a defense of innocent infringement in mitigation of actual or statutory damages; see *id.* § 402(d) for the same rule, with respect to copyrighted sound recordings embodied in phonorecords. Moreover, the inclusion of notice on copies published prior to that date can

At the very least, it would be helpful to know (for example) whether, in our television component hypothetical, the patent notice must be placed on the final product or only on the interior component in order to be effective.

A more radical proposal, designed to avoid the problem of technical compliance with the marking statute that nevertheless fails to convey actual notice to potential infringers, would be to create a registry for commercialized patented inventions; and to provide that registration, rather than marking, constitutes constructive notice for purposes of assessing damages against infringing manufacturers. Suppose, for example, that the patent owner who wishes to register his invention must provide evidence of his actual use of the invention in products or processes. Theoretically, this type of system might provide a more effective notice than marking in cases in which the patent owner markets only a small number of products that might otherwise evade a potential infringer's attention. Moreover, since only a portion of all patents ever result in commercial products, the burden upon manufacturers of checking the registry may well be manageable. (Registration also would allow someone to use patents that are not listed on the registry without having to worry about incurring damages liability unless and until the receipt of an actual notice. Perhaps this sort of "efficient" infringement should be encouraged.) Balanced against these benefits, however, would be the cost of maintaining the registry. These would include not only the costs of setting up and maintaining the system, but also of monitoring its operation to preclude patentees from registering merely token uses.[66] On balance, it seems doubtful that the problem merits such a costly solution.

---

still affect a work's copyright status. See *id.* § 405(a); *Estate of King v. CBS, Inc.*, 194 F.3d 1211, 1214–16 (11th Cir. 1999). Federal regulations set forth some detailed rules for the placement of copyright notice. See 37 C.F.R. § 201.20 that sets forth various examples of adequate notice; *id.* § 202.2 that lists "common defects" in copyright notice, including "a notice is permanently covered so that it cannot be seen without tearing the work apart"; "a notice is illegible or so small that it cannot be read without the aid of a magnifying glass"; "a notice is on a detachable tag and will eventually be detached and discarded when the work is put in use"; and "a notice is on the wrapper or container which is not a part of the work and which will eventually be removed and discarded when the work is put in use."

[66] As noted earlier, under the current system marketing and marking a few token items would appear to suffice under § 287. We view this as a drawback of the current system. If, however, the registry is open only to patent owners who are willing to verify a certain amount of commercialization, akin to (but perhaps more substantial than?) the amount of use that is necessary for establishing federal trademark rights, the administrative cost of this system may well outweigh any potential benefits.

CONCLUSION

We have argued that patent, copyright, and trademark infringement are not strict liability torts after all under a common understanding of that term and that this may be a good thing. In the case of patent law in particular, the applicable rules give the patent owner an incentive to put potential infringers on notice. The precise way in which U.S. law operates nevertheless leaves much to be desired, in that it is both overinclusive (sometimes "innocent" infringers *are* strictly liable) and underinclusive (sometimes requiring the provision of notice to knowing infringers). We have suggested some modest reforms to cure the latter problem. We have also suggested some less modest reforms that would address the former problem, but are less sure of the cost-effectiveness of these solutions.

SIX

Who Is an Infringer?

On a few occasions, we have presented incoming business and law students with the following hypothetical. We asked them to identify, without guessing, which if any of the characters in the hypothetical are liable for patent infringement:

Blair Electronics manufactures components for TV sets. In doing so, it infringed upon someone else's patents. This occurred because Blair Electronics copied some-one else's component, which was protected by a valid patent. Blair's component was purchased by Tom's Television and was installed in all of Tom's TV sets. These sets were sold to Diane Distributor, who sold them to Roger's Retail. Carl Consumer bought a TV set from Roger's Retail.

Typically, although most students are aware of the infringing manufacturer's liability, only a handful know that liability can be imposed solely for the unauthorized sale or use of the patented invention, which means that Tom, Diane, Roger, and even Carl (assuming he turns on the set) are all liable.

In fact, as we noted in Chapter 2, patent law confers upon the patentee a right to exclude others not only from the unauthorized manufacture, but also from the unauthorized sale, offer of sale, use, or importation of the patented invention. By rendering all unauthorized uses of the patented product unlawful, patent law departs from the practice found in trade secret, copyright, and trademark law, all of which proscribe only *some* unauthorized uses of protected material. The rule is also inconsistent with the practice in some other countries, such as Britain and France, which exempt from liability the private noncommercial use of patented inventions.

The good news for consumers is that (as far as we can tell) patent owners rarely if ever bother to sue them for the private, noncommercial users of their inventions. Carl, therefore, is probably safe from suit. There are several good reasons for this. In most cases, finding the infringing end user is unlikely to be worth the hassle; suing unwitting consumers would create a public relations nightmare, even if it were feasible; and the other entities in the chain of distribution are easier to find and are jointly liable for infringement anyway. Patent owners sometimes *do* sue these other entities (e.g., entities analogous to Tom's Television, Diane Distributor, or Roger's Retail) for unauthorized sales. Also, commercial users are not immune from the occasional suit.[1] The question, therefore, arises whether the practice of imposing liability upon sellers and users makes economic sense, and if so, whether it makes sense to follow a different rule in trade secret, copyright, and trademark law.

In the sections that follow, we consider some possible justifications for the patent rule. Before plunging into the abyss, however, a few contextual points are necessary. The first is that the patent owner's right to prevent unauthorized uses and sales has less bite than it might otherwise appear as a result of the first-sale or exhaustion doctrine. As we noted in Chapter 2, the owner of a lawfully made product embodying the patented invention has a right to use and sell that product without having to obtain permission from the patent owner.[2] If Blair's Electronics had obtained permission to manufacture and sell the component in our hypothetical, none of the other actors in the chain would be liable for reselling or using that component. Copyright and trademark law also follow versions of the first-sale doctrine, which insulate from liability the owners of lawfully made copies or products, when those owners distribute or display those copies or products. We noted these rules in Chapter 2 as well. Our discussion in this chapter, therefore, focuses on the situation in which the copy is not lawfully made (or the first-sale doctrine does not apply for some other reason) and asks whether other entities in the chain – who may be unaware of the infringement – should be liable as well.

A second point worth noting is that patent, copyright, and trademark law all impose liability on persons *outside* the chain of distribution under some circumstances. In our previous hypothetical, all of the entities within the chain were *direct* infringers, because each one directly engaged in an

---

[1] See, e.g., *Oiness v. Walgreen Co.*, 88 F.3d 1025 (Fed. Cir. 1996) which involves alleged sales of infringing products; *Clark v. Linzer Prods. Corp.*, 40 U.S.P.Q.2d 1469 (N.D. Ill. 1996) which involves alleged sales of infringing products purchased from overseas manufacturers; see also *J.E.M. AG Supply, Inc. v. Pioneer Hi-Bred Int'l, Inc.*, 534 U.S. 124 (2001) which involves resales allegedly beyond the scope of a license agreement.

[2] This assumes there is no enforceable contractual limitation upon resale or use. In some instances, such limitations may be enforceable. See *Mallinckrodt, Inc. v. Medipart, Inc.*, 976 F.2d 700, 703–9 (Fed. Cir. 1992); Cohen & Lemley (2001; 33–5). Whether the patent owner's rights are exhausted when the product was lawfully manufactured or sold in another country also raises some thorny issues, which go beyond the scope of the present discussion.

unlawful manufacture, or use, or sale. But sometimes a person who enables another person's direct infringement can be liable as an *indirect* infringer. Patent law recognizes two forms of indirect liability, contributory infringement and active inducement; copyright and trademark also recognize their own versions of indirect liability.[3] (Under all of these, someone must be liable for direct infringement before another person can be liable for indirect infringement.) The rationale for indirect liability parallels some of the reasoning we employ later, namely that there may be situations in which (1) the direct infringer is judgment-proof or beyond the court's jurisdiction and (2) it would be socially cost-justified for the indirect infringer to take steps to reduce the probability of direct infringement. Several commentators have recently weighed in with discussions of the economics of indirect liability, particularly as it effects the sharing of music files on the Internet, which we note but will not repeat here.[4] Some of this analysis parallels our discussion

---

[3]   More specifically, under U.S. patent law a person can be liable for actively inducing an infringement, if he intentionally causes another to infringe. See Patent Act § 271(b). A person is liable for contributory infringement if he (1) sells a component that (a) constitutes a material part of a patented invention and (b) is not suitable for substantial noninfringing use and (2) knows or should know that the buyer will use the component to infringe the patent. See Patent Act § 271(c).
      In copyright law, a person is liable for *vicarious* infringement if he has (1) the right and ability to supervise the infringer's conduct and (2) a direct and obvious financial interest in the infringement. See *Fonovisa, Inc. v. Cherry Auction, Inc.*, 76 F.3d 259, 262–63 (9th Cir. 1996). Contrary to normal agency and tort law principles, it is possible for a person to be vicariously liable in copyright for the infringement of persons other than employees and other similar agents. In addition, a person is liable for contributory infringement of a copyright if he knowingly induces, causes, or materially contributes to another's infringement. Knowledge may be direct or constructive. Constructive knowledge would be inferred when a person supplies another with a device that is not capable of a substantial noninfringing use. See *Sony Corp. of Am. v. Universal City Studios, Inc.*, 464 U.S. 417, 442 (1984). In the famous *Sony* case, the U.S. Supreme Court concluded that selling VCRs was not an act of contributory infringement, because VCRs had both infringing and noninfringing uses. Napster also had substantial noninfringing uses, but in that case the defendant was found to have had actual knowledge of some subscribers' infringing conduct. In recent litigation involving peer-to-peer file sharing, the suppliers of Grokster and Morpheus software were able to escape liability under these principles. Aimster, on the other hand, was unable to avoid a preliminary injunction, in part because of the advice it provided on how to use its system to download copyrighted songs, and in part because of a lack of evidence of actual use of the software for noninfringing purposes. See *In re Aimster Copyright Litig.*, 334 F.3d 643 (7th Cir. 2003); *A & M Records, Inc. v. Napster, Inc.*, 239 F.3d 1004 (9th Cir. 2001); *Metro-Goldwyn-Mayer Studios v. Grokster, Ltd.*, 259 F. Supp. 2d 1029 (C.D. Cal. 2003).
      In trademark law, a person is liable for contributory infringement if he (1) intentionally induces another to infringe or (2) continues to supply a product to another who he knows or has reason to know will use it to infringe. See *Inwood Labs., Inc. v. Ives Labs., Inc.*, 456 U.S. 844, 854 (1982).
[4]   See Einhorn (2001); Gilbert & Katz (2001); Landes & Lichtman (2003); Yen (2003). The fundamental problem for IP law, which all of these analysts recognize, is that if the law

of when, if ever, someone other than the first infringer – the manufacturer in the previous patent hypothetical – should be liable. The one difference is that indirect liability almost always hinges on a finding of specific intent, actual knowledge, or at least constructive knowledge on the part of the indirect infringer; our discussion will focus instead on the advantages and disadvantages of more-or-less "strict" liability for persons within the chain of distribution (see Chapter 5).

We will argue that, while there are some plausible reasons for extending modified strict liability to commercial users and sellers, there are no persuasive reasons for imposing liability upon private, noncommercial users. We then consider some possible reasons why the other bodies of intellectual property law have traditionally favored a less expansive scope of liability. We conclude with a brief discussion of some ways in which the Internet has pushed both copyright and trademark law toward the *de facto* adoption of the patent rule with regard to practices such as online browsing and cybersquatting.

PATENTS, COPYRIGHTS, AND TRADEMARKS

As we discussed in Chapter 5, the patentee normally may enjoin the unauthorized manufacture, use, or sale of the invention, regardless of whether the infringer is "innocent" or "willful." Thus, in the preceding hypothetical, every person within the chain of distribution beginning with Blair Electronics is an infringer, because each one is engaging in the unauthorized manufacture, sale, or use of the patented article. (Mere possession of the patented article, however, does not constitute a prohibited use. See 5 Chisum (2001; § 16.02[4][b], at 16–50 to –51).) The patent rule therefore differs from the trade secret rule, which forbids only some uses of trade secret information. Copyright and trademark law also afford much narrower protection against unauthorized uses.

First, although the copyright right of reproduction is analogous to the patentee's right to prevent the unauthorized manufacture of her patented

---

were more strict – for example, if it were illegal to sell a product that had any substantial infringing use, even though the product also had substantial noninfringing uses – fewer infringements would escape detection, but social costs would also rise, perhaps significantly. On the other hand, the less strict the standard for indirect infringement is, the less effective indirect liability becomes as a tool for combating infringement. In the wake of the *Grokster* ruling, for example, the recording industry announced plans to target individual users of file-sharing software (the direct infringers); whether it can pull this off without destroying its fan base remains to be seen.

invention,[5] in some countries the copyright right of distribution may be narrower than the corresponding patent right against unauthorized sales. According to one commentator, the U.S. right of distribution is infringed only by unauthorized "publication" of the work – i.e., by distributing "[s]uch copies as are available . . . to all members of the public who are interested,"[6] whether by sale, gift, or rental.[7] Under this view, the unauthorized sale or gift to one person – or even to a limited class of persons – would not violate the right of distribution, if the work was not offered to the public at large. At least one case, however, broadly holds (although without any analysis) that *any* unauthorized transfer violates the distribution right.[8] An intermediate view, under which the distribution right proscribes unauthorized publication *and* unauthorized sales (whether accompanied by publication or not), may also be possible.[9] Under any of these views, however, the public distribution right is broader than the corresponding patent right in one respect: namely, that copyright liability is not conditioned upon a sale or offer to sell. Rather, the Copyright Act prohibits *any* unauthorized distribution to the public, whether "by sale or other transfer of ownership, or by rental, lease, or lending."[10] This distinction may have little practical import, however, inasmuch as the gift of a patented invention that was manufactured without permission of the patentee would not trigger application of the first-sale

---

[5] The two are not identical, however. The patent owner must prove that the alleged infringer has made a product that incorporates all of the elements of the claimed invention or their equivalent. The copyright owner must prove that the alleged infringer's work is substantially similar to some greater-than-*de-minimis* portion of the owner's protected expression, selection, or arrangement. Thus, the copyright defendant may be liable for infringement even if he does not copy the owner's work in its entirety.

[6] 1 Nimmer & Nimmer (2001; § 4.04, at 4–22.1 to –22.2).

[7] See 2 Nimmer & Nimmer (2001; § 8:11[A], at 8–135). Nimmer and Nimmer note that the scope of the right – "to distribute copies or phonorecords of the copyrighted work to the public by sale or other transfer of ownership, or by rental, lease, or lending," see 17 U.S.C. § 106(3) – corresponds to the definition of "publication," namely, "the distribution of copies or phonorecords of a work to the public by sale or other transfer of ownership, or by rental, lease, or lending." *Id.* § 101. Consequently, the view § 106(3) largely as embodying a right of first publication. See 2 Nimmer & Nimmer (2001; § 8:11[A], at 8–135); see also 2 Goldstein (2001; § 5.5, at 5:98). Not all publications constitute distributions under the current act, however. A publication also may be effected by "offering to distribute copies or phonorecords to a group of persons for purposes of further distribution, public performance, or public display." 17 U.S.C. § 101. One does not infringe the distribution right by merely *offering* to distribute works to the public. See 2 Nimmer & Nimmer (2001; § 8:11[A], at 8–135 Footnote 2).

[8] See *Ford Motor Co. v. Summit Motor Products, Inc.*, 930 F.2d 277, 299 (3d Cir. 1991).

[9] See 2 Nimmer & Nimmer (2001; § 8:11[A], at 8–135 to –136).

[10] 17 U.S.C. § 106(3).

doctrine. The recipient, therefore, would infringe by using the invention, even if the transfer is not infringing (because it's not a "sale").

A second difference between the patent and copyright rules centers on copyright's treatment of unauthorized *uses* of copyrighted material. Unlike patent law, which prohibits all unauthorized uses of patented inventions, copyright generally proscribes only three such uses: (1) the use of the work to prepare derivative works; (2) the public performance of the work; and (3) its public display.[11] Other uses – including the private performance or display of a work, reading an illegally reproduced book, listening to an unlawfully reproduced CD, or viewing a bootleg movie – do not infringe, even though the analogous use of a patented invention would.

Third, copyright provides more liberal exceptions to liability than does patent law with regard to activities that on their face may appear infringing. As we noted in Chapter 2, there are (in addition to the first-sale doctrine) a host of additional exceptions under U.S. law, many of them tailored to very narrow circumstances. But the most famous exception in copyright law is the *fair use* doctrine, which exempts from liability some uses for purposes "such as criticism, comment, news reporting, teaching . . . scholarship, or research."[12] A great deal of copyright scholarship addresses the many applications and purposes of fair use.[13] From an economic perspective, one purpose is to provide an outlet for the would-be user in situations in which the transaction cost of requesting permission to reproduce or adapt the work would outweigh the value of the use. Another is to exempt uses that may give rise to positive externalities (such as some uses for purposes of education, research, news reporting, criticism, and commentary) in excess of the amount the user himself would be willing to pay.[14] Our discussion of fair use is not intended to be exhaustive, but merely to illustrate how fair use

---

[11] As noted in Chapter 2, we put to one side the doctrines of moral rights and neighboring rights, which are of less importance in U.S. law and which, in any event, are usually viewed as embodying more of a natural-law perspective than an economic one.

[12] 17 U.S.C. § 107.

[13] Among the leading works, which we draw upon in our brief discussion above, are Fisher (1988); Gordon (2002); Gordon (1982); Landes & Posner (1989).

[14] To illustrate: in some instances, the amount the user is willing to pay (WTP) exceeds the amount the owner is willing to accept (WTA), but transaction costs (TC) outweigh both: $TC > WTP > WTA$. Absent the fair use exception, the user will forgo the use, even though the uncompensated use would increase social wealth. In other cases, the social value of the use (SV) may exceed the amount the owner is WTA, which in turn exceeds the amount the user is willing to pay: $SV > WTA > WTP$. In this instance, if the user could appropriate more of the social value to himself, he might negotiate a license. If transaction costs or other social obstacles prevent this from happening, however, it may be desirable to excuse the use as fair because, once again, the use enhances social wealth.

renders copyright rights somewhat less secure than patent rights (although, unlike patent rights, few copyright rights are invalidated in court). Fair use exempts many more uses of copyrighted materials than does the analogous (but extremely narrow) experimental use doctrine in patent law, although some recent scholarship argues for expanding the latter, or introducing a fair-use style exemption, in copyright as well.[15]

Trademark law also creates a narrower use proscription than does patent law. For one thing, only the commercial use of a mark – that is, a use in connection with the marketing of products or services – can constitute an actionable infringement or dilution.[16] Thus, while liability extends to all unauthorized *commercial* users within the chain of distribution, where their use gives rise to a likelihood of confusion,[17] merely wearing a counterfeit IZOD shirt should not give rise to liability on the part of the consumer, who is not using the mark to identify a business or to market goods or services. Trademark law also recognizes a "descriptive use" or "fair use" doctrine under which a seller may lawfully use another's mark to describe the seller's own product in a nonconfusing fashion,[18] and it exempts from liability the use of another's mark to market one's own goods (e.g., "IBM-compatible") or for purposes of truthful and nonconfusing comparative advertising.[19]

AN ECONOMIC ANALYSIS OF THE PATENT RULE

There are a variety of reasons why it might make sense to render some persons, in addition to the infringing manufacturer, liable for direct patent

---

[15] See Burk (2000; 154–8); O'Rourke (2000; 1194).

[16] See 15 U.S.C. §§ 1114(1)(a), (b); *id.* §§ 1125(a)(1), (2); *id.*§§ (c)(1), (4); Restatement (Third) of Unfair Competition §§ 20(1), 25(2).

[17] See *Stabilisierungsfonds für Wein v. Kaiser Stuhl Wine Distribs.*, 647 F.2d 200, 207 (D.C. Cir. 1981); 4 McCarthy (2001; § 25:26). An infringer of a registered mark, however, who is "engaged solely in the business of printing the mark or violating matter for others" and who "establishes that he or she was an innocent infringer" is subject only to an injunction against future printing and not to damages liability. See 15 U.S.C. § 1125(2)(A). A similar limitation applies to the publication of infringing advertisements in newspapers and magazines. See *id.* § 1125(2)(B), (C). We know of no authority addressing the issue of whether all persons within the chain of distribution are similarly liable for the dilution of a famous mark; there is nothing in the text of the federal statute that would suggest otherwise, however. See 15 U.S.C. § 1125(c).

[18] See Restatement (Third) of Unfair Competition § 28. An example might be the use of the sentence "Our salad dressings are tasty" in an ad campaign, even though another owns the mark TAS-TEE for a competing brand of dressing. See *Henri's Food Prods. Co. v. Tasty Snacks, Inc.*, 817 F.2d 1303, 1307 (7th Cir. 1987).

[19] See Restatement (Third) of Unfair Competition § 20 cmt. b, § 25 cmt. i.

infringement.[20] None of these reasons necessarily provides a complete justification for the precise contours of the existing rule, although in the aggregate they make a reasonably compelling case for its general scope. The best reason, as we shall see, is the need to ensure the patentee of its expected stream of rents, regardless of the infringing manufacturer's ability to pay or amenability to suit.

The first reason focuses on the fact that an inventor may obtain a patent on a *process* as well as on a machine, manufacture, or composition of matter. Semantically, it seems awkward to refer to a person "making" a process; rather, the person analogous to the manufacturer of an infringing device is one who "uses" the patented process. This observation may provide some explanation for extending liability to the users of patented processes, but the argument fails to explain why liability has extended as well to the unauthorized use of a machine, manufacture, or composition of matter.[21]

---

[20] Schlicher considers the patent rule from the opposite perspective: namely, why does patent law provide a cause of action against anyone *other than* the end user? As Schlicher points out:

> Unauthorized making and selling of patented products would not injure the patent owner, if he had a costless remedy against end users. Unauthorized making of a product does not necessarily reduce the private value of the invention to the patent owner. Someone could make ten million personal computers identical to IBM's PC/2 and store them in a warehouse. The fact that ten million computers are sitting there in boxes does not reduce the consumer demand IBM captures from supplying its PC/2s. Likewise, unauthorized selling does not necessarily reduce the private value of the invention. If a patent owner enjoins each user immediately after the sale, the value of that product to them is zero. If users know that injunction will inevitably and immediately follow the purchase, they will pay a seller nothing for the product. If there is no end user demand for the product prohibiting making and selling serves no purpose. Rights against users seem sufficient.

Schlicher (1998; § 8.02[2] at 8–9). Schlicher argues, however, that providing a cause of action against manufacturers and sellers is efficient because (1) it reduces the cost of enforcing the patentee's rights; (2) it reduces the need – and therefore the concomitant transaction costs – for end users to negotiate indemnification agreements with those farther upstream in the chain of distribution, who typically can discover at lower cost whether the product is patented; and (3) it encourages those who can make the invention at lower cost than the patentee to seek licenses from the patentee. See *id.* at 8–9 to –11.

We agree with Schlicher's analysis, but the question we pose is slightly different. Given the benefits, as cited by Schlicher, from allowing the patentee to sue the manufacturer – as well as the costs associated with allowing her to sue end users and sellers, which we discuss herein – why does the law continue to recognize a cause of action against end users and sellers?

[21] Note also that, under a 1989 amendment to the U.S. Patent Act, "[w]hoever without authority imports into the United States or offers to sell, sells, or uses within the United States a product which is made by a process patented in the United States shall be liable as an infringer, if the importation, offer to sell, sale, or use of the product occurs during the term of such process patent." See 35 U.S.C. § 271(g). This provision may render it

Second, extending liability to users and sellers makes it easier to hold liable an entity that can control another's unlawful manufacture (a parent company, for example) but which might otherwise be able to shield itself by engaging only in the purchase of the infringing product for resale or use. For example, suppose that in our hypothetical Tom's Television, the parent company, bought infringing components manufactured by its thinly capitalized subsidiary, Blair's Electronics. If Tom's Television could not be liable for infringement by virtue of using or selling the components, it would escape liability altogether unless the patent owner could prove some other theory of liability (such as intentional inducement, *respondeat superior*, or piercing-the-corporate-veil). This in turn might provide Tom's with an incentive to set up a corporate structure of this nature to the possible detriment of the patent owner. Once again, however, the "solution" of rendering all users and sellers liable appears more extensive than is necessary to achieve a rather limited purpose of deterring the strategic use of corporate formalities.

A third possible justification for extending liability all the way down the chain of distribution nevertheless builds upon the insight that it may be worthwhile to ensure the patent owner against having only one, possibly judgment-proof, defendant to sue. We argued in Chapter 3 that in order to preserve the incentives to invent, disclose, and commercialize, the applicable damages rules should ensure that the patentee will be no worse off and the infringer no better off as a result of infringement. Consistent with this principle, the patent owner should recover the greater of her own lost profit or the infringer's profit attributable to the infringement. But this remedy will be inadequate if the only available defendant is an infringing manufacturer who happens to be judgment-proof or otherwise beyond the reach of a civil suit for damages.[22] Therefore, the current scope of liability may be

unnecessary in some cases to assert a claim against the mere user of the process, though clearly not in all: a person who uses the process in his own business for purposes other than to generate a product would not be liable under this provision. Oddly enough, this provision, unlike other provisions of the Patent Act, makes it more difficult to sue a private noncommercial user: "In an action for infringement of a process patent, no remedy may be granted for infringement on account of the noncommercial use or retail sale of a product unless there is no adequate remedy under this title for infringement on account of the importation or other use, offer to sell, or sale of that product." *Id.* Section 271(g) also provides that a product will not be considered the product of a patented process if it is "materially changed by subsquent processes" or "becomes a trivial and nonessential component of another product." *Id.*

[22] For example, if the person engaging in the unauthorized manufacture is overseas, he is not violating U.S. patent law. See *Deepsouth Packing Co. v. Laitram Corp.*, 406 U.S. 518, 531–2 (1972). Even so, the patentee would not be without recourse, even in the absence of user and seller liability. For one thing, the patentee would now appear to have a cause of action

seen as preserving the incentive to invent by permitting the patentee to sue the infringer's customers. In this regard, we note that extending liability to sellers and users does not permit duplicative recovery; it merely allows the patentee to sue the most convenient infringer on the list.

An obvious objection to this theory is that sellers and users may not be very well-positioned to prevent infringing merchandise from reaching the public; indeed, it may seem unfair to penalize someone who may be an *unwitting* infringer. But recall that patent law is, in some if not all respects, a strict liability tort. We argued in Chapter 5 that this standard of liability is preferable to the alternatives as long as the would-be defendant is in a better position to avoid the infringement. This is arguably the case here: the users and sellers will often be in a better position to monitor the potentially infringing manufacturer than will be the patentee.[23] The patentee, after all, may be a complete stranger to the transaction between the manufacturer of the infringing component and the manufacturer of the final product; the entity that buys from the infringing manufacturer at least knows something about that manufacturer and could choose to refrain from dealing with a suspicious or unknown company. (Other options for users and sellers to deal with the possibility of infringement liability might be to demand a risk

---

against the person who *imports* the product into the United States under a provision added to the Patent Act in 1995 that allows the patentee to exclude others from importing the patented invention into the United States without permission. See 35 U.S.C. §§ 154(a)(1), 271(a). In addition, the patentee often has the option of obtaining a patent abroad and pursuing an infringement claim there. Finally, if the infringer is practicing another's process abroad, the patentee can sue someone who imports into the United States, or who offers to sell, sells, or uses in the United States, a product made by the process. See 35 U.S.C. § 271(g).

[23] To some extent, the analysis that follows in the text above parallels the analysis of Landes and Posner with regard to products liability. As Landes and Posner note, the law of products liability allows a person who has been injured by a defective component to sue anyone in the chain of distribution from the component manufacturer to the retailer. Every entity within the chain of distribution, however, has an indemnity claim against the entities further up the chain, so that (in theory) the component manufacturer ultimately bears the full extent of liability. Using the terms "general contractor" to refer to the person in the position of the component manufacturer and "subcontractor" to refer to someone further down the chain, Posner and Landes defend this arrangement for the following reasons:

First, it is cheaper for the general contractor to get reimbursement of the plaintiff's damages by way of indemnity from the subcontractor than for the plaintiff to get damages from the subcontractor directly. For example, the general contractor could more easily arrange for the bonding of the subcontractor or some other guarantee of his financial responsibility than could the plaintiff. Second, the general contractor has better information than the plaintiff regarding the identity of the ultimately responsible party.

Landes & Posner (1987; 206). See also Demsetz (1972; 27–8).

premium or a bond from the component manufacturer or to purchase insurance against infringement liability. These options, however, are certainly not costless and may themselves give rise to unintended consequences.) Sellers and users also may be in a better position to pursue a remedy against the illicit manufacturer than is the patentee. Sellers and users of infringing goods might have an indemnity claim against the manufacturer under the Uniform Commercial Code (UCC), which implies such a term in the contract of sale.[24] For these reasons, the deterrent value of seller and user liability, though perhaps weak, may have some small positive effects upon behavior.

One problem with the patent rule is that seller and user exposure creates uncertainty and may have unintended consequences. For example, when a manufacturer of television sets buys a component that could possibly be the product of patent infringement, the cost of the component becomes a random variable; the television manufacturer might be buying a patent lawsuit along with the component. The expected result of this added potential cost is that component buyers will reduce their purchases. Also, if it is difficult to distinguish infringing from noninfringing components in advance, this reduction in purchases of components will hurt both infringing and noninfringing manufacturers. Further complications arise if the manufacturer of the final product is risk-averse, because a risk-averse manufacturer will try to

---

[24] In the United States, a transaction of this nature often will be governed by the Uniform Commercial Code (UCC). Section § 2-312(3) of the UCC states:

Unless otherwise agreed a seller who is a merchant regularly dealing in goods of the kind warrants that the goods shall be delivered free of the rightful claim of any third person by way of infringement or the like but a buyer who furnishes specifications to the seller must hold the seller harmless against any such claim which arises out of compliance with the specifications.

Whether this warranty "runs with the goods" – that is, whether a defendant may file a cross-claim against any of the parties above him in the chain of distribution – or whether he has a claim only against the party from whom he purchased the goods (who might, in turn, have a claim against the party from whom *he* purchase the goods, and so on up to the infringing component manufacturer) is unclear. Compare *Aeroquip Corp. v. United States*, 37 Fed. Cl. 139 (1997), with *Crook Motor Co. v. Goolsby*, 703 F. Supp. 511, 520 (N.D. Miss. 1988); see also 1 White & Summers (1995; § 9–12a, at 534–5). In cases not governed by § 2–312(3) – for example, when the seller is not "a merchant regularly dealing in goods of the kind" – the parties presumably could negotiate a similar warranty obligation that would be binding at least upon the immediate parties to the transaction. *Cf.* Toedt (1998; § 13.05[c]). Whether patent law itself imposes any duty of contribution among joint tortfeasors is uncertain, although the few cases that have addressed this issue have held that it does not. See *Chemtron, Inc. v. Aqua Prods., Inc.*, 830 F. Supp. 314, 316 (E.D. Va. 1993); *Construction Tech., Inc. v. Lockformer Co.*, 781 F. Supp. 195, 201 (S.D.N.Y. 1991); *Motorola, Inc. v. Varo, Inc.*, 656 F. Supp. 716, 717–18 (N.D. Tex. 1986).

mitigate the risk by purchasing even fewer components than its risk-neutral counterpart.

Interestingly, this liability exposure hurts the manufacturer of television sets because the effective cost of the component is higher. But it also hurts the legitimate producers of components because it depresses the demand for their product. To the extent that this leads the manufacturer to deal only with established suppliers with solid reputations, the entry of new suppliers becomes more difficult. This is an unfortunate result, but it is important not to overstate the point. New entrants often have credibility hurdles to overcome. Our only point is that patent law provides one more reason for buyers to be cautious in dealing with newcomers.

The uncertainty that patent law creates for sellers and users adds to the cost of anything that may be the product of infringement. Risk aversion adds to that cost. Risk-shifting mechanisms such as indemnification and insurance therefore might be desirable, but it is important not to overstate this point either. First, we already have risk shifting to the extent that the possibly infringing manufacturer would be liable for indemnification under the UCC. Second, even if the manufacturer is outside the United States, so that the UCC might not protect the customer, sales contracts can be drafted to deal with that problem. Finally, we should note that, even apart from whatever patent law requires, the commercial sellers within the chain of distribution are already in the position of purchasing a potential lawsuit when they purchase products that contain components, as a result of products liability law. Perhaps the incremental risk posed by patent law is minor in comparison with the much more likely probability of incurring a products liability suit from an injured consumer.

In summary, the extension of liability for patent infringement to all sellers and users has costs and benefits. From the perspective of preserving the incentive to invest in inventive activity, this extension appears to be beneficial. It affords the greatest opportunity for recovering lost profits due to infringement. It also does so at least cost because the patentee can sue the most convenient infringer. On the other side of the coin are the costs. The extension of liability to all sellers and users increases the expected costs of economic activity, which leads to a reduced level of such activity. This is not beneficial. Which influence is more important cannot be determined *a priori*. Anecdotal evidence suggests that people are largely unaware of their exposure. If such unawareness is indeed widespread, it would tend to reduce sellers' and users' expected costs. This, in turn, suggests that the benefits of the rule may outweigh the costs.

The preceding analysis nevertheless still leaves two issues unresolved. First, nothing in the analysis thus far provides a strong reason for holding private noncommercial users liable; one would expect that in most cases the effect on incentives of being able to sue a consumer for using a patented invention would be virtually nil. On the other hand, because patentees do not appear in practice to sue consumers for the unauthorized use of their inventions, the extension of liability may do little harm and perhaps it serves to economize on litigation costs; by not distinguishing between commercial users and private consumers, we avoid the cost of having to determine what constitutes a commercial use.[25] Still, the American practice is at odds with that of other countries, such as Britain and France, that specifically exempt private noncommercial use from the scope of liability. Second, if we wish to provide the patentee with a broad range of defendants to sue, in order to maximize the patentee's incentive to invent, why not make it unlawful merely to *possess* a patented invention without consent rather than condition liability upon manufacture, sale, or use? Perhaps the point makes little difference, however, because most people (we assume) do not acquire patented inventions in order to hoard or contemplate them, but rather for the more down-to-earth purposes of use or resale. Moreover, because utility is a condition of patentability, it is probably fair to say that the Patent Act is not designed to encourage the creation of unused inventions (for more on this point, however, see Chapter 8). One who possesses but does not use a patented invention, in other words, is not harming the patentee in a way that the patent scheme is intended to prevent.

WHY IS THE RULE DIFFERENT IN TRADE SECRET, COPYRIGHT, AND TRADEMARK LAW?

Whatever the merits may be of the rule followed in patent cases, the question remains why trade secret, copyright, and trademark law proscribe a much narrower class of unauthorized uses. In the following paragraphs, we suggest some possible reasons for this divergence. We also note some ways in which the Internet is moving copyright and trademark law toward the *de facto* adoption of the patent rule under certain conditions and consider some of the implications of this transformation.

1. Trade Secret Law

The different route chosen by trade secret law is perhaps the easiest to explain. As noted earlier, trade secret law allows one to use another's secret

---

[25] In copyright law, by contrast, the analogous issue of whether a performance is public or private is frequently the subject of litigation.

where the user owes no duty of secrecy and has acquired the secret by lawful means, such as independent discovery or reverse engineering; it also exempts the use of a secret that the user acquired without actual or constructive knowledge that the person from whom it was acquired owed a duty of secrecy. Although these rules differ considerably from the corresponding rules in patent law, they are consistent with an economic rationale for trade secret law developed by Friedman, Landes, and Posner (1991). We alluded to this theory in Chapter 2, but will provide a slightly fuller explication here to illustrate our point.

The Friedman-Landes-Posner theory suggests that it is rational for a creator of useful information to rely upon trade secret protection under three circumstances.[26] First, the creator may believe that the information is patentable but unlikely to be independently discovered or reverse-engineered until the patent term is over, or nearly over; in such a case, she may opt for trade secret protection if the value of the information is low and the cost of keeping it secret is lower than the cost of seeking a patent. Second, if the creator believes that the information is patentable but will be difficult for others to independently discover or reverse-engineer until *after* the patent term has expired, she may opt for the anticipated longer term of trade secret protection. Third, the creator may believe that the information is unpatentable, but that "reinventing it would take so long that he can obtain a substantial return by keeping the invention secret" (e.g., the Coca-Cola syrup recipe). Friedman, Landes, and Posner argue that in these three circumstances

trade secret law supplements the patent system. Inventors choose trade secret protection when they believe that patent protection is too costly relative to the value of their invention, or that it will give them a reward substantially less than the benefit of their invention (as reflected, in part, in the length of time before any[one] else will invent it), either because the invention is not patentable or because the length (or other conditions) of patent protection is insufficient. By successfully maintaining their trade secret they provide evidence that their belief was correct.[27]

In this regard, trade secret law "provides a means of internalizing the benefits of innovation" and thereby encouraging the production of innovation; in doing so, it plugs some of the gaps found in patent law, such as the inability to modify the patent term depending on the social utility of the invention.[28]

---

[26] See Friedman et al. (1991; 63–4).

[27] *Id.* at 64.

[28] See *id.* at 63–64. Of course, there might be other possible responses to some of these circumstances. One possibility would be to provide a shorter patent term for inventions that, while not entirely obvious, are insufficiently nonobvious to merit patent protection. This is exactly what some countries do, under a form of legal protection known as a utility

The cost of this incentive, however, is that some useful information will remain secret, although trade secret law attempts to minimize this cost by allowing access to at least some of the information the incentive generates.

Like patent law, trade secret law may be viewed as a means of encouraging the production of useful information while, at the same time, avoiding the undue limitation of access to that information; the ways in which trade secret law attempts to resolve this incentive-access tradeoff, however, are unique. For example, trade secret law solves the problem of terminating protection in the absence of a fixed term by conferring rights that cease when others lawfully acquire the secret. Friedman, Landes, and Posner argue that the courts take into account the incentive-access tradeoff in determining what counts as a "proper means" of acquisition, "by prohibiting only the most costly means of unmasking commercial secrets," that is, those that would induce costly defensive maneuvers.[29] On this view, trade secret law rightly condemns the acquisition of another's secret by means such as theft and espionage, but not by independent discovery. Similarly, allowing the use of a secret that has been accidentally disclosed is arguably more efficient than the alternative of forbidding such use, because the owner of the secret is likely to be better positioned than are potential users to determine in advance what information is secret and to take the necessary steps to maintain its confidentiality. The legality of reverse-engineering is somewhat more difficult to explain on the basis of this reasoning, inasmuch as the trade secret owner may incur large costs to make its products more difficult to reverse-engineer; reverse-engineering nevertheless may be justified by the fact that the process itself can lead to new discoveries.[30] And, as we noted in the preceding Chapter, the relative weakness of trade secret law in comparison to patent law provides one basis for the U.S. Supreme Court's decision that patent law does not preempt trade secret law.

The Friedman-Landes-Posner hypothesis is clearly not the last word on the economics of trade secret law, as they themselves recognize. As we noted in Chapter 2, Robert Bone argues that, in light of the protections against disclosure that are available under contract and tort law, the benefits of any additional duties of secrecy attributable to trade secret law are outweighed by

---

model. See, e.g., The Protection of Utility Models in a Single Market: Green Paper from the Commission to the European Council, COM(95)370 final at 7–8 (discusses various types of utility model protection available in member nations of European Union); Reichman (1994; 2455–9) (discussing utility models).

[29] See Friedman et al. (1991; 67).

[30] See *id.* at 67, 69.

the costs of inhibiting the disclosure of useful information.[31] The logic of the Friedman-Landes-Posner thesis nevertheless provides some useful insights into why it may make sense for trade secret liability to differ from patent liability in certain ways. To the extent that Bone's alternative approach has merit, it suggests that the liability exceptions found in trade secret law do not go far enough, although presumably they at least tend to reduce some of the inefficiencies to which Bone believes trade secret law gives rise.

2. Copyright

One possible reason for copyright to exempt certain uses from the scope of liability involves the presence of transaction costs. To illustrate, imagine for a moment that the copyright owner *did* have a right to prevent all unauthorized uses of the work that were not otherwise exempt under some exception such as first sale. Even so, one would expect very few copyright owners to exercise their right to prevent others from merely reading infringing books, watching infringing movies, or privately performing works of music (e.g., singing in the shower), due to the enormous transaction costs involved in attempting to enforce such a right. In a sense, exempting certain uses from the scope of liability parallels one of the rationales behind the fair use doctrine – namely, to permit valuable uses of copyrighted material in circumstances in which transaction costs or other bargaining obstacles would preclude voluntary negotiations. Indeed, even if these private uses of copyrighted material were prima facie unlawful, one might expect that many of them would be covered by a rational fair use doctrine. Rendering them prima facie lawful instead (as opposed to prima facie unlawful, though possibly subject to fair use) is therefore likely to have little if any impact upon the incentive to create and to publish works of authorship. Moreover, since the user normally bears the burden of proving fair use, the rule of prima facie legality may be preferable, inasmuch as the alternative of prima facie illegality subject to fair use might deter some risk-averse users from engaging in lawful conduct, thus leading to the suboptimal utilization of copyrighted works.

Nevertheless, this reasoning still does not explain why the copyright and patent rules should differ, inasmuch as the private noncommercial use of a patent is likely to be of as little value to the patentee as the analogous use of a copyright is to the copyright owner. Perhaps a distinction can be made, however, on the ground, which we noted in Chapter 5 in connection

---

[31] See Bone (1998).

with our discussion of independent discovery, that copyrighted works of authorship are much more pervasive than are patented inventions. If every unauthorized use of a copyrighted work of authorship were potentially subject to liability, *some* copyright owners would file suit to prevent some uses that are not permitted – even if, in most circumstances, transaction and detection costs would render this strategy infeasible. This possibility, however, raises the spectre of deterring risk-averse users from engaging in the fair use of copyrighted works, as discussed previously. Moreover, the absence of an exception for private noncommercial use in patent law at least has the virtue of avoiding litigation over the definition of "private noncommercial use." Copyright law, by contrast, is replete with cases examining the meaning of "public performance," a result that could be avoided if all performances required authorization. But, if our previous suggestion is correct – that many private uses of copyrighted works would fit within the fair use exception, even if prima facie unlawful – then perhaps there is less to be gained from attempting to economize on litigation over such issues as the definition of "public performance," since analogous litigation costs would be incurred even if such uses were prima facie illegal.[32]

---

[32] In a sense, this reasoning begs the question of why there is no fair use doctrine in patent law. One possible reason is that (for commercial users, at least) negotiating with the patentee is often not very difficult, due to factors such as the smaller number of works subject to protection; the fact that patents are public records and contain the name of the inventor and assignee, if any; and the shorter term of protection. Perhaps another reason for patent law's lack of a fair use doctrine relates to the fact that the first-sale doctrine in patent law is broader than the first-sale doctrine in copyright. The patent-law doctrine exempts from the scope of liability any sale or use (though not the re-making) of an article embodying the patented invention after the first lawful sale of that article. The copyright doctrine of first sale, by contrast, exempts from liability the further distribution or public display of the work, but not such uses as public performances or adaptations. In practice, however, it may be that the fair use defense is not successful very often in cases involving the public performance or adaptation of a work, which has been lawfully acquired (though occasionally it is, as in, for example, some cases involving parodies); perhaps fair use is invoked more often, or at least succeeds more often, in cases involving the mere reproduction of such works. The owner of the typical patented article, on the other hand, often has little need or interest in reproducing (remaking) the patented invention. For the typical user of a lawfully acquired patented article, a fair use defense would add relatively few benefits beyond what is already available under first-sale. But see 3 Chisum (2001; § 16.03[3]), who discusses case law involving the issue of whether the owner of a patented article has engaged in lawful repair or unlawful making of the invention; see also O'Rourke (2000), who argues that patent law should recognize a fair use defense in cases in which the use of a patented article is necessary to create a new invention.

One factor that arguably cuts against any attempt to rationalize the patent and copyright rules is that private, noncommercial users of patented inventions often have no idea that they are, technically, infringing. In the example we used in our survey, it is unlikely that the

A second likely reason for copyright to follow a different path may be attributed to traditional notions of freedom and privacy. We suspect there would be considerable discomfort over adopting and enforcing a rule that all unauthorized uses of copyrighted works (not otherwise accounted for by an appropriate exception) infringe. The thought of penalizing people for reading books, watching movies, or listening to or making music within the privacy of their own homes arguably grates upon First Amendment and privacy concerns in a way that penalizing people for copying, distributing, or *publicly* performing these works apparently does not. The analogy here is to *Stanley v. Georgia*,[33] a case in which the U.S. Supreme Court held that the First Amendment prohibits the state from rendering the private possession of obscenity unlawful, even though the distribution of such works may be subject to criminal penalties. The reasoning of the case appears to be that government interference with mere possession of reading material threatens to interfere with the autonomy of the individual mind, in a way that merely preventing the sale of such work does not.[34] The speech and privacy interests at stake in using patented inventions, by contrast, would seem in most cases relatively minor.[35] The utilitarian products we use, in other words, may not be as intensely personal as the books we read, the music we listen to, or the films we watch, and in regulating the former but not the latter the state conveys less of an impression of attempting to control the minds of its citizens.

The analogy with *Stanley* is not a perfect one for at least two reasons, however. First, one might argue that the outcome in *Stanley* is attributable not only to First Amendment concerns over governmental intrusion into the

---

average consumer would have any reason to know that the television contains an infringing component. At least some users of infringing copyrighted works, however, clearly have reason to know that these works were produced and sold without consent of the copyright owner; see, e.g., Mann (1998; 57), who discusses the purchase of presumably infringing software at prices of less than 1% of the products' retail value. Yet, the mere purchase and use of these products may be legal. Copying such works, however (for example, onto the hard drive of a computer) does infringe.

[33] 394 U.S. 557 (1969).

[34] See *id.* at 565 that refers to the defendant's assertion of "the right to satisfy his intellectual and emotional needs in the privacy of his own home" and "to be free from state inquiry into the contents of his library" and concludes that "[i]f the First Amendment means anything, it means that a State has no business telling a man, sitting alone in his own house, what books he may read or what films he may watch"; but see *Osborne v. Ohio*, 495 U.S. 103, 108–11 (1990) that hold the state may criminalize mere possession of child pornography and may distinguish *Stanley* on ground that proscription of child pornography is justified by considerations more substantial than the state's paternalistic desire to control private thoughts.

[35] But see Burk (2000), who argues that software patents may implicate First Amendment concerns.

minds of its citizens, but also to Fourth Amendment concerns over the means the government would have to employ to determine whether someone is merely possessing obscenity.[36] To the extent that the Fourth Amendment explanation of *Stanley* is compelling, it may suggest an alternative reason for the copyright exemption for private noncommercial uses: namely, that the only way the copyright owner would be able to detect these activities would be through methods that seem highly intrusive upon individual privacy. A court also would have a difficult time enforcing an injunction against many such uses (e.g., singing in the shower) without seriously invading the user's privacy. The scope of contemporary copyright and patent law, however, makes this explanation for the distinction between copyright and patent liability rules highly suspect today – although it may have had greater force in an era in which relatively few consumer goods were patented and private acts of copying were both cumbersome and time-consuming. It is, after all, a copyright violation to copy a copyrighted videotape that one has rented at the local video emporium – or to download copyrighted music using file-sharing software – even though the act of copying is done in private and cannot easily be detected (though note the recent use of subpoenas against Internet service providers, requiring them to provide the names of persons suspected of illegally downloading music files). Similarly, the mere act of switching on the television containing the infringing component, as described in our survey hypothetical, appears to be an act of infringement even if the activity takes place entirely within the confines of one's private home. If the law's disparate treatment of these private acts, on the one hand, and private acts of reading, watching, listening, or performing, on the other, continues to have any logical force, it does not appear to derive solely from the intrusiveness of the means necessary to detect the violation.[37]

---

[36] The Fourth Amendment states:

> The right of the people to be secure in their persons, houses, papers, and effects, against unreasonable searches and seizures, shall not be violated, and no Warrants shall issue, but upon probable cause, supported by Oath or affirmation and particularly describing the place to be searched, and the persons or things to be seized.

Justice Stewart's concurring opinion in *Stanley* specifically focuses upon the Fourth Amendment.

[37] This is not to suggest that the intrusiveness of the means necessary to detect the violation is entirely unimportant, however. If private acts of reading, watching, performing, or listening are different from private acts of reproducing copyrighted works or using patented inventions, in that control over the latter does not so strongly implicate government regulation of the autonomous individual mind, then relatively intrusive means of detection may seem more appropriate in the latter context than in the former. The driving force behind the classification of means as too intrusive, however, seems to be more the conduct to be

A second reason for doubting the analogy relates to the extension of copyright to utilitarian works such as computer programs. In terms of First Amendment interests, these works may be more similar to patented inventions than to literary works and yet (unless they happen to be patented as well) unauthorized users of these works may enjoy more freedom than do the unauthorized users of patented inventions. The distinction may be more illusory than real, however, insofar as even the private noncommercial use of a computer program may entail actionable copying.[38] As we shall see, this is but one example of the ways in which computer technology is moving copyright law towards the *de facto* adoption of the patent liability rule.

3. Trademarks

Trademark law's exemption from liability of noncommercial uses generally (whether public or private) at first blush appears to be consistent with trademarks' primary function as mechanisms for reducing consumer search costs. By definition, a noncommercial use of a mark (a use not associated with any offer to sell a product or service) does not interfere with this purpose; moreover, the consumer who purchases an infringing product is often himself a victim of the confusion generated by the bogus mark. Indeed, to penalize innocent consumers for merely using products bearing infringing marks would in effect tell them that they *cannot* rely upon trademarks, a message that would tend to undermine the principal purpose of this body of law.

There are, nevertheless, a few situations in which consumers are not innocent victims or in which the unauthorized noncommercial use of a mark could harm the trademark owner. As Judge Alex Kozinski has observed, for example, a person who buys a "Rolex" watch from a street vendor for $20 does so knowing either that the watch is a fake or is stolen.[39] Clearly, the purchaser himself has no cause of action against the seller under these circumstances; but neither is he liable to the trademark owner as long as he confines himself to the noncommercial use of the watch. Similarly, a gift of the fake watch would not appear to be a "use in commerce" and

---

regulated than anything inherent to the search itself. But cf. Colb (1998; 1685 Footnote 166, 1704–23) who argues that the reasonableness of the search should depend in part upon the strength of the privacy interest which the state seeks to invade.

[38] See *MAI Sys. Corp. v. Peak Computer, Inc.*, 991 F.2d 511, 518–19 (9th Cir. 1993), which holds that loading copyrighted software into random access memory, without permission of the copyright owner, causes the copy to be made in violation of the Copyright Act.

[39] See Kozinski (1993; 964).

therefore would not trigger application of trademark liability on the part of the giver. And one can easily imagine other uses normally viewed as being noncommercial that could dilute the value of the mark, such as publishing a dictionary that classifies the mark as a generic term[40] or wearing a tee shirt that degrades a mark.[41]

Like the exclusion of certain noncommercial uses from the scope of copyright liability, the exemption for noncommercial diluting uses of trademarks may be largely attributable to First Amendment and privacy interests.[42] Trademark law's failure to penalize the knowing purchaser of a counterfeit product for merely using that product, however, even when third-party confusion is likely, is difficult to reconcile with the patent rule condemning all unauthorized sales. And while trademark law's refusal to punish the knowing giver of an infringing product (even when the recipient is likely to be confused) is similar to the patent rule under which mere gifts are not actionable, it nevertheless leaves the trademark owner with one less person to sue than would be the case under patent law, because the recipient's noncommercial use is actionable in patent but not in trademark law. Absent some meaningful distinction that has thus far eluded us, then, either the trademark or the patent rule may be efficient – but not both.

4. The Internet

In some respects, the Internet is pushing both copyright and trademark law towards the *de facto* adoption of something that resembles the patent rule in certain respects. In this section, we briefly explore how this change is coming about through the application of copyright law to cyberspace and in connection with domain name disputes in trademark law.

---

[40] The common wisdom is that this conduct is not actionable, largely for First Amendment reasons. See Restatement (Third) of Unfair Competition § 25 cmt. i; *cf.* 3 McCarthy (2001; § 24:76), where it was noted that "the law presently offers no legal remedies," but suggesting that "dilution doctrine might be available for this purpose."

[41] *Cf. Coca-Cola Co. v. Gemini Rising, Inc.*, 346 F. Supp. 1183 (E.D.N.Y. 1972), enjoining manufacturer from selling tee shirts blazoned with logo ENJOY COCAINE in style reminiscent of plaintiff's slogan ENJOY COCA-COLA.

[42] See, e.g., *Cohen v. California*, 403 U.S. 15 (1971) for a ruling that recognized the First Amendment right to publicly wear a shirt bearing the slogan "Fuck the Draft"); see Blair & Cotter (1998; 1692 & n.364) who speculated that the Lanham Act limits damages in dilution cases partly for First Amendment reasons; Denicola (1982; 190–206); but see Coombe (1991), who criticized trademark owners' efforts – sometimes successful – to prevent others' use of owners' symbols to communicate political or other messages.

The merits of applying traditional copyright principles to the Internet remain a matter of intense debate. For the past decade, advocates of expansive copyright protection have recommended a rather "literal" approach. In a 1993 report, for example, the U.S. National Information Infrastructure Task Force stated that a person who accesses a website makes a copy (as defined in the U.S. Copyright Act) of the site's content, because the text is fixed upon the random access memory (RAM) of her computer for "a period of more than transitory duration."[43] The viewer therefore infringes unless the copyright owner has authorized her access.[44] The logic of this position also suggests that when the recipient of an e-mail message forwards that message to another, she induces the other to make an unauthorized copy (and may be violating the owner's distribution right as well).[45] Even the display right – often dormant in the nonvirtual world, due to the first-sale doctrine – may be implicated because the sender, website owner, and Internet service provide (ISP) all (arguably) cause a public display of the work, as defined in the Copyright Act, by transmitting materials over the web.[46] Moreover, the widespread adoption of automated rights management (ARM) technology may allow content providers to monitor access to their websites and to restrict access to those who are willing to pay, regardless of whether the act of accessing the site is infringing.[47] In the United States, the Digital Millennium Copyright Act (DMCA), enacted in 1998, makes it easier for copyright owners to rely upon access restriction measures, by rendering the

---

[43] See National Information Infrastructure Task Force (1993; 64–6) (quoting 17 U.S.C. § 101). There is some case law that supports this position. See, e.g., *MAI Sys. Corp. v. Peak Computer, Inc.*, 991 F.2d 511, 519 (9th Cir. 1993).

[44] A person who properly accesses a website that contains no infringing material presumably would be viewed as having an implied license to view (and hence "copy" onto her RAM) that material. See, e.g., O'Rourke (1998; 655–62). But if the material found on the website is itself infringing, or if the viewer accesses it without proper authorization (by somehow bypassing the viewer monitoring system), access would infringe under the NII view.

[45] See Rowley (1998; 501 n.78). A transmittal that is not directed to the public at large constitutes a "distribution" only under the most expansive definition of that term, however.

[46] See Reese (2001). The Online Copyright Infringement Liability Limitation Act (OCILLA), enacted in 1998, reduces the potential liability of Internet service providers for merely acting as a "conduit" for the transfer of infringing material. See 17 U.S.C. § 512. Even absent OCILLA, ISPs sometimes would be immune from liability as direct or indirect infringers, depending on the facts, but the application of the direct and indirect liability rules in this context remains uncertain. For one court's analysis, see *Religious Tech. Center v. Netcom On-Line Comm. Servs.*, 907 F. Supp. 1361 (N.D. Cal. 1995).

[47] For discussion of ARMs and their effect on copyright, see, e.g., Bell (1998); Cohen (1998).

circumvention of these measures – and the sale of tools that could be used for circumvention – unlawful, even in some instances in which the end use would otherwise be protected as a fair use.[48]

One thing that is interesting about the preceding examples is that many nonelectronic equivalents of the activities at issue – such as privately reading copyrighted materials (whether lawfully copied or not), browsing through such materials (even in a public place, such as a bookstore or newsstand), or publicly distributing lawfully owned copies of literary works – do not infringe under current law. Rendering such uses infringing (or subject to enforceable pay-per-use contracts) in effect moves copyright law closer to the patent model and even beyond it to the extent that the first-sale doctrine does not apply to electronic forwarding. (Recall that, even under patent law, the lawful sale of a patented article exhausts the patentee's right to prevent the use and sale of that article.) As noted, these developments remain highly controversial. On the one hand, many of the objections we raise to the patent rule in the preceding section are attributable to transaction costs that may be minimal or nonexistent in the digital world; moreover, to the extent that the fair use exemption is based upon transaction costs, the need for that doctrine tends to disappear as those costs approach zero.[49] Opponents of an expansive digital copyright, on the other hand, contend that the economic arguments in favor of pay-per-use are incomplete[50] or that noneconomic considerations – including the First Amendment and privacy interests discussed earlier – counsel against the widespread "propertization"

---

[48] See 17 U.S.C. § 1201; *Universal City Studios, Inc. v. Corley*, 273 F.3d 429, 443–44 (2d Cir. 2001); *United States v. Elcom Ltd.*, 203 F. Supp. 2d 1111, 1125 (N.D. Cal. 2002). Commentators have voiced strong concerns about the potential impact of the DMCA upon First Amendment rights, but so far these arguments against application of the DMCA have been largely unavailing in court.

[49] See Bell (1998; 567–73). Bell does not believe that ARMs will eliminate the fair use defense altogether, however; the doctrine will continue to permit uses for which no market can be expected to exist, such as critical reviews. See *id.* at 592–6. And some critics argue that, while the Internet reduces some transaction costs, it increases others, so that arguments based on an assumed reduction of transaction costs must be taken with a grain of salt. See Burk (1999;145–63); Kitch (1999; 889–90).

[50] See, e.g., Cohen (1998) (arguing, *inter alia*, that the "cybereconomists" do not fully account for positive social benefits of fair use); Lunney (2001) who argues that private copying does not deter the production of popular works, and also serves a "civil disobedience" function; Netanel (1996; 337) for a discussion on an argument that "a broad proprietary copyright may lead to the mix of expression desired by those consumers who wish to buy expression, but it will draw resources away from nonexpressive productive activity, resulting in an inefficient allocation of social resources overall" (citations omitted).

of traditionally noninfringing uses.[51] Critics also note the heavy hand of the entertainment industry and other concentrated interest groups in shaping legislative responses to new technologies.[52]

The Internet is also arguably pushing trademark law toward the *de facto* adoption of the patent standard in a few respects. Outside the world of the Internet, it is common – and perfectly legal – for more than one firm to make use of the same trademark as long as there is no likelihood of confusion or dilution. Consider, for example, the concurrent use of the name PRINCE to identify a brand of spaghetti and a brand of tennis racket.[53] The Internet complicates matters, because under the system as it exists today there can be only one website with the address "prince.com" (although there can be multiple sites with slightly different addresses, such as "princespaghetti.com," "princeracket.com," and so on). A business that wants to use its mark as part of its website address, so that people who wish to access the site will be able to do so with little effort, therefore may find that the preferred domain name has already been assigned to someone else. On occasion, the "someone else" is a "cybersquatter" or "cyberpirate," a person who registers names (such as "panavision.com") in the hope of profiting by selling them back to the entities that use those names as trademarks.[54]

The use of trademarks as domain names has given rise to many disputes. In a few early decisions, courts sensibly held that the domain-name use of another's mark to market goods or services in a manner that is likely to give rise to confusion as to source or sponsorship constitutes trademark infringement.[55] In others, courts held that the defendant's use of a famous mark can give rise to a likelihood of dilution. In *Hasbro, Inc. v. Internet Entertainment Group, Ltd.*, for example, the plaintiff (maker of the popular

---

[51] See Netanel (1996; 372–3); Litman (1994; 43). Netanel argues in favor of a middle approach, under which copyright owners would be entitled to compensation for practices such as online browsing, subject to state regulation of user license fees. See Netanel (1996; 373–6).

[52] See Litman (1994; 53–4); see also Sterk (1996), who argues that a public-choice model explains much of copyright law's expansion in recent years.

[53] In fact, a domain name dispute did arise between Prince Sporting Goods, Inc. (makers of the famous tennis rackets) and a British computer company, Prince plc.

[54] For an early case dealing with this phenomenon, see *Panavision Int'l, L.P. v. Toeppen*, 141 F.3d 1316 (9th Cir. 1998).

[55] See, e.g., *Cardservice Int'l, Inc. v. McGee*, 950 F. Supp. 737 (E.D. Va. 1997) for a ruling that enjoins the defendant's use of "cardservice.com" as the name for a website advertising merchant card services, where the plaintiff had a superior right to mark CARDSERVICE for credit-card processing services.

children's game CANDYLAND) was able to enjoin the use of the name candyland.com in connection with a website featuring erotic photographs, on the ground that this use threatened to tarnish the wholesome nature of the mark.[56] In yet other cases, however, courts had to stretch to find a likelihood of confusion or dilution or, for that matter, any "commercial use" of the plaintiff's mark whatever. Although the need to engage in such creative readings of the trademark laws is less pressing now in light of the Anticybersquatting Consumer Protection Act and the Uniform Domain Name Resolution Policy,[57] the early case law remains on the books and may cause problems when applied in other contexts.

In *Intermatic Inc. v. Toeppen*, for example, the plaintiff, a manufacturer of programmable timers, filed suit against Dennis Toeppen, a squatter who operated several websites including one registered as "intermatic.com."[58] For a few days, Toeppen had used the site to advertise a software program he was planning to market under the name INTERMATIC. After Intermatic Inc. complained, however, Toeppen removed the ads and placed a map of Champaign-Urbana on the site instead. Intermatic nevertheless filed suit, alleging claims for trademark infringement and dilution in violation of the Lanham Act.[59] The court denied the plaintiff's motion for summary judgment on the infringement claim, on the ground that there were genuine issues of material fact as to likelihood of confusion, but granted the motion as to the dilution claim.[60] The result is dubious as a matter of trademark law for two reasons. First, it is questionable whether the plaintiff's mark was in fact the sort of "famous" mark that the federal dilution remedy was intended to protect – and imagine the consequences of routinely enjoining the concurrent, nonconfusing use of *non*famous marks.[61] Second, the court

---

[56] 40 U.S.P.Q.2d (BNA) 1479 (W.D. Wash. 1996).

[57] See Anticybersquatting Consumer Protection Act, 15 U.S.C. § 1125(d); ICANN, Uniform Domain Name Resolution Policy, at *http://www.icann.org/udrp/udrp-policy-24oct99.htm*.

[58] 947 F. Supp. 1227, 1229–30 (N.D. Ill. 1996). According to the opinion, Toeppen had registered approximately 240 domain names – including "deltaairlines.com," "eddiebauer.com," and "neiman-marcus.com" – all without permission of the firm that used the name as a trade or service mark. See *id.* at 1230.

[59] See *id.* at 1229, 1233.

[60] See *id.* at 1240–41.

[61] Toeppen did not dispute the fame of the mark. See id. at 1239. The court also asserted that the mark was "a strong fanciful federally registered mark, which has been exclusively used by Intermatic for over 50 years." *Id.* Strength and duration of use are factors that weigh in favor of a finding of fame under the Lanham Act. See 15 U.S.C. § 1125(c)(1)(A), (B). According to the Restatement (Third) of Unfair Competition, however, "a trademark is sufficiently distinctive to be diluted by a nonconfusing use if the mark retains its source significance when encountered outside the context of the goods or services with which the mark is

expressly found that Toeppen had *not* used the name in connection with the sale or advertising of any available goods or services,[62] despite the fact that the Lanham Act (and traditional trademark law as well) requires such a finding as a precondition to liability. Equally questionable is the holding of another case to which Toeppen was a party – this one involving his use of the name panavision.com for a website consisting of an aerial photograph of the town of Pana, Illinois – in which the court was willing to find "commercial use" in Toeppen's use of the website as a means by which he hoped to extract money from the trademark owner.[63] Although Toeppen arguably was engaged in the "business" of extortion, he was not selling extortion services *to others* under the PANAVISION (or any other) mark. But can the use of a mark in connection with a service that one provides exclusively to oneself qualify as a commercial use?

We think that the courts and, later, Congress and the Internet Corporation for Assigned Names and Numbers (ICANN) were right, as a matter of policy, to condemn cybersquatting. For one thing, the practice appears to generate needless transaction costs. In the *Intermatic* and *Panavision* examples noted previously, for example, it seems likely that Toeppen's only reason for operating websites under the names intermatic.com and panavision.com was to profit by selling the rights to those names back to the Intermatic and Panavision firms. Toeppen's use of the plaintiffs' marks, in other words, was not socially productive, but rather threatened to generate

---

used by the trademark owner." Restatement (Third) of Unfair Competition § 25 cmt. e (1995). An example would be KODAK, which "evokes an association with the cameras sold under that mark whether the word is displayed with cameras or simply appears alone." *Id.* Does INTERMATIC retain similar source significance when encountered on products other than electronic timers? For the matter, how many consumers were even aware that the INTERMATIC mark existed?

[62] See 947 F. Supp. at 1233.

[63] See Panavision Int'l, L.P. v. Toeppen, 141 F.3d 1316 (9th Cir. 1998), *aff'g* 938 F. Supp. 616 (C.D. Cal. 1996). The Ninth Circuit addressed the commercial use issue as follows:

Toeppen's "business" is to register trademarks as domain names and then sell them to the rightful trademarks owners. He "act[s] as a 'spoiler,' preventing Panavision and others from doing business on the Internet under their trademarked names unless they pay his fee." Panavision, 938 F. Supp. at 621. This is a commercial use. See Intermatic Inc. v. Toeppen, 947 F. Supp. 1227, 1230 (N.D. Ill. 1996) (stating that "[o]ne of Toeppen's business objectives is to profit by the resale or licensing of these domain names, presumably to the entities who conduct business under these names").

141 F.3d at 1324. Some cases, however, concluded that merely registering a domain name, without more, does not constitute actionable conduct under the Lanham Act. See, e.g., *Avery Dennison Corp. v. Sumpton,* 189 F.3d 868, 880 (9th Cir. 1999).

needless transactions.[64] Many people also seem to have an instinctive reaction that the practice is morally wrong, again perhaps because the cybersquatter's free-riding is not socially productive, but rather parasitical. The question nevertheless remains whether the practice is, technically, illegal under trademark law. The old adage that hard cases make bad law may come back to haunt us if the result of the cybersquatting cases is to dilute (no pun intended) the "commercial use" requirements for liability generally or the standards for finding infringement or dilution in particular. To put the matter another way, we might think twice before asking judges to condemn any unauthorized uses of trademarks that they happen to think are inefficient, if doing so requires a broad expansion of traditional trademark principles.

CONCLUSION

To the extent that patent law renders all parties within the chain of distribution, including unwitting consumers, liable for the unauthorized manufacture, use, or sale of patented inventions, it operates in a manner that may be contrary to the expectations of the average person. This outcome is tempered to some extent by the facts that (1) the first-sale doctrine exempts consumers and others within the chain as long as the first manufacture was authorized by the patent owner; (2) indirect liability requires some showing

---

[64] Professor David Friedman once suggested to one of us that cybersquatting *is* productive, because the cybersquatter helps to ensure that the name ultimately will be used by the person who accords it the highest value. Friedman analogized the cybersquatter to a land speculator who buys a plot of land in an area toward which a city is likely to expand. The speculator thereafter can auction the property off to the person who is willing to pay the most for it, i.e., the person who is able to put the property to its highest-valued use. Friedman argued that, in the absence of speculators, it might be more costly later on to develop the land for use as, say, a shopping center, because lower-value users (such as homeowners) may already have begun inhabiting the land. In the same way, a cybersquatter can facilitate the efficient uses of domain names by making sure that names are not appropriated by lower-value users, who might incur heavy switching costs if they subsequently were to transfer those names to higher-value users. Whatever the merits may be of Friedman's efficiency justification for speculation, however, we find it entirely unconvincing as applied to the practice of cybersquatting. For one thing, in many – probably most – of the cybersquatter cases that have arisen thus far it seems rather obvious who the highest-valued user of a given domain name happens to be. Who would be a higher-value user for the name panavision.com than the Panavision firm itself? Moreover, even if a good-faith user were to accidentally choose a name that is more highly valued by someone else – maybe the tennis racket company values the name "prince.com" more than the spaghetti people, the admirers of the Artist Formerly Known as Prince, or whoever else gets to it first – the potential cost of transferring the name to its highest-valued user do not seem at all comparable with the potential switching costs incurred in the land-use context.

of intent or knowledge on the part of the defendant; and (3) patent owners' self-interest often militates against filing suit against unwitting sellers
and users, particularly consumers. Sellers and users nevertheless are, technically, subject to liability whenever the first-sale doctrine does not apply.
Our analysis suggests that there is a plausible economic rationale for making commercial users and sellers liable, which is in order to ensure that the
patentee will be no worse off as a result of an infringing manufacture. In
this respect, the rule is consistent with our general thesis that patent rules
should have this effect. The extension of this rule to private noncommercial
uses, on the other hand, is more difficult to justify. This difficulty perhaps
explains why some other countries specifically exempt such uses from the
scope of patent liability.

The exemptions recognized under trade secret, copyright, and trademark
law, on the other hand, are largely consistent with what our model would
predict, although in the case of copyright and trademark law free speech considerations also probably play a role in limiting the scope of user liability. As
the Internet reduces transaction costs between users and owners, however,
and as new types of uses for copyrighted and trademarked materials prolif-
erate in the electronic environment, the long-standing distinctions between
patent, copyright, and trademark liability rules are becoming blurred. This
erosion of boundaries may have far-reaching consequences, not only for
electronic uses of intellectual property but also, to some extent, for more
traditional uses that, until now, have appeared to fall outside the scope of
the intellectual property owner's rights.

SEVEN

Who Should Be Entitled to Sue for Infringement?

In this chapter, we examine in some detail the question of standing and joinder – that is, of who is entitled to sue for patent, copyright, or trademark infringement.[1] This question, which is the flipside of the question we examined in the last chapter (who gets sued?), could be answered in a variety of ways, each of which could affect the originator's expected payoff and hence its *ex ante* incentives to create, publish, innovate, and invest in quality control. Although the answer might seem obvious – the owner of the IPR has the right to sue – a moment's reflection suffices to reveal that the question is more complicated. Is an assignor with some sort of ongoing interest in the IPR an "owner"? Does a licensee have a sufficient interest to file suit? If so, must the licensor join the suit? Should all licensees have the same rights or should they vary depending upon one's status as an exclusive or nonexclusive licensee? What exactly does it mean to *be* an exclusive licensee?

A simple – albeit somewhat fanciful – example may help to illustrate these issues. Suppose that a modern-day Dr. Frankenstein applies for a U.S. patent on his process for reanimating a dead body, as well as on the computer software he has used to implement the invention; that he registers his copyright on the software with the U.S. Copyright Office; and that he assigns his patents and copyrights to a corporate entity, Reanimators S.A. Reanimators in turn licenses an American company, Karloff, to provide reanimation

---

[1] In the United States, there is very little case law on the topic of standing to sue for trade secret misappropriation. The few cases that do exist generally follow the patent rules. This approach may make sense if, as we argue in this chapter, the patent rules are explainable in part due to the high risk of patent invalidation. Assertions of trade secret rights, like assertions of patent rights, are often vulnerable to invalidation in litigation. Indeed, merely filing suit for trade secret misappropriation creates some risk that the secret will leak out, even if it is subject to a protective order.

services in the United States using Frankenstein's patented inventions and copyrighted software under his now-famous trademark, FRANKENSTEIN. When Karloff learns of a rival U.S. company, offering similar reanimation services under a similar mark, it files suit in U.S. district court for patent, copyright, and trademark infringement. But is Karloff the appropriate plaintiff? Can it, or must it, join Frankenstein or Reanimators as co-plaintiffs? Does Karloff have any right to participate in the litigation?

As we shall see, the traditional rule in patent law is that only patent owners have "standing" to assert claims for patent infringement. An initial question, therefore, would be whether Reanimators has assigned, or only licensed, the patent to Karloff. An assignment would confer upon Karloff alone the right to sue; an exclusive license might confer upon Karloff a right to file suit, but only if the patent owner also joins; and a nonexclusive license would confer no right upon Karloff at all. Counterintuitively, an exclusive licensing arrangement might permit the *licensor* to initiate suit without necessarily joining the licensee – even though the licensor's rights might be much less economically significant than the licensee's. With respect to the copyright claim, on the other hand, Karloff has a right to file suit on its own initiative and does not necessarily have to join Reanimators or Frankenstein, as long as Karloff is an assignee or exclusive licensee. The fate of the trademark claim may depend upon exactly which statutory provision is at issue. Section 32 of the Lanham Act restricts standing to trademark registrants, but some courts have permitted even nonexclusive licensees to file suit under Lanham Act § 43(a). To further complicate matters, the Federal Rules of Civil Procedure may provide an independent basis for permitting, or requiring, joinder in some cases. At first glance, then, the standing rules in U.S. intellectual property law may appear as much a patchwork as Dr. Frankenstein's monster – and only marginally more coherent.

This chapter is divided into two main parts. In the first part, we present a more detailed overview of the rather complicated standing and joinder rules that apply in U.S. courts. We discuss some possible justifications for and critiques of these rules, and provide some possible reasons for the differences we observe in the way these three bodies of intellectual property law allocate the right to sue for infringement. In the second part, we fine-tune our analysis with some economic models of different assignment and licensing structures, focusing primarily on patents. On closer inspection, we conclude that the traditional rules are not quite as arbitrary and formalistic as they might initially appear to be; but they are at best only approximations for the optimal set of rules to be applied in different settings. We argue that courts and legislatures could improve upon the IP system by focusing more carefully on precisely how an act of infringement is likely to affect the various interests at stake; and that, armed with a better understanding of the economic consequences of infringement, courts would find that the rules of civil procedure provide them with sufficient tools for determining who should, and should not, be a party plaintiff in an infringement action. IP-specific "standing" rules may not be necessary or desirable after all.

STANDING AND JOINDER IN PATENT LAW

As a matter of history, the law of standing to sue for patent infringement has its roots in a series of nineteenth-century U.S. Supreme Court decisions interpreting the Patent Act as it existed at that time. The original U.S. Patent Act of 1790 contemplated that patent owners could assign their rights, and that in such instances the assignee would have standing to sue for patent infringement.[2] The 1793 Act further clarified that it was "lawful for any inventor, his executor or administrator to assign the title and interest in the said invention, at any time," and that "the assignee having recorded the said assignment in the office of the Secretary of State, shall thereafter stand in the place of the original inventor, both as to right and responsibility, and so the assignees of assigns, to any degree."[3] Early case law interpreted the 1793 Act to mean that a person who had been assigned something *less* than an undivided interest in the entire patent *lacked* standing to sue for infringement. In *Tyler v. Tuel*, for example, the Supreme Court held that a transfer of the exclusive right to make, use, and sell the patented invention throughout the entire United States, with the exception of four counties in the State of Vermont, was not an assignment, and that the plaintiffs, therefore, lacked standing to maintain the action in their own names.[4] The U.S. Congress overruled the narrow holding of *Tyler* when it enacted the Patent Act of 1830, which recognized the validity of geographically restricted, but otherwise undivided, patent assignments.[5] With this one modification, however, and subject to the exceptions noted below, the Supreme Court throughout the nineteenth century adhered to the general principle that patent rights were indivisible, such that only an "assignee" of the entire patent

---

[2]   See Patent Act of 1790, 1 Stat. 109–12, Chapter 7, §§ 1, 4.

[3]   Patent Act of 1793, 1 Stat. 318–23, Chapter 11, § 4.

[4]   See 10 U.S. (6 Cranch) 324–7 (1810).

[5]   See Patent Act of 1836, 5 Stat. 117, Chapter 357, § 11; see also *Moore v. Marsh*, 74 U.S. 515, 521 (1868). Similar provisions were included in the next major revision of the Patent Act in 1870 and in 1952, when the current version of the Patent Act went into effect.

had standing to sue for patent infringement; persons known as "licensees," who owned something less than an undivided interest in the entire patent, did not.[6]

The first clear statement of the policy behind the rule is found in Chief Justice Taney's opinion in *Gayler v. Wilder:*

> . . . it was obviously not the intention of the legislature to permit several monopolies to be made out of one, and divided among different persons within the same limits. Such a division would inevitably lead to fraudulent impositions upon persons who desired to purchase the use of the improvement, and would subject a party who, under a mistake as to his rights, used the invention without authority, to be harassed by a multiplicity of suits instead of one, and to successive recoveries of damages by different persons holding different portions of the patent right in the same place.[7]

As we shall see, Taney's concern over the possibility multiple liability remains valid, although it can be accommodated today within the framework of the Federal Rules of Civil Procedure, which govern all civil actions filed in U.S. district courts. Whether Taney's comment about making "several monopolies . . . out of one" suggests that he also had some notion that unrestricted licensing might allow the patentee to "leverage" his one monopoly into additional monopolies is unclear. As we discuss later in Chapter 8, antitrust scholars are often skeptical about the economic viability of claims of monopoly leveraging, but to the extent that the practice does occur it is remediable under contemporary antitrust laws and would not necessarily require any modifications to patent law. Taney's discussion also assumes that all patents are, in fact, monopolies, which is a position with which most modern economists would disagree.

The potential harshness of the patent indivisibility rule was nevertheless tempered by three exceptions which, in modified form, still exist today. The first was that a licensee could join with the patentee as a plaintiff in a suit in equity, at least in cases in which the court deemed this procedure necessary to protect the licensee's interest.[8] The second was that, while an action at law could be commenced only *in the name of the patentee*, the courts sometimes permitted the legal fiction of allowing the licensee to sue in the patentee's

---

[6] See, e.g., *Rude v. Westcott*, 130 U.S. 152, 162–3 (1889); *Birdsell v. Shaliol*, 112 U.S. 485, 486–7 (1884); *Hayward v. Andrews*, 106 U.S. 672, 675–6 (1883); *Paper-Bag Mach. Co. v. Nixon* (*Paper-Bag Cases*), 105 U.S. 766, 771 (1881); *Moore v. Marsh*, 74 U.S. 515, 520–2 (1868); *Gayler v. Wilder*, 51 U.S. 477, 494–5 (1850).

[7] *Gayler*, 51 U.S. (10 How.) 477, 494–5 (1850).

[8] See *Waterman v. Mackenzie*, 138 U.S. 252, 255 (1891); *Birdsell*, 112 U.S. at 486–7; 3 Robinson (1890; § 1098, at 420).

name and to recover his (the licensee's) actual damages.[9] A third exception allowed the licensee to sue in his own right in cases in which the patentee himself was accused of infringing rights granted under the license.[10]

The case that best summarizes these rules, and which U.S. courts still cite as controlling precedent, is *Waterman v. Mackenzie*.[11] In *Waterman*, the inventor had obtained a patent on an improvement for fountain pens and subsequently assigned the patent to his wife. Pursuant to a "license agreement," the wife then granted back to her husband "the sole and exclusive right and license to manufacture and sell fountain pen-holders, containing the said patented improvement, throughout the United States," in exchange for his promise of a twenty-cent royalty for each holder he manufactured. The wife subsequently assigned the patent to the firm of Asa L. Shipman's Sons (subject to the husband's license) in exchange for a loan, along with a promissory note made out by the couple in the amount of the loan, the agreement stating that if the couple paid off the loan within three years the assignment would be null and void. Two years later, while the loan remained outstanding, Mrs. Waterman assigned "all her right, title, and interest in the patent" back to her husband, who then commenced an infringement suit against Mackenzie and Murphy. The district court dismissed the action on the ground that Waterman lacked standing and the Supreme Court affirmed.

Writing for the Court, Justice Gray elaborated on the standing rules the Court had developed over the course of the preceding century:

The patentee or his assigns may, by instrument in writing, assign, grant, and convey, either (1) the whole patent, comprising the exclusive right to make, use, and vend the invention throughout the United States; or (2) an undivided part or share of that exclusive right; or (3) the exclusive right under the patent throughout a specified part of the United States. A transfer of either of these three kinds of interests is an assignment, properly speaking, and vests in the assignee a title in so much of the patent itself, with a right to sue infringers. In the second case, jointly with the assignor. In the first and third cases, in the name of the assignee alone. Any assignment or transfer, short of one of these, is a mere license, giving the licensee no title in the patent, and no right to sue at law in his own name for an infringement. In equity, as in law, when the transfer amounts to a license only, the title remains in the owner of the patent; and suit must be brought in his name, and never in the name of the licensee alone unless that is necessary to prevent an absolute failure of justice, as where the patentee is the infringer, and cannot sue himself. Any rights of the licensee must be enforced through or in the name of the owner of the patent,

---

[9] See *Independent Wireless Tel. Co. v. Radio Corp. of Am.*, 269 U.S. 459, 464–5 (1926); *Goodyear v. Bishop*, 10 F. Cas. 642, 644–6 (C.C.S.D.N.Y. 1861); 3 Robinson (1890; § 938, at 125).
[10] See *Littlefield v. Perry*, 88 U.S. 205, 223 (1874).
[11] 138 U.S. 252 (1891).

and perhaps, if necessary to protect the rights of all parties, joining the licensee with him as a plaintiff.[12]

The Court went on to state that "whether a transfer of a particular right or interest . . . is an assignment or a license does not depend upon the name by which it calls itself, but upon the legal effect of its provisions."[13] An example of an assignment would be "a grant of an exclusive right to make, use, and vend two patented machines within a certain district" that "gives the grantee the right to sue in his own name for an infringement within the district," because the grant "excludes all other persons, even the patentee, from making, using, or vending like machines within the district."[14] "On the other hand," the Court stated, "the grant of an exclusive right under the patent within a certain district, which does not include the right to make, *and* the right to use, *and* the right to sell, is not a grant of a title in the whole patent-right within the district, and is therefore only a license."[15] Examples of the latter would include "a grant of 'the full and exclusive right to make and vend' within a certain district, reserving to the grantor the right to make within the district, to be sold outside of it"; "a grant of 'the exclusive right to make and use,' but not to sell, patented machines within a certain district"; or a grant of " 'the sole right and privilege of manufacturing and selling' patented articles" which does not expressly authorize their use, "because, though this might carry by implication the right to use articles made under the patent by the licensee, it certainly would not authorize him to use such articles made by others."[16]

Applying these principles to the case, the Court concluded that the "license agreement" between the Watermans was, in fact, only a license, for while it granted the husband the exclusive right to make and sell his invention throughout the United States, it "did not include the right to use such pen-holders, at least if manufactured by third persons."[17] Mrs. Waterman therefore retained legal title to the patent until she transferred "all right, title and interest" in it to Asa L. Shipman's Sons (which, in turn, had assigned its rights to Asa Shipman himself). As a result, Shipman was the only person entitled to commence an action for infringement, despite the fact that he held the property as a mortgagee and his interest was subject to defeasance

[12] *Id.* at 255.
[13] See *id.* at 256.
[14] *Id.* at 256 (citing *Wilson v. Rousseau*, 45 U.S. 646, 686 (1846)).
[15] *Id.* (emphasis added).
[16] *Id.* (citations omitted).
[17] *Id.* at 257.

in the event the couple paid off its loan. The Court did not reach the issue of whether, in the event Shipman were to exercise his right to sue, the joinder of Mr. Waterman as a party would be necessary or desirable.

The Court appears not to have noticed two strange consequences of the rules it articulated in *Waterman*. The first is the tension between the Court's conclusion that Mrs. Waterman had assigned the patent subject to Mr. Waterman's exclusive license to make and sell the invention, and its suggestion that a transfer under which the patent owner herself retains rights against the transferee is merely a license.[18] The conclusion that a patent owner can assign a patent that is subject to outstanding third party licenses seems correct – otherwise these patents would be unassignable, and this would deter potentially efficient licensing or assignments or both – but the Court gives no reason why the result should be different if the license is held by the patent owner instead of by a third party.[19] Why couldn't Mrs. Waterman assign the patent to Mr. Waterman, subject to her own right to exclusive use? A second consequence is that the only right Shipman held, despite his status as the "assignee" of the patent, was the right to use the invention, because Mr. Waterman held a license to the exclusive rights to make and sell. Common sense would suggest that Waterman's exclusive rights were a more valuable asset than the one right held by Shipman (recall that Waterman could have sued Shipman for invading Waterman's rights), and yet it was Shipman, not Waterman, who held the right to initiate suit against third parties for infringing the patent.

Subsequent case law has continued to work out the implications of the rules discussed above. For example, the principle that "an assignment . . . vests in the assignee a title . . . with a right to sue infringers" has come to mean that an assignee (buyer) has standing to sue in response to infringements that take place after the assignment, but not before, because an infringement claim belongs to the person who owns the patent at the time the infringement takes place.[20] Under this principle, the assignor retains the right to sue for damages attributable to infringements that occurred prior to assignment but would lack standing to sue in response to those occurring afterward – though in fact some courts have stated that an assignor may at least intervene

---

[18] See *id.* at 256 (stating that "a grant of an exclusive right to make, use, and vend . . . is an assignment . . . because the right . . . excludes all other persons, *even the patentee*, from making, using, or vending like machines") (emphasis added).

[19] The parties might be able to work around this consequence, however, by having the patent owner assign the patent and then having the assignee license the assignor to continue some limited use of the patent – as Mr. Waterman did with respect to Mrs. Waterman.

[20] See *Crown Die & Tool Co. v. Nye Tool & Mach. Works*, 261 U.S. 24, 39–44 (1923).

in an action filed by the assignee, if the assignor still retains some interest in the patent or might otherwise be affected by the litigation.[21] The assignor also may transfer a claim for damages for pre-assignment infringements, but only if the transfer is express and is accompanied by an assignment of the underlying patent.[22] The upshot is that assigning your patent to someone else does not all by itself transfer any claims you may have for past infringements; merely transferring a claim for past infringements is ineffective, unless you also assign the patent.

A second implication of the standing rules is that courts often must determine whether a transfer is an assignment, in which case standing is conferred upon the transferee or a license, in which case it remains with the transferor. To this end, the courts try to "ascertain the intention of the parties and examine the substance of what was granted."[23] The parties' own description of the transfer as either a license or an assignment is not dispositive: courts have found agreements titled "licenses" to be assignments, and vice versa. Several factors may be relevant to the determination. First, a transfer is an assignment if it transfers "all substantial rights" in the patent[24] – including the right to exclude the patentee himself from making, using, and selling the invention – at least within a specific geographic area.[25] Second, an express transfer of the right to sue for infringement also suggests, but does not necessarily prove, that the agreement is an assignment.[26] Third, other factors may be relevant, including whether (1) the transferor expressly retains the right to bring suit for infringement; (2) he retains the right to prevent or limit the transferee's assignment of the patent to another;

---

[21] See *Hook v. Hook & Ackerman*, 187 F.2d 52, 59 (3d Cir. 1951); *Pennsalt Chems. Corp. v. Dravo Corp.*, 240 F. Supp. 837, 839–40 (E.D. Pa. 1965).

[22] See *Crown Die & Tool*, 261 U.S. at 41–3; *Arachnid, Inc. v. Merit Indus., Inc.*, 939 F.2d 1574, 1579 n.7 (Fed. Cir. 1991).

[23] *Vaupel Textilmaschinen KG v. Meccanica Euro Italia, S.p.A.*, 944 F.2d 870, 874 (Fed. Cir. 1991).

[24] *Id.*

[25] See *Waterman*, 138 U.S. at 256; *Abbott Lab. v Diamedix Corp.*, 47 F.3d 1128, 1131 (Fed. Cir. 1995). Although a geographically limited transfer of all substantial rights is deemed an assignment, a transfer that is limited in scope – for example, of all substantial rights with respect to one claim of a multiclaim patent – is not. See *Pope Mfg. Co. v. Gormully & Jeffery Mfg. Co.*, 144 U.S. 248, 249–52 (1892). Similarly, a transfer of the exclusive right to make, use, and sell the invention for one purpose (or "field of use") but not others is a license, see *Channel Master Corp. v. JFD Electronics Corp.*, 260 F. Supp. 568, 571–72 (E.D.N.Y. 1966), unless the field of use restriction is commensurate with all commercially viable uses of the patent, see *McNeilab, Inc. v. Scandipharm, Inc.*, No. 94-1508, 1996 WL 431352, at *2–3 (Fed. Cir. July 31, 1996), *rev'g* 862 F. Supp. 1351 (E.D. Pa. 1994).

[26] See *Vaupel*, 944 F.2d at 874–6; *Abbott Labs.*, 47 F.3d at 1132.

(3) the transfer is made subject to the rights of prior licensees.[27] All of these would tend to suggest that the transfer is a license, but may not be dispositive. Recall that the Court in *Waterman* described the transfer from Mrs. Waterman to Asa L. Shipman & Sons as an assignment, even though that transfer was subject to Mr. Waterman's exclusive license to make and sell the invention.[28] A third development emerged as courts began to recognize that some licensees have a greater interest than others in preventing third parties from infringing a patent. As previously noted, the early decisions acknowledged that in some instances a licensee might have a right to sue for damages in the patentee's name, or to join the patentee in a suit in equity. Over time, courts began to expressly restrict the enjoyment of these rights to "exclusive" licensees, and to deny them to the nonexclusive variety.[29] Courts today essentially follow the former equity practice, by allowing an exclusive licensee to sue, but (subject to an exception discussed below) only if he and his licensor are coplaintiffs; nonexclusive licensees, by contrast, lack standing to sue either alone or in conjunction with their licensors.[30]

The best articulation of the distinction between exclusive and nonexclusive licenses, and of the reason for treating them differently, is found in a 1930 decision of the U.S. Court of Appeals for the Second Circuit, *Western Electric Co. v. Pacent Reproducer Corp.*[31] Defining a nonexclusive license as one that "grants to the licensee merely a privilege that protects him from a claim of infringement by the owner of a patent monopoly," such that the patentee "may freely license others, or may tolerate infringers," the court reasoned that a nonexclusive licensee lacks standing because infringement does not cause him to suffer any legal injury (though he may suffer some pecuniary loss).[32] On the other hand, the court recognized that "a license to practice the invention may be accompanied by the patent owner's promise

---

[27] See *Abbott Lab.*, 47 F.3d at 1132–3.

[28] Other factors might seem more consistent with a license than with an assignment, but are not necessarily inconsistent with a characterization of the transfer as an assignment. These include: (1) the transferor's retention of the right to veto the transferee's choice of sublicensees; (2) the transferor's right to receive royalties on sales made by the transferee; (3) the fact that the patent may revert to the transferor upon the occurrence of specified conditions; and (4) the inclusion of a provision conferring upon the transferor the right to receive a portion of any damages the transferee recovers in an infringement action. See *Rude v. Westcott*, 130 U.S. 152, 162–3 (1889); *Vaupel*, 944 F.2d at 875.

[29] See *Overman Cushion Tire Co. v. Goodyear Tire & Rubber Co.*, 59 F.2d 998, 1000 (2d Cir. 1932); *Deitel v. Chisholm*, 42 F.2d 172, 173 (2d Cir. 1930); *Western Elec. Co. v. Pacent Reproducer Corp.*, 42 F.2d 116 (2d Cir. 1930).

[30] See *Abbott Lab.*, 47 F.3d at 1131.

[31] 42 F.2d 116 (2d Cir. 1930).

[32] *Id.* at 118.

that others shall be excluded from practicing it within the field of use wherein the licensee is given leave" and that in such a case the licensee "is obviously prejudiced by an infringement of the patent, for the patentee's sufferance of an unauthorized practice of an invention is as harmful to his promisee as would be the grant of a license in direct violation of the contract."[33] Under these circumstances, "the licensee . . . must have the right of joinder in a suit to restrain infringement, or of suing in the patentee's name if the patentee refuses to join in the litigation.[34] Distinguishing between exclusive and nonexclusive licensees therefore is a matter of substance, not form:

> The definition of an exclusive license . . . might be thought to imply that an "exclusive licensee" is a sole licensee. But we do not so understand it. A bare license might be outstanding in one when the patent owner grants a license to another accompanied by the promise that the grantor will give no further licenses. In such a case, the second licensee needs the protection of the right of joinder in a suit against infringers as much as though he were the sole licensee.[35]

Modern courts continue to follow this approach, stating that a licensee may join an action commenced by the licensor – and may recover damages for his own losses attributable to the infringement – but only when the licensor has promised the licensee exclusive rights.[36]

To state that an exclusive licensee has standing to join an action commenced by his licensor naturally raises the question of how the licensee can protect himself when his licensor is unwilling to file suit. The Supreme Court had addressed that question, however, just a few years prior to *Western Electric* in *Independent Wireless Telegraph Co. v. Radio Corp. of America.*[37] At issue in *Independent Wireless* were two patents owned by DeForest Radio Telephone & Telegraph Company (DeForest) and subject to an exclusive license for the benefit of Radio Corporation of America (RCA). DeForest having refused to join in an infringement suit against Independent Wireless Telegraph Company, RCA filed suit on its own and named DeForest as an *involuntary* plaintiff. The Supreme Court had to decide if this novel procedure was permissible. Reading the Patent Act as requiring the patentee to be a party to any action for infringement, the Court first brushed aside the

---

[33] *Id.*
[34] *Id.*
[35] *Id.* at 119.
[36] See *Textile Productions, Inc. v. Mead Corp.*, 134 F.3d 1481, 1484 (Fed. Cir. 1998); *Weinar v. Rollform Inc.*,744 F.2d 797, 807 (Fed. Cir. 1984). Note that an agreement promising to protect the patent against infringement, but not limiting the number of authorized licensees, appears to be viewed as a nonexclusive license. See Strickland (1998; 582–3).
[37] 269 U.S. 459 (1926).

suggestion that an exclusive licensee should be able to sue for an injunction or damages without bothering to join the patentee. Nevertheless, the Court agreed that the licensee must have a way of forcing the patentee into the litigation, stating that the latter "holds the title to the patent in trust for such a licensee [and] must allow the use of his name as plaintiff in any action brought at the instance of the licensee . . . for the injury to his exclusive right."[38] Thus, "[i]f the owner of a patent, being within the jurisdiction, refuses or is unable to join an exclusive licensee as coplaintiff, the licensee may make him a party defendant by process, and he will be lined up by the court in the party character which he should assume."[39] Alternatively, if the patentee is outside the jurisdiction (as was the case here), and therefore not amenable to service of process, the licensee may join the patentee as an involuntary plaintiff – though only after he has declined a request to join voluntarily. Moreover, the Court noted, as an involuntary plaintiff the patentee who is aware of the action and of his obligation to join it would be bound by any judgment in the case, whether he chose to participate or not. On this basis, the Court affirmed the involuntary joinder of DeForest.[40]

Waterman and *Independent Wireless* appear to remain good law in the United States, although the matter may not entirely settled. A few courts have suggested that the Federal Rules of Civil Procedure, enacted in 1938, partially displace *Waterman* and – perhaps – *Independent Wireless* as well.[41] Because this position overlaps to some extent with our own, we shall examine it in some detail, even though it remains for now a minority view among the courts. Our principal focus will be on Federal Rule 19.[42]

---

[38] *Id.* at 469.

[39] *Id.* at 468. Lining the defendant up "in the party character he should assume" means that, for example, if the licensee and licensor are both citizens of State A, and the defendant of State B, joining the licensor as a party defendant will not defeat the court's exercise of diversity jurisdiction. See 7 Wright et al. (2002; § 1605, at 69–70). It is not clear, however, why this procedure would matter in a patent infringement case, which is supported by federal question jurisdiction.

[40] See *Independent Wireless*, 269 U.S. at 475.

[41] See, e.g., *Parkson Corp. v. Fruit of the Loom Inc.*, 28 U.S.P.Q.2d (BNA) 1066, 1068–70 (E.D. Ark. 1992), which concluded that Rule 19 displaces *Independent Wireless*); *Rainville Co. v. Consupak, Inc.*, 407 F. Supp. 221, 223 (D.N.J. 1976), which concluded that Rule 19 displaces *Waterman*); *Catanzaro v. International Tel. & Tel. Corp.*, 378 F. Supp. 203, 208–9 (D. Del. 1974); *Tycom Corp. v. Redactron Corp.*, 380 F. Supp. 1183, 1185–91 (D. Del. 1974). Even those courts that continue to apply *Waterman* and *Independent Wireless*, however, sometimes conduct a Rule 19 analysis as well. See, e.g., *Abbott Lab.*, 47 F.3d at 1130–3; *Pfizer Inc. v. Elan Pharmaceutical*, 812 F. Supp. at 1370–5; *Micro-Acoustics Corp. v. Bose Corp.*, 493 F. Supp. 356, 359–61 (S.D.N.Y. 1980).

[42] Several provisions of the Federal Rules of Civil Procedure deal with the issue of who is a proper party to a civil action. Rule 17(a) provides that "[e]very action shall be prosecuted

As originally enacted, Rule 19 created a two-step procedure for determining whether a person should be made a party to an action and, if so, how the court should respond to his nonjoinder. First, Rule 19(a) stated that, subject to the limitations set forth in Rule 19(b) and in Rule 23 (relating to class actions), "persons having a joint interest shall be made parties and be joined on the same side as plaintiffs or defendants," and that if "a person who should join as a plaintiff refuses to do so, he may be made a defendant or, in proper cases, an involuntary plaintiff."[43] With regard to the latter, the Advisory Committee Notes to the rule cited *Independent Wireless* as an "example of a proper case for involuntary plaintiff."[44] Second, Rule 19(b) advised that if such a person was "not indispensable" and he "ought to be [a] part[y] if complete relief is to be accorded between those already parties," the court should order him to be summoned to appear in the action, if he was subject to service and his presence in the action would not deprive the court of jurisdiction or venue.[45] Alternatively, if the person was not subject to process or his presence would defeat jurisdiction or venue, the court in its discretion could proceed without making him a party.[46] By negative implication, if the person was "indispensable" and could not be made a party due to service, jurisdiction, or venue problems, the court was required to dismiss the action.

In response to criticism over the rule's confusing terminology, as well as the absence of written guidelines for the exercise of judicial discretion under Rule 19(b), the Supreme Court in 1966 approved a substantial revision of the

in the name of the real party in interest," thus abolishing the type of legal fiction to which courts sometimes had resorted to allow exclusive licensees to file an action at law in the name of the patentee. Rules 19 and 20 address the issue of which persons may or must be joined as parties to an action. More specifically, Rule 19, the mandatory joinder provision, addresses the twin issues of which persons must be joined as parties when their joinder is feasible, and how the court should proceed when their joinder is not feasible due to problems of jurisdiction or venue. Rule 20 then sets forth the circumstances under which certain other persons may join the action either as plaintiffs or defendants. Rules 22, 23, 23.1, and 23.2 deal with the joinder of parties in a variety of specialized procedures, including interpleader and class actions. Rule 24 allows certain other interested persons to intervene in an action, either as a matter of right or by permission of the court, whereas Rule 25 provides for the substitution of parties in the event of death, incompetency, transfer of interest, or separation from office of a public official. Finally, Rule 12(b)(7) authorizes the court to dismiss an action for failure to join a party under Rule 19, whereas Rule 21 cautions that *mis*joinder (as opposed to *non*joinder) is not a ground for dismissal and that the court may drop or add parties "at any stage of the action and on such terms as are just."

[43] FED. R. CIV. P. 19(a) (1938 version).

[44] FED. R. CIV. P. 19 advisory committee's note (1938 version).

[45] FED. R. CIV. P. 19(b) (1938 version).

[46] See *id.*

rule. In its present form, Rule 19(a), titled "Persons to be Joined if Feasible," reads as follows:

A person who is subject to service of process and whose joinder will not deprive the court of jurisdiction over the subject matter of the action shall be joined as a party to the action if (1) in the person's absence complete relief cannot be accorded among those already parties, or (2) the person claims an interest relating to the subject of the action and is so situated that the disposition of the action in the person's absence may (i) as a practical matter impair or impede the person's ability to protect that interest or (ii) leave any of the persons already parties subject to a substantial risk of incurring double, multiple, or otherwise inconsistent obligations by reason of the claimed interest. If the person has not been so joined, the court shall order that the person be made a party. If the person should join as a plaintiff but refuses to do so, the person may be made a defendant, or, in a proper case, an involuntary plaintiff. If the joined party objects to venue and joinder of that party would render the venue of the action improper, that party shall be dismissed from the action.

Rule 19(b) goes on to state that if the person described in the preceding paragraph "cannot be made a party, the court shall determine whether in equity and good conscience the action should proceed among the parties before it, or should be dismissed, the absent person being thus regarded as indispensable."

The rule then lists four factors the court should consider in determining whether a person is indispensable. These are: (1) the extent to which "a judgment rendered in the person's absence might be prejudicial to the person or those already parties"; (2) "the extent to which, by protective provisions in the judgment, by the shaping of relief, or other measures, the prejudice can be lessened or avoided"; (3) "whether a judgment rendered in the person's absence will be adequate"; and (4) "whether the plaintiff will have an adequate remedy if the action is dismissed for nonjoinder." Emphasizing the "pragmatic" and "practical" thrust of the amended Rule 19, the Supreme Court in *Provident Tradesmens Bank & Trust Co. v. Patterson* (a non-patent case) stated that a court applying the rule should avoid "undue preoccupations with abstract classifications of rights or obligations."[47] Instead, the court should focus on "factors varying with the different cases, some such factors being substantive, some procedural, some compelling by themselves, and some subject to balancing against opposing interests," "examin[ing] each controversy to make certain" that the purported interests at stake really exist.[48]

---

[47] 390 U.S. 102, 116 n.12 (1968) that quoted FED. R. CIV. P. 19 advisory committee's note (1966 version).

[48] *Id.* at 119.

A few courts have concluded that Rule 19 abolishes *Waterman*'s categorical approach to standing in preference for a more open-ended inquiry. For example, in *Tycom Corp. v. Redactron Corp.*,[49] an alleged infringer moved to dismiss on the ground that the plaintiff Tycom had failed to join an indispensable party: the patent owner, Holmes. Concluding that Rule 19 has shifted the focus away from the "per se *Waterman* test," the court determined, first, that Holmes was a person who should be joined if feasible, because he held legal title to the patent and his agreement with Tycom entitled him to royalties and to half of all damages recovered in any infringement action.[50] Second, the court stated that "no showing has been made . . . that Holmes is subject to service of process of this Court";[51] it did not address whether the involuntary plaintiff procedure might apply, however. Third, the court considered whether the action could proceed "in equity and good conscience" absent Holmes, noting (among other things) the costs associated with multiple litigation, and the fact that Tycom would not be prejudiced if the action were dismissed because its contract gave it the right to force Holmes to participate in any patent litigation.[52]

The more difficult question with regard to "equity and good conscience" was whether Holmes's absence would prejudice either the defendant or Holmes himself, in light of applicable principles of collateral estoppel. The general rule followed by the federal courts is that an issue decided on the merits in one action will be binding against a person who was a party to that action, or someone in privity with him, in a subsequent action.[53] Thus, if a patentee files suit against Defendant A but the court determines that the patent is invalid, the judgment of invalidity would be binding in a subsequent suit between the patentee and Defendant B. In this instance, the issue was whether Tycom and Holmes were so closely allied that an adverse judgment would be binding against Holmes in future litigation. While not conclusively resolving this issue, the court believed there was a "strong probability" that the two were in privity, given their "concurrent interest" in the same property and the fact that their agreement purported to grant Tycom the right to

---

[49] 380 F. Supp. 1183 (D. Del. 1974).
[50] See *id.* at 1187–8.
[51] *Id.* at 1188.
[52] See *id.* at 1190.
[53] See, e.g., *Parklane Hosiery Co. v. Shore*, 439 U.S. 322, 326–33 (1979); *Blonder-Tongue Labs. v. University of Ill. Found.*, 402 U.S. 313, 320–7, 349–50 (1971). In *Blonder-Tongue* – itself a patent case – the Court abandoned the "mutuality of estoppel" requirement under which collateral estoppel would not apply "unless both parties (or their privies) in the second action are bound by a judgment in the prior case."

sue, at its sole discretion, for any infringement of the patent. Nevertheless, the possibility that a future court might disagree left open the possibility that the defendant might prevail in the present action, only to have to defend itself again in a subsequent suit by the patentee.[54] Holmes himself, on the other hand, might be prejudiced if collateral estoppel *did* apply to an unfavorable judgment rendered in his absence. And even if collateral estoppel did not apply, the stare decisis effect of the first action might be adverse to his interests. Perceiving no obvious way to eliminate the potential prejudice to either Holmes or the defendant, the court dismissed the action – interestingly, the same result it would have reached under the "per se" *Waterman* rule.[55]

A few courts also have concluded that a literal reading of amended Rule 19(a) affects the *Independent Wireless* rule that allows an exclusive licensee to join his licensor as an involuntary plaintiff.[56] As noted earlier, Rule 19(a) states that "If the person should join as a plaintiff but refuses to do so, the person may be made a defendant, or, in a proper case, an involuntary plaintiff." The antecedent of the word "person" appears to be the first words of the rule, namely "[a] person who is subject to service of process;" and if so read, the amended rule would preclude a licensee from forcing a licensor who is beyond the court's jurisdiction to participate in the suit. On the other hand, the rule clearly contemplates the continued vitality of an involuntary plaintiff rule, and this rule would be unnecessary if it applied only to persons subject to the court's jurisdiction: these parties could be made involuntary *defendants* instead, and simply "lined up by the court in the party character which [they] should assume."[57] Other courts and commentators have rejected the literal interpretation, though without extended analysis of why it is wrong.[58]

The Rule 19 issues discussed in the preceding paragraphs normally arise at the instigation of an alleged infringer who is urging the court to dismiss

---

[54] See *Tycom*, 380 F. Supp. at 1189–90.

[55] See *id.* at 1190–91.

[56] See *Parkson Corp. v. Fruit of the Loom Inc.*, 28 U.S.P.Q.2d (BNA) 1066, 1068–70 (E.D. Ark. 1992); *Catanzaro v. Int'l Tel. & Tel. Corp.*, 378 F. Supp. 203, 209 (D. Del. 1974); Heines (1976; 249–51) who argues that Rule 19 modifies *Independent Wireless*. The *Catanzaro* court also questioned the constitutionality of a rule that would render a judgment binding against a party who is beyond the court's jurisdiction. See 378 F. Supp. at 209.

[57] *Independent Wireless*, 269 U.S. at 468.

[58] See *Joy Technologies, Inc. v. Flakt, Inc.*, No. 93–1419, 1995 WL 408631, at *1 n.3 (Fed. Cir. Oct. 11, 1995) that states amended Rule 19(a) "did not fundamentally change the meaning of the term 'involuntary plaintiff'"; 4 Moore et al. (2002; ¶ 19.04[4][b], at 19–77 to –78); 7 Wright et al. (2002; § 1606, at 72–4).

the action for failure to join the patent owner. On occasion, however, the issue arises whether Rule 19 requires the joinder of the exclusive *licensee* in an action filed by the patent owner. Although the exclusive licensee is clearly a proper party, the courts have reached varying conclusions as to whether he is someone who should be joined if joinder is feasible under Rule 19(a), and whether he is someone in whose absence the litigation should not proceed.[59] When an assignee or a licensee *wants* to join an action, Federal Rules 20 or 24 may come into play instead. Rule 20 provides for the permissive joinder of persons as plaintiffs if, among other things, they assert some common right to relief. Although there is little case law on point, it seems reasonably clear that Rule 20 would be the proper vehicle for the exclusive licensee to join the patentee in an infringement action.[60] And there are a few cases stating that an assignor who retains some interest in a patent (for example, a reversionary interest) may intervene pursuant to Rule 24.

A final aspect of the *Waterman* line of cases involves the issue of whether the parties to an assignment or licensing agreement can modify or waive the standing rules discussed above. Not surprisingly, the courts have held that parties cannot create standing by agreement; thus, a provision that purports to give a nonexclusive licensee a right to sue for future infringements would be void.[61] Similarly, as we have noted, a patent owner cannot transfer a right to sue for past infringements absent an assignment of the patent itself. Whether an exclusive licensee's purported waiver of his right to join in an infringement action is enforceable is less clear. One recent decision from the Federal Circuit suggests in dicta that it is not, although there are other possible interpretations of the court's rather cryptic comment.[62] A nonwaivable right, however, may be more consistent with the statement in *Independent Wireless* that the licensor "holds title to the patent in trust for such a licensee [and] must allow the use of his name as plaintiff in any

---

[59] See *Independent Wireless*, 269 U.S. at 466 describing the licensor and exclusive licensee as "generally necessary parties in the action in equity"; *In-Tech Marketing Inc v. Hasbro, Inc.*, 685 F. Supp. 436, 438–41 (D.N.J. 1988).

[60] See 7 Wright et al. (2002; § 1656, at 424).

[61] See *Textile Productions*, 134 F.3d at 1485.

[62] See *Ortho Pharmaceutical*, 52 F.3d at 1034 that states "a licensee with sufficient proprietary interest in a patent has standing regardless of whether the licensing agreement so provides." Although a broad interpretation of this sentence would suggest that the licensee's right to sue is not waivable, the court may only have meant that the exclusive licensee has standing, regardless of whether the contract purports to confer this right upon him or not. See Lee et al. (1997; 22–5). Lee et al. claim that the "narrow reading preserves the long-standing assumption between licensors and licensees that right to sue clauses are a valid means to regulate, and even deny, litigation rights between them." *Id.*

action brought at the instance of the licensee . . . for the injury to his exclusive right."[63]

A number of arguments can be (and have been) made to justify the standing rules described above. One is that the Patent Act itself authorizes suit only in the name of the patentee or a "successor in title," and that a licensee, being neither, therefore lacks standing. This argument is not particularly compelling, however, given the act's lack of a definition of the term "successor in title" and the courts' longstanding practice of allowing exclusive licensees to sue, as long as they join their licensors. And even if the argument were persuasive as a matter of statutory interpretation, it would still beg the question of whether the Patent Act itself is right to limit the standing of licensing. A better argument might be that infringement causes exclusive licensees to suffer legal injury but has no effect upon nonexclusive licensees for reasons discussed in *Western Electric*; but this insight sheds no light on why exclusive licensees are forbidden to sue alone.

There nevertheless may be some good reasons for qualifying the licensee's right to sue. In an often-quoted passage, Learned Hand noted two of them – namely, the patentee's interest in choosing his own forum, and concerns over multiple litigation involving the same patent:

> It is indeed true that a mere licensee may have an interest at stake in such a suit; his license may be worth much more to him than the royalties which he has agreed to pay, and its value will ordinarily depend on his ability to suppress the competition of his rivals. The reason why he is not permitted to sue is not because he has nothing to protect. But against that interest is the interest of the infringer to be immune from a second suit by the owner of the patent; and also the interest of the patent owner to be free to choose his forum – the same interest which exists here. Indeed, the owner may have granted a number of licenses, and it would be exceedingly oppressive to subject him to the will of all his licensees. These two interests in combination have been held to overweigh any interest of the licensee. . . . [64]

Of course, one might question whether these concerns really do "overweigh" the exclusive licensee's interest in protecting the value of his license. Deferring to the patentee's choice of forum in particular might not seem terribly important until we take into account the likelihood that the alleged infringer will raise the affirmative defense of patent invalidity and that he may succeed on that defense. Until recently, the invalidity defense was successful in about 65% of the reported patent decisions in which it was raised, and in

---

[63] *Independent Wireless*, 269 U.S. at 469; see also *Ethicon, Inc. v. United States Surgical Corp.*, 135 F.3d 1456, 1468 n.9 that states the licensor "stands in a relationship of trust to his licensee and must permit the licensee to sue in his name."

[64] *A.L. Smith Iron Co. v. Dickson*, 141 F.2d 3, 6 (2d Cir. 1944).

some circuits it succeeded as often as 90% of the time.[65] Even today, after the consolidation of all patent appeals within the relatively patent-friendly confines of the Federal Circuit, a substantial plurality of all litigated patents are declared invalid.[66] Nor is it difficult to imagine that in some instances the licensee might be tempted to *provoke* litigation in the hope that the patent will be declared invalid, thus freeing the licensee from the obligation to continue paying royalties to the licensor.[67] This possibility goes a long way toward explaining why the patentee is an indispensable party to infringement litigation.

Similarly, one might question the multiple litigation rationale on the ground that a person whose conduct tortiously harms two or more parties normally should be subject to suit by either or both of them. Moreover, if the patentee and the licensee were to file separate suits, each would be entitled to recover only his own lost profit or royalty, but presumably not any damages accruing to one another – thus precluding the possibility of duplicative recoveries. But neither of these objections is very persuasive. With regard to the first, it is certainly not unusual to compel commonly injured parties to litigate together, for reasons of economy and consistency; to this end, we have not only the Federal Rules relating to mandatory joinder of parties and intervention, but also such mechanisms as class actions and consolidation. Requiring the joinder of licensee and patentee is not inconsistent with procedures of this nature. Furthermore, patent litigation is very costly.[68] As the Supreme Court suggested in *Blonder-Tongue*, a defendant who is subject to successive lawsuits may bear a disproportionate part of the total cost, because in each action the patent initially will be presumed valid and the defendant will bear the burden of overcoming this presumption by clear and convincing evidence. Rather than beat back successive challenges, then, the defendant might find it more cost-effective simply to give up and purchase a license from the patent owner.[69] But if, in fact, the patent is invalid (meaning, more or less, that the Patent Office erred in concluding

---

[65] See Allison & Lemley (1998; 191–2 & nn. 11, 12; 206 & n.53).

[66] See *id.* at 205–7; Moore (2000; 391); *supra* p. 2–6 n.11.

[67] This possibility of opportunistic behavior on the part of the licensee probably should not be overemphasized, however; after all, the licensee *himself* can challenge the validity of the patent. See *Lear, Inc. v. Adkins*, 395 U.S. 653, 669–71 (1969) for a rejection of the doctrine of "licensee estoppel," under which the licensee was precluded from challenging the validity of the patent in a suit between the licensee and its licensor.

[68] See AIPLA (2003; 21–2) where it was found that the average cost through trial of a patent infringement ranged from $500,000 to almost $4 million, depending upon the amount of money at stake.

[69] See *Blonder-Tongue*, 402 U.S. at 335–48.

that the invention satisfied all of the patentability requirements), then the social costs flowing from the licensee's acceptance of the patentee's exclusive rights would seem to outweigh the social benefits.[70] These fears will not be realized if collateral estoppel bars the second action; but the issue of whether collateral estoppel applies in a second action filed by the licensor remains unsettled. And if collateral estoppel *does* apply, the patentee who is absent from the first suit may be prejudiced by a judgment of invalidity entered in his absence.

The objection based upon the nonavailability of duplicative recoveries is weak for similar reasons. First, unless collateral estoppel applies to the second action, there is no guarantee that Court Number One and Court Number Two will assess damages in a consistent manner. And even if collateral estoppel does apply there may be problems, as the following example shows. Suppose, for simplicity, that the licensee and infringer face the same marginal cost curves for the production of the patented item; that the licensee suit proceeds to trial first; and that the licensee recovers, as his damages, a reasonable royalty equal to 100% of the net profits earned from the defendant's sales of infringing merchandise. If the licensee's contract requires him to pay his licensor 50% of his *own* net profits earned from sales of licensed merchandise, he is actually better off as a result of the infringement, unless the contract also requires him to share his damages with his licensor. On the other hand, if the contract does not require sharing, the licensor will argue in the second action that he is entitled to recover 50% of the infringer's profits; an award in this amount, however, will subject the defendant to multiple damages for the same offense. Court Number One, of course, could take these factors into account in setting damages in the first action (by reducing the licensor's damages by 50%), but even so it seems much more efficient simply to join licensor and licensee as parties in one single action.

On the basis of our analysis thus far, a few aspects of the standing rules in patent law – including the rule requiring the exclusive licensee to join his licensor, and the practice some courts have followed of allowing an assignor who retains some interest in the patent to intervene – seem eminently sound. A few others, such as the rule precluding nonexclusive licensees from participating in infringement suits, also may seem persuasive, although (as we discuss later) the logic of cases such as *Western Electric* is not quite as airtight as it might at first. Yet other problems are not clearly resolved by

[70] But see Dreyfuss (1986; 681, 745–6 & n.244) who argues that the effect of *Blonder-Tongue* could be to induce inventors to protect their inventions as trade secrets rather than to seek patent protection and to deter innovation by making patent protection risky.

the standing rules, including not only definitional issues (how much of a commitment to protect the patent is necessary on the part of the patentee in order for the license to be deemed exclusive?) but also the issue of whether the licensor must join his exclusive licensee to an action for infringement. Finally, nothing we have discussed thus far directly addresses the merits of the rule that a geographically restricted assignee has standing to sue without joining his assignor.

COPYRIGHTS

Until fairly recently, U.S. courts took the position that copyrights, like patents, were indivisible, meaning that the copyright owner, like the patent owner, could assign only an undivided interest in her property; a transfer of anything less than an undivided interest in the entire copyright was a license, not an assignment. As a result of this emphasis on indivisibility, copyright courts followed the same standing rules as did courts in patent cases: assignees had standing to sue for copyright infringement without joining their assignors; exclusive licensees also could sue, but only if they joined the copyright owner; an exclusive licensee could join the copyright owner against her will as a defendant or, in a proper case, as an involuntary plaintiff; a licensor could sue without necessarily joining his exclusive licensee; and nonexclusive licensees had no standing to sue at all.[71]

As Nimmer and Nimmer have noted, however, the indivisibility rule eventually proved disadvantageous to copyright owners:

When the doctrine of indivisibility was first enunciated the only effective manner in which copyrighted materials could be exploited was through the reproduction of copies. Hence no great hardship resulted from the doctrine that limited assignments to transfers of all rights under the copyright because there was little incentive to reserve rights other than the reproduction right. The subsequently developed media of communications completely altered this situation. Today the value of motion picture rights in a novel will often far exceed the value of the right to publish the work in book form. Moneys derived from performing and recording popular songs are greatly in excess of the value of "copying" such songs in sheet music form.... [A]s a matter of commercial reality, "copyright" is now a label for a collection of diverse indivisibility rights each of which is separately marketable. The doctrine of

---

[71] See 2 Goldstein (2002; § 13.5, at 13:35 n.5, 13:36 n.6; § 13.5.1.2, at 13:41 n.28); 3 Nimmer (2002; § 10.01[A], at 10–6; § 10.01[C][1], at 10–12 to –13; § 12.02[A], at 12–51 to –52). The copyright rules may have been even more restrictive than the patent rules, insofar as there was some case law suggesting that a transfer of all of the exclusive rights to a copyright was not an assignment if it was limited to a specific geographic area. See Nimmer (2002; § 10.01[B], at 10–8 to –9).

indivisibility did not prevent commercial dealings in such separate rights, but it greatly impeded such dealings, and produced technical pitfalls for both buyers and sellers.[72]

In response to these perceived inadequacies, Congress abolished the copyright indivisibility rule when it enacted the Copyright Act of 1976. Several provisions of the current act reflect this abolition.

First, under § 101, a "transfer of copyright ownership" is defined as "an assignment, mortgage, exclusive license, or any other conveyance, alienation or hypothecation of copyright or of any of the exclusive rights comprised in a copyright, whether or not it is limited in time or place of effect, but not including a nonexclusive license."[73] This section also defines a "copyright owner, with respect to any one of the exclusive rights comprised in a copyright," as "the owner of that particular right."[74] To be effective, a transfer of ownership must be in writing;[75] absent a writing, the would-be transfer may be deemed a nonexclusive license.[76] Section 201(d) provides that copyright ownership "may be transferred in whole or in part" and that "[a]ny of the exclusive rights comprised in a copyright, including any subdivision of any of the rights specified by section 106, may be transferred . . . and owned separately."[77] Section 201(d)(2) also states that the owner of any one or more of these rights is entitled to "all of the protection and remedies accorded to the copyright owner by this title."[78] Section 501(b) implements this latter provision in the following terms:

The legal or beneficial owner of an exclusive right under a copyright is entitled, subject to the requirements of section 411, to institute an action for any infringement of that particular right committed while he or she is the owner of it. The court may require such owner to serve written notice of the action with a copy of the complaint upon any person shown, by the records of the Copyright Office or otherwise, to have or claim an interest in the copyright, and shall require that such notice be served upon any person whose interest is likely to be affected by a decision in the case. The court may require the joinder, and shall permit the intervention, of any person having or claiming an interest in the copyright.[79]

---

[72] 3 Nimmer (2002; § 10.01[A], at 10–6 to –7).
[73] 17 U.S.C. § 101.
[74] *Id.*
[75] See *id.* § 204(a).
[76] See *Jacob Maxwell, Inc. v. Veeck*, 110 F.3d 749, 752–53 (11th Cir. 1997).
[77] 17 U.S.C. § 201(d).
[78] *Id.*
[79] *Id.* § 501(b).

The transferee may record the transfer, but he is not required to do so in order to commence an action for infringement.[80]

The standing rules that flow from these provisions of the Copyright Act can be summarized briefly. First, because the copyright owner may assign an interest in one or more of the exclusive rights that comprise the copyright in its entirety, the assignee of any one or more of these rights may commence an action for infringement without necessarily joining any other persons as plaintiffs (although the court may require or allow their joinder pursuant to the Rules of Civil Procedure). Second, an exclusive licensee of one or more of these rights may do the same, subject to the same qualification.[81] Third, § 501(b) confers standing upon a "beneficial owner" of a copyright, ostensibly "without any grant of priority to the legal owner."[82] Nimmer and Nimmer suggest that a beneficial owner would include someone for whom another holds a copyright in trust;[83] in addition, the legislative history states by way of example that a beneficial owner would include "an author who had parted with legal title to the copyright in exchange for percentage royalties based on sales or license fees."[84] This suggests that an assignee with a continuing interest in the assigned property may commence an infringement action in his own right, which is something that appears to be impossible in patent law.[85] Fourth, nonexclusive licensees lack standing to sue either by themselves or in conjunction with the copyright owner.[86] Finally, some authorities interpret § 501(b), which confers standing only upon copyright *owners*, to mean that copyright claims, like patent claims, can be assigned only with the copyright itself.[87]

---

[80] See *id.* § 205. From 1978 to 1988, however, the 1976 Copyright Act required the recordation of a transfer as a precondition to the transferee being permitted to file suit.

[81] See *Eden Toys, Inc. v. Florelee Undergarment Co.*, 697 F.2d 27, 36 (2d Cir. 1982).

[82] 3 Nimmer (2002; § 12.02[C], at 12–57).

[83] See *id.*

[84] H. Rep. No. 94-1476, at 159, 1976 U.S.C.C.A.N. at 5775. See also 2 Goldstein (2002; § 13.5.1.2, at 13:40–:41), who noted other persons courts have found to have beneficial ownership include "authors who have retained a royalty interest in the exploitation of their works," "copyright owners who have conveyed legal security title in their copyright to secure a debt" and "purchasers under a yet unperformed contract for the sale of copyright."

[85] See 2 Goldstein (2002; § 13.5.1.2, at 13:40–:41). Nimmer and Nimmer contend, however, that possession of a "mere contingent reversionary interest in a copyright is inadequate to confer standing," because "otherwise all parties who could conceivably claim a renewal reversion or a termination of transfer decades hence . . . would enjoy current standing, an absurd result." See Nimmer (2002; § 12.02[C], at 12–59).

[86] See *I.A.E., Inc. v. Shaver*, 74 F.3d 768, 775 (7th Cir. 1996); *Eden Toys, Inc. v. Florelee Undergarment Co.*, 526 F. Supp. 1187, 1190 (S.D.N.Y 1981), *aff'd in part, rev'd and remanded in part on other grounds*, 697 F.2d 27 (2d Cir. 1982).

[87] See *Eden Toys*, 697 F.2d at 32 n.3.

Unfortunately, nothing in the Copyright Act tells judges how to distinguish among assignments, exclusive licenses, and nonexclusive licenses. As far as the standing rules are concerned, however, there is often little need to distinguish between assignments and exclusive licenses, because the consequence of either transaction is that the transferee may sue without necessarily joining the transferor. As for the distinction between exclusive and nonexclusive licenses, the former must be in writing,[88] whereas the latter can be oral. And at least one court, citing *Western Electric*, has stated that the distinction between an exclusive and a nonexclusive copyright license is that the former "permits the licensee to use the protected material for a specific use and further promises that the same permission will not be given to others."[89] Other authorities, however, evidence confusion among assignments, exclusive licenses, and nonexclusive licenses.[90]

Although the differences between the copyright and patent standing rules probably reflect in part the greater influence that formal distinctions continue to have in patent law, there are nevertheless a few reasons to expect the rules, or at least the standard practice, to differ somewhat from one body of law to the other. For one thing, the indivisibility rule, which underlies the *Waterman* line of standing doctrine, is probably less of a hindrance in patent law than it would be in contemporary copyright law. We suspect (although we know of no relevant empirical data) that the type of transaction at issue in *Waterman*, in which the licensor transferred to the licensee the exclusive right to make and sell, but not to use, the patented invention, is relatively uncommon, and that most patent licenses transfer the rights to make, use, *and* sell, though perhaps subject to various restrictions. In other words, a rule under which one who owns only the exclusive right (say) to make the invention is considered a licensee, rather than an assignee, is not particularly troublesome if the rule does not need to be invoked very often. By contrast,

[88] See 17 U.S.C. § 204(a).

[89] *I.A.E.*, 74 F.3d at 775.

[90] See, e.g., *Zenix Indus. USA, Inc. v. King Hwa Indus. Co.*, Nos. 88–5760, 89–55720, 88–5936, 1990 WL 200234, at **2 (9th Cir. Oct. 3, 1990) that states "in order for the license to be exclusive . . . the licensor . . . must also give up the rights granted to" the licensee; *Althin CD Med., Inc. v. West Suburban Kidney Ctr.*, S.C., 874 F. Supp. 837, 842–3 (N.D. Ill. 1994), which held that an agreement under which the licensor retained "sole right to determine whether or not any infringement actions would be brought" and "gave the licensee no right to transfer or assign the license agreement with only a very narrow exception," was not an exclusive license. In both cases, the factors cited strongly suggest that the arrangement was a license, not an assignment, but – assuming that the *Western Electric* standard applies in copyright as well as patent cases – they should have had no bearing on whether the license was exclusive or nonexclusive.

in copyright law the various exclusive rights can be quite valuable even when separately owned. A second point is that copyrights probably are invalidated in litigation much less frequently than are patents.[91] If so, a rigid adherence to the rule that the licensor must be a party to any infringement action makes more sense in patent than in copyright cases, and it is not surprising that the latter have abandoned this requirement. There also would be relatively little risk that the owner of a given copyright right would inadvertently succeed in having the copyright invalidated in litigation, to the possible detriment of the other owners of other divisible rights in the same work; in this sense, the abolition of indivisibility would go hand in hand with the lower invalidation risk.

TRADEMARKS

Trademark actions in the United States can be litigated in either state or federal court, but in this section we will focus our attention on standing to sue in federal court under the Lanham Act. Section § 32(1) of the Lanham Act states that "[a]ny person who shall, without the consent of the registrant," infringe a federally registered mark "shall be liable in a civil action by the registrant."[92] Section 45 then defines the word "registrant" to "embrace the legal representatives, predecessors, successors and assigns of such . . . registrant."[93] The owner or assignee of a registered mark is clearly a proper party under § 32(1), and very likely a necessary and indispensable party as well for purposes of Rule 19.[94] There is also some authority suggesting that an exclusive licensee might have standing under § 32(1), although this rule may be limited to so-called exclusive licensees who are functionally indistinguishable from assignees.[95] Nonexclusive licensees, on

---

[91] *Cf.* Heald (1994; 271) who noted that "[m]any patents are declared invalid in litigation, mostly on nonobviousness grounds, a challenge that is unavailable against a copyright" and suggested that for this reason licensees should have a "greater degree of reliance . . . on the validity of a copyright" than on the validity of a patent. Unfortunately, we are unaware of any statistics concerning exactly how often litigated copyrights are invalidated.

[92] 15 U.S.C. § 1114(1).

[93] *Id.* § 1127.

[94] See *Fin. Inv. Co. (Berm.) Ltd. v. Geberit AG,* 165 F.3d 526, 531 (7th Cir. 1998); *Association of Co-Operative Members, Inc. v. Farmland Indus.,* 684 F.2d 1134, 1143 (5th Cir. 1982).

[95] See *Finance Inv. Co.,* 165 F.3d at 531–2; *Quabaug Rubber Co. v. Fabiano Shoe Co.,* 567 F.2d 154, 159 (1st Cir. 1977). The fact that trademark law continues to require assignments and licenses to comply with different formalities tends to simplify the task of distinguishing between the two. See Restatement (Third) of Unfair Competition § 33 & cmts. b, c; § 34 & cmts. b, f.

the other hand, clearly do not have standing under this provision.[96] A few courts also have held that licensees are not indispensable parties to a § 32(1) action, although this rule may be limited to nonexclusive licensees only.[97] And while there is little case law on point, it seems likely that a court would impose restrictions on the transfer of claims for trademark infringement under § 32(1) similar to those that apply in patent and copyright law.[98] The same rules that apply under § 32(1) probably also apply to federal claims for trademark dilution.[99]

Much of what § 32 denies the licensee is nevertheless available under § 43(a). In relevant part, § 43(a) states:

Any person who, on or in connection with any goods or services, or any container for goods, uses in commerce any word, term, name, symbol, or device, or any combination thereof, or any false designation of origin, false or misleading description of fact, or false or misleading representation of fact, which –

(A) is likely to cause confusion, or to cause mistake, or to deceive as to the affiliation, connection, or association of such person with another person, or as to the origin, sponsorship, or approval of his or her goods, services, or commercial activities by another person, or

(B) in commercial advertising or promotion, misrepeents the nature, characteristics, qualities, or geographic origin of his or her or another person's goods, services, or commercial activities,

shall be liable in a civil action by any person who believes that he or she is or is likely to be damages by such act.

Courts have construed the final clause of § 43(a) as conferring standing upon any person who has a "reasonable commercial interest," which the offending conduct threatens.[100] Several courts that have confronted the issue have concluded that exclusive trademark licensees have such an interest, and therefore have standing to sue for trademark infringement under this

---

[96] See *Finance Inv. Co.*, 165 F.3d at 531–2; *Quabaug*, 567 F.2d at 159 & n.6.

[97] See *National Bd. of Young Women's Christian Ass'n of U.S.A. v. Young Women's Christian Ass'n of Charleston*, 335 F. Supp. 615, 627 (D.S.C. 1971); *Volkswagen Aktiengesellschaft v. Dreer*, 224 F. Supp. 744, 745–6 (E.D. Pa. 1963).

[98] See *International Soc'y for Krishna Consciousness, Inc. v. Stadium Auth.*, 479 F. Supp. 792, 796–7 (W.D. Pa. 1979), which held the assignee of a chose in action is not a "registrant" for purposes of § 32(1)).

[99] See 15 U.S.C. § 1125(c)(1) (stating that "[t]he *owner* of a famous mark shall be entitled" to protection against dilution) (emphasis added); *STX, Inc. v. Bauer USA, Inc.*, 43 U.S.P.Q.2d (BNA) 1492, 1495–6 (N.D. Cal. 1997).

[100] See, e.g., *Waldman Publ. Corp. v. Landoll, Inc.*, 43 F.3d 775, 784 n.6 (2d Cir. 1994).

provision.[101] Moreover, at least two courts have held that *nonexclusive* licensees also have standing under § 43(a),[102] although in neither case did the court provide much in the way of explanation, or spell out exactly how the alleged infringement threatened to injure the licensee. Other cases suggest that an assignor who retains a right to a running royalty would have standing to sue as well.[103] The only categorical limitation appears to be the rule, formulated by some courts, that a licensee cannot sue its own licensor for trademark infringement when the latter uses the mark in violation of the license (though he may have a claim for breach of contract).[104] Given the rules in patent and copyright law, it also seems doubtful whether courts would permit the assignment of § 43(a) claims, although we are aware of no cases on point; and at least one court has held, albeit without explanation, that licensees *may* waive their right to sue under this provision.[105]

If there is any logic to the liberality of the trademark standing rules in comparison with those in copyright and especially in patent law, it probably stems from the fact that trademarks are intended largely to serve a consumer protection function. Encouraging the producers of goods and services to invest in quality control by providing them with trademark rights is simply a means of achieving this latter end. Because the ultimate beneficiaries of trademark rights are not trademark owners, a somewhat looser application of standing rules may fit the law of trademarks and unfair competition better than it would the law of patents and copyrights. On the other hand, experience suggests – though we are aware of no relevant empirical evidence – that trademarks are invalidated in litigation more frequently than are copyrights but less frequently than are patents. If so, this differential invalidation risk might suggest that the trademark rules should be more liberal than the patent rules but less so than the copyright rules – although judicious

---

[101] See, e.g., *Martin's Herend Imports, Inc. v. Diamond & Gem Trading USA Co.*, 112 F.3d 1296, 1301 n.10 (5th Cir. 1997); *STX*, 43 U.S.P.Q.2d at 1495.

[102] See *Quabaug*, 567 F.2d at 160; *Traditional Living, Inc. v. Energy Log Homes, Inc.*, 464 F. Supp. 1024, 1026 (N.D. Ala. 1978); see also *National Lampoon, Inc. v. American Broad. Cos.*, 376 F. Supp. 733, 737, 746 (S.D.N.Y. 1974) that held that the plaintiff, who appears to have been a nonexclusive licensee, had standing to sue under § 43(a). The court in *Quabaug* also appears to have held, though without explanation, that the licensor is not an indispensable party for purposes of Rule 19. See 567 F.2d at 158, 160.

[103] See *PPX Enters. v. Audiofidelity, Inc.*, 746 F.2d 120, 124 (2d Cir. 1984); *Tri-Star Pictures, Inc. v. Leisure Time Prods., B.V.*, 749 F. Supp. 1243, 1245–6, 1249–50 (S.D.N.Y. 1990), *aff'd*, 17 F.3d 38 (2d Cir. 1994).

[104] See, e.g., *Gruen Marketing Corp. v. Benrus Watch Co.*, 955 F. Supp. 979, 983–4 (N.D. Ill. 1997); *Tap Publications, Inc. v. Chinese Yellow Pages (New York) Inc.*, 925 F. Supp. 212, 217 (S.D.N.Y. 1996).

[105] See *Finance Inv. Co.*, 165 F.3d at 532.

application of Rule 19, coupled with a rule allowing trademark licensees to waive their right to sue under § 43(a), might alleviate the potential risk to trademark owners.

TOWARD A THEORY OF RATIONAL STANDING RULES

In this part, we develop some simple economic models to illustrate the impact of infringement upon intellectual property transferors and transferees under a variety of assignment, exclusive licensing, and nonexclusive licensing arrangements. We shall argue that understanding the ways in which infringement can affect the various interests at stake, and then applying that knowledge within the context of the flexible procedures such as those embodied in the Federal Rules of Civil Procedure, can more readily accommodate these interests than can intellectual property-specific rules of the type articulated in *Waterman.* In addition, this more nuanced approach may render intellectual property rights (and the licensing thereof) of marginally greater value.

THE ASSIGNOR-ASSIGNEE RELATIONSHIP

As we have seen, the three branches of IP law under consideration here all accord the assignee the right to sue for infringement without requiring him to join the assignor as a party – though some courts have allowed the latter to intervene when she retains an interest in the patent, such as the right to receive the patent back from the assignee after a period of years. Allowing the assignor to intervene in cases of this nature clearly makes sense, even though she may be unable to prove any damages attributable to the infringement, because of her interest in monitoring the conduct of litigation that could affect her future rights. As noted earlier, almost half of all patents are invalidated in litigation. A similar deference may not be warranted in copyright cases, however, to the extent that copyrights are invalidated much less frequently than are patents. Moreover, since trademark rights exist only in connection with an ongoing line of products and services, it seems unlikely that there would be many instances in which a trademark assignor retains a reversionary interest sufficient to warrant intervention in a subsequent infringement suit. Nevertheless, to the extent that a copyright or trademark assignor does retain an interest in the property which might be jeopardized in litigation, allowing the assignor to join or intervene in the suit on a case-by-case basis – as permitted in the U.S. under Rules 19, 20, or 24 of the Federal Rules of Civil Procedure – is probably a more intelligent response to the problem than trying to resolve it by fitting the assignor within some preconceived category.

The more interesting question, which we take up in this section, is whether the assignor of a patent, copyright, or trademark should be allowed to intervene in cases in which she has transferred the property in exchange for a lump-sum payment, a series of payments, or an ongoing royalty that is tied to units sold or produced, but otherwise retains no ongoing interest in the property itself. We shall demonstrate that, in the first two cases, according standing only to the assignee adequately safeguards the value of the property, and should have no impact on the assignor's *ex-ante* incentives. In the third case, however, in which the assignor sells the property in exchange for a "running" royalty, according her a waivable right to sue infringers can increase the value of the property, and thus marginally enhance the relevant incentives. The assignee, on the other hand, clearly has an interest in participating in any litigation that might result in the invalidation of the property he now owns.

LUMP-SUM FEES

Suppose that a firm has a patent on an invention that comprises an entire product market and that the use of the patent will confer monopoly rights in that market. As we saw in Chapter 3, the firm maximizes profit by equating marginal revenue with marginal cost, that is, by selling Q_1 at a price of P_1. (We reproduce Figure 3.1 from Chapter 3 as Figure 7.1.) The total profit is the mark-up over cost, $P_1 - MC$, times the quantity, Q_1. This total profit, $(P_1 - MC)Q_1$, represents the value of the patent. The problem for the inventor whose expertise lies in invention, rather than in production, distribution, and marketing, is how to extract that potential value through licensing, assignment, or vertical integration.

For the inventor who wishes to assign the patent the best strategy is to announce that the patent is available for sale and then to assign it to the highest bidder.[106] Competitive bidding among equally efficient potential licensees or assignees will drive the price of the patent up to its full

---

[106] The analysis that follows assumes zero information and transaction costs; when those costs are not zero, the patentee will not be able to extract the full value of the patent. For purposes of this section, however, the assumption of zero information and transaction costs simplifies the analysis without altering the basic conclusion: namely, that a patentee who has extracted whatever value there is to be extracted from the patent, and who retains no ongoing interest in the patent, has no reason to participate in any subsequent infringement litigation.

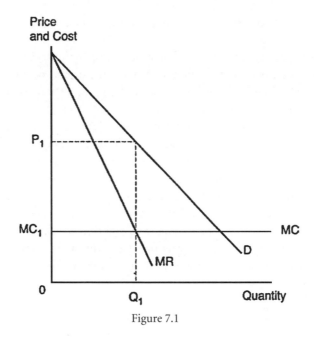

Figure 7.1

value.[107] Extracting this full value, however, leaves the patentee with no residual interest in the patent and no reason to join in any future infringement action. Thus, the patentee's *ex-ante* incentive to engage in inventive activity is completely protected, because by selling the patent for a lump sum she extracts the invention's full value regardless of any future infringement.

The story is quite different for the assignee who is the real victim of infringement. Again, as we saw in Chapter 3, an equally efficient infringer can produce at a cost of MC but without incurring any license fee. Given the assignee's production of a quantity equal to Q_1, the profit maximizing quantity for the infringer to produce is equal to one-half of Q_1. This production will increase the total output to Q_2, which will cause the price to fall to P_2. The assignee's injury then is equal to the reduction in the price times the output that it produced: $(P_1 - P_2)Q_1$. The assignee is entitled to recover these lost profits. We should note that the patentee's incentives are protected and promoted by conferring standing on the assignee. If the assignee were

---

[107] If the auction proceeds as a first-price English auction, the price is bid up to the transaction price. In a Dutch auction, the patentee would announce a willingness to sell and the price would fall until there was a buyer. If all potential buyers are equally efficient manufacturers, either auction form will yield the full value because everyone values the patent equally. For a classic treatment of auctions, see Cassady (1967; 56–63).

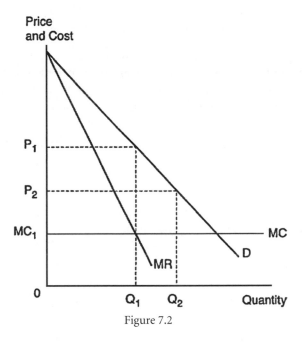

Figure 7.2

unable to fully recover its lost profits due to infringement, the value of the patent to the assignee would be lower than $(P_1 - MC)Q_1$ and, therefore, the patentee would be unable to extract the full value of the patent through the assignment.[108]

---

[108] See also *infra* pp. 236–9, where we return to a Cournot oligopoly model in which the parties compete on the basis of quantity. Alternatively, the parties could compete on the basis of price (a Bertrand model) or could accommodate one another (a Chamberlinian model). For examples, see *supra* p. 51, *infra* pp. 239–41. Note that the model presented above is *not* a single period model (compare *infra* pp. 236–7). Instead, one can think of the results described above as representing production and profits in one year. Then the value can be determined by calculating the discounted present value of the future stream of profits. The life of a patent is not a single year and, therefore, the value of the patent is equal to the sum of the profits generated during the life of the patent. Due to the time value of money, the value of a stream of future profits is the present value of that stream:

$$PV(\pi) \equiv \frac{\pi 1}{1 + r} + \frac{\pi 2}{(1 + r)^2} + \cdots + \frac{\pi T}{(1 + r)^T}$$

where π denotes profit, r is the discount rate, and T is the patent life. One can compress the notation by using the summation notation:

$$PV(\pi) = \sum_{t=1}^{T} \frac{\pi 1}{(1 + r)^t}$$

In the preceding discussion, we implicitly assumed that the lump-sum assignment fee was equal to the present value of the future profit stream. Suppose, however, that the assignee

CONTINUING ROYALTY PAYMENTS

When the patentee assigns the patent in exchange for a lump-sum payment, she has no continuing (or residual) interest in the patent and, accordingly, her incentive to invent is unaffected by post-assignment infringement. But suppose instead that she assigns the patent in exchange for a continuing (or "running") royalty. A running royalty is a fee that depends upon the performance of the assignee.[109] In this case, the profits of the patentee are equal to the sum of the royalties

$$R = fQ$$

where R denotes the total royalties, f is the license fee per unit of output, and Q is the assignee's total output. For the assignee, its profit is

$$\pi = PQ - CQ - FQ$$

where P is the price of the output and C is the constant marginal (and average) cost of production. The assignee will maximize its profits by producing that output where marginal revenue equals the sum of the marginal cost of production and the per unit royalty. The patentee will offer the license at a fee that will maximize the sum of the royalties subject to the profit maximizing behavior of the assignee.[110] By substituting the profit maximizing

---

agreed to pay this amount over time. The same sort of competitive bidding that would drive the price of the assignment to $PV(\pi)$ will drive the annual payments to π_t per period. Although the form is somewhat different, analytically this is the same as the lump-sum payment because the payment is not tied to actual performance; it is not a running royalty. In other words, at the contract negotiation stage, the assignee commits to paying π_t per period irrespective of its actual performance. Clearly, this is the same thing as agreeing to a lump-sum payment equal to the present value of the future profits. (Really, the patentee is financing the purchase of the patent right. This "mortgage" contract is distinct from the sale of the patent.) In this case, we have continuing payments over the life of the patent, but the patentee's only continuing interest is that the assignee be able to sue for infringement. In the event that the patent is infringed, the patentee will lose nothing – provided, of course that the assignee does not default on its obligations to make the periodic payments. Consequently, any loss that is suffered will be incurred by the assignee.

[109] See 3 Milgrim (2002; § 18.06, at 18–12). A running royalty may be expressed as a percentage of sales or as a percentage of units produced or sold; or it may be based upon the resulting production of some other good that uses the patented invention, or even plant capacity multiplied by a percentage of time in operation. See *id.* §§ 18.06, 18.24.

[110] For the assignee,

$$\pi = PQ - CQ - FQ$$

and

$$\frac{d\pi}{dQ} = P + Q\frac{dP}{dQ} - C - f = 0$$

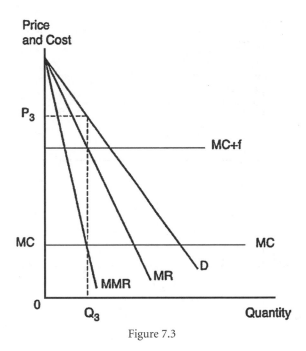

Figure 7.3

condition of the assignee into its own royalty function, the patentee can solve for the optimal (i.e., royalty-maximizing) license fee. In Figure 7.3, we have identified the optimal price to the consumer as P_3, the quantity as Q_3, and the optimal license fee as MR−MC.

In contrast to the preceding case of a lump-sum license fee, the running royalty per unit of output seems inefficient. First, it is socially inefficient since output is lower and price is higher. Second, it is privately inefficient because the total royalties to the patentee are lower than with a lump-sum fee. We might, therefore, expect to find few uses of running royalties in exchange for patent assignments or exclusive licenses Empirically, however, this prediction is not borne out. One likely reason is that information costs often

Since $P + QdP/dQ$ is marginal revenue, the condition for profit maximizing is satisfied where $MR = C + f$. For the patentee, royalties are

$$R = fQ$$

And $f = MR - C$. Thus, we can write the royalties as

$$R = (MR - C)Q.$$

In order to maximize the royalty revenue, the patentee will set the license fee such that

$$\frac{dR}{dQ} = \frac{dMR}{dQ} - C = 0$$

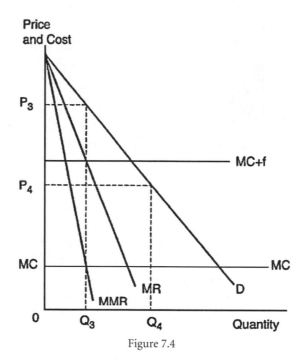

Figure 7.4

make it very difficult to estimate the proper value of a lump-sum royalty.[111] If so, the parties may prefer a running royalty that at least will bear some relation to the value of the property. In any event, under our model the total royalties received by the patentee are

$$R = fQ = (MR - MC)Q_3.$$

As for the licensee, its profit will be equal to

$$\pi = (P_3 - MC - f)Q_3.$$

Both the patentee and its exclusive licensee earn positive profits with running royalties. Because of the inefficiency noted above, however, the sum of these profits is less than the lump-sum fee analyzed earlier.

Consider now what happens when an infringer enters and pays no royalty. As depicted in Figure 7.4, its costs are equal to MC. Given the assignee's production of Q_3, the infringer will find it optimal to produce a sum equal to $Q_4 - Q_3$. Because total output is now Q_4, the price will fall to P_4 and

[111] See, e.g., Bessy & Brousseau (1998; 464); Caves et al. (1983; 257–9); Gallini & Wright (1990; 149–52).

the assignee will experience losses. In the first period, the assignee's output will be unchanged and, therefore, the royalty payment will still be fQ_3. But the assignee's optimal response to the presence of the infringer is to reduce its output in subsequent periods. This, of course, will lead to lower royalties and thereby injure the assignor. Thus, in the case of running royalties, infringement injures both assignor and assignee.[112]

One might argue in response to the preceding analysis that, if the contract of assignment does not contain an explicit promise on the part of the assignee to prosecute all material infringers – assuming that such a promise is not itself inconsistent with the status of being an "assignee" – then an infringement does not really injure the assignor, because she could have had no expectation *ex ante* of receiving any continuing stream of royalties. The assignor, in other words, would have known that the assignee would be legally free to tolerate infringers – and that in some cases he may decide it is better to do so than to risk having the patent invalidated in litigation.[113] Moreover, even if the assignee has promised to prosecute infringers, one might argue that the assignor's only reasonable expectation is that such infringers will be enjoined, but not that she (the assignor) will recover damages for any loss incurred prior to the entry of the injunction. On this logic, as long as the assignee fulfills his obligation to sue infringers, neither he nor the infringers owe any further duty to the assignor, though one might consider whether the assignor should be able to pursue an infringement action if the assignee breaches his obligation to sue.

This reasoning is not persuasive, however, because the assignor's expectations will themselves be a product, at least in part, of the applicable legal

---

[112] Much the same results hold qualitatively for a royalty levied on total revenue. This *ad valorem* license fee generates royalties of

$$R = kPQ,$$

where k is the royalty rate and, of course, $0 < k < 1$. As a result, the licensee's net profit function

$$\pi = (1 - k)PQ - C(Q)$$

From the patentee's perspective, the optimal value of k will maximize total royalties. At the optimum, both the patentee and the licensee will earn positive profits. Infringement will lead to a reduction in the licensee's optimal output. As a result, both the licensee and the patentee will suffer losses due to infringement.

[113] See Choi (1990; 1250, 1255–8). In Choi's model, a patent owner may find it optimal to tolerate a first infringer because of the risk of invalidation, but not to tolerate subsequent infringers because with each additional infringement the cost of toleration (forgoing potential royalties) outweighs the benefit (avoiding the risk of invalidation). The patent owner's toleration of the first infringer, therefore, does not necessarily invite subsequent infringement.

rules. Thus, if the law provides her with a right to recover any royalties she loses as a result of an infringement, then she *will* have the expectation of recovering those damages, notwithstanding the contract's failure explicitly to address this issue, or the right of the assignee, as patent owner, to tolerate infringements. Certainly the case for the assignor's participation will be *stronger* if the assignee has promised to prosecute infringers, because in such instances it is clear that the parties' intent was that the assignee would not permit others to infringe. Allowing the assignor to sue in cases in which the assignee has not made this commitment, on the other hand, might conceivably contravene the parties' intent that the assignee would have the final say on whether litigation should proceed; and it is also somewhat difficult to square with the language of the Patent Act, which confers a right to sue upon patentees and successors in title, neither of which sobriquets fits comfortably upon the shoulders of an assignor. The analysis above nevertheless suggests that, as long as the parties are free to modify or waive the assignor's right to sue, in instances in which conferring standing upon the assignor would appear not to serve their common interest,[114] a default rule permitting the royalty-accruing assignor to litigate would be preferable, because it would allow them to capture a greater portion of the profit attributable to the innovation.[115] We, therefore, conclude that, absent a waiver, the royalty-accruing

---

[114] We see little reason why a waiver of this nature should not be enforceable, because it might be in the parties' common interest to forgo some potential value in exchange for reducing the expected cost of litigation and the risk of invalidation. Moreover, if the parties agree that the assignee alone will have the right to sue, but must share any damages recovery with his assignor, the ultimate outcome may be exactly the same as if the assignor himself participates in the suit. Specifically, if the assignee recovers as damages a reasonable royalty that is equal to both his and his assignor's lost income, then both parties will be at least as well off as when both participate and recover separate judgments. To the extent that the assignee's potential damages recovery is uncertain, however, the parties may prefer instead a rule that allows either or both to commence (or at least participate in) litigation. But if this rule is difficult to establish by contract, then the better default rule is initially to confer a waivable right to sue upon both parties.

[115] The Coase Theorem, of course, predicts that, in the absence of transaction costs and other obstacles to bargaining, the choice of default rule does not matter, because the parties can contract around whatever the rule happens to be. See Coase (1960). Thus, if the rule permits assignor participation but the parties do not view this rule as serving their interest – perhaps because the potential benefits of assignor participation outweigh the potential risk that the assignor will stir up litigation that results in patent invalidation – the assignee can require the assignor to waive her right to participate. If, on the other hand, the rule does not permit the assignor to participate, the parties can confer this right by contract if they believe that doing so will enhance the patent's value. The courts' unwillingness to allow the parties to confer "standing" by agreement, however, coupled with the restrictions they impose on assigning causes of action, suggest that the latter strategy might not work unless these other rules were abandoned or modified. Given the present state of the law, then,

assignor should be allowed not only to intervene in litigation commenced by the assignee, but also to initiate such litigation herself – although the high risk of patent invalidation, as well as the potential drawbacks of multiple litigation and duplicative recoveries, should result in the mandatory joinder of the assignee as well, pursuant to Rule 19.[116]

The preceding analysis nevertheless still leaves two questions open: namely, why the transfer of a single patent right is considered to be only a license (thus conferring no right to sue without joining the licensor), whereas the transfer of a single copyright right is considered an assignment conferring upon the assignee the right to sue alone;[117] and why the transfer of all patent rights within a single geographic area is nevertheless considered an assignment conferring full standing rights upon the assignee. We have already suggested a response to the first question, however, when we noted that transfers of single copyright rights are likely to be more common – and probably more valuable – than transfers of single patent rights; the owner of a single copyright right, therefore, may have a greater need to initiate litigation without having to obtain consent or approval from, or coordination with, another party. At the same time, if the risk of invalidation is much lower for copyrights than for patents, the need to join the party who transferred the copyright right may be less substantial than the need to join the patent licensor. In this respect, the difference between the rules anticipates our observations in the following subsection about the standing of exclusive licensors.

The second question is more difficult to answer, although we can think of two possible reasons for this rule. The first is that a rule conferring assignee status upon a person who owns all of the rights to a patent within one jurisdiction but not in others, and thereby permitting her to sue without necessarily joining the "assignor" who retains those rights in other jurisdictions, might possibly have made sense in an era when travel was difficult and expensive; requiring the assignor/patent owner to participate in distant states, in other words, might have imposed an undue burden upon her. In

---

the better default rule is probably for the royalty-accruing assignor initially to possess a waivable right to sue.

[116] By contrast, the assumed lower risk of invalidation for copyrights might make it less than necessary for the copyright assignor to join the assignee. However, even in the copyright arena the risk of multiple litigation, duplicative recoveries, and the potential preclusive effects of judgments might counsel in favor of requiring, or at least permitting, the joinder of the assignee.

[117] This sort of issue cannot arise in trademark cases in which the only rights at stake – the right to prevent infringement and, in some instances only, the right to prevent dilution – cannot be separated from one another without divorcing the trademark from the goodwill it represents.

the modern world, however, the assignor's inconvenience might seem fairly minimal in comparison with the possible preclusive effect of an adverse judgment. A second possible reason for the rule is that the risk of duplicative recoveries and multiple litigation is minimal in cases of this nature, because the patent owner herself suffers no injury if an infringer competes with the licensee within the licensee's exclusive territory only. But this is not necessarily true when the licensor is entitled to royalties from the licensee's sale of patented goods, as discussed above. Once again, procedural rules (such as those embodied in the Federal Rules of Civil Procedure) may be capable of efficiently melding the relevant party interests, without the need for standing rules that depend upon a party's ontological status.

THE LICENSOR-EXCLUSIVE LICENSEE RELATIONSHIP

At first blush, the preceding analysis would appear to apply just as well to the licensor-exclusive licensee relationship as it does to assignor-assignee relationship. Thus, if the intellectual property owner licenses another to be her exclusive licensee in exchange for a lump-sum amount, an infringement injures the licensee but does not appear to affect the licensor, who has already been paid for the property. If, instead, the owner licenses her property for a running royalty, notwithstanding the efficiency problems discussed previously, the parties will maximize the value of that property if both licensor and licensee are able to recoup their losses attributable to the infringement. In light of our analysis with respect to assignors and assignees, therefore, the questions remain why the licensor has standing when she transfers the property for a lump sum (and in fact is, arguably, the *only* necessary plaintiff in an infringement suit); and why the law requires her to be a party when she licenses the property for a running royalty, but does not even clearly permit her to be a party when the transaction takes the form of an assignment.

To the extent there is a rational answer to these questions, it resides in the fact that a license does not entail a transfer of ownership in the underlying property; or, to state the matter another way, a person who is classified as a licensor typically retains greater control over the property than does a person who is classified as an assignor. As we have seen, a court is likely to find that a transaction is a license, and not an assignment, when (in the patent context) it involves a transfer of fewer than all of the patentee's rights within a given geographic area; or when the IPR owner purports to retain a right to sue for infringement or to prevent or limit the transferee's assignment of the property to another; or when the transfer is made subject to existing licenses. In each of these contexts, it is clear that the transferor retains significant rights in the property, and in this sense his situation is similar to that of the assignor who retains a reversionary interest.[118] This would suggest that, in patent cases at least, the licensor should normally be a party to the litigation, because her remaining interest in the property is at risk in most infringement suits. The need to join her in copyright and trademark cases, on the other hand, may depend upon the relative probability of invalidation, which we believe to be lower than in patent law.

The preceding section also demonstrates, however, that infringement threatens the assignee, regardless of whether the transaction involves a lump sum or a running royalty, and there is no reason why this analysis should not apply to exclusive licensees as well (except in cases in which the licensee and infringer operate in entirely different markets). Notwithstanding *Waterman*, then, there appears to be no excuse for not routinely requiring the exclusive licensee to participate in infringement litigation, absent a waiver of his right to participate. Those courts that have required the joinder of exclusive licensees have had good grounds for doing so.

One final observation on the use of exclusive licenses is that, when the property owner employs a running royalty and licenses a single licensee, a successive monopoly may be created. Successive monopoly is a market structure in which there is both an upstream and a downstream monopoly.[119] In the case in which the intellectual property owner is the upstream monopolist whose position is protected by her property, and the downstream monopolist is the only producer (by virtue of his license contract) of the product that embodies that property, the owner does not extract the full value of her property. In fact, the sum of her profits and the licensee's profits falls short of the full profit potential because the resulting market structure is inefficient. It is, therefore, necessary for both parties to have standing or the profits will deviate even further and thereby reduce the incentive to invent.

A more interesting question, however, is why would a patentee or other intellectual property owner create such an inefficient market structure. The answer is apt to involve economies of scale. The scale of the licensee's operation may well be large relative to the demand and, therefore, there may not be room for more than one licensee to produce at an efficient scale of operation. In other words, there are elements of natural monopoly in

---

[118] That is not to say that he is entitled to damages, however, if he has transferred the license in exchange for a lump sum. Nor does this analysis explain why the licensor is a necessary party for purposes of Rule 19 but the assignor with a reversionary interest, whose interest might be of equal weight, may have a right to intervene but is generally not viewed as a necessary party.

[119] See Schlicher (1998; § 1.01(e)).

production. This explanation, however, does not end the matter. Having determined that it is most efficient to have a single licensee, why would the owner opt for a running royalty rather than a lump-sum fee? The answer may involve one of two things. First, it may be that the licensee is wealth constrained and cannot pay a lump-sum fee equal to the full present value of the future profits; this does not explain, however, why that sum cannot be borrowed either in the capital market or from the owner herself. Second, it may be that the demand is uncertain, i.e., the owner and the licensee cannot predict the commercial success of the product. As a result, the owner may be willing to accept a running royalty If the demand is higher than expected, then she will share in that success.

NONEXCLUSIVE LICENSEES

We next consider the effect of infringement upon the nonexclusive licensee when the transfer involves a lump-sum payment and when it involves a running royalty. Our analysis will assume that these licensees will be able to compete with one another in the output market; and that, irrespective of the form that the royalty takes, the patentee will attempt to set the royalty at a level that maximizes the sum received by the patentee. We shall demonstrate that, contrary to the outcome that obtains in the exclusive licensee situation, the use of running royalties in connection with nonexclusive licenses is more efficient than the use of lump-sum fees. Moreover, our analysis suggests that in both the lump-sum and running royalty situation, the aggregate expected profits accruing to licensor and licensee would increase if the licensee had standing to sue for infringement. The law's refusal to confer standing on the nonexclusive licensee nevertheless might be justifiable in light of the difficult proof problems that would surround the calculation of the licensee's damages.

LUMP-SUM FEES

If a patentee is going to issue nonexclusive licenses, it will be difficult to use lump-sum royalties because they will induce inefficient production. Figure 7.5 displays the cost curves of a typical competitive firm. The average and marginal cost curves are denoted by AC and MC, respectively. In order to extract the full potential profit, the patentee would like each firm to produce efficiently. This means producing q_1 at the minimum point on the average cost curve. A lump-sum fee of F_1, however, shifts the average cost from AC to AC + F, but does not affect the firm's marginal cost. As a result, competition will lead firms to produce q_2. Note that at an output of q_2, the height of

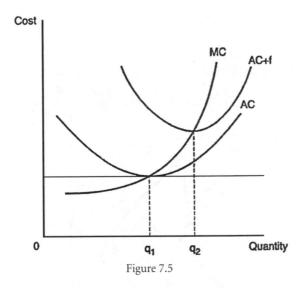

Figure 7.5

the average cost curve AC is above the height at q_1. This means that the output is being produced inefficiently, i.e., at greater than minimum cost. To the extent that production costs are higher than the minimum, the profit available for the patentee is reduced.

If the patentee nevertheless employs a lump-sum nonexclusive royalty, an infringement will not directly affect her, just as we saw in the cases involving lump-sum assignments and exclusive licenses. As in the exclusive license scenario, however, the patentee still has a strong interest in participating in any infringement litigation, because (by definition) she retains some ongoing interest in the patent and the threat of invalidation is always serious. The need for copyright and trademark licensors to participate, on the other hand, is less substantial, if our assumption is correct that copyright and trademarks are much less frequently invalidated than are patents. In all cases, however, infringement appears to injure the nonexclusive licensees by increasing output and reducing price below the minimum point on AC + F. Thus, the revenue that each nonexclusive licensee earns will fall below the sum of the production cost of the output produced plus the amortized lump-sum royalty.

PER-UNIT ROYALTIES

If a patentee charges a per-unit royalty on a nonexclusive basis, she can extract the full value of the patent. In panel a of Figure 7.6, the industry demand curve is given by D and the associated marginal revenue is MR. Under conditions of constant costs, the long-run supply curve will be

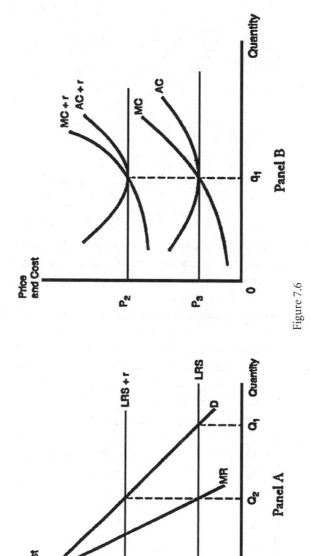

Figure 7.6

200

horizontal. This is also an industry marginal cost curve. The patentee will observe that the maximum available profit will be generated if the licensees will collectively produce Q_2 and sell it at P_2. The resulting profit will be $(P_2 - P_1)Q_2$. Now, the trick is to select a per unit royalty that will extract this profit. The patentee will charge a per unit royalty of $P_2 - P_1$, which will have the effect of increasing the typical firm's cost curves from AC and MC to AC $+$ r and MC $+$ r. As can be seen in panel b of Figure 7.6, the minimum point of AC $+$ r occurs at the same output as AC. The licensee fee does not distort productive efficiency. Each firm is producing efficiently and, therefore, the patentee can extract all of the available profit.

If an infringer enters, he does not pay the per-unit royalty and thereby has lower costs. He will produce as long as the industry price exceeds its marginal cost. This additional output will increase industry supply and thereby reduce price. As long as the resulting price is above the average variable cost (including the royalty) of the licensee, the infringer will continue to produce. Note, however, that the nonexclusive licensee will experience losses as AC $+$ r will exceed the price it receives for the product. In Figure 7.7, we have reproduced panel b of Figure 7.6. Suppose that infringement leads to a price reduction from P_2 to P_3. A typical licensee would maximize profits (i.e., minimize losses) by producing q_3 units of output. At this production level, the average cost of production is above P_2 due to an inefficient level of output. That is, the licensee is using the plant at a rate of output that is too low to fully exploit economies of scale. Thus, the nonexclusive licensee is injured by infringement.

At the same time, the patentee is also injured by infringement. The licensees will reduce their output levels and, consequently, the royalties are declining.

PROFIT-SHARING

A third possibility is that the royalty could be specified as a share of the licensee's profits. In this case, the patentee's royalties would be

$$R = \alpha\pi$$

where $0 < \alpha < 1$ defines the share going to the patentee. The licensee's net profits (π_N) would be

$$\pi_N = (1 - \alpha)\pi.$$

Because the license royalty is levied on profits, the licensee has an incentive to maximize its profits. In other words, the royalty does not influence the

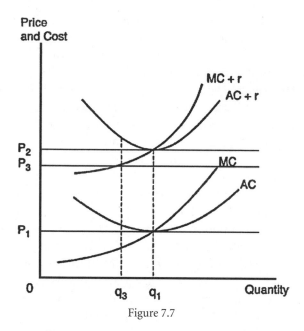

Figure 7.7

incetives of the licensee.[120] This result is somewhat counterintuitive, but it follows because the royalty is levied on the profits, and $(1 - \alpha)$ of the maximum profit is more than $(1 - \alpha)$ of any other profit.

As we saw in the analysis of Figure 7.1, infringement will expand output and reduce price. This will reduce the licensee's profits and, accordingly, will reduce the royalties earned by the patentee. Once again, both the patentee and the licensee have suffered damages due to infringement.

OBJECTIONS

An objection similar to the one we considered in connection with the assignor-assignee relationship can be raised in connection with the

---

[120] The net profit for the licensee is

$$\pi_N = (1 - \alpha)\pi$$
$$= (1 - \alpha)(PQ - C(Q))$$

To maximize net profits, the licensee must produce where

$$\frac{d\pi}{dQ} = (1 - \alpha)(MR - MC) = 0$$

This requires that the licensee produce where marginal revenue equals marginal cost, which is precisely the same output that maximizes profits in Figure 7.1 in the text.

preceding analysis regarding nonexclusive licensees: namely, that in the absence of a commitment by the patentee to defend the patent and to expressly limit the number of licensees, the licensees can have no reasonable expectation of profit *ex ante*, and therefore are not harmed in any meaningful sense by the infringement. This is essentially the reasoning of cases such as *Western Electric*. As we have suggested, however, the parties' expectations are themselves a function of the applicable legal rule. Moreover, the question arises why, if aggregate expected profits might be higher under a licensee-standing rule, the courts refuse to confer standing upon nonexclusive licensees, at least as a default rule subject to modification or waiver by the parties.

Indeed, as the following example illustrates, one might question whether there is any meaningful economic distinction between exclusive and nonexclusive licenses; if not, the difference between standing rules will be difficult to justify. Suppose that the patentee commits to a specific number of licensees and also to sue for infringement, i.e., to protect her intellectual property. If there is infringement and the patentee sues, the patentee's injuries will be compensated. If the licensees do not have standing to sue for their injuries, then their losses will go uncompensated. Since there is some positive probability of infringement, there is an expected cost due to infringement that is not zero. This added cost will be reflected in the value of the patent being lower than without this added cost. At the margin, then, denying standing to these licensees will reduce the incentive to invent. But the result appears to be the same, regardless of whether the patentee promises to limit the number of licensees to n or sets a license fee and permits the free flow of resources to yield n licensees. As can be seen in Figure 7.6, the optimal per unit royalty is $P_2 - P_1$. If the licensees have identical cost curves, the optimal (i.e., profit maximizing) number of licensees is $n = Q_2/q_1$.[121] If the patentee simply announced that the royalty would be $P_2 - P_1$, licensees would earn supracompetitive profits until n licensees entered the industry. Consequently, one would expect the same number of licensees whether the patentee committed to a specific number or not. In either case, permitting the licensees to sue for their losses will increase the value of the patent and thereby increase the incentive to invent. Under the current rules, however, licensees have standing to sue only when the patentee expressly limits their

---

[121] Based on the quest for maximum profits, the patentee has determined that Q_2 is the optimal output that the licensees should produce. Now, it is imperative that Q_2 be produced as efficiently as possible. Thus, the patentee will want the licensees to be producing at minimum average cost. This means that each licensee produce q_1. As a result, the optimal (i.e., profit-maximizing) number of licensees will be $n = Q_2/q_1$.

number; if she relies on market forces to limit the number, then the licensees are deemed to be nonexclusive and are denied standing.

Not according standing to the nonexclusive licensee nevertheless still may be justified, once we consider the effect of uncertainty upon the parties' expectations. Although one might expect the licensee to be willing to pay more for a license if he knows that he will be no worse off as a result of an infringement, the very nature of a nonexclusive license is that the patentee *can* license as many others as he wishes; the licensee arguably cannot have any expectation of a given level of profit. The previous analysis suggests, however, that the market will limit the number of nonexclusive licensees to some number n; so the argument would be that the licensee does have an expectation of receiving the profits associated with being one of that number n. The problem lies in determining what n is. As others have noted, the business of licensing technology – especially a new and unproven technology – is fraught with uncertainty.[122] *Ex ante*, neither the patentee nor the licensees know how commercially successful the venture will be. Our analysis also assumes that the patentee will set the license fee at a level that seeks to maximize profit, but in reality, a number of forces may constrain the patentee from attaining this goal. First, there is a disparity of information between patentee and potential licensees. The patentee probably knows more about the technology than do the licensees, and she may not be willing to disclose all of this information before an agreement is signed.[123] The dilemma is to disclose enough information about the innovation so that potential licensees will want to purchase a license, but not so much that the information becomes common knowledge; not being able to disclose all of the information in advance, however, lowers the potential value of the license.[124] Second, the price of the license is constrained by the possibility that potential licensees may be able to discover substitutes for the invention.[125] Third, the demand for licenses may be interdependent, meaning that a licensee's willingness to

---

[122] See, e.g., Schlicher (1996; § 1.8(g), at 53); Bessy & Brousseau (1998; 460–70).

[123] As we noted in Chapter 2, patent law requires the inventor to disclose enough information to enable a person ordinarily skilled in the art to practice the invention, and to reveal his "best mode" of practicing the invention as of the time the application is filed. See 35 U.S.C. § 112. But it does not require him to disclose any later discoveries relating to the means of practicing the invention, and often this subsequent know-how will be necessary for the successful exploitation of the technology. Patent law may reduce Arrow's Information Paradox by providing a framework for the transfer of know-how, but it does not eliminate it.

[124] See Schlicher (1996; § 1.8(g), at 53–4); Arrow (1962; 614–16); Bessy & Brousseau (1998; 463); Gallini & Wright (1990; 148).

[125] See Schlicher (1996; § 1.8(g), 53); Gallini & Wright (1990;148).

purchase a given cost-reducing innovation may depend upon how many of his competitors are doing the same.[126] Fourth, licensees are free to challenge the validity of the patent and may be tempted to do so if the cost of the license fee is too high. The result of these various imperfections is that licensors typically receive only a portion of the total profit of their innovation; one study shows an average of 40%.[127] The lower the licensor's royalty is, however, the closer output will move to the competitive level of Q_1; and as Q increases, so too does n. This suggests that trying to reconstruct what the optimal number n was expected to be at the time the contract was executed – and thereby of determining the nonexclusive licensee's expected profit – is likely to be extremely difficult. Prohibiting nonexclusive licensees from suing therefore may be attributable more to the difficulty of calculating the *amount* of their harm than to the *lack* of any discernible harm.[128] (We've seen this principle before – it was the reason, right or wrong, for eliminating restitution in patent cases and probably one reason for limiting restitution to willful infringement in trademark cases.) Exclusive licensees, by contrast, do not suffer under the same disability, because the number of such licenses is (by definition) constrained in advance. In cases in which the optimal number of licensees can be determined in advance, the patentee can easily provide her licensees with a right to sue, if this appears to be in her interest, by opting for the use of exclusive licenses.

---

[126] See Katz & Shapiro (1986; 569).

[127] See Caves et al. (1983; 258).

[128] On the other hand, one might argue that, even if the nonexclusive licensee's damages will be difficult to prove, a license that includes a right to sue for those damages will be more valuable than one than does not. But perhaps not by much: absent the infringement, the infringer might have purchased a nonexclusive license and thereby lawfully have competed with the other nonexclusive licensees. Moreover, if the typical nonexclusive licensing arrangement involves a larger number of licensees than the typical exclusive licensing arrangement (which may or may not be the case, however), the potential cost of conferring upon each of those nonexclusive licensees a right to initiate litigation (and therefore potentially jeopardize the patent) may be relatively high. Finally, as noted earlier, if the parties wish to confer a right to sue upon the licensees, they can do so by expressly limiting the number of those licensees. Although the analysis somewhat speculative, these considerations may, on balance, weigh in favor of precluding nonexclusive licensees from suing in most cases.

Conceivably, one could create a default rule that allows nonexclusive licensees, absent an agreement to the contrary, to sue for injunctive relief but not damages. Such a rule might be consistent with the traditional dictum that injunctive relief is available only when damages or other "legal" remedies are inadequate. But if the patentee has committed to prosecute infringers, the need for conferring a parallel right upon nonexclusive licensees to sue for injunctive relief only should be unnecessary.

A related point is that uncertainty may compel the patentee to prefer nonexclusive licenses even if the standing rules threaten to reduce the profitability of the venture to some extent. Suppose, for example, that the patentee expects the optimal number of licenses to be $n = Q_2/q_1$ and commits to offer n licenses. If the patentee commits to this number and the patented product is not as successful as had been anticipated, the patentee will still receive nearly all of the rents attributable to the patent. If it is more successful than expected, however, the licensees will share in those rents because there are too few licensees. By not committing to a specific number of licensees, the patentee can allow market forces to increase the number of licensees when product demand is higher than expected.[129] In that case, the patentee will extract more of the additional rents than she would if the number of licensees were limited to n. Thus, this uncertainty can explain why a patentee may opt for nonexclusive licensees even when doing so would appear to reduce the value of the patent.

CONCLUSIONS

The analysis above leads to the following specific conclusions with respect to standing:

1. In patent cases, the assignee virtually always has an interest in participating in infringement litigation, and the assignor may as well in cases in which the latter retains a reversionary interest in the patent, or is entitled to a running royalty tied to sales or production, or continues to own the patent outside the assignee's territory. At the very least, the assignor who possesses such an interest should be allowed to intervene in infringement litigation pursuant to Federal Rule 24. Moreover, we have argued that when the patentee has assigned the patent in exchange for a running royalty, her interest is sufficiently great that the default rule should be that she has a waivable right to initiate litigation herself. In addition, we would expect that in most cases the licensor *and* exclusive licensee of a patent would have a substantial interest in participating in infringement litigation, and that mandatory joinder under Rule 19 is likely to be the most appropriate vehicle for protecting those interests without giving rise to multiple litigation. We also (weakly) concur with the traditional rule against conferring standing upon nonexclusive licensees, although

---

[129] If demand is higher than anticipated, the licensees will earn supracompetitive returns, which will attract entry.

more for reasons relating to the difficulty of proving the extent of injury than for lack of injury altogether.

2. The liberalization of standing rules in copyright cases probably makes sense, in light of the differing economic value of individual copyright rights as opposed to individual patent rights, and in light of what is probably a much lower risk of property invalidation in copyright litigation. Our only word of caution is that courts must be alert to the possibility that persons not named as parties to the original suit may nevertheless have an interest, depending on the specific circumstances of the case, in being required or allowed to participate pursuant to Rules 19, 20, or 24.

3. The standing rules in trademark law probably should largely track those in patent law, because trademark rights, like patents but unlike copyrights, are not practically separable the one from the other. It may also be the case that trademarks are invalidated in litigation more often than are copyrights. If so, this fact would suggest that both parties to an assignment or exclusive licensing arrangement may be indispensable parties for purposes of Rule 19. On the other hand, to the extent that trademark law operates as a consumer protection system as well as a means for inducing trademarks owners to engage in socially desirable behavior, a more liberal standing regime – perhaps even allowing nonexclusive licensees to initiate litigation – may be warranted, as some courts apparently have concluded.

Two other conclusions necessarily follow from what we have discussed above. The first, which we have repeated throughout, is that there is no overriding need for the type of rigid standing rules exemplified by *Waterman*. The decision whether a person must, may, or may not participate in infringement litigation should instead focus upon a realistic assessment of the person's interest and on the consequences on her nonparticipation, rather than upon her amenability to classification as an assignor, assignee, licensor, or licensee. The second is the need for further empirical study of copyright and trademark invalidation. As we have noted, some features of the current standing rules make more sense if our hypothesis is correct that copyrights are invalidated only rarely and trademarks perhaps somewhat more frequently but still less commonly than patents. Although this hypothesis is consistent with anecdotal observation derived from the case law, a more rigorous empirical inquiry would allow us more accurately to measure the rationality of the standing rules courts now employ.

EIGHT

Calculating Monetary Damages

We return in this penultimate chapter to the question of damages. To put this chapter in context, we proposed in Chapter 3 a general rule under which the IPR owner is entitled to recover from the infringer the greater of her lost profit or the defendant's profit attributable to the infringement, subject to adjustment up or down to avoid over – and underdeterrence. In Chapter 4, we considered whether further refinements to the model are necessary or at least justifiable when more specific consideration of the nature of patents, copyrights, and trademarks is brought to bear. We then took up, in Chapters 5, 6, and 7 some related issues concerning the standard of liability and identifying the proper defendants and plaintiffs. We now return to the damages question, focusing on the more concrete issue of how damages should be calculated. Our principal concern will be the calculation of compensatory damages – lost profits or reasonable royalties – in patent cases, although much of our analysis could be applied to calculating restitutionary damages as well. It also could be extended to trade secrets, copyrights, and trademarks. In general, however, the case law on damages calculation in these bodies of law is much less developed than in patent law. In copyright, this may be due in part to the availability (in the United States) of statutory damages, and perhaps to the lower stakes at issue in the average case (in comparison with patent law). In trademark, no damages are available at all absent a showing of actual confusion, and restitutionary damages are usually limited to cases of willful infringement. These limitations reduce the importance of monetary damages to some extent, and (in the case of the latter limitation) may be attributable in part to the impossibility of accurately apportioning the harm caused by the infringement in all but the most egregious cases. Nevertheless, in an appropriate case, the principles we develop in this chapter should be equally applicable to all of the various bodies of IP law.

THE PROBLEM IN PERSPECTIVE

A hypothetical may help to illustrate some of the problems that can arise when one sets out to quantify the harm caused by an act of infringement. An intriguing problem in the field of computer science is the development of speaker-independent voice recognition technology. At present, this technology is in general only about 80% accurate, and scientists expect that it will not materially improve in the absence of a major breakthrough, perhaps in our understanding of how the mind processes sound. Suppose, however, that a few years down the road a scientist (call her Alice) makes such a discovery and embodies it in a computer programmed to understand and transcribe English speech; she then markets her invention to, among others, television networks that provide closed-caption programming for the hearing impaired. A competitor, Bruce, markets a rival system that infringes Alice's device. Alice normally will be entitled to an injunction forbidding Bruce from making, using, or selling Alice's patented invention, but what damages should a court award for the period from the beginning of the infringement to the entry of the injunction?

Although a facile analysis might suggest that Alice has lost a sale for every sale made by Bruce, and that she should be awarded her normal profit margin on those sales – or, in the alternative, the customary royalty she charges others who wish to license and market her technology – neither standard necessarily provides an accurate measure of Alice's economic loss. First, with respect to lost profits, it is not at all clear that Alice would have made a sale for every infringing sale made by Bruce. As we have seen, one party may produce the product at higher or lower marginal cost than the other, or may serve different markets. Whether the parties will compete, during the infringement phase, on the basis of price, quantity, or both is a matter that cannot be assumed *a priori*. A complete analysis also must take into account that a variety of nonpatented technologies may be substitutable, if only imperfectly so, for Alice's new machine. If Bruce priced his infringing product below the price charged by Alice, some customers who bought machines from Bruce might have preferred a less advanced but lower-priced nonpatented technology to the higher-priced patented machine, in the absence of infringement. Alice's lost profit therefore will be a function of the likely reaction of consumers in light of these nonpatented alternatives. Estimating the precise state of the world absent infringement can be a difficult task, albeit one that can be aided by the tools of economic analysis.

Further complications arise if we conclude that Alice would have licensed the technology to Bruce for a price, rather than marketing it herself. We argued above that, when the defendant is the more efficient user of the patented technology, courts should be allowed to award the defendant's profit attributable to the infringement. Estimating this number is the flipside of estimating the patentee's lost profits, because the profit attributable to the infringement *and not to other causes* will be a function of market demand and existence of other alternatives. If instead the law permits only an award of reasonable royalties, different complications ensue. If Alice does not have a standard royalty she charges all potential licensees, a court might try to estimate the royalty the parties would have agreed to (if any) in the absence of infringement. But this task is not easy either, given that it is likely that the parties would have negotiated a royalty in light of factors similar to those that are relevant to the lost profits analysis, including the profit one could expect to earn from alternative, unpatented technologies.

Still more difficulties will ensue if Alice seeks damages for other losses allegedly caused by the infringement. Should she be able to recover lost profits on lost sales of unpatented goods that she normally would have sold along with the patented product? What if Alice makes more money selling or licensing a less advanced technology and therefore lets her patent remain idle for some time? If the infringement causes her to lose sales on unpatented products that compete with infringing products, should she recover her lost profits on those sales or should the patentee's own marketing of the patented product be a precondition to lost profits damages? Or what if Alice's patent is instead for a component that constitutes only a small part of a final product that Alice markets (say, a new device that marginally improves the quality of television reception)? Should Alice recover lost profits on lost sales of television sets generally, or should her recovery be apportioned so as to avoid conferring a windfall recovery? Alternatively, how much of the defendant's profit is attributable to the infringing component, and how much to other factors?

The correct answers to these questions are both simpler and more difficult than one might think. They are simpler, in the sense that traditional tort-law doctrines of cause-in-fact and proximate cause can serve a useful purpose in the present context; patent law and the other bodies of IP law do not require materially different legal standards for assessing the fact, and quantity, of harm for which the plaintiff is to be compensated. But the answers to these questions are also more difficult than is sometimes assumed, because careful application of economic analysis is not easy, and sometimes leads to counterintuitive results.

In the sections that follow, we begin with an overview of how U.S. courts approach the problem of estimating lost profits and reasonable royalties in patent cases. In particular, we note the historic shift from an approach focused on apportionment – the question of how much of the value of a product is attributable to some patented feature – to an approach that attempts simply to calculate the profit the plaintiff would have earned, but for the infringement. The but-for approach, as we shall see, focuses more on the realities of the marketplace, and in particular on the existence of economic (not necessarily technological) substitutes for the patented invention among the relevant class of consumers and other users. We provide a rationale for a general "but-for" causation standard and demonstrate how this standard might result in different amounts of damages, depending on market structure. The amount of but-for damages may differ, for example, in a market characterized by Cournot oligopoly (in which the patentee and infringer compete with respect to quantity), as opposed to one characterized by Bertrand oligopoly (in which they compete with respect to price).

We also discuss the legal concept of proximate cause – a doctrine that, for policy reasons, limits the amount of damages that otherwise would be recoverable in tort under the but-for standard – and what it might mean in the context of patent infringement. In particular, we consider a variety of arguments suggesting that the doctrine of proximate cause should limit the patent owner from recovering its lost profits on sales of complementary products, or on sales of unpatented products that compete with the infringing good, because allowing patent owners to recover these damages might facilitate anticompetitive schemes of preemptive patenting, tying, or bundling. We reject the more sweeping of these arguments, but express agreement that proximate cause should rein in lost profits on sales of complementary goods in at least *some* cases – and that the Federal Circuit's (somewhat vague) criteria for determining which cases fall into this category are essentially sound.

COMPENSATORY DAMAGES IN U.S. PATENT CASES

The easiest case for calculating damages would be one in which the patent owner already licenses the patent to others for a standard or "established" royalty, because in such a case (as the 1793 Patent Act explicitly recognized) it may be appropriate to conclude that the infringement deprived the patent owner of that fee. Unfortunately, this type of case is relatively uncommon. For one thing, the conditions under which a patent owner licenses its technology may vary so widely that there is no established royalty.[1] Furthermore, even when an established royalty exists, it may not accurately reflect the fee the patent owner would have charged the defendant, because the defendant's use of the invention (1) may differ in some material respect from that of the established licensees or (2) may itself have reduced the established royalty below what it otherwise would have been. Thus, in cases in which the established royalty either does not exist or would not be an appropriate measure of the patent owner's actual damages – including the case in which the patent owner does not license others at all, but rather uses the patent herself – the court must engage in the more difficult task of estimating the patent owner's lost profits or the amount of a reasonable royalty.

Infringement can reduce the patent owner's profit in a number of ways. First, and most obviously, the infringer may divert sales from the patent owner. Second, competition from the infringer may cause the patent owner to reduce her own price (or to forgo an increase) and thus earn lower profits on those goods she continues to sell. This is sometimes referred to as "price erosion."[2] The first two effects can be seen in Figures 3.2 and 3.3 from Chapter 3. A third possible effect is that the infringement causes the patentee to suffer additional costs, such as increased advertising and marketing expenditures. Courts also on occasion have awarded or considered awarding damages for other asserted harms – such as lost future profits, injury to the patent owner's reputation resulting from the sale of poor-quality infringing goods, and the infringer's accelerated entry into the marketplace once the patent expires – but these latter injuries are more commonly perceived either as being subsumed in one or more of the other categories, or as being too remote or speculative. Finally, patent owners sometimes claim damages for lost sales of other goods, not covered by the patent at issue, that typically would have been sold in connection with the patented product or that were sold in competition with the infringing product. We take up the issue of whether these latter harms should be compensable in subsequent sections

---

[1] The U.S. courts recognize this problem. Thus, for a royalty to qualify as "established," it must satisfy four conditions: (1) it "must be paid or secured before the infringement complained of"; (2) it "must be paid by such a number of persons as to indicate a general acquiescence in its reasonableness by those who have occasion to use the invention"; (3) it "must be uniform at the places where the licenses are issued"; and (4) it should not be paid in settlement of another infringement claim. *Rude v. Westcott*, 130 U.S. 152, 165 (1889).

[2] Note, however, that if the price goes down, the quantity sold normally will increase, albeit at a lower profit margin; accurate price erosion damages therefore should account not only for the reduction in price, but also for the increase in quantity caused by the reduction in price. See Addanki (1998; 852); Werden et al. (1999; 312–16).

of this chapter. For now, we shall focus exclusively on the complications that arise from estimating lost sales of products that embody, or were made by use of, the patented invention.

Two methods the U.S. courts have sometimes used for estimating the patent owner's lost sales are problematic. The first is simply to subtract the number of units the patent owner sold after the infringement from the number she sold before and to infer that the infringement caused whatever difference may exist. This sort of *post hoc, ergo propter hoc* reasoning is valid, however, only if demand and cost conditions have remained stable during the period of infringement, which is often unlikely.[3] A second method is to use the *defendant's* actual sales of the infringing products as a surrogate for the sales the *plaintiff* would have made absent the infringement. Courts sometimes make this assumption today, though typically only when the plaintiff and defendant are the only two suppliers of the product at issue (the so-called two-supplier market scenario).[4] This method was much more common in the nineteenth century, however – and sometimes courts took the analysis one step further, not only considering the defendant's actual sales but also using the defendant's actual *profits* as a surrogate for the profits the plaintiff would have earned but for the defendant's improper use.[5] To be sure, the better reasoned decisions cautioned against presuming that the defendant's profits were identical to the plaintiff's lost profits; at the very least, the plaintiff would have to prove that she was ready and able to supply the defendant's customers. Moreover, either party could try to show that the plaintiff's and defendant's profit margins differed, though normally a different profit margin worked in favor of the plaintiff.[6] Efforts to calculate the defendant's profit attributable to the infringement, however, whether used as a surrogate for actual damages or as an end in itself, tended to focus the courts' attention on two problems that continue to cause difficulties today: namely, substitutability and apportionment.

---

[3] See Werden et al. (1999; 316).

[4] See *Pall Corp. v. Micron Separations, Inc.,* 66 F.3d 1211, 1222 (Fed. Cir. 1995).

[5] See *Seymour v. McCormick,* 57 U.S. 480, 489 (1853). Note that this use of defendant's profits as an estimate of the plaintiff's actual damages was different in purpose from awarding the defendant's profits in their own right, as restitution. Until 1870, a court of equity could award restitutionary but not compensatory damages, and somewhat different procedures governed the estimation methods used at law and in equity.

[6] See *Pitts v. Hall,* 19 F. Cas. 754, 758 (C.C.N.D.N.Y. 1851) which notes that the infringer might be able to tolerate a lower profit margin than the patent owner, who must recoup its research and development costs (cited in Curtis (1867; § 338, at 345–6); 3 Robinson (1890; § 1062, at 350).

Substitutability

The substitutability problem centers upon whether there are noninfringing substitutes that the defendant could have used instead of the patented invention. When the infringer has access to substitute technologies, the inference that he caused the patent owner to lose any profits may be false – and a reasonable royalty may then be a more appropriate form of compensation – because the infringer could have made comparable sales and profits, and thereby deprived the patent owner of comparable sales and profits, by using those substitutes. But it is not always easy to determine whether one product is a substitute for another. Whether one product substitutes for another depends not only upon the function of the two products, but also upon the prices at which they are offered to the public.[7] Under the cost and demand conditions that prevail in the developed world today, for example, most people would not view automobiles and horse-drawn carriages as reasonable substitutes, but if the price of automobiles were to increase one-million-fold relative to carriages, the demand for carriages would undoubtedly rise significantly. In addition, as this example itself suggests, substitutability is not necessarily an all-or-nothing phenomenon: given an increase of $x in the price of Good 1, *some* consumers may switch to Good 2, while others remain loyal to Good 1. Thus, an infringer who could have used an alternative that *some* consumers would have viewed as an adequate substitute for the patented invention would have siphoned off *some* sales from the patent owner, even in the absence of infringement, and courts should take this fact into account in estimating the latter's lost profits damages. Unfotunately,

---

[7] As an economic matter, products A and B are substitutes if an increase in the price of good B, which leads to reduced consumption of B, results in an increase in the quantity demanded of good A, as consumers substitute A for B. See Pindyck & Rubinfeld (1998; 109); Schlicher (1999; § 9.05[2][l], at 9–92 (1999)).

    A formal way of capturing the degree of substitutability is provided by the cross-elasticity of demand. In general form, the cross-elasticity of demand (ε_{AB}) is defined to be

$$\varepsilon_{AB} = \frac{\partial Q_A}{\partial P_B} \bullet \frac{P_B}{Q_A}.$$

Because the price of good B and the quantity of good A must necessarily be positive, the cross-elasticity of demand will be positive for substitutes because $\partial Q_A/\partial P_B$ is positive if A and B are substitutes. The larger the cross-elasticity of demand, the stronger the degree of substitutability. On intuitive reasoning, we would expect large values for ε_{AB} when examining Coke v. Pepsi, Bud v. Miller, and Burger King v. McDonald's. Similarly, we would expect lower values of ε_{AB} when examining automobiles v. motorcycles, PCs v. typewriters, and light bulbs v. candles. The actual values of ε_{AB} are, of course, an empirical matter. In other words, the data will tell us to what extent goods A and B are substitutes.

this understanding of the economics of substitution has only occasionally taken hold in IP cases.

Apportionment

The apportionment problem arises from the recognition that not all of the infringer's actual profit, or the patent owner's lost profit, is necessarily attributable to the use of the patented invention. To illustrate, suppose that a television manufacturer owns a patent for a component that, when incorporated into television sets, improves the picture quality of television broadcasts; that a rival manufacturer (the nefarious Blair Electronics from Chapter 6) infringes this patent by incorporating an identical component into its (otherwise noninfringing) sets, without permission of the patent owner; and that the patent owner then sues Blair for infringement. The intuition that not *all* of the plaintiff's or defendant's profit is attributable to the patented component and that the plaintiff, therefore, should recover only for the *incremental* gain attributable to the patent seems compelling, although in searching for an explanation for this intuition the courts sometimes succeed only in further muddying the waters. Historically, the courts' principal concern seems to have been that awarding the plaintiff any more than the lost profit attributable to the component (or, under a restitutionary theory, any more than the defendant's profit attributable to the component) would in effect expand the scope of the plaintiff's patent to encompass the entire final product.[8] Consistent with their often-expressed concern over the "monopolistic" nature of patents, sometimes expressed in maxims calling for narrow patent construction, courts strove to avoid this result, but with the consequence of requiring them to apportion the profits attributable to the patented and unpatented components of a unitary invention. From an economic standpoint, however, trying to determine what portion of the profits earned from a multicomponent product are attributable to any one component, or combination of components, is often a meaningless inquiry. In our television hypothetical, for example, the patent owner (let's say it's Sony) presumably earns a certain amount of its profit from the sale of Sony TVs. But how much of that profit can be attributed to any one component?

---

[8] See, e.g., *Philp v. Nock*, 84 U.S. 460, 462 (1873) which states that "[w]here the infringement is confined to a part of the thing sold, the recovery must be limited accordingly. It cannot be as if the entire thing were covered by the patent. . . . " Moreover, as suggested in *Seymour v. McCormick*, 57 U.S. 480, 490 (1853), a contrary rule might be particularly troublesome in a case in which the final product incorporates two or more patents, as it might imply duplicative damages claims.

In principle, these questions could be answered if Sony marketed enough different models, each containing different combinations of components, but in reality firms usually cannot offer hundreds or thousands of models of a standard commodity; they will instead rely upon a few profit-maximizing configurations, and ignore the rest.

A more sophisticated analysis might assume that, in the typical case, the defendant would have sold some television sets, and earned some profit, even if it had avoided using the infringing component. This is just another way of saying that a set without the picture-enhancing component is, at some price and for some consumers, an imperfect albeit reasonable substitute for a set with the component. Under this analysis, the only sales the plaintiff loses as a result of the infringement are sales to those consumers for whom the picture-enhancing component is a decisive factor in their purchasing decision. Thus, rather than having to determine which portion of the profits earned by the defendant, or lost by the plaintiff, are attributable to the component, a court using this approach would have to determine only what sales were lost and award the plaintiff all the profit she would have earned on those sales.

The inadequacy of the apportionment framework the courts actually employed nevertheless soon became apparent in cases in which a patented component clearly *was* the principal reason that most buyers of a multicomponent product were interested in buying that product. Using our television example, suppose that the component at issue revolutionized television technology in some way – say, by allowing the user to access thousands of stations from around the globe, without using cable or a satellite dish, and at a fraction of the cost – that effectively made ordinary televisions obsolete. In such a case, one might surmise that the infringer would have made *no* sales if he had refrained from infringing, and that awarding the patent owner only a portion of the profits she would have earned on sales of the final product would leave her worse off than if the infringement had never occurred. To deal with such cases, U.S. courts developed what has come to be known as the "entire market value rule" (EMVR).[9] According to its most recent articulation, the rule allows the patent owner to recover the entire profit she would have earned on sales of a final product incorporating a patented component, when the patented component is the "basis for customer demand" for that product.[10] Despite its vagueness, courts have

[9] For early articulations of the rule, see, e.g., *Garretson v. Clark*, 111 U.S. 120, 121 (1884); *Fay v. Allen*, 30 F. 446, 447–48 (C.C.N.D.N.Y. 1887).

[10] *Tec Air Inc. v. Denso Mfg. Mich. Inc.*, 192 F.3d 1353, 1362 (Fed. Cir. 1999) that quotes *State Indus. v. Mor-Flo Indus.*, 883 F.2d 1573, 1580 (Fed. Cir. 1989).

continued to cite the rule to the present day, viewing it either as an exception to the apportionment principle, or as an application of that principle in cases in which 100% of the profit properly can be attributed to the patented component.[11]

The *Panduit* Factors

In a famous 1978 decision, *Panduit Corp. v. Stahlin Bros. Fibre Works, Inc.*, the United States Court of Appeals for the Sixth Circuit summarized many of the rules we have examined in the preceding pages. The court set forth the following four factors to establish lost profits damages in a patent infringement case:

(1) demand for the patented product, (2) absence of acceptable noninfringing substitutes, (3) his manufacturing and marketing capability to exploit the demand, and (4) the amount of the profit he would have made.[12]

U.S. courts continue to recite and apply the *Panduit* factors today, though they also caution that it may not be necessary for the plaintiff to prove every factor in every case. Moreover, each factor has its own peculiar characteristics. To satisfy the third factor, for example, the patent owner may need to present evidence of such things as excess manufacturing capacity, ability to obtain financing, and ability to market additional units of the product.[13] Disputes most frequently center, however, on the application of the second factor that relates to the presence or absence of adequate noninfringing substitutes and we shall examine this factor in some detail. (The first factor, proof of demand for the patented invention, is often not contested; when it is, it is usually satisfied by proof of substantial sales of products incorporating the patented invention or else it is subsumed within the second factor.)

In assessing the adequacy of noninfringing substitutes, courts traditionally have considered whether the infringer had access to an alternative comprising the same advantages as the patented device. As we noted previously, however, in determining whether *consumers* would view one product as a substitute for another, it is necessary to consider not only function but also

---

[11] See, e.g., *Velo-Bind, Inc. v. Minnesota Mining & Mfg. Co.*, 677 F.2d 965, 973 (9th Cir. 1981) that refers to EMVR as an exception to the apportionment principle.

[12] 575 F.2d 1152, 1156 (6th Cir. 1978).

[13] See, e.g., *Gargoyles, Inc. v. United States*, 113 F.3d 1572, 1577–8 (Fed. Cir. 1997); *Kori Corp. v. Wilco Marsh Buggies & Draglines, Inc.*, 561 F. Supp. 512, 526–27 (E.D. La. 1981), *aff'd*, 761 F.2d 649 (Fed. Cir. 1985).

price. In some cases, courts have begun to consider both factors[14] and, more generally, to apply explicitly economic criteria to the issue of whether one product is an adequate substitute for another. In *SmithKline Diagnostics, Inc. v. Helena Corp.*, for example, the court rejected the plaintiff's argument that noninfringing products lacking one or more features of the patented invention cannot be adequate substitutes for that invention, noting that non-infringing products "by definition . . . do not represent an embodiment of the invention."[15] Instead, the analysis should center on whether, but for the infringement, purchasers would have bought the patented product or would have been satisfied with products lacking the patented product's unique features. Similarly, in *Grain Processing Corp. v. American Maize-Products Co.*, the Court of Appeals affirmed the district court's decision not to award lost profits, based upon a finding that, in the absence of infringement, the defendant would have resorted to an alternative, noninfringing process for manufacturing a type of food additive.[16] Even so, patent litigants rarely estimate the cross-elasticity of demand between the infringing product and the noninfringing alternative, despite the potential usefulness of this information in determining whether the infringement has cost the patentee any sales.[17]

With respect to the fourth element – the amount of profit the patent owner would have made, absent the infringement – U.S. courts for the most part recognize that they should take into account not only the price at which the patent owner would have made these sales, but also any additional costs he would have incurred in connection with these sales. In estimating costs, courts typically use an "incremental income" approach, which

recognizes that it does not cost as much to produce unit N + 1 if the first N (or fewer) units produced already have paid the fixed costs. Thus fixed costs – those costs which do not vary with increases in production, such as management salaries, property taxes, and insurance – are excluded when determining profits.[18]

---

[14] See, e.g., *BIC Leisure Prods., Inc. v. Windsurfing Int'l, Inc.*, 1 F.3d 1214, 1219 (Fed. Cir. 1993).

[15] 926 F.2d 1161, 1166 (Fed. Cir. 1991).

[16] 185 F.3d 1341 (Fed. Cir. 1999), *aff'g* 979 F. Supp. 1233 (N.D. Ind. 1997).

[17] As noted previously, if the cross-elasticity of demand is very large, then the patentee may not have suffered much in the way of damages; its loss of sales and profits would be due primarily to the infringing firm's entry rather than the infringement. Unless the patentee can separate out the effect of entry, its claim for damages should fail. In contrast, if the cross-elasticity of demand is very low, then it is reasonable to infer, all else being equal, that lost sales and profits are due to infringement rather than entry. Damages claims in such cases should fare much better than in cases where the cross-elasticity of demand is quite large. For discussion of some methods for estimating elasticities indirectly, see Addanki (1998; 856–7); Krosin & Kozlowski (1990; 72–3); Werden et al. (1999; 317–18).

[18] *Paper Converting Mach. Co. v. Magna-Graphics Corp.*, 745 F.2d 11, 31–2 (Fed. Cir. 1984). Litigation often centers on whether certain costs should be classified as fixed or variable.

Courts also recognize, however, that if the volume of diverted sales is sufficiently large, these sales would have entailed additional costs (such as the cost of additional manufacturing facilities) which, although usually categorized as fixed, must be deducted as well to achieve an accurate estimate of lost profits.[19] Finally, taxes that would have been paid on revenues earned from additional sales are not deductible, in light of the fact that the damages award itself will be taxed.[20]

Use of this methodology can sometimes result in lost profits awards that are much higher than one might expect. To see why, consider Paul Janicke's example of a firm that owns a patent on a formula for a household soap:

Fixed costs, principally advertising campaigns and marketing overhead, may run 90% of revenue for an item like a patented household soap formulation. Suppose the soap sells at wholesale for $0.60 per bar. Fixed costs would then be $0.54. Variable costs, e.g., labor, materials, and shipping, are so called because they vary rather directly with volume. Suppose that in our soap example they run 5% of revenue, or $0.03, leaving a 5% net profit, also $0.03.

If an infringer diverts sales of this soap from the patentee, the infringer will be liable for $0.60 (lost revenue) minus $0.03 (variable costs), or $0.57 per bar.[21]

Although at first glance this result may seem perverse, it is economically sound. In the absence of infringement, the patentee would have amortized the fixed costs over a larger number of sales, such that the profit per unit sold would have been higher. To illustrate, suppose that, in Janicke's example, the patent owner sold 10,000 bars at $0.60 each during the period of infringement. It thereby earned $6,000 in gross revenue which, minus $5,400 in fixed costs, leaves $600. Subtracting $300 in variable costs (5% of gross revenue) leaves a profit on goods actually sold of $300. Ignoring

---

See, e.g., *Kalman v. Berlyn Corp.*, 914 F.2d 1473, 1485 (Fed. Cir. 1990); *W. R. Grace & Co.–Conn. v. Intercat, Inc.*, 60 F. Supp. 2d 316, 326 (D. Del. 1999). Parties may prove the amount of fixed and variable costs by subjecting the patent owner's profit and loss statements to a line-by-line analysis, or by using regression analysis. See, e.g., *Stryker Corp. v. Intermedics Orthopedics, Inc.*, 891 F. Supp. 751, 825–32 (E.D.N.Y. 1995), *aff'd*, 96 F.3d 1409 (Fed. Cir. 1996); *Schneider (Europe) AG v. Scimed Life Sys., Inc.*, 852 F. Supp. 813, 859 (D. Minn. 1994), *aff'd mem.*, 60 F.3d 839 (Fed. Cir. 1995).

[19] See *Schneider (Europe) AG v. Scimed Life Sys., Inc.*, 852 F. Supp. 813, 847 (D. Minn. 1994), *aff'd mem.*, 60 F.3d 839 (Fed. Cir. 1995); *In re Mahurkar Double Lumen Hemodialysis Catheter Patent Litig.*, 831 F. Supp. 1354, 1385 (N.D. Ill. 1993), *aff'd*, 71 F.3d 1573 (Fed. Cir. 1995).

[20] See *Kalman*, 914 F.2d at 1482.

[21] Janicke (1993; 708–09). In other words, as Skenyon et al. note, "the patent owner's 'lost profit' for each infringing sale is necessarily *greater* than the actual profit the patent owner earned for each patented item it actually did make and sell." Skenyon et al. (2002; § 2:46, at 2–74) (emphasis in original).

for now the effect of price erosion, and assuming for simplicity that the patent owner faces a constant marginal cost curve, let us assume that, in the absence of infringement, the patent owner would have sold 1000 more bars at the same price, earning an additional $600 in gross revenue. Subtracting 5% of this additional gross revenue, or $30, leaves a lost profit of $570. On these facts, it is easy to show that the sum of the patent owner's lost profit ($570) and its actual profit ($300) is exactly what the patent owner would have earned absent the infringement: 11,000 bars sold at $0.60 each would have generated $6,600 in gross revenue; subtracting $5,400 in fixed costs would have left $1,200; and further subtracting variable costs of 5% of gross revenue, or $330, would have left total profits of $870.

LOST PROFITS: TOWARD ADOPTION OF A "BUT FOR" STANDARD

Perhaps the most important development in the law of patent damages over the past two decades or so has been the gradual, albeit incomplete, adoption of an alternative framework to the miscellany of rules examined in the preceding section. In this section, we show how U.S. courts began, in the mid-1980s, to supplement (and in some cases, override) the traditional perspective with cause-in-fact and proximate cause standards borrowed from the law of torts, and how in doing so they have modified the law concerning both apportionment and the recovery of lost profits on so-called convoyed and derivative goods. Although in some ways these developments herald a much simpler analysis, they also require courts to apply a greater degree of economic sophistication.

Championing this approach, more or less, has been the U.S. Court of Appeals for the Federal Circuit, which has heard all appeals in patent cases since the early 1980s. Citing dicta from two Supreme Court cases interpreting the 1952 Patent Act,[22] the court has adopted a more flexible standard, under which the patent owner is, in general, entitled to recover whatever profits she would have earned but for the infringement.[23] In two circumstances in particular, this "but-for" standard can result in much more generous damages awards than would be permitted under a strict reading of *Panduit*: first,

---

[22] The two cases are *Aro Manufacturing Co. v. Convertible Top Replacement Co.* (*Aro II*), 377 U.S. 476 (1964), and *General Motors Corp. v. Devex Corp.*, 461 U.S. 648 (1983).

[23] See, e.g., *Grain Processing Corp. v. American Maize-Prods. Co.*, 185 F.3d 1341, 1349–50 (Fed. Cir. 1999); *Rite-Hite Corp. v. Kelley Co.*, 56 F.3d 1538, 1544–45 (Fed. Cir. 1995) (en banc).

in cases in which the patent owner can prove a partial, but not complete, absence of adequate noninfringing substitutes for the patented item (*Panduit* factor two) and, second, in cases in which the patent owner can prove that the infringement has cost it sales of unpatented products (thus, in some cases, obviating the need to prove *Panduit* factor three, demand for the patented product). With respect to the first class of cases, the court has permitted the recovery of damages on a market-share basis. The second class of cases raises more difficult policy questions, and for this reason has been more controversial.

Market-Share Damages and the Death of Apportionment

A case that illustrates the market-share approach is *State Industries v. Mor-Flo Industries.*[24] The plaintiff in *State Industries* owned a patent on a method of using polyurethane for insulating water-heater tanks, and it had a 40% share of the market for energy-efficient residential gas water heaters from 1984 to 1986. After finding that the defendant Mor-Flo had infringed the patent, the district court assessed lost profits damages based upon the assumption that, but for the infringement, State would have made 40% of Mor-Flo's infringing sales during the relevant period of time. Overlooking a mathematical error on the part of the district court, the Court of Appeals affirmed.[25] Subsequent case law has recognized that this market-share principle in effect creates an exception to *Panduit* factor two, since it assumes that, in a market characterized by a range of imperfect substitutes, infringement is likely to deprive the patent owner of some of the sales made by the infringing party, but that other (lawful) competitors probably would have earned some of those sales as well.[26] For that matter, a court may entertain evidence that the infringer itself would have earned some

---

[24] 883 F.2d 1573 (Fed. Cir. 1989).

[25] See *id.* at 1578–81. The mathematical error arises from the court's assumption that, absent the infringement, Mor-Flo would have retained the 40% market share that it enjoyed during the period of infringement. As others have noted, this assumption probably underestimates the amount of State's lost profits. To illustrate, suppose that during the period of infringement State had a 40% market share and that Mor-Flo and three other companies each had 15%. If Mor-Flo were eliminated from the picture, and if each of the other firms had retained a market share equal to 37.5% of State's market share, then in the absence of infringement State would have had a 47.1% market share and the three remaining competitors each 17.6%. See Cox (1998; 145–6) who describes the correct method; Evans (1995; 616–17); Jarosz & Page (1993; 318 n. 23); Krosin & Kozlowski (1990; 81–82); Werden et al. (1998; 319).

[26] See, e.g., *BIC Leisure Products v. Windsurfing Int'l, Inc.*, 1 F.3d 1214, 1217–19 (Fed. Cir. 1993).

share of the market by selling a noninfringing substitute product, had it not infringed.[27]

Cases like *State Industries* pose a serious challenge to the continued viability of the apportionment principle. Borrowing from our previous example, suppose that a firm owns a patent on a component that it incorporates into a final product, television sets; that a rival manufacturer incorporates an infringing component into its sets; and that these are the only two firms within the relevant market. As we have seen, traditionally the general rule is said to be that the patent owner is entitled only to the lost profits that are directly attributable to the patented component, rather than the entire profit it would have earned on lost sales of television sets; the exception arises when demand for the sets is driven by the presence of the patented component, in which case the EMVR entitles the patent owner to its entire lost profit. But when does the "general rule" ever apply? Suppose, first, that a television without the component is not an adequate noninfringing substitute for a television with the component. As we have seen, the more recent decisions recognize that the question of whether one product is an adequate substitute for another depends upon consumer demand, not technical interchangeability. To say that there are no adequate noninfringing substitutes, then, essentially means that the rival manufacturer would have made no sales absent the infringement. In such a case, however, the patented component "drives the demand" for the product, and the EMVR should entitle the patent owner to its entire lost profit on forgone sales of TVs. Alternatively, if a television without the component *is* an adequate noninfringing substitute for a set with the component, a straightforward reading of *Panduit* suggests that the patent owner is entitled to no lost profits damages at all. Analysis of this nature has led some observers to conclude – we think correctly – that the apportionment rule is a dead letter under U.S. law.[28]

Lost Profits on Sales of Unpatented Goods

A second principal consequence of the courts' move toward adopting a but-for standard has been the evolution of case law permitting the patent owner to recover lost profits on sales of unpatented items – including unpatented components, unpatented goods that are sold along with patented goods

---

[27] See *Atlantic Thermoplastics Co. v. Faytex Corp.*, 970 F.2d 834, 847 (Fed. Cir. 1992).

[28] See *W. L. Gore & Assocs. v. Carlisle Corp.*, 198 U.S.P.Q. (BNA) 353, 364–5 (D. Del. May 17, 1978); Conley (1987; 371); Rabowsky (1996; 294–5).

(so-called convoyed sales or collateral goods), and unpatented spare parts (sometimes referred to as "derivative goods") – if those losses are traceable to an act of patent infringement. In this regard, a trio of cases is of particular significance: *Paper Converting Machine Co. v. Magna-Graphics Corp.*, *Rite-Hite Corp. v. Kelley Co.*, and *King Instrument Co. v. Perego.*

In *Paper Converting*, a U.S. District Court had held that the defendant infringed a reissue patent claiming an improvement in a machine used to manufacture rolls of toilet paper, and awarded the patent owner lost profits not only on the sales of two of these machines but also on the sales of other, separate, machinery that was used in the manufacturing process.[29] In affirming the damages calculation, the Court of Appeals cited with approval two earlier cases in which the United States Court of Claims had suggested that the EMVR applies whenever an unpatented good has "financial and marketing dependence on the patented item," or the patentee normally can anticipate selling the patented and unpatented items together. Applying this standard, the court noted that every firm within the industry, including the purchasers of the two infringing machines at issue in this case, almost always bought an entire line of products from the manufacturer of the rewinder machine. This restatement of the EMVR, as depending upon the patent owner's reasonable expectations, departed from the more traditional articulation of the rule as applying only when the patented feature is the "basis for demand" for the unpatented feature. As John Schlicher has noted, however, the two ways of stating the rule are hardly identical.[30]

The second case, *Rite-Hite Corp. v. Kelley Co.*, simultaneously expanded and reduced the patent owner's ability to recover under the standards announced in *Paper Converting*. At issue was a patent covering "a device for securing a vehicle to a loading dock to prevent the vehicle from separating from the dock during loading or unloading." The patent owner, Rite-Hite, used this device in an inexpensive vehicle restraint known as the MDL-55, but it also sold a more expensive motorized restraint, the ADL-100, that made use of a different patent or patents. The defendant Kelley marketed a restraint known as the Truk-Stop, which infringed the '847 Patent and which competed against both the MDL-55 and the ADL-100. The district court awarded Rite-Hite lost profits not only on 80 lost sales of the MDL-55, but also on 3,243 lost sales of the ADL-100 and on 1,692 lost sales of "dock levelers," an unpatented device that Rite-Hite typically sold with the restraints and that was used as a bridge platform between the vehicle and the

---

[29] *Paper Converting Co. v. Magna-Graphics Corp.*, 745 F.2d 13–14, 22 (Fed. Cir. 1984).
[30] See Schlicher (2002; § 9.05[2][m], at 9–99).

restraint. In a divided ruling, the Federal Circuit affirmed the award with respect to the ADL-100 but reversed as to the dock levelers.[31]

With regard to the ADL-100, a majority of the court agreed that claims of patent infringement are subject to the same cause-in-fact and proximate cause standards as are other tort claims, and that, as a general matter, these standards entitle a patent owner to recover damages for the reasonable, objectively foreseeable consequences of the infringement.[32] Thus, while some consequences may be "too remote to justify compensation," the lost sales of the ADL-100, a product that directly competed with the infringing product, were "reasonably foreseeable" and therefore compensable. The court also suggested that allowing the patent owner to recover under these circumstances would be consistent with the constitutional policy of promoting R & D.[33]

The court rejected three arguments against allowing Rite-Hite to recover for the ADL-100 sales. First, the court concluded that recovery would not conflict with "antitrust law condemning the use of a patent as a means to obtain a 'monopoly' on unpatented material," reasoning that the present case did not risk "expanding the limits of the patent grant" or "exclud[ing] competitors from making, using, or selling a product not within the scope of" the '847 Patent, but rather "simply asks, once infringement of a valid patent is found, what compensable injuries result from that infringement, i.e., how may the patentee be made whole."[34] Second, the court rejected Kelley's argument "that, as a policy matter, inventors should be encouraged by the law to practice their inventions," noting that the government issues patents in exchange for inventors' disclosure (rather than use) of their inventions, and that the Patent Act does not require inventors to practice their patents.[35] Finally, the court rebuffed Kelley's argument that the case law, as reflected by *Panduit*, "uniformly requires that 'the intrinsic value of the patent in suit is the only proper basis for a lost profits award.'"[36] The court concluded that it could find no reason in "the statute, precedent, policy, or logic to limit the compensability of lost sales of a patentee's device that

---

[31] See *Rite-Hite Corp. v. Kelley Co.*, 56 F.3d 1538, 1543 (1995) (en banc). Kelley did not contest the award with respect to the MDL-55. See *id.*

[32] See *id.* at 1544–46.

[33] *Id.* at 1547, which quotes U.S.Const. art. I, § 8, cl. 8.

[34] *Id.* at 1547.

[35] See *id.* The court suggested, however, that in cases in which the failure to practice the invention "frustrates an important public need," a court may exercise its equitable powers to deny injunctive relief against infringement. See *id.* at 1547–8 (citations omitted).

[36] *Id.* at 1548.

directly competes with the infringing device if it is proven that those lost sales were caused in fact by the infringement."[37]

A majority of the court nevertheless also voted to vacate with respect to the dock levelers, for which the district court had awarded lost profits damages based upon the EMVR. Judge Lourie downplayed those statements in *Paper Converting* that "articulated the entire market value rule in terms of the objectively reasonable probability that a patentee would have made the relevant sales," and that "emphasized the financial and marketing dependence of the unpatented component on the patented component."[38] That language, Judge Lourie wrote, should be read in the overall context of the general principle, as applied in *Paper Converting*, that permits the recovery of lost profits on unpatented components only when those components and the patented components "function together . . . in some manner so as to produce a desired end product or result," in a manner "analogous to components of a single assembly or . . . parts of a complete machine, or . . . constitute a functional unit."[39] In the present case, the dock levelers – which could be used independently of the vehicle restraints (and vice versa), but which were sold together merely "as a matter of convenience or business advantage" – did not meet this test.[40] Judge Lourie distinguished the court's decision to allow damages on the unpatented ADL-100's on the ground that the latter were competitive with the infringing device, thus formulating a rule that damages may not be recovered "for items that are neither competitive with nor function with the patented invention."[41]

The third case, *King Instrument Corp. v. Perego*,[42] goes so far as to permit the recovery of lost profits even when the patent owner does not market *any* product embodying the patented invention. At issue in *King Instrument* was, among other things, the '461 Patent, which read on an assembly for connecting magnetic audio- or videotape to nonmagnetic "leader" tape connected to the hubs of a cassette. Both the patent owner, King, and the defendant Tapematic marketed tape loaders – machines that spliced and wound magnetic tape into videocassettes – but there were significant differences between their products. In particular, Tapematic's model included

---

[37] *Id.* at 1548–9.

[38] *Id.* at 1550.

[39] *Id.*; see also *id.* where it is stated that the patentee may recover lost profits on sales of unpatented components when the patented and unpatented components together are "considered part of a single assembly" or are "analogous to a single functioning unit."

[40] *Id.* at 1550–1.

[41] *Id.* at 1551.

[42] 65 F.3d 941 (Fed. Cir. 1995).

a so-called double pancake reel changer, which consisted of "two reels of magnetic tape so that when one reel is empty the machine is automatically fed from the second reel of magnetic tape thus avoiding down time for changing reels."[43] The district court found this feature of the product to infringe the '461 Patent. King's competing model was a "single pancake loader" that lacked this feature and, therefore, did not embody King's '461 Patent. The court nevertheless awarded King lost profits on the sales of its machine, based on the following assumptions. First, as a first approximation, the court concluded that King had a 70% share of the tapeloader market prior to Tapematic's infringement and that but for the infringement customers would have purchased these machines "according to the other sellers' market shares." Second, taking into account the differences between the Tapematic and King devices, the court reduced the number of lost sales from 54 to 49. The court also awarded lost profits on spare parts that King would have sold, and a reasonable royalty on sales of "acceptable noninfringing alternatives" that would have been made by the competitors who controlled the remaining 30% of the market, but for the infringement.[44]

Affirming as to both liability and damages, the Court of Appeals rejected Tapematic's argument that a patent owner may recover lost profits only when it markets a product embodying the patent at issue. In reaching this conclusion, the court framed its analysis in quasi-economic terms:

The market may well dictate that the best use of a patent is to exclude infringing products, rather than market the invention. A patentee, perhaps burdened with costs of development, may not produce the patented invention as efficiently as an infringer. Indeed, the infringer's presence in the market may preclude a patentee from beginning or continuing manufacture of the patented product. Thus, as apparent in this case, the patentee may acquire better returns on its innovation investment by attempting to exclude infringers from competing with the patent holder's nonpatented substitute.

Under this situation, the Patent Act is working well. The patentee is deriving proper economic return on its investment in acquiring a patent right. The public benefits from the disclosure of the invention and the ability to exploit it when the patent term expires.[45]

Unfortunately, the court did not explain why, if the patentee is less efficient, it would be in her interest to let the patent remain idle rather than to license the would-be user. If either party could earn the same return from using the

---

[43] *King Instrument Corp. v. Perego*, 737 F. Supp. 1227, 1241 n.11 (D. Mass. 1990), *aff'd*, 65 F.3d 941 (Fed. Cir. 1995); see also *King Instrument*, 65 F.3d at 946; *id.* at 955–6 (Nies, J., dissenting).

[44] See *King Instrument*, 65 F.3d at 953.

[45] *Id.* at 950.

next-best alternative to the patent, the patentee has an incentive to license the would-be user if the latter can earn more from the use of the patented product than can the patentee. On the other hand, if the patentee can earn more from the alternative than from either using the patent herself or licensing the would-be user, she will allow it to remain idle, but whether this result is consistent with the goals of the patent system deserves more consideration than the court devoted to it, as we shall see. Second, the court considered a hypothetical in which the patent owner is more efficient than the would-be user. In such a case, the court recognized, "[t]he patentee profits more by supplying the demand itself than by granting a license on terms which would allow the competitor to reasonably operate," and "[t]he value of exercising the right to exclude is greater than the value of any economically feasible royalty."[46] Asserting that a patentee who recovers only a reasonable royalty in this situation does not receive adequate compensation, the court apparently concluded that, *a fortiori*, where the patentee can make an even greater profit by neither using nor licensing the patent, a reasonable royalty does not provide adequate compensation.[47] Whether a reasonable royalty is "adequate," in light of the goals of patent law, when the patentee has disclosed *but not used* that invention is a much more difficult question than the court appears to have realized. As we'll discuss later, we are inclined to agree with the court's conclusion, but the question is a very close one.

In addition, on its facts *King Instrument* does not present a compelling case for an award of lost profits under the but-for causation principle. The court specifically held that adequate noninfringing substitutes for the patented device were available,[48] but if so then it is not at all clear that Tapematic's infringement cost King any sales. More likely, absent the infringement, Tapematic (like the competitors who purportedly made up the other 30% of the market) would have sold the noninfringing substitute, rather than vanishing altogether. Indeed, the court's finding that only five out of fifty-four customers would have purchased nothing if the defendant had not been selling its "double pancake" loader[49] suggests that the patented reel changer had relatively little to do with demand for either plaintiff's or defendant's products. Whatever the merits of the court's policy analysis, it seems doubtful that King should have been awarded any lost profits even under a standard causation test. If anything, the case highlights the dangers of a wooden, fact-insensitive application of market-share analysis.

---

[46] See *id.*
[47] See *id.*
[48] See *id.* at 953.
[49] See *King Instrument*, 737 F. Supp. at 1242, *aff'd*, 65 F.3d 941 (Fed. Cir. 1995).

REASONABLE ROYALTIES

In cases in which the patent owner cannot prove the fact or amount of its lost profit or of an established royalty, the U.S. Patent Act authorizes an award of "a reasonable royalty for the use made of the invention by the infringer." Although the governing legal rules with respect to reasonable royalties are somewhat more straightforward than the rules relating to lost profits, courts have aptly described the actual calculation of the royalty as "'involv[ing] more the talents of a conjurer than those of a judge.'"[50]

Perhaps the most frequently-cited modern case on reasonable royalties is a 1970 district court opinion, *Georgia-Pacific Co. v. United States Plywood Co.*,[51] which catalogued some fifteen factors that courts over the years had considered in assessing reasonable royalties.[52] In any given case, however,

---

[50] *Trell v. Marlee Elecs. Corp.*, 912 F.2d 1443, 1447 (Fed. Cir. 1990) (quoting *Fromson v. Western Litho Plate & Supply Co.*, 853 F.2d 1568, 1574 (Fed. Cir. 1988)).

[51] 318 F. Supp. 1116 (S.D.N.Y. 1970), *mod'd*, 446 F.2d 295 (2d Cir. 1971).

[52] See *Georgia Pacific*, 318 F. Supp. at 1120. The entire list of factors is as follows:

1. The royalties received by the patentee for the licensing of the patent in suit, proving or tending to prove an established royalty.
2. The rates paid by the licensee for the use of other patents comparable to the patent in suit.
3. The nature and scope of the license, as exclusive or nonexclusive; or as restricted or nonrestricted in terms of territory or with respect to whom the manufactured product may be sold.
4. The licensor's established policy and marketing program to maintain his patent monopoly by not licensing others to use the invention or by granting licenses under special conditions designed to preserve that monopoly.
5. The commercial relationship between the licensor and licensee, such as, whether they are competitors in the same territory in the same line of business; or whether they are inventor and promoter.
6. The effect of selling the patented specialty in promoting sales of other products of the licensee; the existing value of the invention to the licensor as a generator or sales of his nonpatented items; and the extent of such derivative or convoyed sales.
7. The duration of the patent and the term of the license.
8. The established profitability of the product made under the patent; its commercial success; and its current popularity.
9. The utility and advantages of the patent property over the old modes or devices, if any, that had been used for working out similar results.
10. The nature of the patented invention; the character of the commercial embodiment of it as owned and produced by the licensor; and the benefits to those who have used the invention.
11. The extent to which the infringer has made use of the invention; and any evidence probative of the value of that use.
12. The portion of the profit or of the selling price that may be customary in the particular business or in comparable businesses to allow for the use of the invention or analogous inventions.

a court is likely to focus on only a small number of these factors, such as other royalty rates to which the patent owner and willing licensees have agreed, or the hypothetical amount to which a willing licensor and licensee *would* have agreed at the time of infringement. In the alternative, some courts have applied the so-called analytical approach, under which the defendant's average return on noninfringing merchandise is subtracted from his average return on infringing goods, and the resulting sum, multiplied by the number of infringing sales, awarded as a reasonable royalty.[53] These various approaches are not necessarily mutually exclusive. The amount a willing licensee would have agreed to pay, after all, is constrained by the amount he could have expected to earn on the sales of other goods; and the willing licensor/licensee approach itself may be viewed more as a matter of emphasis than as a rejection of the other factors set forth in *Georgia-Pacific*.

As a matter of logic, the willing licensor/licensee approach suggests that the range of possible royalties the parties would have agreed to (assuming that they would have agreed to anything – an important qualification, as we shall see), as of the date the infringement began, should fall between the maximum incremental profit (or cost saving) the infringer could have expected to earn from use of the invention, and the maximum profit the patentee could have expected to earn from her next-best alternative to licensing the invention. Courts generally seem to recognize this logic[54] with two important exceptions. The first is that, for purposes of these hypothetical negotiations, the patent is presumed to be valid and the defendant's

13. The portion of the realizable profit that should be credited to the invention as distinguished from nonpatented elements, the manufacturing process, business risks, or significant features or improvements added by the infringer.

14. The opinion testimony of qualified experts.

15. The amount that a licensor (such as the patentee) and a licensee (such as the infringer) would have agreed upon (at the time the infringement began) if both had been reasonably and voluntarily trying to reach an agreement; that is, the amount which a prudent licensee – who desired, as a business proposition, to obtain a license to manufacture and sell a particular article embodying the patented invention – would have been willing to pay as a royalty and yet be able to make a reasonable profit and which amount would have been acceptable by a prudent patentee who was willing to grant a license.

Id. For an even more comprehensive list of potentially relevant factors, see Conley (1987; 387).

[53] See *Snellman v. Ricoh Co.*, 862 F.2d 283, 289 (Fed. Cir. 1988).

[54] *Georgia-Pacific*, 318 F. Supp. at 1121, provides what is perhaps the best articulation of this logic in the case law. Taken to its logical conclusion, this reasoning would seem to suggest that if the patented invention has no advantages (either technological, or solely in terms of consumer perceptions) over the next-best alternative – i.e., its incremental value to the defendant is zero – the amount of the reasonable royalty should be zero.

proposed use infringing, despite the fact that the parties to real negotiations almost certainly would have discounted the value of the license to reflect uncertainty with respect to both validity and infringement.[55] The presumption nevertheless makes economic sense, because an award that reflected the parties' uncertainty at the time of the hypothetical negotiations in effect would require the plaintiff to bear the risk of uncertainty twice: first, at the time of those negotiations, and second when deciding whether to proceed to trial.[56] Second, courts sometimes take into account events that have occurred after the infringement, such as the patent's having met with commercial success, despite the fact that this success may have been unanticipated at the time of the hypothetical negotiations.[57] As Sherry and Teece (1999; 426–8) point out, this use of hindsight is analogous to awarding the owner of a stolen lottery ticket the *ex post* value of the ticket (either $0 or $1,000,000, depending on whether the ticket was a winner) rather than its expected value *ex ante* ($1,000,000, discounted by the very low probability of its being a winner). In theory either *ex ante* or *ex post* damages should be sufficient to deter infringement,[58] although the use of such "ex post" data

---

[55] As we noted in Chapter 7, a substantial plurality of litigated patents are invalidated. See Allison & Lemley (1998; 205–7); Moore (2000; 391).

[56] Kalos & Putnam (1997; 4–5) use the following example to illustrate this point. Suppose that, at the time of infringement, the defendant would have agreed to license the patent for $1,000,000 discounted to reflect an 80% probability of validity and a 70% probability of infringement. Assuming that the latter two probabilities are independent, the resulting license fee to which the parties would have agreed would have been $560,000 (that is, $1,000,000 × 0.7 × 0.8). The patent owner's expected payoff prior to trial, however, also must be discounted to reflect the uncertainty surrounding validity and infringement. For example, if the patent owner's pretrial estimation of the probabilities of validity and infringement are the same as the estimated probabilities of these events at the time of infringement, the patent owner's expected payoff is only .56 of her best estimate of the damages she is likely to be awarded. Thus, if she is entitled to recover $1,000,000 in the event that she prevails at trial, and has a .56 chance of prevailing at trial, she should be indifferent between licensing the patent *ex ante* and recovering damages *ex post*. If instead she were entitled to recover only $560,000 in the event she prevailed at trial, her expected payoff from litigating would be only $313,600 ($560,000 × 0.7 × 0.8). She would, in other words, be worse off as a result of the infringement. See *id.*

[57] See *Fromson*, 853 F.2d at 1575–6. As Janicke notes, courts have declined to apply this principle in reverse, that is, to reduce the amount of the royalty based upon the infringer's lower-than-expected earnings. See Janicke (1993; 726).

[58] To illustrate, suppose that the would-be infringer expects that there is a 50% chance he could earn $1,000,000 in profit from using the patented device, and a 50% chance that he will earn only $100,000. His expected profit is therefore $550,000 and a reasonable royalty is (let us say, for purposes of exposition) half that, or $275,000. If he knows at the time of his proposed use that his use will be detected and that he will have to pay $275,000 in damages

may be more consistent with most people's intuitive sense of justice and fair play.

Critics nevertheless have perceived two major problems with using the willing licensor-licensee standard to estimate the amount of a reasonable royalty. The first is that the standard may not have a sufficient deterrent effect, to the extent that an award of what the defendant would have paid absent the infringement leaves him no worse off for having infringed. This critique, however, does not take account of the defendant's litigation costs and attorney's fees or of his potential exposure (in cases of willful infringement) for treble damages and plaintiff's attorney's fees. Moreover, this critique does not recognize the substantial costs that accompany an injunction, which thereby renders the infringer's inventory valueless. Finally, at least one court has responded to this argument by emphasizing that under *Georgia-Pacific*, the willing licensor/licensee concept is only one factor to be considered among others in setting the amount of the royalty[59] (although the Federal Circuit has also cautioned against awarding a "kicker" as a means of compensating the patent owner for litigation and other expenses).[60] The second, more fundamental critique is that a willing buyer and seller might not have reached agreement on *any* royalty *ex ante*, because the patent owner would have expected to earn more from making, using, or selling the invention than from licensing it to the defendant. Of course, in such a case, the patent owner should be entitled to recover her lost profit *unless*, for some reason, she is unable to prove the amount of the lost profit with the requisite degree of certainty.[61] In this instance, a reasonable royalty is really a substitute for the patent owner's lost profit, rather than compensation for some actual forgone royalty,[62] and logically should exceed the infringer's expected profit. In fact, courts sometimes

---

in the event that he is found liable for infringement, he is no better off choosing to infringe over choosing to pay the license fee. If instead he knows, at the time of his proposed use, that his use will be detected and that he will have to pay damages equal to half of the profits he has earned from the patent, he still is no better off choosing to infringe over choosing to pay the license fee. His expected damages in this latter instance, at the time he must make his decision, are still $275,000.

[59] See *Maxwell v. J. Baker, Inc.*, 86 F.3d 1098, 1109–10 (Fed. Cir. 1996).

[60] See *Mahurkar v. C. R. Bard, Inc.*, 79 F.3d 1572, 1580–1 (Fed. Cir. 1996).

[61] As in antitrust litigation, the plaintiff who can prove the fact of injury is held to a somewhat lesser standard in proving the amount of that injury. Nevertheless, there are bound to be cases in which the patent owner's proof of the amount of her lost profit fails even this minimal standard.

[62] See Schlicher (2002; § 9.04[5], at 9–45 to –46); Skenyon et al. (2002: § 1:11, at 1–18 to –19).

have suggested that it may be appropriate for a reasonable royalty to exceed the profit the infringer could have expected to earn from the use of the invention, though without explaining the economic logic behind this conclusion.[63]

A final issue that arises from time to time is whether the royalty should reflect the profit expected to be earned on sales of an entire product, in cases in which the patent covers only a component (or on sales of complementary goods, in cases in which such goods are typically sold along with the patented product). In such instances, courts apply the EMVR in the same way as when dealing with lost profits; thus, a component that is the "basis for the demand" for an entire product should result in a royalty based upon the profit earned from the entire product.[64] Where the patented invention does not have this effect, courts sometimes claim to base the royalty on the invention's more limited contribution to the infringer's profits, that is, to apply an apportionment principle.[65] Even here, however, the use of an apportionment principle as traditionally understood – that is, as entitling the patentee to a recovery based only on the patented features of an invention comprising patented and nonpatented components – is problematic. If the use of the patented component is expected to increase the licensee's sales of the final product (because some consumers want a final product that incorporates that component) or reduce his costs (and, concomitantly, increase some sales for that reason as well), thereby making him better off than he otherwise would have been in the amount of $x, an agreed-upon royalty should be some portion of $x. If the apportionment principle means only that "x" will be a small number if the patented component is a relatively minor innovation, we have no quarrel with it, but again this is not apportionment in the traditional sense.

The preceding discussion has shown that the transition toward a but-for and proximate causation framework in patent law has been anything but smooth, both in terms of the justification for this framework and in terms of its application. In the following sections, we present an economic

---

[63] For example, in *State Industries v. Mor-Flo Industries*, 883 F.2d 1573 (Fed. Cir. 1989), the court approved a 3% royalty despite evidence that the infringer's "net profit margin was 2.1% for the seventeen months preceding issuance of the patent" (that is, for a period of time during which the defendant used the plaintiff's invention lawfully), stating that "[t]here is no rule that a royalty be no higher than the infringer's net profit margin." *Id.* at 1580.

[64] See, e.g., *Fonar Corp. v. General Elec. Co.*, 107 F.3d 1543, 1552–3 (Fed. Cir. 1997).

[65] See, e.g., *Slimfold Mfg. Co. v. Kinkead Indus.*, 932 F.2d 1453, 1458–59 (Fed. Cir. 1991); *Procter & Gamble Co. v. Paragon Trade Brands, Inc.*, 989 F. Supp. 547, 612–13 (D. Del. 1997); 7 CHISUM (2002; § 20.03[3][b][vii]).

argument for applying the standard tort-law concepts of but-for and proximate causation in patent law. This approach radically simplifies the law, by rendering the EMVR, and *Panduit*-like standards irrelevant, while at the same time demanding a much more sophisticated understanding of the economic consequences of infringement.

CAUSE-IN-FACT

The argument in favor of a general cause-in-fact or "but-for" causation standard in patent cases is straightforward. If, as we have argued throughout, damages rules should preserve the incentive structure embedded in the Patent Act, they must leave the patent owner no worse off than she would have been absent the infringement. This is essentially a restatement of but-for causation: the plaintiff is entitled to be restored to the position she would have been in, but for the infringement. This restoration requires, most obviously, an accurate calculation of either lost profits or lost royalties, with lost profits defined as the difference between the profits the patentee actually earned and the amount that she would have earned but for the infringement, and lost royalties as the sum of the royalties the parties would have agreed to but for the infringement. With respect to lost profits, the (relatively) easy task is to measure the patentee's actual profits. The more difficult job is to estimate the amount that would have been earned absent the infringement, although as noted above once the plaintiff has proven fact of injury she faces a somewhat lower burden in proving the amount of damages suffered.[66] With respect to lost royalties, as discussed above, it may be feasible to assess the *range* of possible royalties the parties would have considered, although the reconstruction of the actual agreed-upon royalty may involve some guesswork concerning the parties' relative bargaining strength.

A few straightforward implications of the but-for rule are only imperfectly reflected in the governing legal standards. The first is that a pure system of but-for damages would take account of the fact that litigation is expensive by awarding the patent owner all of the costs of litigation, including attorney's and expert witness fees, out-of-pocket expenses for filing, copying, and the like, and the opportunity costs of the plaintiff's time. In fact, patent litigation

---

[66] An inherent difficulty is that of separating out the effect of the infringement from other factors that may have influenced the patentee's financial performance, such as managerial mishaps and changed market conditions. For a discussion of analogous problems that arise in the context of antitrust litigation, see Blair & Page (1995; 423). See also Stewart (1995; 325–8), who discusses a method for estimating but-for profits in patent litigation in the context of market share damages; Werden et al. (1999; 323–7), who propose a method for estimating but-for profits in patent litigation using a logit demand function.

is said to be the most expensive type of litigation that exists, outpacing even other likely candidates such as antitrust.[67] Although there is little case law on point, U.S. courts appear to interpret the statutory mandate to award the prevailing plaintiff "costs as fixed by the court"[68] as encompassing only such commonplace items as docket and witness fees.[69] We are aware of no cases (in this or any other field) in which courts have awarded opportunity cost damages. Moreover, in keeping with the so-called American rule,[70] the U.S. Patent Act authorizes awards of attorney's fees only in "exceptional cases,"[71] generally meaning only when the defendant has willfully infringed.[72] (Many other countries, however, routinely award the prevailing party its attorneys' fees.)

U.S. law is consistent with a second implication of the but-for rule, which is to account for the passage of time that elapses from the date of infringement to the date of judgment, and from the date of judgment to the date of payment. U.S. courts normally should award pre- and postjudgment interest to the prevailing plaintiff in a patent infringement suit,[73] and it is possible for damages to extend into the future beyond the time of trial.[74] In such cases, courts properly reduce these future damages to present value so as to avoid overcompensating the patentee.

[67] See Blair & Cotter (2000; 1363 n.187) (citing sources).
[68] 35 U.S.C. § 284.
[69] See, e.g., *Amsted Indus. v. Buckeye Steel Castings Co.*, 23 F.3d 374, 375–9 (Fed. Cir. 1994) (holding that, in general, a court may award the prevailing party in a patent infringement suit her expert witness fees pursuant only to 28 U.S.C. §§ 1821(b) and 1920, which limit recovery to $40 per day); *American Safety Table Co. v. Schreiber*, 415 F.2d 373, 380 (2d Cir. 1969) (approving inclusion of master's fee as costs); *Sarkes Tarzian, Inc. v. Philco Corp.*, 351 F.2d 557, 560–1 (7th Cir. 1965) (reversing award of costs for triplicate depositions); see also Skenyon et al. (2002; § 1:16, at 1–27) (noting that, "[w]ith the exception of expert witness fees, little significant case law has developed relating to "the assessment of costs in patent cases"). Note also that § 284 does not authorize the awarding of costs to the prevailing defendant. With respect to defendants, U.S. courts instead resort to Rule 54 of the Federal Rule of Civil Procedure. See FED. R. CIV. P.54(d) (stating that costs "shall be allowed as of course to the prevailing party unless the court otherwise directs"); 10 Wright et al. (1998; § 2670, at 259) that states when courts award costs pursuant to Rule 54(d), they typically include docket fees and other items listed in 28 U.S.C. § 1920); Skenyon et al. (2002; § 1:16, at 1–26 to –27).
[70] See, e.g., *Alyeska Pipeline Serv. Co. v. Wilderness Soc'y*, 421 U.S. 240, 245 (1975), which notes the "general 'American rule' that the prevailing party may not recover attorneys' fees as costs or otherwise," subject to certain exceptions.
[71] 35 U.S.C. § 285.
[72] See, e.g., *Standard Oil Co. v. American Cyanamid Co.*, 774 F.2d 448, 455 (Fed. Cir. 1985) (stating that "exceptional circumstances" justifying an award of attorney's fees may include the patentee's fraud or inequitable conduct in procuring the patent, "willful infringement, misconduct during litigation, vexatious or unjustified litigation, or a frivolous suit").
[73] See *General Motors Corp. v. Devex Corp.*, 461 U.S. 648, 651–3 (1983).
[74] See our discussion at p. 212.

LOST PROFITS: SOME MATHEMATICAL EXAMPLES

The Patent Act provides for a damages award that is adequate to compensate for the infringement. We have argued that, as a general matter, this standard requires a "but for" measure of damages equal to the difference between the patentee's actual profits and the profits that would have been earned but for the infringement. In this section, we examine this measure with the assistance of some standard economic models. For the moment, we abstract from the litigation costs. As we shall see, there is no simple formula for capturing the damages suffered. The actual damages depend upon the behavior of the infringing entrant, the behavior of the patentee, cost conditions, and the reactions of buyers. In all of our examples, we assume that the defendant who infringed had appropriate notice, either actual or constructive, as discussed in Chapter 5.

Let us begin with a relatively simple case and a concrete numerical example. The patentee produces widgets at a constant marginal (and average) cost of $40. The demand for widgets can be expressed as

$$P = 100 - 0.1Q \tag{1}$$

where P denotes price and Q represents the number of widgets. The negative coefficient on Q means that the demand curve has the customary negative slope indicating that larger quantities will be demanded at lower prices. Assuming that the patentee has a legal monopoly of the production and sale of widgets, the patentee will maximize its profit (π), which is the difference between total revenue and total costs

$$\pi = (100 - 0.1Q)Q - 40Q, \tag{2}$$

by producing where marginal revenue and marginal cost are equal. In this case, the patentee will produce where

$$100 - 0.2Q = 40. \tag{3}$$

Solving this equation for Q yields the optimal (i.e., profit maximizing) quantity, which is 300. Substituting this quantity into the demand function (Equation (1)) provides the profit maximizing price, which is 70. The patentee's maximum profit is then

$$\pi = 70(300) - 40(300)$$

or $9,000. This is the patentee's maximum profit if there is no infringement and, therefore, it provides a benchmark for comparison.

Infringement: The Cournot Case

If infringement occurs, we must know something about the behavior of the infringer and the patentee to determine the economic effect of infringement. As we saw in Chapters 3 and 7, there are several cases to consider. We build upon those cases here, beginning with the Cournot case in which the firms compete by setting quantities.[75] For analytical simplicity, suppose that the infringing entrant can produce widgets at the same cost as the patentee. The impact of infringing entry depends upon the appropriate time horizon. We investigate two cases: first, where the patentee discovers the infringement immediately, but was unaware of the impending entry and second, where the patentee was aware of the impending entry, but is initially unaware that the entrant will infringe.

Hit-and-Run Infringement. Consider the case where the infringer plans on being in the market for a single period, perhaps because he expects to be detected quickly. Under these conditions, the infringer must select an output that provides maximum profit for that one-shot infringement. Suppose that the infringer has observed the patentee producing 300 units prior to its entry. If neither cost nor demand changes, the infringer will expect the unwary patentee to continue producing 300 units. In that event, the infringer observes a residual demand of

$$P = 70 - 0.1Q_I,$$

where Q_I is the output of the infringing entrant,[76] and will find it optimal to produce an output of 150.[77] Since the patentee will produce 300, the

---

[75] The Cournot duopoly model was first proposed in Cournot (1883). Modern treatments are available in standard textbooks. See, e.g., Carlton & Perloff (2000; 153–93). See also *supra* pp. 188–9.

[76] The demand curve is $P = 100 - 0.1Q$ and the patentee will produce 300 units. Thus, the demand facing the entrant is the residual:

$$P = 100 - 0.1(300 + Q_I)$$

where Q_I represents the infringing entrant's output. Algebra yields

$$P = 100 - 0.1(300) - 0.1Q_I$$

or

$$P = 70 - 0.1Q_I.$$

[77] For the infringer,

$$\pi_I = (70 - 0.1Q_I)Q_I - 40Q_I$$

total quantity in the market will be 450. Substituting 450 into the demand function (equation (1)), we find that the price has fallen to 55. As a result, the patentee's profit will fall to

$$\pi = 55(300) - 40(300)$$

or $4,500, which is one-half of its former level.

There are several things to note here. First, the patentee's damages are equal to the difference between her actual profit of $4,500 and the "but for" profit of $9,000, i.e., damages are equal to $4,500. Second, the profit to the infringer[78] is only $2,250, which means that the damages suffered by the patentee are much larger than the illicit gains of the infringer. Thus, restitution, which is not currently an option, would undercompensate the patentee and thereby fail to fully restore the incentive for inventive effort. Finally, the damage is entirely due to price erosion. The patentee continues to sell its pre-infringement quantity, but because of the infringer's production the price is reduced.

These results can be seen quite clearly in Figure 8.1. Demand and the associated marginal revenue are shown as D and MR, respectively. The constant marginal (and average) production cost is shown as MC. Profit maximization leads the patentee to produce 300 units of output because marginal revenue equals marginal cost at that quantity. The price will be $70 while the unit cost is $40. The profits, which are ($70 − $40)(300) = $9,000, are shown in Figure 8.1 as area abdc. Infringement leads to a total output of 450–300 units will be produced by the patentee and 150 by the infringer. For this quantity, the price will be $55 and the patentee's profit will fall to ($55 − $40)(300) = $4,500, which is shown as area efdc. Infringement causes the patentee's profits to drop by area abfe. It is obvious from the graph that this loss is due to price erosion as quantity is 300 in either case while price has fallen from $70 to $55.

Multiperiod Infringement. Instead of hit-and-run infringement, the infringer may establish a presence in the market before the fact of infringement is known. In this case, the patentee will know about the existence of

and

$$d\pi_I/dQ_I = 70 - 0.2\,Q_I - 40 = 0$$

implies an optimal output of 150.

[78] For the infringing entrant,

$$\pi_I = 55(150) - 40(150) = \$2,250.$$

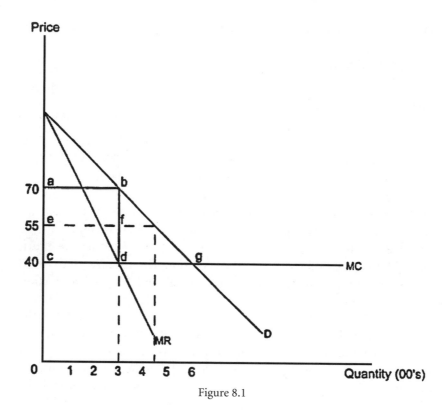

Figure 8.1

the infringer, but will be unaware that the new entrant's product actually infringes its presumably valid patent. If the patentee and the infringer compete in quantities, then they have to adjust their outputs while taking into account the presence of one another. The patentee's profit function will be

$$\pi_P = (100 - 0.1(Q_P + Q_I))Q_P - 40Q_P. \tag{4}$$

Similarly, the infringer's profit function will be

$$\pi_I = (100 - 0.1(Q_P + Q_I))Q_I - 40Q_I. \tag{5}$$

In order to maximize profits, the firms will want to produce where marginal revenue equals marginal cost:

$$100 - 0.1Q_I - 0.2Q_P = 40 \tag{6}$$

and

$$100 - 0.1Q_P - 0.2Q_I = 40. \tag{7}$$

The interdependence of the two firms can be seen quite clearly by solving conditions (6) and (7) for Q_P and Q_I, respectively:

$$Q_P = \frac{100 - 0.1\,Q_I - 40}{0.2} \qquad (8)$$

and

$$Q_I = \frac{100 - 0.1\,Q_P - 40}{0.2}. \qquad (9)$$

Obviously, the optimal (i.e., profit maximizing) output of each firm depends on the output of the other firm.

An equilibrium exists when neither firm has an incentive to change its own output given the output of the other firm. This can be found by solving (8) and (9) simultaneously. The result is that each firm will produce 200 units and, therefore, total output will be 400. Substituting this into the demand function yields a Cournot equilibrium price of $60.

Damages to the patentee equal the difference between the "but for" profit of $9,000 and the actual profit when its quantity equals 200 and the price is $60. This will be

$$\pi = \$60(200) - \$40(200) = \$4,000.$$

Thus, the damage due to infringement will be $5,000. In this case, the damage is partly due to the fall in price from $70 to $60 and partly due to a reduction in output from 300 to 200.

These results can be seen in Figure 8.2. The preinfringement output is 300 and price is $70. As before, profit is shown in Figure 8.2 as area abdc. Infringement leads to a Cournot equilibrium with price equal to $60 and the patentee producing 200 units. Thus, the new profit level is represented by area efgc. In the graph, the difference between the actual profit and the "but for" profit is the irregular area abdgfe. If there were some point to attributing this loss to price erosion, sales diversion, and quantity accretion, one could do so.[79] But this is an unnecessary exercise.

Infringement: The Bertrand Case

If the patentee and the infringing entrant compete on price rather than quantity, they exhibit Bertrand behavior (see *supra* pp. 51–2). Here the

[79] For an excellent attempt to calculate damages in a case in which price erosion likely had occurred, see Judge Easterbrook's opinion in *In re Mahurkar Double Lumen Hemodialysis Catheter Patent Litigation*, 831 F. Supp. 1354, 1392–3 (N.D. Ill. 1993), *aff'd*, 71 F.3d 1573 (Fed. Cir. 1995).

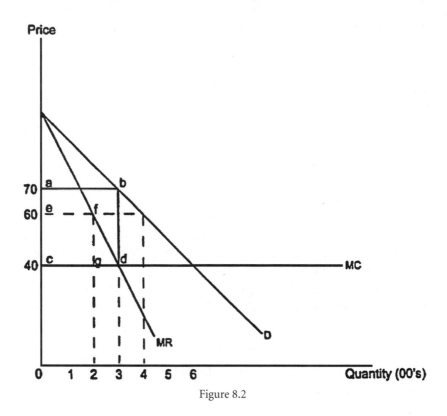

Figure 8.2

result is the same for hit-and-run infringement and for a more permanent sort of infringing entry: the patentee's actual profit falls to zero. Assuming that the goods produced by the patentee and the infringing entrant are identical and buyers see them as being perfect substitutes, the hit-and-run strategy will be to reduce price just below the patentee's price. Since the products are homogeneous, everyone will switch to the entrant's product. The patentee will sell nothing and, therefore, will earn no profits. In this case, the difference between the actual profit and the "but for" profit will equal the full "but for" profit. The infringing entrant will earn slightly less than the "but for" profit of $9,000 due to the slightly lower price that is charged. In this case, restitution would be a fairly close approximation of the damages suffered by the patentee.

Interestingly, the result is the same for the patentee when the infringing entrant establishes a more permanent presence. In that case, the two firms know that the firm with the lower price will make all of the sales. The best strategy for the patentee to adopt is to sell at the competitive price, which is

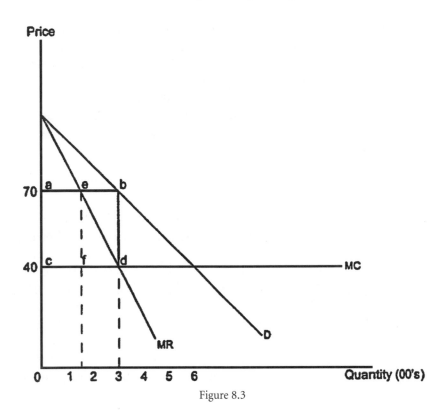

Figure 8.3

equal to marginal (and average) cost. In our example, the patentee will sell
at a price equal to $40. As a result, the patentee's profits will fall from the pre-
infringement level of $9,000 to zero. Again, the damage due to infringement
is equal to the "but for" profit of $9,000. In this case, however, restitution
will not be an adequate measure of damages because the infringing entrant
earns no profit either.

Infringement: Chamberlinian Behavior

Dissatisfied with the state of duopoly theory, Edwin Chamberlin suggested
that the firms might optimally take into account each other's presence by
mutual accommodation.[80] Presumably, both firms know that competition
will lead to smaller total profits than the preentry level of profits. This
means that the firms might rationally restrain their competitive impulses
and each produce one-half of the preentry output. In Figure 8.3, we can see

[80] See Chamberlin (1962; 46–55). See also *supra* p. 51.

that the preinfringement profit was area abdc, which equals $9,000. If the patentee and the infringing entrant each produce 150 units, total output will remain at 300 units and price will remain at $70. The total profit of $9,000 will be split evenly. Thus, the patentee's actual profit of $4,500 will be half of the "but for" profit of $9,000 and, therefore, the damage will be equal to $4,500. In this case, there is no price erosion. All of the damage is due to sales diversion, but putting a label on the nature of the loss is unnecessary if one adopts a "but for" measure of damages.

Summary

We can see from the examples above that the extent of the damages suffered depends upon the economic behavior of the patentee and the infringing entrant. These examples do not exhaust the possibilities, as there are other reactions to entry that we have not explored here. Moreover, the results will be different if the two firms have different costs of production. The results will also be different if the production costs increase with increases in output. We have also assumed that the infringing product is identical to the patented product and that buyers so view them. This, of course, may not be true. Product differentiation – real or imagined – will require further modification. But whatever the essential features are, they can be modeled and the difference between the actual profits and the "but for" profits can be used as the measure of damages.

REASONABLE ROYALTIES REVISITED

As we have seen, a "reasonable royalty" can mean one of two things in patent law. First, it may mean the royalty that the parties would have agreed to *ex ante* had the defendant chosen not to infringe. Accurately calculating this amount will depend in large part upon the reconstruction of actual market conditions along the lines discussed in the preceding pages. For example, in cases in which the parties proceeded as Cournot oligopolists, the calculation of the reasonable royalty should be conducted in light of the profit each could have expected to earn from operating in this fashion. Presumably, the patent owner would have agreed to a royalty equal to no less than the profit she could have expected to earn from manufacturing the invention herself; the infringer would have agreed to a royalty equal to no more than the amount he could have expected to earn from using a noninfringing alternative. Of course, this framework makes economic sense only in cases in which the infringer is at least as efficient as the patentee. If the patentee can earn higher profits from manufacturing the product than from licensing it, the parties would not have agreed to any licensing agreement and the proper relief should be lost profits, if lost profits can be adequately proven.

A second type of reasonable royalty is awarded precisely in the latter type of case, when the patentee is unable to prove with the requisite certainty the amount of her lost profit. With regard to this type of award, economic analysis has relatively little to say, other than that the award should be greater than the amount of the defendant's expected profit attributable to the infringement (which may be very difficult to estimate, to be sure). By making infringement unprofitable, an award of this nature should deter infringement and thereby preserve the incentive to invent. Ideally, a court should award the patentee the court's best estimate of her lost profit, suitably discounted in light of the uncertainty that prevents the patentee from recovering directly under a lost-profits theory. In light of the inherently deficient information, however, there is little doubt that exercise will be plagued by measurement error.

PROXIMATE CAUSE: SOME GENERAL CONSIDERATIONS

An important principle in tort law is that, even when the defendant breaches a duty owed to the plaintiff and this breach is the cause-in-fact (but-for cause) of the plaintiff's injury, the defendant is not liable unless the breach was also the "proximate" or "legal" cause of the injury. Courts frequently state that the proximate cause doctrine screens out claims that are "unforeseeable," "indirect," "remote," or "speculative," or that are barred for "policy considerations," without much analysis beyond the use of these conclusory terms. A standard law-and-economics account of proximate cause is that the doctrine serves to prevent recovery in cases in which the defendant's conduct (for example, the failure to take a safety step), though a but-for cause of the plaintiff's injury, did not materially increase the risk of injury *ex ante*.[81] In such a case, the social costs of imposing liability may exceed the social benefit of a reduction in injury, because the imposition of liability when the probability of injury is very low will have little if any *ex ante* deterrent effect, and may impose substantial administrative costs.[82] At first blush, this

---

[81] See Landes & Posner (1983; 119–20, 125–33); Shavell (1980; 481, 490–3).

[82] See Landes & Posner (1983; 119–23, 125–34); Shavell (1980; 484, 490–3). For example, in *Berry v. Sugar Notch Borough*, 43 A. 240 (Pa. 1899), a motorman was injured when a tree fell onto the roof of the trolley that the motorman was running at excessive speed. In his subsequent action against the municipality that was responsible for maintaining the tree, the defendant asserted that the cause of the accident was the motorman's excessive speed. Although the motorman's speed was a but-for cause of his injury, speed did not increase the *ex ante* probability of being injured by a falling tree.

reasoning suggests that patent infringement should be viewed as not only the but-for cause but also the proximate cause of the patentee's lost profits in two problematic but recurring situations: first, when the infringement causes the patentee to lose profits on sales of goods (either unpatented or covered by another patent) that compete with the infringing product (as in *Rite-Hite* and, supposedly, *King Instrument*) and second, when the infringement causes the patentee to lose profits on sales of complementary goods (as in *Paper Converting* and *Rite-Hite*). Presumably, the user's conduct (if defined as the infringement of the patent) materially increases the risk that the patentee will suffer harm of this nature. Although the administrative costs of assessing the amount of damages are not trivial, they are perhaps no more significant than the cost of assessing lost profits damages generally.

John Schlicher (2000; 527–9) nevertheless offers a critique of the application of proximate cause analysis to patent infringement cases and argues that some harms foreseeably caused by an act of infringement should be uncompensable. To illustrate, Schlicher suggests the example of a patent owner who (1) sells 100 units of unpatented "Model A" for $100 each and (2) owns a patent on "Model B," which costs the same amount to produce as Model A and can also sell for $100. Now suppose that another company sells 50 units of Model B for $100 each, such that the patentee's sales of Model A fall to 50 units. On these facts, the patentee should recover no lost profit damages, because his patent has no economic value, that is, no advantage over the next best alternative.[83] Schlicher therefore concludes that, although foreseeability of harm "is useful in tort and contract cases where the law is trying to create appropriate financial incentives to avoid harming others and to perform contracts," it "has little to do with identifying the lost value of an invention and awarding that value to the patent owner."[84]

Schlicher has identified a real problem, but it can be resolved in at least two ways that allow the concept of proximate cause to remain in place. The first is that, in Schlicher's hypothetical, the availability of a noninfringing

---

[83] As Schlicher notes, the result is easier to intuit when we consider the case in which the user starts by selling 50 units of the unpatented Model A for $100 each, which reduces the patentee's sales from 100 to 50 units (at $100 each). Clearly there is no liability in this instance, because the user is not infringing. Now assume that the user switches to the patented Model B, in the false hope that it will sell more. (It does not, because it has no advantage, price or otherwise, over Model A.) The result is exactly the same as when the user sold the unpatented Model A: namely, each party sells 50 units at $100 each. Schlicher concludes that "awarding damages equal to the patent owner's lost profits in selling A seems more clearly to be a pure windfall to the patent owner, and too large a compensation for the valueless B invention." *Id.*

[84] *Id.* at 527.

alternative (Model A) means that the infringer has not "caused" any harm at all, because the patent owner would have suffered the same loss absent the infringement. In this regard, the user's taking the "safety step" of not infringing would not have increased the *ex ante* probability of harm and, therefore, should not be viewed as the proximate cause of the patentee's lost profit. A second response to the problem relates to the definition of "harm." Again, the patentee in Schlicher's example would have suffered exactly the same harm even if the infringer had used the noninfringing substitute Model A; in other words, the patentee suffered no harm beyond the competitive harm that she would have suffered in the absence of infringement. If we borrow the concept of "antitrust injury" from U.S. antitrust law, the patentee in Schlicher's example does not suffer "patent injury" in the sense of an "injury of the type the [patent] laws were intended to prevent."[85] Incorporating a "patent injury" requirement into the analysis should be sufficient to avoid the type of problem Schlicher has identified, without discarding the concept of proximate causation altogether.

It still remains to determine, however, whether the harm suffered by the patentee when she loses profits on the sale of unpatented or complementary goods should be viewed as harm of the type the patent laws were intended to prevent, assuming that this harm would not have been incurred in the absence of infringement. In the remaining parts of this chapter, we discuss these issues in turn. We conclude, first, that awarding lost profits on the sale of unpatented goods, when the patentee does not market any goods covered by the patent, raises some difficult issues but is (probably) consistent with the purpose of the patent laws. Second, we conclude that awarding lost profits on the sales of complementary goods is consistent with that purpose, at least in cases in which the degree of complementarity is relatively high. Somewhat surprisingly, the Federal Circuit's vague rule permitting the recovery of lost profits on sales of complementary goods only when those goods are functionally integrated with the patented device may be as good an articulation as any of the appropriate proximate cause standard. We also reject the view that the recovery of complementary-good profits threatens to facilitate anticompetitive tying arrangements.

---

[85] See *Brunswick Corp. v. Pueblo Bowl-O-Mat, Inc.*, 429 U.S. 477, 489 (1977) (holding that antitrust plaintiff must demonstrate "antitrust injury," meaning "injury of the type the antitrust laws were intended to prevent," and not merely competitive harm). In *Rite-Hite*, Judge Nies advocated use of the antitrust injury analogue, although she concluded that the lost profits at issue were *not* injuries of the type the patent laws were intended to prevent. See *Rite-Hite*, 56 F.3d at 1559–60, 1574–5 (Nies, J., dissenting).

THE CASE OF THE IDLE PATENT

The first case we consider involves the measurement of damages in cases in which the patentee neither uses the patented invention herself nor authorizes anyone else to do so. Because the idle patent directly generates no income, one might expect that the patentee's recovery would be limited to a reasonable royalty for any infringement that occurred prior to the entry of an injunction prohibiting the defendant from further use of the invention. As the Federal Circuit recognized in *Rite-Hite* and *King*, however, it is possible for an infringement to cause the patentee to lose sales, and hence profit, with respect to those goods that she does make, use, or sell. For example, suppose that Alice makes machine X, which is covered by her patent, Patent 1, and that she also owns, but does not use, Patent 2, which reads on a slightly less marketable variation, X'. If Bruce infringes Patent 2, by making and selling quantities of X', he does not cause Alice to lose any sales of X', which Alice was not marketing anyway. To the extent that X and X' are substitutes for one another, however, Bruce may cost Alice sales of X. According to *Rite-Hite* and *King*, Alice may recover her profit on lost sales of X that are attributable to the infringement.[86] The question is whether this result is sound (or, if not, what the appropriate remedy should be). Two of the more insightful analyses of this question were offered by Julie Turner (1998) and Brent Rabowsky (1996).[87]

Following Turner and Rabowsky, we agree that the best place to begin the analysis is by considering why the patent owner may choose not to commercialize her patent. Possible reasons include (1) the patented technology is not commercially viable, due to factors such as lack of demand, cost, lack of

---

[86] Alternatively, suppose that machine X is unpatented, but that Alice nevertheless finds it to be a more marketable product than the product covered by her patent, X'. Alice, therefore, neither makes, uses, nor sells product X'. Bruce-perhaps because he is more efficient at making X' than is Alice-infringes by making and selling X'. To the extent that X and X' are substitutes, Bruce's sales of X' reduce the quantity of X that Alice can sell. Should Alice be able to recover lost profits on her lost sales of X? Although *King* suggests that the answer is yes, this result is more difficult to reconcile with a but-for causation standard. But for the infringement Bruce most likely would have made, used, or sold the unpatented alternative X, unless X is protected by some other form of intellectual property protection, such as trade secrets. Unless Alice can prove that she would have lost fewer sales of X under this scenario, she should not recover any lost profits.

[87] Rabowsky would affirm the result in *Rite-Hite* (but not *King*), on the ground that the plaintiff in the former case was marketing some products under the infringed patent. See Rabowsky (1996; 303). Although Turner's principal focus is on whether courts should award the nonmanufacturing patent owner injunctive relief or damages only, she acknowledges that her reasoning, if adopted, would overrule *Rite-Hite*. See Turner (1998; 207).

financing, inability to develop a marketable embodiment, or underestimation of its commercial value; (2) the technology is commercially viable but less promising than other technologies the patent owner is investigating; (3) the technology lacks commercial applications within the area of the patent owner's expertise; (4) the patent owner has overestimated the value of the patent and, therefore, has been unable to find a willing licensee; and (5) the patent owner resists commercialization, because the new invention would compete against some other product the patent owner currently markets.[88] As we shall see, it is only when the patent owner fails to commercialize for reason number (5) that the recovery of lost profits is even tenable; whether it is desirable as a matter of policy may depend upon how frequently reason number (5) forms part of an anticompetitive scheme on the part of a patent monopolist.

Economic logic strongly suggests that the patent owner who has failed to commercialize for reasons (1) through (4) should recover only a reasonable royalty, not lost profits. Consider first the patent owner who has failed to commercialize because she does not believe the invention to be commercially viable for one or more of the suggested reasons. On these facts, Bruce is likely to infringe only if he disagrees with Alice's assessment of the demand for, cost, or value of the patent, or if Bruce is better able to obtain financing or to envision a commercial embodiment of the invention. Absent the infringement, it would have made sense for the parties to have agreed to a royalty (since Bruce expected to earn more from the use of the patent than did Alice) and a court can attempt to estimate the amount of this royalty. Second, suppose that Alice allows the patent to remain idle for reasons two or three, but not for reasons four or five also. For example, suppose that Alice is not manufacturing the invention because some other technology looks more promising to her, but that Alice has not overvalued the patent (reason four) and is not concerned about possible competition from another's use of it (reason five). In such a case, we again would expect the parties to reach agreement in the absence of infringement, as long as Bruce expects to earn more from the patented technology than from his next-best alternative.[89] Similarly, if Alice is not commercializing the patent because it has no commercial applications in her field, but Bruce wants to

---

[88] See Rabowsky (1996; 324); Turner (1998; 182–3).

[89] Of course, it is possible that the parties would not have reached agreement due to stubbornness or mistake, even in the absence of overvaluation (reason four) or concerns about potential competition (reason five). Nevertheless, there is a range of royalties that would have made both parties better off and that reasonable parties would have agreed to, even if these did not.

use it because it *does* have commercial applications in his field, then again we would expect rational parties to reach agreement, which the court can attempt to reconstruct. Third, suppose that Alice is not licensing the patent because she overestimates its value (reason four), but not because she fears the effect of such licensing upon her profits from other products she sells (reason five). Presumably, Alice is not using the patent herself for one of the other reasons above (e.g., it is less promising than other technologies she is investigating). Normally, we would expect a license in this situation, but for Alice's imperfect information. Once again, a court can award a reasonable royalty based upon its superior, hindsight information about the true value of the patent.

When, however, the patent owner refuses to use a commercially viable, properly valued invention or to license it to a willing licensee due to the effect that such commercialization is expected to have upon the patentee's profit from sales of other goods, a lost profits theory is plausible. On these assumptions, a rational patent owner would allow her patent to remain idle if she expected that doing so would result in more profit (from sales of other goods) than either using the invention herself or licensing it to someone else (who will be willing to pay no more than what he expects to earn from the use of the invention). Thus, the patent owner's expected lost profits on the other goods must exceed the amount of the royalty to which the parties would have agreed. If the patent owner can prove actual lost profits consistent with these expectations, then under *Rite-Hite* and *King* she may recover damages in excess of a reasonable royalty. Turner and Rabowsky both contend that this remedial scheme should be modified in order to reduce the patent owner's incentive to allow her patent to remain idle.

In support of this thesis, Rabowsky argues, among other things, that awarding lost profits to the nonmanufacturing patent owner may facilitate the anticompetitive practice of "preemptive patenting."[90] To understand the concept of preemptive patenting, suppose that Alice has a monopoly over the proverbial widget either because she owns a patent for which there are initially no close substitutes or for other reasons. Sensing, however, that a substitute product (call them schmidgets) may be technologically viable, and that this product if developed could compete with widgets, Alice engages in a patent race with her potential competitor, Bruce, to be the first to develop and patent schmidgets. If Alice wins the race, she may conclude that she is

---

[90] See Rabowsky (1996; 315–17, 328). For theoretical analyses of when preemptive patenting is possible and when it is not, see Fudenberg et al. (1983); Gilbert & Newbery (1982); Gilbert (1981); Reinganum (1983); Salant (1984); and Vickers (1985).

better off letting her schmidget patent sit idle, as long as her profits from selling only widgets are expected to exceed her potential profits or licensing revenues on schmidgets, along with profits on reduced sales of widgets. By winning the race, she is able to prolong her monopoly, to the detriment of consumers. Although allegations of preemptive patenting abound,[91] the theoretical literature suggests that Alice is likely to succeed in such a scheme only if both (1) the race is conducted against only one or a small number of potential competitors[92] and (2) the payoff from investing in research and development into the new invention is relatively certain.[93] Rabowsky

[91] See, e.g., Blair (1972); Crew (1998; 416–17); Turner (1998; 179–81). The view among mainstream economists, however, is that preemptive patenting is uncommon. See, e.g., Scherer (1980; 452); Gilbert (1981; 211, 239–57, 269); Gilbert & Newberry (1982; 514); Rabowsky (1996; 324 & n.218); Reinganum (1983; 746).

[92] See Gilbert & Newbery (1982; 522–25); Gilbert & Sunshine (1995; 578). The intuition behind this condition is that, as the number of potential entrants increases, the likelihood that one or more of them will discover either a way to "invent around" the patent or a patentable opportunity that has escaped the notice of the patent owner also increases, thus reducing the probability that the preemptive patenting strategy will succeed. See Gilbert & Newbery (1982; 523–4). Salant also argues that preemptive patenting will not occur as long as transaction costs are sufficiently low for the dominant firm and its rival(s) to negotiate an assignment or licensing of patent rights. See Salant (1984; 247–50). If correct, this suggests that even when the number of potential competitors is small, preemptive patenting will be rare because in such cases transaction costs are likely to be small, *ceteris paribus*, relative to the costs that would arise in an industry characterized by a large number of potential competitors.

[93] See Gilbert & Sunshine (1995; 578); Reinganum (1983; 745–6). As Reinganum observes, the intuition behind this condition is that

> when the inventive process is stochastic [i.e., random] the incumbent firm continues to receive flow profits during the time preceding innovation. This period is of random length but is stochastically shorter the greater the firms' investments in R & D. Since a successful incumbent merely "replaces himself" (albeit with a more profitable product), the incumbent firm has a lower marginal incentive to invest in R & D than does the challenger.

Reinganum (1983; 741, 745–6). Similarly, Fudenberg et al. show that when the R & D process is stochastic and occurs in multiple stages or when firms have imperfect information about their competitors' R & D activities, even a monopolist with a headstart in a patent race may be unable to prevent a latecomer from "leapfrogging" into first place in the race. See Fudenberg et al. (1983; 10–21).

As a general rule, one would expect that the patent owner would not suppress a technology that is superior (lower-cost) to the one she is marketing, because she could earn more from the exploitation of the superior technology. Karp and Perloff (1996), however, have shown that the patent owner may be better off leaving idle a superior technology if, *inter alia*, consumers are unaware that the superior technology exists. For the latter condition to hold, however, the superior technology would have to remain secret, thus ruling out the possibility of patenting it. Theory therefore suggests that preemptive *patenting* is unlikely to occur when the suppressed technology is inferior to the technology currently in use.

nevertheless observes that awarding lost profits to the nonmanufacturing patent owner increases the incentive for engaging in preemptive patenting schemes.

Turner and Rabowsky also argue that none of the principal reasons for having a law of patents support the current remedial scheme with respect to *unused* patents. Turner is dubious about the efficacy of the patent system *in general* as a means of inducing invention, and would argue against having a patent system if this were its only justification. As we noted in Chapter 2, we do not believe that skepticism over the patent system in general provides a reasoned basis for tailoring damages awards, although there may be good reasons to question the merits of the patent system in the context of preemptive patenting in particular. As discussed earlier, preemptive patenting is assumed to occur (if it occurs at all) within the context of a race between Alice (a monopolist) and Bruce (a potential competitor) to develop a new technology. Conferring a patent reward upon Alice, if she wins the race, may provide little if any net social benefit in cases in which (1) Alice chooses not to commercialize the technology and (2) she expected the loser (Bruce) to develop the same technology within a short time. In other words, there may be no compelling reason to provide Alice with an incentive to invent and file first and then suppress the invention, if another party would have invented and then commercialized the invention shortly thereafter.[94] Second, both Turner and Rabowsky reject the argument that rewarding nonmanufacturing patentees advances the goal of public disclosure of new technologies, regardless of their exploitation. Turner reasons that an inventor who does not expect her competitors to independently discover the new technology and who does not intend to use or license it herself will prefer to keep it secret.[95] On the other hand, one who does anticipate independent discovery and who, therefore, patents to forestall competition would perform a greater disclosure service by commercializing the invention, because a commercial embodiment often discloses more information

---

[94] Thus, even if one believes, *contra* Turner, that patents *do* provide a significant incentive to invent, in the context of preemptive patenting it may be socially optimal to confer that incentive upon the potential competitor, rather than upon the monopolist. This assumes, however, that the would-be preemptive patentee's assumption that someone else was about to invent and patent the new technology was correct. If the patentee is wrong and if denying her a patent (or limiting the enforceability of her patent) reduces her incentive to invent, then society loses out because no one invents and discloses the new technology. It also assumes that one can readily distinguish preemptive patenting from other situations in which the patent owner decides not to commercialize her patent. This, too, is a questionable assumption.

[95] See Turner (1998; 191).

than can be gleaned from the patent.[96] Third, both Turner and Rabowsky assume that patents *do* encourage commercialization and they, therefore, conclude that a rule that rewards the noncommercializing inventor undermines this goal.[97] Fourth, both authors note Kitch's "prospect" theory, under which the patent system enables the owner of a "pioneering" patent to efficiently coordinate investment in follow-up inventions, thereby reducing the social cost of inefficient rent-seeking. To the extent (if any) that the patent system serves this purpose, it is undermined when the patent owner uses the patent not for the purpose of coordinating investment in follow-up inventions, but rather for the purpose of forestalling others' use of that technology.[98]

Taken together, the logic of these arguments might suggest that unused patents should not be enforceable at all – and indeed some countries do have "working" requirements that can result in the forfeiture or compulsory licensing of patents that are not exploited within a given period of time. This outcome might be difficult to sustain under the laws of the United States and some other industrialized nations, however. The U.S. Supreme Court on several occasions has refused to invalidate patents on the ground of failure to work and the U.S. Patent Act itself refuses to equate nonuse with misuse.[99] Similarly, U.S. courts have held that, as a general rule, a patent owner does not violate the antitrust laws by unilaterally refusing to license her patent.[100] This reasoning would suggest that a unilateral refusal to use would similarly not constitute the offense of monopolization.[101] Turner, therefore, recommends that courts enforce unused patents, but that they do so pursuant to a liability rule (meaning that the defendant must pay damages, but will not be enjoined from further infringement) rather than pursuant to a property rule (under which the court enters an injunction).[102] Turner argues that this outcome is more efficient than a property rule in this context and that (despite the general presumption of injunctive relief in patent cases) it could be accommodated under current patent law. Finally, although Turner professes

---

[96] See *id.*; Rabowsky (1996; 312–13).

[97] See Rabowsky (1996; 311–14); Turner (1998; 191–4).

[98] See Rabowsky (1996; 314–15); Turner (1998; 194–5).

[99] *See* 35 U.S.C. § 271(d)(4).

[100] See *In re Indep. Servs. Org. Antitrust Litig.*, 203 F.3d 1322, 1325–7 (Fed. Cir. 2000), which holds that the refusal to sell or license a patented product does not violate the antitrust laws; but see *Image Tech. Servs. v. Eastman Kodak Co.*, 125 F.3d 1195, 1218 (9th Cir. 1997), which holds that a refusal to license may violate the antitrust laws if, among other things, the refusal lacks a valid business justification.

[101] See Chin (1998; 444–6); Cohen & Burke (1998; 428–31).

[102] See Turner (1998; 196–209).

agnosticism over whether the damages she envisions would encompass reasonable royalties or lost profits, our previous discussion suggests that an award of lost profits would tend to have the same effect as injunctive relief. In this scenario, the patent owner's lost profits would likely exceed any royalty to which the defendant would have agreed *ex ante*, thus making it unprofitable for the defendant to infringe in the first place. Turner's reasoning suggests that the nonmanufacturing patent owner should recover a royalty only – not lost profits or injunctive relief – and that this royalty should be less than the amount of her lost profit. Rabowsky, in contrast, does not suggest the elimination of injunctive relief, but he does recommend the more limited step of limiting nonmanufacturing patent owners' damages to a reasonable royalty.[103]

Three problems with the analyses presented by Turner and Rabowsky nevertheless mandate caution in adopting a rule that denies the nonmanufacturing patent owner a lost profits award. The first relates back to the argument that enforcing nonmanufacturing patent owners' rights does not promote the public disclosure of new technologies, because an inventor who anticipates the independent discovery of a new technology by her competitors would still have an incentive both to patent *and to commercialize* that technology, rather than to keep it secret, if her rights were unenforceable (or less enforceable) in the absence of commercialization. As Turner herself recognizes, however, inventors who are uncertain of the likelihood of independent discovery may not have the same incentive structure to patent and commercialize; for this class of inventors, a rule that penalizes patent nonuse could be the decisive factor in choosing secrecy, in which case the public loses the benefit of disclosure unless and until independent discovery does take place.[104] Although this disclosure may not be as extensive as that which would accompany commercialization, it is still preferable to no disclosure at all.

A second problem relates to Rabowsky's preemptive patenting argument. As noted, preemptive patenting occurs when a patent owner/monopolist patents and then suppresses technology 2, specifically for the purpose of preserving the monopoly that arises from the patent on technology 1. Preemptive patenting schemes can succeed, however, only when all of the necessary conditions – including the possession of market power in the market supported by the patent on technology 1, the absence of other substitute technologies, a small number of potential competitors, and a relatively

---

[103] See Rabowsky (1996; 316–17, 328).
[104] See Turner (1998; 191).

deterministic research and development process – are met.[105] But even if it makes sense to limit the enforceability of preemptive patents, it is not clear that *all* nonmanufacturing patent owners should be subject to a rule of limited damages. To illustrate the possible consequences of such a rule, suppose that a firm must decide whether to develop and patent technology 1, technology 2, or both, and that it does not know which technology is likely to have more commercial applications. In addition, the firm knows that if it patents both but subsequently winds up using only technology 1, it will not be able to recover its lost profits (or injunctive relief, under Turner's proposal) from the sale of products embodying technology 1 when the patent on technology 2 is infringed. In effect, this rule (1) encourages others to infringe technology 2 and (2) threatens to leave the firm worse off than it otherwise would have been absent that infringement. These effects in turn have two possible consequences. The first is that they might encourage the firm to decide early in the development process to develop and patent only one technology and to suppress the other.[106] This would be unfortunate, not only because of the technology suppression, but also because the firm may pick the wrong technology, thus depriving consumers of the more commercially useful product. Balanced against this incentive, however, is the fact that not patenting both technologies leaves the firm vulnerable to competitors who themselves may discover and patent the suppressed technology; in addition, there may be adequate market incentives to avoid locking oneself into the "wrong" technology too early, regardless of the potential remedies that may be available in some hypothetical future patent litigation.[107] Alternatively, the firm could decide to patent both technologies and to commercialize both to some extent in order to preserve its ability to recover lost profits on the sale of either, but this may not be an efficient use of resources. Once again, however, the market incentive to sell commercially

---

[105] See *id.* At least one of those conditions, however – the existence of market power in the market served by technology 1 – is likely to be met in cases in which the patent owner can prove lost profits. Under *Panduit* and subsequent cases, the owner of multiple, potentially substitutable patents will be able to prove lost profits only when its ownership of these patents confers some degree of market power, because otherwise the existence of adequate noninfringing alternatives would entitle her only to a reasonable royalty.

[106] In this regard, allowing a patent on technology 2 regardless of its commercialization might provide an incentive to invent and disclose, if the firm does not expect others to duplicate that technology independently. In the case of preemptive patenting, the firm generally assumes that someone else will duplicate unless the preemptive patentee acts first.

[107] Rabowsky (1996; 282–3) notes that a large number of patents are not commercialized for benign reasons.

useful products may be stronger than the incentive provided by a hypothetical patent recovery. Nevertheless, to the extent that it may be important to distinguish between preemptive and nonpreemptive nonmanufacturing patent owners, the need to make this distinction adds further costs both administratively and in terms of potential errors.[108]

A third problem – more of a practical than an economic one – is that even the modified enforceability regimes advocated by Turner and Rabowsky would be difficult to square with existing law in those countries that do not impose working requirements. Turner's proposal to award nonmanufacturing patent owners only damages is functionally the equivalent of a working requirement coupled with compulsory licensing since, for reasons stated earlier, a lost profits recovery would tend to have the same effect as injunctive relief, which Turner wishes to avoid. For similar reasons Rabowsky's plan, which would couple injunctive relief with an interim royalty, may encourage some interim infringement in exchange for (what is effectively) a compulsory licensing fee. U.S. law nevertheless has consistently avoided working requirements, as well as the compulsory licensing of patents (except when the government itself wants to use a patent and in a few other discrete situations). As with the Ayres and Klemperer proposal we considered in Chapter 3, we question whether it would be appropriate for the courts in countries that generally eschew working requirements and compulsory licenses to manipulate the law of damages in order to, in effect, impose these policies. For these reasons, we think that policymakers should remain moderately skeptical of proposals to deny the nonmanufacturing patent owner her lost profits in all cases.

COMPLEMENTARY GOODS

A second issue is whether the patentee should be able to recover lost profits on lost sales of complementary goods, whether they be collateral (convoyed) or derivative (spare parts) products, if these losses are the but-for consequence

---

[108] Turner thinks it would be relatively easy to distinguish between patent owners who fail to commercialize for reasons (1) through (4) from those who fail for reason (5). See Turner (1998; 209) (suggesting that courts should "look[ ] to whether the patent owner is taking reasonable and diligent steps toward commercializing the patented technology"). Neither she nor Rabowsky, however, addresses the issue of distinguishing preemptive from nonpreemptive nonmanufacturing patent owners. This latter distinction might prove particularly difficult. See Gilbert & Newbery (1982; 525), who state that "[p]reemption would be very hard to identify in any practical situation because it is difficult to distinguish product development that is the result of superior foresight and technological capabilities from development that is motivated by entry deterrence."

of infringement. As we have seen, the Federal Circuit has taken the position that the patentee must prove that these complementary goods function with the patented product, but the court has not provided a clear definition of that term. The correct resolution of this issue depends in part on *how* complementary the products are, although this factor cannot be easily quantified either.

Complementarity is the flipside of substitutability, which we discussed earlier in the chapter. To illustrate complementarity, assume that the demand for a patented product A can be depicted as

$$Q_A = Q_A(P_A, P_B, P_C, P_X, \ldots, M, \ldots)$$

where Q_A denotes quantity; P_B, P_C, P_X represent prices of related goods; M is income; and the dots represent other variables that we have not specified.

If the quantity of A demanded falls when the price of B rises (that is, if $\partial Q_A/\partial P_B < 0$), products A and B are *complements*. The intuition is easy to grasp. For example, people eat peanut butter and jelly sandwiches. If the price of jelly rises due, for example, to a Concord grape crop failure, the quantity demanded of jelly will fall. As less jelly is consumed, less peanut butter will be consumed. Thus, the increase in the jelly price causes a decrease in the quantity of peanut butter demanded because peanut butter and jelly are consumed together.

To get a sense of how complementary two products are, we again look to the cross-elasticity of demand:

$$\varepsilon_{AB} = \frac{\partial Q_A}{\partial P_B} \bullet \frac{P_B}{Q_A}.$$

Because P_B and Q_A must be positive, the sign of γ_{AB} is determined by the sign of $\partial Q_A/\partial P_B$. When A and B are complements, $\partial Q_A/\partial P_B$ will be negative by definition and, therefore, γ_{AB} will be negative for complements. It will be positive for substitutes, as we saw above.

The larger in absolute value is the cross-elasticity of demand; the stronger is the degree of complementarity. For example, if $\gamma_{AB} = -1$, then a five percent increase in the price of B will lead to a five percent reduction in the quantity demanded of A. In contrast, if $\gamma_{AB} = -2$, then a five percent increase in the price of B will lead to a 10% decline in the quantity of A demanded. When $\gamma_{AB} = -2$, the degree of complementarity between A and B is stronger than when $\gamma_{AB} = -1$. An extreme case is that of *perfect* complements, in which two products are consumed in fixed proportions. Classic examples of perfect complements include right and left shoes (or gloves).

The argument in favor of awarding the patentee her lost profits on sales of complementary goods that she would have made, but for the infringement, is the same one we have made earlier in connection with lost profits generally: namely, that this measure of damages preserves the incentive to invent, by ensuring that the patentee is no worse off as a result of the infringement, and discourages would-be infringers by ensuring that they will be no better off when they infringe. Awarding lost profits on sales of complementary goods when those goods are only weakly complementary, however, may be problematic. Indeed, even when the goods are strongly complementary, it is not clear that infringement will necessarily reduce the patentee's sales of the complementary good. Somewhat surprisingly, the Federal Circuit's vague "functionality" test may be as good as any to delimit the circumstances under which the patentee should recover lost profits on sales of complementary goods.

To illustrate, consider a hypothetical case in which the cross-elasticity of demand between good A (unpatented) and good B (patented) is -1, and in which the aggregate quantity demanded of good A (Q_A) preinfringement is 100. Using our examples from a few pages back, consider first the case of hit-and-run infringement. In our earlier example, the quantity of good B supplied by the patentee remains at 300 units, the quantity of good B supplied by the infringer is 150 units, and the price of good B (P_B) falls from \$70 to \$55. On these facts, Q_A increases from 100 to 121.43 units.[109] The effect of this change in Q_A upon the patentee is clear. Although the patentee may benefit from the increase in demand for good A, if she is a supplier of that good, any increase in profits on sales of good A cannot offset her loss of profits on sales of good B. (Unless the patentee has market power in the market for unpatented good A, her profits on sales of good A would equal the normal rate of return.) If reduced profits on sales of B could be more than offset by increased sales of A, the patentee would have reduced the price of B and expanded quantity on her own. Alternatively, if the patentee and the infringer are the only two suppliers of good A and if they sell in proportion to their sales of good B, the patentee will be worse off, as her sales of good A fall from 100 units to 80.96.[110] Or she may not be affected at all, if suppliers other than the infringer and the patentee are the only producers of good A. Thus, the mere fact that goods A and B are moderately complementary does

---

[109] That is, if $\varepsilon_{A,B} = \Delta Q_A / \Delta P_B \times P_B / Q_A$, then $\Delta Q_A / -15 \times 70/100 = -1$. $\Delta Q_A = -1500/70 = 21.43$.

[110] That is, the patentee now sells 2/3 of the quantity demanded of good B (300 units out of 450 total), as well as 2/3 of the quantity demanded of good A (80.96 out of 121.43). The infringer sells 1/3 of the quantity demanded of both goods (150 units of good B and 40.48 units of good A).

not tell us whether the patentee is likely to gain sales of good A, lose sales of good A (and if so, at what profit margin), or be unaffected as a result of the infringement.

Second, consider the result if the infringement results in a multiperiod Cournot equilibrium. In our example, Q_B supplied by the patentee falls from 300 to 200 units, while Q_B supplied by the infringer rises from 0 to 200; meanwhile, P_B falls from \$70 to \$60. On these facts, again assuming a cross-elasticity of demand of -1 and an initial Q_A of 100, Q_A increases by 14.3 units.[111] Once again, the effect on the patentee will depend upon whether consumers typically buy good A from the supplier of good B or from other sources. If, prior to the infringement, consumers purchased good A exclusively from the patentee and afterwards in equal quantities from both patentee and infringer, the patentee will see her sales of good A decrease from 100 units to 57.2. On the other hand, if consumers continue to buy good A exclusively from the patentee, the patentee will increase her sales of that product. If they buy from other sources, she may not be affected at all. Of course, she loses profits on sales of B in any event.

Third, consider the results under a Bertrand equilibrium. If the infringement is hit-and-run, the patentee sells nothing, the infringer makes all the sales of good B, and the price of good B declines slightly. Whether this outcome affects the patentee's sales of good A, if any, cannot be determined solely from these facts. Alternatively, if the infringement forces the patentee to sell at the competitive price and quantity, Q_A increases from 100 to 142.9.[112] Whether the patentee makes any of these additional sales and, if so, at what profit, will depend on other facts. Finally, if the infringement results in Chamberlinian behavior, both infringer and patentee produce half of the patentee's former output of 300 units of good B, while the price remains the same. There will be no change in Q_A, but whether the patentee retains her previous share (if any) of the market for that good or must split it as well with the infringer is uncertain.

Interestingly, under some circumstances the patentee may suffer a loss even if the goods are not functionally related at all. For example, suppose that $\epsilon_{A,B}$ is zero but that consumers typically engage in "one-stop shopping," buying all of good A they need from the purveyor of good B. (In this case, goods A and B are by assumption not complements in consumption. The "one stop shopping" phenomenon indicates *transactional* complementarity, which would not be obvious from a functionality perspective.) Under any of

---

[111] That is, $-1 = \Delta Q_A / -10 \times 70/100 = 14.3$.
[112] That is, $-1 = \Delta Q_A / -30 \times 70/100 = 42.9$.

the scenarios in which the patentee loses sales of good B to the infringer, she will also lose sales of good A, even though the goods are not complementary in the traditional sense of that term.

What we might expect to observe, then, are really two effects, one relating to (traditional) complementarity and the other to transactional complementarity. The more complementary the goods are in the traditional sense (that is, the higher the cross-elasticity of demand), the greater the demand will be for the unpatented good A under some infringement scenarios. This increase in demand could exacerbate or reduce the patentee's loss, depending upon (1) whether she gains or loses sales of good A and (2) the profit margin from those sales (which will probably be lower as output increases); or it may have no effect whatsoever, if she does not supply good A. In addition, if the one-stop shopping effect is significant, the infringement may cause the patentee to lose some sales of good A even if the goods are not consumed together. The question is whether these losses should be viewed as proximately caused by the infringement and are therefore compensable.

To answer this question, we need again to fall back upon first principles, namely that damages rules should (1) preserve the patent incentives to invent, disclose, and commercialize and (2) deter infringement by channeling would-be users into voluntary transactions. In this regard, awarding the patentee her lost profits on lost sales of weakly complementary (or non-complementary) goods due to the one-stop shopping effect may be hard to justify in terms of the incentive to invent. It would require considerable foresight on the patentee's part to invest in inventing good B with the expectation that she will thereafter profit from sales of unpatented (and possibly unrelated) good A as well. At the same time, denying her these damages is unlikely to provide would-be users with an incentive to infringe, because it is unlikely that the profits they would earn from increased sales of unpatented good A would exceed their potential damages liability for sales of good B (in addition to litigation and sunk costs). Indeed, the prospect of ruinous liability might lead to overdeterrence in cases in which there is some uncertainty or some risk of adjudicatory error with respect to the issue of whether the accused device actually infringes. At the same time, even if the goods are strongly complementary, this does not necessarily mean that the patentee's *ex ante* expectation is to capture a significant share of the market for good A. And even when it does, it is possible for her market share (though not necessarily her profit margin) of good A to increase post-infringement.

What this analysis seems to suggest is that the Federal Circuit may have had the correct intuition when it decided, in *Rite-Hite*, that lost profits on sales of collateral goods should be limited to cases in which those goods and the patented article "constitute a functional unit." In such a case, the goods are likely to exhibit a high degree of both consumption and transactional complementarity, which means that consumers buy the products together due to both functional advantages and convenience. Moreover, in such a case it is at least somewhat more plausible that the patentee may have invented, or at least commercialized, in the expectation of profiting from sale of the complementary good, and the inability to recover these damages might in some cases make it profitable to infringe.[113] Finally, to award lost profits in other cases involving complementary goods might give rise to high administrative costs of determining whether a gain or loss in sales of good A is attributable to infringement or to other, lawful causes. Perhaps one way to give content to the court's vague standard is along these lines: the patentee may recover lost profits on the sales of collateral goods only when those goods exhibit a relatively high degree of both consumption and transactional complementarity, because only in these cases would recovery serve the purposes of the Patent Act. Although the application of this standard may seem as vague as the functionality standard, it at least provides a rationale for adopting a limitation of this kind.

TYING

A final argument *against* permitting the recovery of lost profits on sales of complementary goods is that this rule encourages the patentee to market these goods along with the patented article and that this joint marketing may have anticompetitive consequences. Specifically, the rule may reward the patentee who tries to leverage her patent "monopoly" into a monopoly in the market for the complementary product by tying sales of the patented and complementary products.[114] In our view, however, this concern should not

---

[113] For example, suppose that a patentee were limited to recovering lost profits only on the patented good. A potential infringer may expect to earn, say, $1,000 by infringing on patented good A and an additional $1,000 on collateral sales of B that he would not otherwise have made. If the damages suffered by the patentee due to lost profits on good A are less than $2,000, say, $1,500, there is an incentive for infringement. The potential infringer will net $500 if he earns $2,000 by infringing, but must only pay $1,500 in damages.

[114] By definition, the patentee makes complementary sales according to a tying arrangement if she agrees to sell patented good A only on the condition that the buyer also purchase

affect the patent damages rules for two reasons. The first is that the patentee's marketing of complementary goods is unlikely to have anticompetitive
consequences in the majority of cases. The second is that the damages rule
advocated previously is likely to provide little incentive for engaging in anticompetitive conduct, especially in light of existing antitrust laws and the
patent misuse doctrine.

With respect to anticompetitive consequences, again the theory is that
the patentee can leverage her patent "monopoly" into the market for good
B if she coerces buyers to purchase good B as a condition of buying good A.
Absent proof of such coercion, however, there is no anticompetitive conduct
and, thus, no reason grounded in competition policy for denying the patentee lost profits on sales of good B, as long as the elements of cause-in-fact
and proximate cause are met.[115] Moreover, even when the patentee has tied
the goods together, the tie may serve a neutral or procompetitive purpose,
such as the assurance of quality control (and, for that reason, may be exempt
from antitrust scrutiny).[116] Further, when the market for the tied product
is competitive, economic analysis strongly suggests that the patentee *cannot*
leverage her patent monopoly into a monopoly in the market for the tied
product.[117] Although antitrust doctrine may still impose liability in some
such cases, in order to satisfy noneconomic goals, a patent damages rule
grounded in economic analysis need not be based upon a faulty economic
premise.

A second reason for rejecting the argument is that existing antitrust law
and the patent misuse doctrine are likely sufficient to address the relatively
infrequent situation in which the patent owner is capable of leveraging
one monopoly into another. Economic theory suggests that tying schemes
can facilitate monopoly leveraging (or deter entry into the market for the
tied good) when, *inter alia*, the monopolist begins with some degree of

---

some other good B. In that event, good A is said to be the *tying* good, whereas good B is
deemed to be the *tied* good. Under some circumstances, tying arrangements may violate
competition laws, such as (in the U.S.) the Sherman Act. The term "bundling" is used
when two products are sold as a package at a price below the price charged for both goods
separately. In some cases, bundling also may violate competition laws, to the extent it
constitutes an act of monopolization.

[115] See, e.g., Keyes et al. (1999; 43), who discern a general rule under U.S. law "that where
two products normally are sold together as a matter of customary market practices, or
because most buyers find it convenient to buy the combination from one source at a time,
the courts will not condemn the seller who refuses to split up the package when the buyer
demands it, and will instead conclude that there is only a single product made up of
multiple parts" (citations omitted).

[116] See Meese (1997; 61–6); Whinston (1990; 838).

[117] See Bork (1976; 356–81); Director & Levi (1956); Bowman (1957).

market power in the market for the tied good.[118] Moreover, the return on investing in such a scheme is likely to be higher when the two goods are complementary.[119] Thus, it is precisely those cases in which the patent owner may be able to prove significant collateral damages – namely, cases in which the patent confers a degree of market power because there are few if any good substitutes for it, the collateral good is highly complementary, and the patentee is one of the few suppliers of that good – that are the most susceptible to anticompetitive ties. But when these conditions are present, the incentive to tie is likely to be substantial regardless of what sort of recovery the patent damages rules would permit in a patent infringement suit. The profitability of the tie is due to the market power the monopolist possesses in goods A and B, which allows her to credibly deter entry into both markets, and not to her ability to recoup lost profits on sales of good B in the event of an infringement of good A. Of course, if this is true then one might argue that the patentee has an incentive to market good B regardless of any potential damages recovery for lost sales of good B in a suit alleging infringement of good A. The choice then is whether to (1) forbid the recovery of these damages in all cases; (2) forbid them only in cases in which the patentee engages in an anticompetitive tie; or (3) permit them in all cases and leave it to other legal doctrines, including antitrust law and the patent misuse doctrine, to regulate the tying problem.

Two factors suggest that choice (3) may be the best option. First, to the extent that ties can be pro- as well as anticompetitive, solutions (2) and (3) are both preferable to solution (1), which (at the margin) might deter some beneficial conduct on the part of the patentee or encourage infringement for the reasons stated in the preceding section. Second, to the extent that solution (2) would impose high administrative costs in all cases in which the patentee seeks collateral damages, solution (3) may be preferable to (2). In cases in which the tie is anticompetitive, the defendant will normally have an ample incentive to litigate that issue, either by means of an antitrust counterclaim or pursuant to the patent misuse defense. To deny the patent owner any recovery of collateral lost profits solely to deter the relatively infrequent case of an anticompetitive tie would be overkill in light of these existing remedies.

---

[118] The economic analysis generally focuses on two effects. The first is that, under some conditions, the monopolist may be able to deter entry into the market for the tied good by precommitting to a strategy of intense competition in the event that a rival were to enter that market. See Blair & Kaserman (1982); Whinston (1990). The second is that the monopolist may be able to strategically price the bundle in such a way as to deter entry into the market for either good A or B. See Aron & Wildman (1999); Nalebuff (1999).

[119] See Nalebuff (1999; 24–27).

Finally, if we accept the Federal Circuit's functionality doctrine as a limitation upon the patentee's ability to recover collateral damages, the potential harm from rewarding anticompetitive ties should be minimized. To describe the relationship between two products as "functional" may suggest that the tie is not coerced, but rather is a matter of consumer demand, or alternatively that the procompetitive aspects outweigh the anticompetitive potential.

NINE

Concluding Remarks

Intellectual property law, which covers patents, trade secrets, copyrights, and trademarks, confers a set of exclusive rights in a variety of subject matter, including inventions, useful information, creative expression, and commercial symbols. This subject matter is often the product or embodiment of investments of scarce resources such as human capital, time, energy, money, and a vast array of other resources. These investments must be made before any return can be realized. In some cases, the investment may be nominal – some songs may be written in an afternoon. In other cases, the investments may be quite substantial. For example, a pharmaceutical manufacturer may have to invest hundreds of millions of dollars over many years before it receives the first dime of sales revenue. The fundamental assumption of our system of IPRs is that social welfare is enhanced by conferring exclusive rights on those who produce or disseminate these forms of information. Because exclusive rights may enable the owner to control quantity and price, however, access to the resulting creation may be restricted. Thus, a socially optimal system of IPRs will strike a delicate balance between encouraging investment, on the one hand, and insuring access, on the other. With the exception of a few caveats sprinkled here and there, we have proceeded on the (perhaps heroic) assumption that our current system of IPRs is, in fact, socially optimal. Although we recognize that this assumption may be incorrect, that issue is the subject of a very different book.

In this book, our focus has been on the law and economics of remedies and closely related issues in IP law. Our inquiry was framed by the various IP statutes and their judicial interpretations. We presented a simple model of IPRs to discern the optimal damages rules. In this model, damages play two roles: first, to compensate the victims of infringement in order to protect the relevant incentive; and second, to deter would-be infringers from such activity. In this regard, we found that the successful plaintiff should be awarded her profits lost as a result of infringement or the profits earned by the defendant due to its infringement, whichever is greater. In some instances, the award would be enhanced (or reduced) to provide the optimal deterrent effect. In some respects, existing IP law conforms to this conclusion, although it fails to do so in other respects.

Although U.S. trade secret law is almost entirely consistent with our conclusions regarding optimal damages, damages rules in patent, copyright, and trademark law often depart from the optimum our model predicts. We cannot fully explain the logic of the U.S. patent law's departure, that is, the rule precluding the patentee from an award of restitution when the infringer's gain exceeds the patentee's lost profit. Accordingly, we argued that restitution should be a recovery option as it is in some other nations. We also acknowledge that there may be serious problems in proving either lost profits or the ill-gotten gains *due to the patent infringement.* Isolating the influence of infringement is apt to be a daunting empirical problem, but it must be done to avoid overcompensation of the patentee. The departures followed by U.S. copyright and trademark law, by contrast, may be justified by the difficulty of detecting many acts of copyright infringement, in the first instance, and of determining the amount of profit attributable to nonwillful trademark infringement *and not to other causes,* in the second, although we cannot claim any precise correlation of cause and effect.

We also noted that IP law often has the appearance of being a body of strict liability law and is often referred to as such. Contrary to the conventional wisdom, however, we concluded that infringement is not truly a strict liability tort under U.S. patent, copyright, and trademark law, and that the law's departure from a true strict liability system is probably sound. In this regard, the primary issue is whether inadvertent (i.e., unwitting, "innocent") infringement should be subject to a damages recovery. Does or should the infringer's *intent* play a critical role in determining guilt or not? For the most part, intent is not dispositive, but potential infringers must be forewarned. U.S. patent law gives patentees an incentive to put potential infringers on notice through the marking requirement. The details of U.S. law, however, could use some improvement, insofar as some inadvertent infringers are strictly liable while some knowing infringers escape for want of notice. Similarly, copyright and trademark law in various ways mitigate, but do not eliminate, damages liability for nonintentional infringement.

Also somewhat surprisingly, the *scope* of liability varies across the various bodies of IP law. Patent law has the broadest scope. A manufacturer of a product who infringes the valid patent of another is, of course, liable. But so are other manufacturers who incorporate the offending product in their own outputs, distributors of offending products, all resellers (wholesalers and retailers), and even final consumers. To a marked degree, the scope of liability is more limited under trade secret, copyright, and trademark law, which proscribe only some unauthorized uses of protected subject matter. Our admittedly informal surveys suggest that the reach of patent law all the way to the final consumer may come as an unpleasant surprise to innocent parties who have sold or used an infringing product. Most of these people will be unaware of potential complaints and, therefore, their unwitting infringements cannot be deterred. This, of course, raises the question of how sensible it is for patent law to enjoy such an extended reach. We have argued that extending liability to commercial users and sellers helps to insure that the patentee's interests are fully protected, which may be necessary to preserve the incentive to invent in the first place. Including private, noncommercial uses within the scope of liability, however, is not compelling. Nevertheless, for the most part end users are not sued for patent infringement – the costs of such a suit no doubt typically outweigh the injury suffered.

Having examined who can be sued for infringement, we turned our attention to who can sue for damages due to infringement, i.e., who has standing. It turns out that this deceptively simple question has a complicated answer, due primarily to the fact that intellectual property may be assigned or licensed by the creator to another. Our legal and economic analysis led to several conclusions regarding standing. First, in patent cases, the assignee almost always has an interest in participating in infringement litigation. The assignor may also be interested when it retains a reversionary interest in the patent, or is entitled to a running royalty tied to sales or production, or continues to own the patent, or is entitled to a running royalty tied to sales or production, or continues to own the patent outside the assignee's territory. At the very least, the assignor who possesses such an interest should be allowed to intervene in infringement litigation. In addition, we have argued that when the patentee has assigned the patent in exchange for a running royalty, her interest is sufficiently great that the default rule should be that she has a waivable right to initiate litigation herself. Furthermore, we would expect that in most cases the licensor *and* exclusive licensee of a patent would have a substantial interest in participating in infringement litigation. Mandatory joinder is likely to be the most appropriate vehicle for protecting those interests without giving rise to multiple litigation. We also (weakly) concur with the traditional rule against conferring standing upon *nonexclusive* licensees, primarily for reasons relating to the difficulty of proving the extent of injury.

In contrast to patent law, the standing rules in copyright are quite flexible and we suggested two reasons for this difference: first, the differing economic value of individual copyright rights as opposed to individual patent rights and second, the much smaller risk of copyright invalidation. Finally, the standing rules in trademark law are less clear in their application, but arguably should fall somewhere in between what we find in patent and in copyright law, because (1) trademark rights (unlike copyright rights) are not easily separable from one another and (2) trademarks (we suspect) are more likely to be invalidated than copyrights but less likely than patents. In sum, our analysis suggests that there is no overriding need for the type of rigid standing rules exemplified by the old *Waterman* case. The decision whether a person must, may, or may not participate in infringement litigation should be driven by a realistic assessment of the person's interest and on the consequences of her nonparticipation rather than upon her amenability to classification as an assignor, assignee, licensor, or licensee.

Finally, we examined the problem of calculating compensating monetary damages in a patent infringement suit. This exercise is of some interest because the case law is not entirely coherent from an economic perspective. A great deal of confusion can be swept away if one proceeds on the assumption that damages in patent cases should be computed in the same way as in any other tort case: that is, by requiring the plaintiff to prove that the defendant's conduct is both a but-for and a proximate cause of the plaintiff's asserted injury. This is not to say that these calculations will be easy and uncomplicated. But incorporating these doctrines from tort law clears away much of the clutter and thereby makes the calculations as simple as a complicated world will permit.

Bibliography

Cases

A. L. Smith Iron Co. v. Dickson, 141 F.2d 3 (2d Cir. 1944)

A&M Records, Inc. v. Napster, Inc., 239 F.3d 1004 (9th Cir. 2001)

Abbott Lab. v. Diamedix Corp., 47 F.3d 1128 (Fed. Cir. 1995)

Advanced Display Systems, Inc. v. Kent State Univ., 212 F.3d 1272 (Fed. Cir. 2000)

Aeroquip Corp. v. United States, 37 Fed. Cl. 139 (1997)

Althin CD Med., Inc. v. West Suburban Kidney Ctr., S.C., 874 F. Supp. 837 (N.D. Ill. 1994)

American Medical Sys., Inc. v. Medical Engineering Corp., 6 F.3d 1523 (Fed. Cir. 1993)

Amsted Indus., Inc. v. Buckeye Steel Castings Co., 24 F.3d 178 (Fed. Cir. 1994)

Apple Computer, Inc. v. Articulate Systems, Inc., 234 F.3d 14 (Fed. Cir. 2000)

Arachnid, Inc. v. Merit Indus., Inc., 939 F.2d 1574 (Fed. Cir. 1991)

Aro Manufacturing Co. v. Convertible Top Replacement Co. (Aro II), 377 U.S. 476, (1964)

Aronson v. Quick Point Pencil Co., 440 U.S. 257 (1979)

Association of Coop. Members, Inc. v. Farmland Indus., Inc., 684 F.2d 1134 (5th Cir. 1982)

Atlantic Thermoplastics Co. v. Faytex Corp., 970 F.2d 834 (Fed. Cir. 1992)

Augustine Med., Inc. v. Gaymar Indus., 181 F.3d 1291 (Fed. Cir. 1999)

Avery Dennison Corp. v. Sumpton, 189 F.3d 868 (9th Cir. 1999)

Berry v. Sugar Notch Borough, 43 A. 240 (1899)

BIC Leisure Prods. v. Windsurfing Int'l, Inc., 1 F.3d 1214 (Fed. Cir. 1993)

Birdsell v. Shaliol, 112 U.S. 485 (1884)

Blonder-Tongue Lab., Inc. v. University of Ill. Found., 402 U.S. 313 (1971)

Bouchat v. Baltimore Ravens, Inc., 241 F.3d 350 (Fed. Cir. 2001)

Branch v. Ogilvy & Mather, Inc., 772 F. Supp. 1359 (S.D.N.Y. 1991)

Brenner v. Manson, 383 U.S. 519 (1966)

Bright Tunes Music Corp. v. Harrisongs Music, Ltd., 420 F. Supp. 177 (S.D.N.Y. 1976)

Broadcast Music, Inc. v. Star Amusements, Inc., 44 F.3d 485 (7th Cir. 1995)

Broadcast Music, Inc. v. Entertainment Complex, Inc., 198 F. Supp 2d 1291 (N.D. Ala. 2002)

Brunswick Corp. v. Pueblo Bowl-O-Mat, Inc., 429 U.S. 477 (1977)

Canopy Music, Inc. v. Harbor Cities Broad., Inc., 950 F. Supp. 913 (E.D. Wis. 1997)

Campbell v. Acuff-Rose Music, Inc., 510 U.S. 569 (1994)

Cardservice Int'l, Inc. v. McGee, 950 F. Supp. 737 (E.D. Va. 1997)

Catanzaro v. International Tel. & Tel. Corp., 378 F. Supp. 203 (D. Del. 1974)

Celanese International Corp. B.P. Chemicals Ltd (1999) R.P.C. 203

Central Point Software, Inc. v. Nugent, 903 F. Supp. 1057 (E.D. Tex. 1995)

Champion Spark Plug Co. v. Sanders, 331 U.S. 125 (1947)

Channel Master Corp. v. JFD Elecs. Corp., 260 F. Supp. 568 (E.D.N.Y. 1966)

Chemtron, Inc. v. Aqua Prods., Inc., 830 F. Supp. 314 (E.D. Va. 1993)

Chi-Boy Music v. Charlie Club, Inc., 930 F.2d 1224 (7th Cir. 1991)

Clark v. Linzer Prods. Corp., 40 U.S.P.Q.2d 1469 (N.D. Ill. 1996)

Coca-Cola Co. v. Gemini Rising, Inc., 346 F. Supp. 1183 (E.D.N.Y. 1972)

Cohen v. California, 403 U.S. 15 (1971)

Construction Tech., Inc. v. Lockformer Co., 781 F. Supp. 195 (S.D.N.Y. 1991)

Crook Motor Co. v. Goolsby, 703 F. Supp. 511 (N.D. Miss. 1988)

Crown Die & Tool Co. v. Nye Tool & Mach. Works, 261 U.S. 24 (1923)

Crystal Semiconductor Corp. v. Tritech Microelectronics Int'l, Inc., 246 F.3d 1336 (Fed. Cir. 2001)

Davis v. Gap, Inc., 246 F.3d 152 (2d Cir. 2001)

DeAcosta v. Brown, 146 F.2d 408 (2d Cir. 1944)

Deepsouth Packing Co. v. Laitram Corp., 406 U.S. 518 (1972)

Deitel v. Chisholm, 42 F.2d 172 (2d Cir. 1930)

Diamond v. Diehr, 450 U.S. 175 (1981)

Douglas Press, Inc. v. Arrow International, Inc., No. 95 C 3863, 1997 WL 441329 (N.D. Ill. July 30, 1997)

Dreamwerks Production Group, Inc. v. SKG Studio, 142 F.3d 1127 (9th Cir. 1998)

Eden Toys, Inc. v. Florelee Undergarment Co., 526 F. Supp. 1187 (S.D.N.Y. 1981), *aff'd in part and rev'd in part*, 697 F.2d 27 (2d Cir. 1982)

Eden Toys, Inc. v. Florelee Undergarment Co., 697 F.2d 27 (2d Cir. 1982)

E. I. du Pont de Nemours & Co. v. Christopher, 431 F.2d 1012 (5th Cir. 1970)

Eldred v. Ashcroft, 537 U.S. 186 (2003)

Estate of King v. CBS, Inc., 194 F.3d 1211 (11th Cir. 1999)

Ethicon, Inc. v. United States Surgical Corp., 135 F.3d 1456 (1998)

Fay v. Allen, 30 F. 446 (C.C.N.D.N.Y. 1887)

Feist Publications, Inc. v. Rural Tel. Serv., 499 U.S. 340 (1991)

Feltner v. Columbia Pictures Television, Inc., 523 U.S. 340 (1998)

Festo Corp v. Shoketsu Kinzoku Kogyo Kabushiki Co., 535 U.S. 722 (2002)

Finance Inv. Co. (Berm.) Ltd. v. Geberit AG, 165 F.3d 526 (7th Cir. 1998)

First Jewelry Co. of Can., Inc. v. Internet Shopping Network, LLC, 53 U.S.P.Q.2d (BNA) 1838 (S.D.N.Y. 2000)

Flaminio v. Honda Motor Co., 733 F.2d 463 (7th Cir. 1984)

Florentine Art Studio, Inc. v. Vedet K. Corp., 891 F. Supp. 532 (C.D. Cal. 1995)

Fonar Corp. v. Gen. Elec. Co., 107 F.3d 1543 (Fed. Cir. 1997)

Fonovisa, Inc. v. Cherry Auction, Inc., 76 F.3d 259 (9th Cir. 1996)

Ford Motor Co. v. Summit Motor Products, Inc., 930 F.2d 277 (3d Cir. 1991)

Fromson v. Western Litho Plate & Supply Co., 853 F.2d 1568 (Fed. Cir. 1988)

Gargoyles Inc. v. United States, 113 F.3d 1572 (Fed. Cir. 1997)

Garretson v. Clark, 111 U.S. 120 (1884)

Gayler v. Wilder, 51 U.S. 477 (1850)

General Motors Corp. v. Devex Corp., 461 U.S. 648 (1983)

Georgia-Pacific Corp. v. United States Plywood Corp., 318 F. Supp. 1116 (S.D.N.Y. 1970), *modified*, 446 F.2d 295 (2d Cir. 1971)

Gertz v. Robert Welch, Inc., 418 U.S. 323 (1974)

Goodyear v. Bishop, 10 F. Cas. 642 (C.C.S.D.N.Y. 1861)

Grain Processing Corp. v. American Maize-Products Co., 185 F.3d 1341 (Fed. Cir. 1999), *aff'g* 979 F. Supp. 1233 (N.D. Ind. 1997)

Gruen Marketing Corp. v. Benrus Watch Co., 955 F. Supp. 979 (N.D. Ill. 1997)

Hamilton-Brown Shoe Co. v. Wolf Bros. & Co., 240 U.S. 251 (1916)

Hanson v. Alpine Valley Ski Area, Inc., 718 F.2d 1075 (Fed. Cir. 1983)

Hasbro Inc. v. Internet Entertainment Group, 40 U.S.P.Q.2D (BNA) 1479 (W.D. Wash. 1996)

Hayward v. Andrews, 106 U.S. 672 (1883)

Henri's Food Products, Co. v. Tasty Snacks, Inc., 817 F.2d 1303 (7th Cir. 1987)

Hewlett-Packard Co. v. Bausch & Lomb Inc., 909 F.2d 1464 (Fed. Cir. 1990)

Hook v. Hook & Ackerman, 187 F.2d 52 (3d Cir. 1951)

I. A. E., Inc. v. Shaver, 74 F.3d 768 (7th Cir. 1996)

Image Tech. Servs. v. Eastman Kodak Co, 125 F.3d 1195 (9th Cir. 1997)

In re Aimster Copyright Litig., 334 F.3d 643 (7th Cir. 2003)

In re Indep. Servs. Org. Antitrust Litig., 203 F.3d 1322 (Fed. Cir. 2000), *cert. denied*, 121 S. Ct. 1077 (2001)

In re Mahurkar Double Lumen Hemodialysis Catheter Patent Litig., 831 F. Supp. 1354 (N.D. Ill. 1993), *aff'd*, 71 F.3d 1573 (Fed. Cir. 1995)

In-Tech Mktg. Inc. v. Hasbro, Inc., 685 F. Supp. 436 (D.N.J. 1988)

Independent Wireless Tel. Co. v. Radio Corp. of Am., 269 U.S. 459 (1926)

Intermatic Inc. v. Toeppen, 947 F. Supp. 1227 (N.D. Ill. 1996)

International House of Pancakes, Inc., v. Elca, Corp., 216 U.S.P.Q. (BNA) 521 (T.T.A.B. 1982)

International Soc'y for Krishna Consciousness, Inc. v. Stadium Auth., 479 F. Supp. 792 (W.D. Pa. 1979)

International Star Class Yacht Racing Ass'n v. Tommy Hilfiger, U.S.A., Inc., 80 F.3d 749 (2d Cir. 1996)

International Star Class Yacht Racing Ass'n v. Tommy Hilfiger, U.S.A., Inc., 959 F. Supp. 623 (S.D.N.Y. 1997), *rev'd* 146 F.3d 66 (2d. Cir. 1998)

International Star Class Yacht Racing Ass'n v. Tommy Hilfiger, U.S.A., Inc., 146 F.3d 66 (2d Cir. 1998)

International Star Class Yacht Racing Ass'n v. Tommy Hilfiger, U.S.A., Inc., No. 94 CIV 2663 (RPP), 81980,1999 WL 108739 (S.DN.Y. Mar. 3, 1999), *aff'd mem.*, 205 F.3d 1323 (2d Cir. 2000)

Inwood Laboratories, Inc. v. Ives Laboratories, Inc., 456 U.S. 844 (1982)

Jacob Maxwell, Inc. v. Veeck, 110 F.3d 749 (11th Cir. 1997)

Jacobs Wind Elec. Co. v. Department of Transportation, 626 So. 2d 1333 (Fla. 1993)

J. E. M. AG Supply, Inc. v. Pioneer Hi-Bred Int'l, Inc., 534 U.S. 124 (2001)

Jordan v. Time, Inc., 111 F.3d 102 (11th Cir. 1997)

Joy Technologies, Inc. v. Flakt, Inc., No. 93-1419, 1995 WL 408631 (Fed. Cir. Oct. 11, 1995)

Kalman v. Berlyn Corp., 914 F.2d 1473 (Fed. Cir. 1990)

Kewanee Oil Co. v. Bicron Corp., 416 U.S. 470 (1974)

King Instrument Corp. v. Perego, 737 F. Supp. 1227 (D. Mass. 1990), *aff'd*, 65 F.3d 941 (Fed. Cir. 1995)

King Instrument Corp. v. Perego, 65 F.3d 941 (Fed. Cir. 1995)

King of the Mt. Sports, Inc. v. Chrysler Corp., 185 F.3d 1084 (10th Cir. 1999)

Knitwaves Inc. v. Lollytogs Ltd., 71 F.3d 996 (2d Cir. 1996)

Kori Corp. v. Wilco Marsh Buggies & Draglines, Inc., 561 F. Supp. 512 (E.D. La. 1981), *aff'd*, 761 F.2d 649 (Fed. Cir. 1985)

Lans v. Digital Equip. Corp., 252 F.3d 1320 (Fed. Cir. 2001)

Lear, Inc. v. Adkins, 395 U.S. 653 (1969)

Lipton v. Nature Co., 71 F.3d 464 (2d Cir 1995)

Littlefield v. Perry, 88 U.S. 205 (1874)

Livesay Window Co. v. Livesay Industries, 251 F.2d 469 (5th Cir. 1958)

MAI Sys. Corp. v. Peak Computer, Inc., 991 F.2d 511 (9th Cir. 1993)

Mahurkar v. C.R. Bard, Inc., 79 F.3d 1572 (Fed. Cir. 1996)

Mallinckrodt, Inc. v. Medipart, Inc., 976 F.2d 700 (Fed. Cir. 1992)

Manville Sales Corp. v. Paramount Sys., 917 F.2d 544 (Fed. Cir. 1990)

Martin's Herend Imports, Inc. v. Diamond & Gem Trading USA, Co., 112 F.3d 1296 (5th Cir. 1997)

Maxwell v. J. Baker, Inc., 86 F.3d 1098 (Fed. Cir. 1996)

McNeilab, Inc. v. Scandipharm, Inc., 1996 WL 431352 (Fed. Cir. July 31, 1996), *rev'g* 862 F. Supp. 1351 (E.D. Pa. 1994)

Memphis Community Sch. Dist. v. Stachura, 477 U.S. 299 (1986)

Micro-Acoustics Corp. v. Bose Corp., 493 F. Supp. 356 (S.D.N.Y. 1980)

MGM Studios, Inc. v. Grokster, Ltd., 259 F. Supp. 2d 1029 (C.D. Cal. 2003)

Money Store v. Harriscorp Fin., Inc., 689 F.2d 666 (7th Cir 1982)

Moore v. Marsh, 74 U.S. 515 (1868)

Moseley v. V Secret Catalogue, Inc. 537 U.S. 418 (2003)

Motorola, Inc. v. Varo, Inc., 656 F. Supp. 716 (N.D. Tex. 1986)

N. A. S. Import, Corp. v. Chenson Enters., Inc., 968 F.2d 250 (2d Cir. 1992)

National Bd. of Young Women's Christian Ass'n v. Young Women's Christian Ass'n, 335 F. Supp. 615 (D.S.C. 1971)

National Lampoon, Inc. v. American Broad. Cos., 376 F. Supp. 733 (S.D.N.Y. 1974)

New York Times Co. v. Tasini, 533 U.S. 483 (2001)

Nichols v. Universal Pictures Corp., 45 F.2d 119 (2d Cir. 1930)

Nike Inc. v. Wal-Mart Stores, Inc., 138 F.3d 1437 (Fed. Cir. 1998)

Oiness v. Walgreen Co., 88 F.3d 1025 (Fed. Cir. 1996)

Ortho Pharmaceutical Corp. v. Genetics Inst., Inc., 52 F.3d 1026 (Fed. Cir. 1995)

Osborne v. Ohio, 495 U.S. 103 (1990)

Overman Cushion Tire Co. v. Goodyear Tire & Rubber Co., 59 F.2d 998 (2d Cir. 1932)

Pall Corp. v. Micron Separations, Inc., 66 F.3d 1211 (Fed. Cir. 1995)

Palsgraf v. Long Island R.R. Co., 162 N.E. 99 (N.Y. 1928)

Panavision Int'l, L.P. v. Toeppen, 141 F.3d 1316 (9th Cir. 1998)

Panavision Int'l, L.P. v. Toeppen, 141 F.3d 1316 (9th Cir. 1998), *aff'g* 938 F. Supp. 616 (C.D. Cal. 1996)

Panduit Corp. v. Stahlin Bros. Fibre Works, Inc., 575 F.2d 1152 (6th Cir. 1978)

Paper Converting Mach. Co. v. Magna-Graphics Corp., 745 F.2d 11 (Fed. Cir. 1984)

Parklane Hosiery Co. v. Shore, 439 U.S. 322 (1979)

Parkson Corp. v. Fruit of the Loom Inc., 28 U.S.P.Q.2d (BNA) 1066 (E.D. Ark. 1992)

Peer Int'l Corp. v. Luna Records, Inc., 887 F. Supp. 560 (S.D.N.Y. 1995)

Pennsalt Chems. Corp. v. Dravo Corp., 240 F. Supp. 837 (E.D. Pa. 1965)

Pfizer, Inc. v. Elan Pharmaceutical Research Corp., 812 F. Supp. 1352 (D. Del. 1993)

Philp v. Nock, 84 U.S. 460 (1873)

Pitts v. Hall, 19 F. Cas. 754 (C.C.N.D.N.Y. 1851)

Pope Mfg. Co. v. Gormully & Jeffery Mfg. Co., 144 U.S. 248 (1892)

PPX Enters. v. Audiofidelity, Inc., 746 F.2d 120 (2d Cir. 1984)

Pritikin v. Liberation Publications, Inc., 83 F. Supp. 2d 920 (N.D. Ill. 1999)

Procter & Gamble Co. v. Paragon Trade Brands, Inc., 989 F. Supp. 547 (D. Del. 1997)

Provident Tradesmens Bank & Trust Co. v. Patterson, 390 U.S. 102 (1968)

Quabaug Rubber Co. v. Fabiano Shoe Co., 567 F.2d 154 (1st Cir. 1977)

Qualitex Co. v. Jacobson Prods. Co., 514 U.S. 159 (1995)

Radio Steel & Mfg. Co. v. MTD Prods., Inc., 788 F.2d 1554 (Fed. Cir. 1986)

Rainville Co. v. Consupak, Inc., 407 F. Supp. 221 (D.N.J. 1976)

Read Corp. v. Portec, Inc., 970 F.2d 816 (Fed. Cir. 1992)

Religious Tech. Ctr. v. Netcom On-Line Commun. Servs., 907 F. Supp. 1361 (N.D. Cal. 1995)

Rite-Hite Corp. v. Kelley Co., 56 F.3d 1538 (Fed. Cir. 1995)

Rosso & Mastracco, Inc. v. Giant Food Inc., 720 F.2d 1263 (Fed. Cir. 1983)

Rude v. Westcott, 130 U.S. 152 (1889)

Rutherford v. Trim-Tex, Inc., 803 F. Supp. 158 (N.D. Ill. 1992)

Schneider (Europe) AG v. Scimed Life Sys., Inc., 852 F. Supp. 813 (D. Minn. 1994), *aff'd mem.*, 60 F.3d 839 (Fed. Cir. 1995)

SecuraComm Consulting Inc. v. Securacom Inc., 166 F.3d 182 (3rd Cir. 1999)

Selle v. Gibb, 741 F.2d 896 (7th Cir. 1984)

Sessions v. Romadka, 145 U.S. 29 (1892)

Seymour v. McCormick, 57 U.S. 480 (1853)

Sheldon v. Metro-Goldwyn Pictures Corp., 81 F.2d 49 (2d Cir. 1936)

Sheldon v. Metro-Goldwyn Pictures, 106 F.2d 45 (2d Cir. 1939)

Shields-Jetco Inc. v. Torti, 314 F. Supp. 1292 (D.R.I. 1970), *aff'd on other grounds*, 436 F.2d 1061 (1st Cir. 1971)

Slimfold Mfg. Co. v. Kinkead Indus., 932 F.2d 1453 (Fed. Cir. 1991)

Smithkline Diagnostics, Inc. v. Helena Laboratories Corp., 926 F.2d 1161 (Fed. Cir. 1991)

Snellman v. Ricoh Co., 862 F.2d 283 (Fed. Cir. 1988)

Songmaker v. Forward of Kansas, Inc., No. 90-4156-SAC, 1993 WL 484210 (D. Kan. 1993)

Sony Corp. of Am. v. Universal City Studios, Inc., 464 U.S. 417 (1984)

SRI Int'l, Inc., v. Advanced Tech. Labs, Inc., 127 F.3d 1462 (Fed. Cir. 1997)

Stabilisierungsfonds Fur Wein v. Kaiser Stuhl Wine Distributors Pty., Ltd., 647 F.2d 200 (D.C. Cir. 1981)

Stanley v. Georgia, 394 U.S. 557 (1969)

State Indus., Inc. v. Mor-Flo Indus., Inc., 883 F.2d 1573 (Fed. Cir. 1989)

Stryker Corp. v. Intermedics Orthopedics, Inc., 891 F. Supp. 751, 825–32 (E.D.N.Y. 1995), *aff'd*, 96 F.3d 1409 (Fed. Cir. 1996)

STX, Inc. v. Bauer USA Inc., 43 U.S.P.Q.2d (BNA) 1492 (N.D. Cal. 1997)

Tap Publications, Inc. v. Chinese Yellow Pages (N.Y.) Inc., 925 F. Supp. 212 (S.D.N.Y. 1996)

Taylor v. Meirick, 712 F.2d 1112 (7th Cir. 1983)

Tec Air, Inc. v. Denso Mfg. Mich. Inc., 192 F.3d 1353 (Fed. Cir. 1999)

Textile Productions, Inc. v. Mead Corp., 134 F.3d 1481 (Fed. Cir. 1998)

The Paper-Bag Cases, 105 U.S. 766 (1881)

Thomas v. American Cystoscope Makers, Inc., 414 F. Supp. 255 (E.D. Pa. 1976)

Toys "R" Us, Inc. v. Akkaoui, 40 U.S.P.Q.2d (BNA) 1836 (N.D. Cal. 1996)

Traditional Living, Inc. v. Energy Log Homes, Inc., 464 F. Supp. 1024 (N.D. Ala. 1978)

Trell v. Marlee Elecs. Corp., 912 F.2d 1443 (Fed. Cir. 1990)

Tri-Star Pictures, Inc. v. Leisure Time Prods., B.V., 749 F. Supp. 1243 (S.D.N.Y. 1990), *aff'd*, 17 F.3d 38 (2d Cir. 1994)

Trussell Mfg. Co. v. Wilson-Jones Co., 50 F.2d 1027 (2d Cir. 1931)

Twin Peaks Prods., Inc. v. Publications Int'l, Ltd., 996 F.2d 1366 (2d Cir. 1993)

TWM Manufacturing Co. v. Dura Corp., 789 F.2d 895 (Fed. Cir. 1986)

Ty, Inc. v. GMA Accessories, Inc., 132 F.3d 1167 (7th Cir. 1997)

Tycom Corp. v. Redactron Corp., 380 F. Supp. 1183 (D. Del. 1974)

Tyler v. Tuel, 10 U.S. 324 (1810)

United States v. Elcom Ltd., 203 F. Supp. 2d 1111 (N.D. Cal. 2002)

United States Football League v. National Football League, 644 F. Supp. 1040 (S.D.N.Y. 1986), *aff'd*, 842 F.2d 1335 (2d Cir. 1988)

Universal City Studios, Inc. v. Corley, 273 F.3d 429 (2d Cir. 2001)

Vaupel Textilmaschinen KG v. Meccanica Euro Italia, S.p.A., 944 F.2d 870 (Fed. Cir. 1991)

Velo-Bind, Inc. v. Minn. Mining & Mfg. Co., 647 F.2d 965 (9th Cir. 1981)

Video Aided Instruction, Inc. v. Y & S Express, Inc., No. 96- CV-518-CBA, 1996 WL 711513 (E.D.N.Y. 1996)

Volkswagenwerk Aktiengesellschaft v. Dreer, 224 F. Supp. 744 (E.D. Pa. 1963)

W. R. Grace & Co.-Conn. v. Intercat, Inc., 60 F. Supp. 2d 316 (D. Del. 1999)

W. L. Gore & Assocs. v. Carlisle Corp., 198 U.S.P.Q. (BNA) 353 (D. Del. 1978)

Wal-Mart Stores, Inc. v. Samara Bros. Co., 529 U.S. 205 (2000)

Waldman Publ'g Corp. v. Landoll, Inc., 43 F.3d 775 (2d Cir. 1994)

Walt Disney Co. v. Video 47 Inc., 40 U.S.P.Q.2d (BNA) 1747 (S.D. Fla. 1996)

Warner-Jenkinson Co. v. Hilton Davis Chem. Co., 520 U.S. 17 (1997)

Waterman v. Mackenzie, 138 U.S. 252 (1891)

Weinar v. Rollform Inc., 744 F.2d 797 (Fed. Cir. 1984)

Western Elec. Co. v. Pacent Reproducer Corp., 42 F.2d 116 (2d Cir. 1930)

Wildlife Express Corp. v. Carol Wright Sales, Inc., 18 F.3d 502 (7th Cir. 1994)

Wilson v. Rousseau, 45 U.S. 646 (1846)

Wine Ry. Appliance Co. v. Enter. Ry. Equip. Co., 297 U.S. 387 (1936)
Woods v. Universal City Studios, Inc., 920 F. Supp. 62 (S.D.N.Y. 1996)
Yale Lock Manufacturing Co. v. Sargent, 117 U.S. 536 (1886)
Zazu Designs v. L'Oreal, S.A., 979 F.2d 499 (7th Cir. 1992)
Zenix Indus. USA, Inc. v. King Hwa Indus. Co., No. 88–5760, 1990 WL 200234 (9th Cir. Oct. 3, 1990)

Books, Articles, and Treatises

American Intellectual Property Law Association, Report of the Economic Survey (2003)

Michael Abramowicz, *Perfecting Patent Prizes*, 56 Vand. L. Rev. 115 (2003)

Sumanth Addanki, *Economics and Patent Damages: A Practical Guide*, 532 PLI/Pat 845 (1998)

Martin J. Adelman, *Property Rights Theory and Patent-Antitrust: The Role of Compulsory Licensing*, 52 NYU L. Rev. 977 (1977)

Richard P. Adelstein & Steven I. Peretz, *The Competition of Technologies in Markets for Ideas: Copyright and Fair Use in Evolutionary Perspective*, 5 Int'l Rev. L. & Econ. 209 (1985)

George A. Akerlof *The Market for "Lemons": Quality Uncertainty and the Market Mechanism*, 84 Q.J. Econ. 488 (1970)

John R. Allison & Mark A. Lemley, *Empirical Evidence on the Validity of Litigated Patents*, 26 AIPLA Q. J. 185(1998),

David A. Anderson, *Reputation, Compensation, and Proof*, 25 Wm. & Mary L. Rev. 747 (1984)

Debra J. Aron & Steven S. Wildman, *Economic Theories of Tying and Foreclosure Applied-and Not Applied-in Microsoft*, 14 Antitrust 48 (Fall 1999)

Kenneth J. Arrow, *Economic Welfare and the Allocation of Resources for Invention, in The Rate and Direction of Inventive Activity: Economic and Social Factors* (1962)

Ian Ayres & Paul Klemperer, *Limiting Patentees' Market Power Without Reducing Innovation Incentives: The Perverse Benefits of Uncertainty and Non-Injunctive Remedies*, 97 Mich. L. Rev. 985 (1999)

Ian Ayres & Eric Talley, *Solomonic Bargaining: Dividing a Legal Entitlement to Facilitate Coasean Trade*, 104 Yale L.J. 1027, (1995)

Margreth Barrett, *Functionality*, 61 Wash. & Lee L. Rev. 79 (2004)

Roger L. Beck, *The Prospect Theory of the Patent System and Unproductive Competition*, 5 Res. L. & Econ. 193 (1983)

Tom W. Bell, *Fair Use vs. Fared Use: The Impact of Automated Rights Management on Copyright's Fair Use Doctrine*, 76 N.C. L. Rev. 557 (1998)

Joseph Bertrand, *Theorie Mathematique de la Richesse Sociale*, 67 Journal des Savants 499 (1883)

Christian Bessy & Eric Brousseau, *Technology Licensing Contracts Features and Diversity*, 18 Int'l Rev. L. & Econ. 451 (1998)

John M. Blair, Economic Concentration (1972)

Roger D. Blair & David L. Kaserman, *A Note on Dual Input Monopoly and Tying*, 10 Economics Leters 494 (1982)

Roger D. Blair & Lawrence W. Kenny, *Microeconomics for Managerial Decision Making* (1982)

Roger D. Blair & Thomas F. Cotter, *An Economic Analysis of Damages Rules in Intellectual Property Law*, 39 Wm. & Mary L. Rev. 1585 (1998)

Roger D. Blair & Thomas F. Cotter, *The Elusive Logic of Standing Doctrine in Intellectual Property Law*, 74 Tulane L. Rev. 1323 (2000)

Roger D. Blair & Thomas F. Cotter, *Rethinking Patent Damages*, 10 Tex. Intell. Prop. L.J. 1 (2001)

Roger D. Blair & Thomas F. Cotter, *An Economic Analysis of Seller and User Liability in Intellectual Property Law*, 68 U. Cin. L. Rev. 1 (1999)

Roger D. Blair & William H. Page, *"Speculative" Antitrust Damages*, 70 Wash. L. Rev. 423 (1995)

Michele Boldrin & David K. Levine, *The Case Against Intellectual Property*, 92 Am. Econ. Rev. (Papers and Proceedings) 209–12 (May 2002)

Robert G. Bone, *A New Look at Trade Secret Law: Doctrine in Search of Justification*, 86 Calif. L. Rev. 241 (1998)

Terry R. Bowen, *The Federal Trademark Dilution Act of 1995-Does It Address the Dilution Doctrine's Most Serious Problems?*, 7 DePaul-LCA J. Art & Ent. L. 75 (1996)

William M. Borchard, *Reverse Passing Off-Commercial Robbery or Permissible Competition?*, 67 Trademark Rep. 1 (1977)

Robert H. Bork, *The Antitrust Paradox: A Policy at War with Itself* (1976)

Ward S. Bowman, *Tying Arrangements and the Leverage Problem*, 67 Yale L.J. 19 (1957)

Dan L. Burk and Mark A. Lemley, *Is Patent Law Technology-Specific?*, 17 Berkeley Tech. L.J. 1155 (2002)

Dan L. Burk, *Muddy Rules for Cyberspace*, 21 Cardozo L. Rev. 121 (1999)

Dan L. Burk, *Patenting Speech*, 79 Tex. L. Rev. 99 (2000)

Dan L. Burk, *The Trouble with Trespass*, 4 J. Small & Emerging Bus. L. 27 (2000)

Dennis W. Carlton & Jeffrey M. Perloff, *Modern Industrial Organization* (3d ed., 2000)

Stephen L. Carter, *The Trouble with Trademark*, 99 Yale L.J. 759 (1990)

Ralph Cassady, Jr., *Auctions and Auctioneering* (1967)

Richard E. Caves et al., *The Imperfect Market for Technology Licenses*, 45 Oxford Bull. Econ. & Stat. 249 (1983)

Edward H. Chamberlin, *The Theory of Monopolistic Competition* (8th ed. 1962)

Yee Wah Chin, *Unilateral Technology Suppression: Appropriate Antitrust and Patent Law Remedies*, 66 Antitrust L.J. 441 (1998)

Donald S. Chisum, *Chisum on Patents* (2002)

Jay Pil Choi, *Patent Litigation as an Information-Transmission Mechanism*, 88 Am. Econ. Rev. 1249 (1998)

Dane S. Ciolino & Erin A. Donelon, *Questioning Strict Liability in Copyright*, 54 Rutgers L. Rev. 351 (2002)

R. H. Coase, *The Lighthouse in History*, 17 J.L. Econ. 357 (1974)

R. H. Coase, *The Problem of Social Cost*, 3 J.L. Econ. 1 (1960)

Joel M. Cohen & Arthur J. Burke, *An Overview of the Antitrust Analysis of Suppression of Technology*, 66 Antitrust L.J. 421 (1998)

Julie E. Cohen, *Lochner in Cyberspace: The New Economic Orthodoxy of "Rights Management,"* 97 Mich. L. Rev. 462 (1998)

Julie E. Cohen & Mark A. Lemley, *Patent Scope and Innovation in the Software Industry,* 89 Calif. L. Rev. 1 (2001)

Wesley M. Cohen et al., *Protecting Their Intellectual Assets: Appropriability Conditions and Why U.S. Manufacturing Firms Patent (Or Not),* NBER Working Paper No. 7552 (Feb. 2000)

Sherry F. Colb, *The Qualitative Dimension of Fourth Amendment "Reasonableness,"* 98 Colum. L. Rev. 1642 (1998)

Jules L. Coleman & Jody Kraus, *Rethinking the Theory of Legal Rights,* 95 Yale L.J. 335 (1986)

Matthew J. Conigliaro et al., *Foreseeability in Patent Law,* 16 Berkeley Tech. L.J. 1045 (2001)

Ned L. Conley, *An Economic Approach to Patent Damages,* 15 AIPLA Q.J. 354 (1987)

Robert Cooter & Thomas Ulen, *Law and Economics* (1988)

Carlos M. Correa & Abdulqawi A. Yusuf, *Intellectual Property and International Trade, The TRIPs Agreement* (1998)

Carlos M. Correa, *Intellectual Property Rights, the WTO and Developing Countries* (2000)

Rosemary J. Coombe, *Objects of Property and Subjects of Politics: Intellectual Property Laws and Democratic Dialogue,* 69 Tex. L. Rev. 1853 (1991)

Thomas F. Cotter, *Conflicting Interests in Trade Secrets,* 48 Fla. L. Rev. 591 (1996)

Thomas F. Cotter, *Do Federal Uses of Intellectual Property Implicate the Fifth Amendment?,* 50 Fla. L. Rev. 529 (1998)

Thomas F. Cotter, *An Economic Analysis of Enhanced Damages and Attorneys' Fees for Willful Patent Infringement,* 14 Federal Circuit Bar Journal (forthcoming 2004)

Thomas F. Cotter, *Gutenberg's Legacy: Copyright, Censorship, and Religious Pluralism,* 91 Calif. L. Rev. 323 (2003)

Thomas F. Cotter, *Intellectual Property and the Essential Facilities Doctrine,* 44 Antitrust Bull. 211 (1999)

Thomas F. Cotter, *Owning What Doesn't Exist, Where it Doesn't Exist: Rethinking Two Doctrines from the Common Law of Trademarks,* 1995 U. Ill. L. Rev. 487 (1995)

Thomas F. Cotter, *Pragmatism, Economics, and the Droit Moral,* 76 N.C.L. Rev. 1 (1997)

Thomas F. Cotter, *Market Fundamentalism and the TRIPs Agreement,* 22 Cardozo Arts & Enter. L.J. 307 (2004)

Augustin A. Cournot, *Recherches sur les Principes Mathematiques de la Theorie des Richesses* (1838)

Larry Coury, *C'est What? Saisie! A Comparison of Patent Infringement Remedies Among the G7 Economic Nations,* 13 Fordham Intell. Prop. Media & Ent. L.J. 1053 (2003)

Alan J. Cox, *Antitrust and Intellectual Property Market Definition,* 524 PLI/Pat 129 (1998)

Richard Craswell, *Deterrence and Damags: The Multiplier Principle and its Alternatives,* 97 Mich. L. Rev. 2185 (1999)

Richard Craswell & John E. Calfee, *Deterrence and Uncertain Legal Standards,* 2 J.L. Econ. & Org. 279 (1986)

Eugene Crew, *Foreword: Symposium on Antitrust and the Suppression of Technology in the United States and Europe: Is There a Remedy?*, 66 Antitrust L.J. 415 (1998)

George Ticknor Curtis, *A Treatise on the Law of Patents for Useful Inventions: As Enacted and Administered in the United States* (3d ed. 1867)

Kenneth W. Dam, *The Economic Underpinnings of Patent Law*, 23 J. Legal Stud. 247 (1994)

Harold Demsetz, *When Does the Rule of Liability Matter?*, 1 J. Legal Stud. 13 (1972)

Robert C. Denicola, *Trademarks as Speech: Constitutional Implications of the Emerging Rationales for the Protection of Trade Symbols*, Wis. L. Rev. 158 (1982)

Aaron Director & Edward H. Levi, *Law and the Future: Trade Regulation*, 51 Nw. U. L. Rev. 281 (1956)

Dan B. Dobbs, *Law of Remedies* (2d ed. 1993)

Rochelle Cooper Dreyfuss, *Dethroning Lear: Licensee Estoppel and the Incentive to Innovate*, 72 Va. L. Rev. 677 (1986)

Michael A. Einhorn, *Copyright, Prevention, and Rational Governance: File-Sharing and Napster*, 24 Colum.-VLA J.L. & Arts 449 (2001)

Niva Elkin-Koren & Eli M. Salzberger, *Law and Economics in Cyberspace*, 19 Int'l Rev. L. & Econ. 553 (1999)

David S. Evans, *Market Definition in Antitrust and Patent Litigation*, 414 PLI/Pat 595 (1995)

Joel R. Feldman, Note, *Reverse Confusion in Trademarks: Balancing the Interests of the Public, the Trademark Owner, and the Infringer*, 8 J. Tech. L. & Pol'y 163 (2003)

William W. Fisher III, *Reconstructing the Fair Use Doctrine*, 101 Harv. L. Rev. 1659, (1988)

David D. Friedman et al., *Some Economics of Trade Secret Law*, 5 J. Econ.Perspectives 61 (1991)

Drew Fudenberg et al., *Preemption, Leapfrogging and Competition in Patent Races*, 22 Eur. Econ. Rev. 3 (1983)

Nancy T. Gallini, *Patent Policy and Costly Imitation*, 23 RAND J. Econ. 52 (1992)

Nancy T. Gallini & Brian D. Wright, *Technology Transfer Under Asymmetric Information*, 21 Rand J. Econ. 147 (1990)

Richard J. Gilbert, *Patents, Sleeping Patents, and Entry Deterrence, in Strategy, Predation, and Antitrust Analysis* (Steven C. Salop ed., 1981)

Richard J. Gilbert & Michael L. Katz, *Perspectives on Intellectual Property: When Good Value Chains Go Bad: The Economics of Indirect Liability for Copyright Infringement*, 52 Hastings L.J. 961 (2001)

Richard J. Gilbert & David M.G. Newbery, *Preemptive Patenting and the Persistence of Monopoly*, 72 Am. Econ. Rev. 514 (1982)

Richard J. Gilbert & Steven C. Sunshine, *Incorporating Dynamic Efficiency Concerns in Merger Analysis: The Use of Innovation Markets*, 63 Antitrust L.J. 569 (1995)

Paul Goldstein, *Copyright* (2d ed. 2002)

Paul Goldstein, *Copyright's Highway: From Gutenberg to the Celestial Jukebox* (Hill & Wang 1994)

Wendy J. Gordon, *Excuse and Justification in the Law of Fair Use: Commodification and Market Perspectives, in* The Commodification of Information (Niva Elkin-Koren & Neil Weinstock Netanel eds., 2002)

Wendy J. Gordon, *Fair Use as Market Failure: A Structural and Economic Analysis of the Betamax Case and its Predecessors*, 82 Colum. L. Rev. 1600 (1982)

Mark F. Grady & Jay I. Alexander, *Patent Law and Rent Dissipation*, 78 Va. L. Rev. 305 (1992)

Bronwyn H. Hall & Rosemarie Ham Ziedonis, *The Patent Paradox Revisited: An Empirical Study of Patenting in the U.S. Semiconductor Industry, 1979–1995*, 32 Rand J. Econ. 101 (2001)

I. Trotter Hardy, *The Ancient Doctrine of Trespass to Web Sites*, 1996 J. Online L. art. 7 (1996)

Paul J. Heald, Comment, *Money Damages and Corrective Advertising: An Economic Analysis*, 55 U. Chi. L. Rev. 629 (1988)

Paul J. Heald, *Payment Demands for Spurious Copyrights: Four Causes of Action*, 1 J. Intell. Prop. L. 259 (1994)

M. Henry Heines, *Indispensable Parties in Patent Litigation*, 58 J. Pat. Off. Soc'y 232 (1976)

Michael A. Heller & Rebecca S. Eisenberg, *Can Patents Deter Innovation? The Anticommons in Biomedical Research*, 280 Science 698 (1998)

Molly A. Holman & Stephen R. Munzer, *Intellectual Property Rights in Genes and Gene Fragments: A Registration Solution for Expressed Sequence Tags*, 85 Iowa L. Rev. 735 (2000)

Ethan Horwitz & Lester Horwitz, *Patent Litigation: Procedure & Tactics* (2001)

Paul M. Janicke, *Contemporary Issues in Patent Damages*, 42 Am. U. L. Rev. 691 (1993)

John C. Jarosz & Erin M. Page, *The Panduit Lost Profits Test After BIC Leisure v. Windsurfing*, 3 Fed. Cir. B.J. 311 (1993)

Stephen H. Kalos & Jonathan D. Putnam, *On the Incomparability of "Comparable": An Economic Interpretation of "Infringer's Royalties,"* 9 No. 4 J. Proprietary Rts. 2 (1997)

Larry S. Karp & Jeffrey M. Perloff, *The Optimal Suppression of a Low-Cost Technology by a Durable-Good Monopoly*, 27 Rand J. Econ. 346 (1996)

Michael L. Katz & Carl Shapiro, *How to License Intangible Property*, 101 Q.J. Econ. 567 (1986)

Jeffrey J. Keyes et al., *Tying, Exclusive Dealing, and Franchising Issues*, 1117 PLI/Corp. 9 (1999)

F. Scott Kieff, *Property Rights and Property Rules for Commercializing Inventions*, 85 Minn. L. Rev. 697 (2000)

F. Scott Kieff, *The Case for Registering Patents and the Law and Economics of Present Patent-Obtaining Rules* (in draft 2003)

Edmund W. Kitch, *Can the Internet Shrink Fair Use?*, 78 Neb. L. Rev. 880 (1999)

Edmund W. Kitch, *The Nature and Function of the Patent System*, 20 J.L. & Econ. 265 (1977)

Benjamin Klein et al., *The Economics of Copyright "Fair Use" in a Networked World*, 92 Am. Econ. Rev. (Papers and Proceedings) 205 (May 2002)

John B. Koegel, *Bamboozlement: The Repeal of Copyright Registration Incentives*, 13 Cardozo Arts & Ent. L.J. 529 (1995)

Alex Kozinski, *Trademarks Unplugged*, 68 N.Y.U.L. Rev. 960 (1993)

Kenneth E. Krosin & Holly D. Kozlowski, *Patent Damages*, 300 PLI/Pat 53 (1990)

Raymond Shih Ray Ku, *The Creative Destruction of Copyright: Napster and the New Economics of Digital Technology*, 69 U. Chi. L. Rev. 263 (2002)

William M. Landes, *Optimal Sanctions for Antitrust Violations*, 50 U. Chi. L. Rev. 652 (1983)

William M. Landes & Richard A. Posner, *Causation in Tort Law: An Economic Approach*, 12 J. Legal Stud. 109 (1983)

William M. Landes & Richard A. Posner, *An Economic Analysis of Copyright Law*, 18 J. Legal Stud. 325 (1989)

William M. Landes & Richard A. Posner, *The Economic Structure of Intellectual Property Law* (2003)

William M. Landes & Richard A. Posner, *The Economic Structure of Tort Law* (1987)

William M. Landes & Richard A. Posner, *Indefinitely Renewable Copyright*, 70 U. Chi. L. Rev. 471 (2003)

William F. Lee et al., *When an Exclusive License Is Not an Exclusive License: The Standing of "Exclusive" Patent Licensees to Sue After Ortho Pharmaceutical Corp. v. Genetics Institute, Inc.*, 7 Fed. Circuit B.J. 1 (1997)

John S. Leibovitz, Note, *Inventing a Nonexclusive Patent System*, 111 Yale L.J. 2251 (2002)

Mark A. Lemley, *The Economics of Improvement in Intellectual Property Law*, 75 Tex. L. Rev. 989 (1997)

Mark A. Lemley & David McGowan, *Legal Implications of Network Economic Effects*, 86 Calif. L. Rev. 479 (May 1998)

Mark A. Lemley, *Rational Ignorance at the Patent Office*, 95 Nw. U.L. Rev. 1495 (2001)

Mark A. Lemley & Eugene Volokh, *Freedom of Speech and Injunctions in Intellectual Property Cases*, 48 Duke L.J. 147 (1998)

Richard C. Levin et al., *Appropriating the Returns from Industrial Research and Development*, 3 Brookings Papers on Economic Activity 783 (1987)

Douglas Gary Lichtman, *The Economics of Innovation: Protecting Unpatentable Goods*, 81 Minn. L. Rev. 693 (1997)

Douglas Lichtman & William Landes, *Indirect Liability for Copyright Infringement: An Economic Perspective*, 16 Harv. J. Law & Tech. 395 (2003)

Lyrissa Barnett Lidsky, *Defamation, Reputation, and the Myth of Community*, 71 Wash. L. Rev. 1 (1996)

Jessica Litman, *The Exclusive Right to Read*, 13 Cardozo Arts & Enter. L.J. 29 (1994)

Clarisa Long, *Patent Signals*, 69 U. Chi. L. Rev. 625 (2002)

Glynn S. Lunney, Jr., *The Death of Copyright: Digital Technology, Private Copying, and the Digital Millennium Copyright Act*, 87 Va. L. Rev. 813 (2001)

Charles C. Mann, *Who Will Own Your Next Good Idea*, Atlantic Monthly 57 (Sept. 1998)

Edwin Mansfield et al., *Imitation Costs and Patents: An Empirical Study*, 91 Econ. J. 907 (1981)

James M. Markarian, *Can the Marking Requirements for a Patented Article Be Circumvented by Obtaining a Process Patent?*, 17 J. Pat. & Trademark Off. Soc'y 365 (1997)

Stephen M. Maurer & Suzanne Scotchmer, *The Independent Invention Defense in Intellectual Property*, 69 Economica 535 (2002)

J. Thomas McCarthy, *McCarthy on Trademarks and Unfair Competition* (4th ed. 2003)

Donald G. McFetridge & Douglas A. Smith, *Patents, Prospects, and Economic Surplus: A Comment*, 23 J. Law & Econ. 197 (1980)

Alan J. Meese, *Tying Meets the New Institutional Economics: Farewell to the Chimera of Forcing*, 146 U. Pa. L. Rev. 1 (1997)

Michael J. McKeon, The *Patent Marking and Notice Statute: A Question of "Fact" or "Act"?*, 9 Harv. J.L. & Tech. 429 (1996)

Robert P. Merges, *Contracting into Liability Rules: Intellectual Property Rights and Collective Rights Organizations*, 84 Cal. L. Rev. 1293, 1296 (1996)

Robert P. Merges, *Intellectual Property Rights and Bargaining Breakdown: The Case of Blocking Patents*, 62 Tenn. L. Rev. 75 (1994)

Robert P. Merges, *Patent Law and Policy: Cases and Materials* 1097 (2d ed. 1997)

Robert P. Merges, *Rent Control in the Patent District: Observations on the Grady-Alexander Thesis*, 78 Va. L. Rev. 359 (1992)

Robert P. Merges & Richard R. Nelson, *On the Complex Economics of Patent Scope"*, 90 Colum. L. Rev. 839 (1990)

David J. Meyer, *Patent Marking Statute May Need Major Overhaul*, Nat'l L.J., Dec. 24, 2001, at C5

Roger M. Milgrim, *Milgrim on Licensing* (2003)

James William Moore et al., *Moore's Federal Practice* (3d ed. 1999)

Kimberly A. Moore, *Judges, Juries, and Patent Cases – An Empirical Peek Inside the Black Box*, 99 Mich. L. Rev. 365 (2001)

Preston Moore & Jackie Nakamura, *The United States Patent Marking and Notice Statute*, 22 AIPLA Q.J. 85 (1994)

Dale A. Nance, *Guidance Rules and Enforcement Rules: A Better View of the Cathedral*, 83 Va. L. Rev. 837 (1997)

Barry Nalebuff, *Bundling* (November 22, 1999). Yale ICF Working Paper Series No. 99–14. (available at *http://ssrn.com/abstract=185193*)

Neil Weinstock Netanel, *Copyright and a Democratic Civil Society*, 106 Yale L.J. 283 (1996)

Walter Nicholson, *Microeconomic Theory* (5th ed. 1992)

David Nimmer, *Copyright in the Dead Sea Scrolls: Authorship and Originality*, 38 Hous. L. Rev. 1 (2001)

Melville B. Nimmer & David Nimmer, *Nimmer on Copyright* (2003)

Markus Nolff, *TRIPs, PCT and Global Patent Procurement* (2001)

Note, *Trade Secret Misappropriation: A Cost-Benefit Response to the Fourth Amendment Analogy*, 106 Harv. L. Rev. 461 (1992)

William F. Ogburn & Dorothy Thomas, *Are Inventions Inevitable? A Note on Social Evolution*, 37 Pol. Sci. Q. 83 (1922)

Carl Oppedahl, *Patent Marking of Systems*, 11 Santa Clara Computer & High Tech. L.J. 205 (1995)

Maureen O'Rourke, *Fencing Cyberspace: Drawing Borders in a Vertical World*, 82 Minn. L. Rev. 609 (1998)

Maureen O'Rourke, *Toward a Doctrine of Fair Use in Patent Law*, 100 Colum. L. Rev. 1177 (2000)

Gideon Parchomovsky & Peter Siegelman, *Towards an Integrated Theory of Intellectual Property*, 88 Va. L. Rev. 1455 (2002)

William F. Patry, *The Fair Use Privilege in Copyright Law* (1985)

Shira Perlmutter, *Freeing Copyright from Formalities*, 13 Cardozo Arts & Ent. L.J. 565 (1995)

Laura B. Pincus, *The Computation of Damages in Patent Infringement Actions*, 5 Harv. J.L. & Tech. 95 (1991)

Robert S. Pindyck & Daniel L. Rubinfeld, *Microeconomics* (4th ed. 1998)

Richard A. Posner, *An Economic Theory of the Criminal Law*, 85 Colum. L. Rev. 1193 (1985)

Richard A. Posner, *Economic Analysis of Law* (4th ed. 1992)

George L. Priest, *What Economists Can Tell Lawyers About Intellectual Property: Comment on Cheung*, 8 Res. L. & Econ. 19 (1986)

Brent Rabowsky, *Note, Recovery of Lost Profits on Unpatented Products in Patent Infringement Cases*, 70 S. Cal. L. Rev. 281 (1996)

R. Anthony Reese, *The Public Display Right: The Copyright Act's Neglected Solution to the Controversy Over RAM "Copies,"* 2001 U. Ill. L. Rev. 83

J. H. Reichman, *Legal Hybrids Between the Patent and Copyright Paradigms*, 94 Colum. L. Rev. 2432 (1994)

Jennifer F. Reinganum, *The Timing of Innovation: Research, Development, and Diffusion*, Handbook of Industrial Organization (Richard Schmalensee & Robert D. Willig eds., 1989)

Jennifer F. Reinganum, *Uncertain Innovation and the Persistence of Monopoly*, 73 Am. Econ. Rev. 741 (1983)

Edward W. Remus et al., *Prerequisites to Recovery of Damages: Importance of Marking and Notice of Infringement*, CA15 ALI-ABA 413 (Nov. 9, 1995)

William C. Robinson, *The Law of Patents for Useful Inventions* (1890)

Fred Anthony Rowley, Jr., *Note, Dynamic Copyright Law: Its Problems and a Possible Solution*, 11 Harv. J.L. & Tech. 481 (1991)

Stephen Salant, *Preemptive Patenting and the Persistence of Monopoly: Comment*, 74 Am. Econ. Rev. 247 (1984)

F. M. Scherer, *Industrial Market Structure and Economic Performance* (2d ed. 1980)

F. M. Scherer et al., *Patents and the Corporation: A Report on Industrial Technology Under Changing Public Policy* (2d ed. 1959)

F. M. Scherer, *Competition Policy, Domestic and International* (Edward Elgar 2000)

John W. Schlicher, *Licensing Intellectual Property: Legal, Business, and Market Dynamics* (1996)

John W. Schlicher, *Measuring Patent Damages by the Market Value of Inventions – The Grain Processing, Rite-Hite, and Aro Rules*, 82 J. Pat. & Trademark Off. Soc'y 503 (2000)

John W. Schlicher, *Patent Law: Legal and Economic Principles* (2002)

Suzanne Scotchmer, *Incentives to Innovate, in Palgrave Encyclopedia of Law & Economics* 273 (1998)

Suzanne Scotchmer, *Standing on the Shoulders of Giants: Cumulative Research and the Patent Law*, J. Econ. Persp. (Winter 1991)

Steven C. Seberoff, *New Requirements in Patent Marking and Notice*, 76 J. Pat. & Trademark Off. Soc'y 793 (1994)

Carl Shapiro, *Antitrust Limits to Patent Settlements*, 34 Rand J. Econ. (forthcoming 2003)

Steven Shavell, *An Analysis of Causation and the Scope of Liability in the Law of Torts*, 9 J. Legal Stud. 463 (1980)

Edward F. Sherry & David W. Teece, *Some Economic Aspects of Intellectual Property Damages*, 573 PLI/Pat 399 (1999)

Herbert Simon, *Theories of Decision-Making in Economics and Behavioral Science*, 49 Am. Econ. Rev. 253, (1959)

John M. Skenyon et al., *Patent Damages Law & Practice* (2002)

Stewart E. Sterk, *Rhetoric and Reality in Copyright Law*, 94 Mich. L. Rev. 1197 (1996)

Marion B. Stewart, *Calculating Economic Damages in Intellectual Property Disputes: The Role of Market Definition*, 77 J. Pat. & Trademark Off. Soc'y 321 (1995)

J. Michael Strickland, Note, *Nonexclusive Patent Licensees Unite: Use Bankruptcy Committees to Sue for Patent Infringement*, 48 Duke L.J. 571 (1998)

C. T. Taylor & Z. A. Silbertson, *The Economic Impact of the Patent System* (1973)

Mark A. Thurmon, *The Rise and Fall of Trademark Law's Functionality Defense*, 56 Fla. L. Rev. 243 (forthcoming 2004)

Jean Tirole, *The Theory of Industrial Organization* (1988)

D. C. Toedt, *The Law and Business of Computer Software* (1998)

Julie S. Turner, Comment, *The Nonmanufacturing Patent Owner: Toward a Theory of Efficient Infringement*, 86 Cal. L. Rev. 179 (1998)

John Vickers, *Pre-Emptive Patenting, Joint Ventures, and the Persistence of Oligopoly*, 3 Int'l J. Indus. Org. 261 (1985)

Joel Voelzke, *Patent Marking Under 35 U.S.C. 287(a): Products, Processes, and the Deception of the Public*, 5 Fed. Cir. B.J. 317 (1995)

R. Polk Wagner, *(Mostly) Against Exceptionalism* (2002 draft)

R. Polk Wagner, *Reconsidering Estoppel: Patent Administration and the Failure of Festo*, 151 U. Pa. L. Rev. 159 (2002)

Richard Watt, *Copyright and Economic Theory: Friends or Foes?* (2000)

Gregory J. Werden et al., *Economic Analysis of Lost Profits from Patent Infringement With and Without Noninfringing Substitutes*, 27 AIPLA Q.J. 305 (1999)

Ray D. Weston Jr., *A Comparative Analysis of the Doctrine of Equivalents: Can European Approaches Solve an American Dilemma?*, 39 IDEA 35 (1998)

Michael D. Whinston, *Tying, Foreclosure, and Exclusion*, 80 Am. Econ. Rev. 837 (1990)

James J. White & Robert S. Summers, *Uniform Commercial Code* (4th ed. 1995)

Charles Alan Wright et al., *Federal Practice and Procedure* (3d ed. 2002)

Shusato Yamamoto & John A. Tessensohn, *Doctrine of Equivalents Adds Torque to Japanese Patent Infringement*, 81 J. Pat. & Trademark Off. Soc'y 483 (1999)

Alfred C. Yen, *What Federal Gun Control Can Teach Us About the DMCA's Anti-Trafficking Provisions*, Wis. L. Rev. 649 (2003)

U.S. Constitutional, Statutory, and Other Legislative Materials

United States Constitution

Art. I, § 8, cl.8
Fourth Amendment

Plant Variety Protection Act, 7 U.S.C.

§§ 2321–2582

Lanham Act, 15 U.S.C.

§ 1051	§ 1115	§ 1115
§ 1072	§ 1116	§ 1125
§ 1111	§ 1117	§ 1127
§ 1114	§ 1118	

Copyright Act, 17 U.S.C.

§ 101	§ 201	§ 505
§ 104	§ 204	§ 512
§ 106	§ 205	§ 602
§ 107	§ 401	§ 611
§ 108	§ 402	§ 1101
§ 109	§ 405	§ 1117
§ 110–122	§ 412	§ 1201
§ 111	§ 501	18 U.S.C. § 2320
§ 114	§ 504	

Patent Act, 35 U.S.C.

§ 101	§§ 171–173	1 Cong. ch. 15, 1 Stat.
§ 102	§ 271	124 (May 31, 1790)
§ 103	§ 284	Patent Act of 1790
§ 112	§ 285	Patent Act of 1793
§ 154	§ 287	Patent Act of 1836
§§ 161–164		

Federal Rules of Civil Procedure

Rule 12	Rule 20	Rule 23
Rule 17	Rule 21	Rule 24
Rule 19	Rule 22	Rule 25

Federal Rules of Civil Procedure (1938)

Rule 19

37 C.F.R.

§ 201.20
§ 202.2

Uniform Commercial Code (UCC)

§2–312

Uniform Trade Secrets Act (UTSA)

§ 1	§ 3
§ 4	§ 2

Other Materials

Agreement on Trade-Related Aspects of Intellectual Property Rights, Apr. 15, 1994, Marrakesh Agreement Establishing the World Trade Organization, Annex 1C, art. 28, Legal Instruments – Results of the Uruguay Round vol. 31, 33 I.L.M. 1197 (1994)

House Report No. 79-1587 (1946), *reprinted in* 2 U.S.C.C.A.N. 1387 (1946)

House Report No. 94-1476, at 159, *reprinted in* 1976 U.S.C.C.A.N. at 5775

House Report No. 104-556, *reprinted in* 996 U.S.C.C.A.N. 1074

ICANN, Uniform Domain Name Resolution Policy, *http://www.icann.org/udrp/ udrp-policy-24oct99.htm*

Information Infrastructure Task Force, Intellectual Property and the National Information Infrastructure: The Report of the Working Group on Intellectual Property Rights (1995)

The Protection of Utility Models in the Single Market: Green Paper from the Commission to the European Council, COM(95)370 final

Restatement (Second) of Torts (1959)

§§ 504–524

Restatement (Third) of Unfair Competition (1995)

§ 5	§ 29	§ 37
§ 20	§ 33	§ 40
§ 24	§ 34	§ 44
§ 25	§ 36	§ 45
§ 28		

Senate Report No. 79-1503 (1946), *reprinted in* 2 U.S.C.C.A.N. 1387 (1946)

Index

absolute novelty rule, 8
abstractions test, 28
access restriction measures, 153
accused device, 10
active inducement, 127, 134
actual damages. *See also* damages
　authorized by the Lanham Act, 84
　considered in calculating statutory, 81
　for copyright infringement, 30
　recovering in trademark law, 88
actual dilution, 36. *See also* dilution
actual knowledge standard, 126, 128
actual notice, 101. *See also* notice
actual profit. *See also* profit
　versus expected, 73
　lost profit greater than, 219
adaptation right, 28
ADL-100 motorized restraint, 223
affixation, 101
Aimster, 134
allocative welfare loss. *See* deadweight loss
alternative compensation schemes, 40
American rule, 234
Amsted Industries v. Buckeye Steel Castings Co., 127
analytical approach for awarding a
　reasonable royalty, 229
anticipated by the prior art, 8
anticompetitive consequences of joint
　marketing, 259
anticompetitive ties, 261, 262
Anticybersquatting Consumer Protection
　Act, 156
antidilution laws, 35
anti-free-riding theory, 38
antitrust injury, 245

antitrust laws, 251
apportionment, 211, 215–217
　basing a reasonable royalty on, 232
　in copyright infringement, 75
　in copyright law, 76
　death of, 222
　EMVR as an exception to, 217
　inadequacy for patented components,
　　216
archival purposes, home videotaping for,
　78
ARMs (automated rights management
　technology), 153
Arrow, Kenneth, 15
Arrow's Information Paradox, 204
assignee
　mandatory joinder of, 195
　of a registered trademark, 183
　right to sue for infringement, 186
　standing of, 166
　standing under copyright law, 161
　threatened by infringement, 197
　as a victim of infringement, 188
assignment
　versus a license in copyright law, 179–183
　of patents, 161, 164, 187
　standing under copyright law, 182
　transfer as an, 167
assignor
　allowing to intervene, 186
　retaining a reversionary interest, 197
　standing of, 166
assignor-assignee relationship, 186–187
attorney's fees, 12, 38
auctions, 188
Australia, innovation patents, 21

author, 27, 181
authorship, 27, 104
automated rights management (ARM)
    technology, 153
Ayers-Klemperer thesis, 61–66

bad faith, infringement in, 87
basis for the demand, component as, 232
beneficial owner of a copyright, 181
benefits of a patent system, 17, 20
Bertrand behavior, 239–241
Bertrand equilibrium, 257
Bertrand oligopoly, 211
bidding for a patent, 187
biotechnology, cost of follow-up inventions,
    18
Blair Electronics hypothetical example, 132
blocking patents problem, 10
Blonder-Tongue, effect of, 177
blurring, dilution by, 36
bootleg videocassettes, 82
Bright Tunes Music Corp. v. Harrisongs
    Music, Ltd., 91
broad patent scope, 21
Broadcast Music, Inc. v. Entertainment
    Complex, Inc., 82
Broadcast Music, Inc. v. Star Amusement,
    Inc., 82
bundling, 260
but-for approach, 211
but-for causation standard, 233–234
but-for measure of damages, 235
but-for profit, equaling damages in a
    Bertrand case, 241
but-for rule, 233
but-for standard, 220–227
buyouts of patents, 15

Canopy Music, Inc. v. Harbor Cities
    Broadcasting, Inc., 82
Category 1 cases, 81, 82
Category 2 cases, 82
Category 3 cases, 82
cause-in fact. *See* but-for causation
    standard
Celanese International Corp. v. BP Chemicals
    Ltd, 71
Central Point Software, Inc. v. Nugent, 81
chain of distribution, 133
Chamberlinian behavior, 241, 257
Champion Spark Plug Co. v. Sanders, 85

Chi-Boy Music v. Charlie Club, Inc., 82
child pornography, 149. *See also* obscenity
chilling effect, 88
Choi's model, 193
civil action, proper party to, 170
"clean room" procedures, 110
Coase Theorem, 194
Coca-Cola
    formula for, 25
    syrup recipe, 145
    use of SURGE trademark, 91
collateral estoppel, 173, 178
collateral goods. *See* convoyed sales
collateral products, 254
colors as a source signifier, 32
commercial use
    determining, 144
    of trademarks, 157
commercial users
    sometimes sued for patent infringement,
        133
    trademark liability extending to all
        unauthorized, 138
commercialization
    of a patent, 246
    patents encouraging, 251
commercialized patented inventions,
    creating a registry for, 130
common defects in copyright notice, 130
common-law copyright, 27
comparative advertising, 138
compensatory damages, 208, 211–220
competition
    from the infringer, 212
    between a patentee and an infringer, 50
competitive impulses in Chamberlinian
    behavior, 241
complementarity, 255
complementary goods
    recovering lost profits on sales of, 245,
        254–259
    sales of, 232
complements, 255
compliance costs of an injunction, 46
component buyers, reducing purchases,
    142
component manufacturer, ultimate liability
    of, 141
component patent, incremental gain
    attributable to, 215
components, marking, 119

compulsory licensing
  consistently avoided by U.S. patent law, 254
  of copyrights instead of an injunction, 30
  of patents, 39
  schemes, 40
  working requirement coupled with, 254
computer programming techniques, 31
computer programs
  extension of copyright to, 151
  first-side doctrine not applicable to, 29
  source code and the object code of, 27
computer technology, moving copyright law towards the patent liability rule, 151
confidentiality, duty of, 106
confusion
  likelihood of, 85
  in trademark cases, 35
constructive knowledge, 134
constructive notice, 99
  deeming sufficient, 123
  of patent infringement, 101
  potential infringers always on, 124
consumer goodwill, encouraged by trademarks, 38
consumer protection system, trademark law operating as, 207
consumer surveys in trademark litigation, 105
consumers
  extension of patent liability to, 144
  ignorance of infringement exposure, 148
  preferring brand names, 67
  rarely sued for patent infringement, 132
  trademarks lowering search costs for, 38
consumption complementarity, 259
continuing royalties, 190–196. *See also* running royalties
contractual limitations on resale or use, 133
contributory infringement, 127, 128, 134. *See also* willful infringement
contributory negligence, 118–120
convoyed products. *See* collateral products
convoyed sales, 223
copying
  cost of, 15
  as an element of copyright infringement, 91

inferring from similarity, 103
  liability in copyright law contingent on, 102–104
copying equipment, imposing a tax upon, 31
copyright
  beneficial owner of, 181
  as a collection of diverse indivisibility rights, 179
  as a component to larger products, 73
  doctrines preventing interference with free speech, 77
  extension to computer programs, 151
  forfeiture of, 27
  as indivisible, 179–180
  invalidated in litigation much less frequently than patents, 183
  liberalization of standing rules, 207
  registration of, 27, 107
  right of production, 135
  term, 27
Copyright Act
  abolishment of the copyright indivisibility rule, 180
  damages rules, 69
  highly technical provisions, 29
  registration requirement, 83
  standing rules flowing from, 181
  unauthorized distribution to the public and, 136
copyright infringement
  copying as an element of, 91
  cost of detecting acts of, 77
copyright law, 26–32
  contributory infringement, 134
  damages calculation, 208
  exempting certain uses from liability, 147–151
  extending the patent damages model to, 66
  first-sale doctrine, 133, 148
  independent discovery defense, 107
  liability contingent upon proof of copying, 102–104
  liability for persons other than employees, 134
  moving closer to the patent model, 154
  providing more liberal exceptions to liability, 137
  scope of liability, 265
  standing rules, 182, 266

copyright law (*cont.*)
  standing to an assignee or exclusive
    licensee, 161
  statutory damages, 74–80
  vicarious infringement, 134
copyright notice, 129
copyright owner
  burden of proof, 136
  defined in the Copyright Act, 180
  indivisibility rule disadvantageous to, 179
  rights of, 28
copyright ownership
  registration and, 83
  transfer of, 180
copyright protection
  assigning or licensing, 28
  expansion over time, 27
copyright right, transfer of, 195
copyright system, administrative costs of,
    31
copyrighted material, unauthorized uses of,
    137
copyrighted software, loading, 151
copyrighted works, knowledge by users of
    infringing, 149
corrective advertising awards, for trademark
    cases, 90
cost
  additional for the patent owner, 218
  calculating a royalty or corrective
    advertising award, 90
  detecting acts of copyright infringement,
    77
  detecting trademark infringement, 79
  determining profit attributable to
    trademark infringement, 89
  maintaining a commercialized patents
    registry, 130
  patent system, 20
cost curves, 65
"costs as fixed by the court," 234
counterfeit trademarks, 36, 85
counterfeiting as a trademark infringement,
    34
Cournot case, 236
Cournot duopolist, 108
Cournot duopoly model, 236
Cournot equilibrium price, calculating, 239
Cournot oligopoly, 211, 242
Court of Appeals for the Federal Circuit,
    championing the but-for standard, 220

courts
  application of the statutory damages rule,
    80
  awarding statutory damages, 81
  determining the optimal amount of
    search, 116
  manipulating the rules of enforcement
    and procedure, 6
  methods for estimating lost sales, 213
creative activity, 54
cross-elasticity of demand, 214, 218, 255
cross-licensing agreements in the
    semiconductor industry, 116
cumulative nature of invention, 17
cyberpirate, 155
cybereconomists, accounting for fair use,
    154
cyberspace, application of copyright law to,
    152–155
cybersquatter, 155
cybersquatting, 157, 158

damages. *See also* actual damages; punitive
    damages; statutory damages
  awarding future, 234
  awarding in a suit for patent
    infringement, 12
  but-for standard compared to *Panduit*,
    220
  calculating for nonexclusive licensees, 205
  compensatory, 208, 211–220
  for copyright infringement, 30
  due to multiperiod infringement, 239
  ex ante versus ex post, 230
  in a federal trademark infringement
    action, 36
  law of, 2
  liability for, under patent law, 100
  liability immunizing knowing infringers,
    125
  no simple formula for capturing, 235
  nominal, 76
  opportunity cost, 234
  presumed, 76, 77
  restitutionary, 73, 84–95
  roles of, 263
  strict liability as precondition to recovery,
    120–130
  substantial limitations upon recoveries,
    98
  for a trade secret misappropriation, 25

damages multiplier, 71
damages rules
  constructing a simple model of optimal,
    42–69
  devising to leave NPV unchanged, 45
  governing patent, copyright, and
    trademark law, 69
  necessary to preserve th incentive
    structure, 42
  optimal, 57
  preserving the incentive structure of
    patent law, 233
  preserving the incentive structure of
    trademark law, 66
deadweight loss, 18, 63
  lost aggregate profits as, 52
  reducing, 62
  reducing during the patent term, 67
defamation law, 76
  impact upon protected speech, 88
  vagueness of, 88
defendants
  actual profits as an estimation of
    damages, 213
  actual sales as an estimation of damages,
    213
  involuntary, 174
  in a patent infringement action, 11
DeForest Radio Telephone & Telegraph
  Company, 169
demand, cross-elasticity of, 214, 218,
  255
demand curve, 235
derivative goods, 223
derivative revenues, 31
derivative works
  preparing, 137
  right to prepare, 28
description requirement under patent
  law, 9
descriptive use or fair use doctrine in
  trademark law, 138
design patents
  award of the defendant's profit, 71
  law of, 7
detection of infringement, 48
deterrent effect of the willing
  licensor-licensee standard, 231
development costs for a new invention, 43
Digital Millennium Copyright Act
  (DMCA), 153

dilution, 35
  actual, 36
  by blurring, 36
  federal trademark statute, 95
  likelihood standard, 36
  by tarnishment, 36
  vagueness of the concept, 95
  willful, 95
direct infringers, 133, 135
disclosure requirements, imposed by patent
  laws, 9
discrete products, competitive market for,
  19
display right, 28, 153
diverted sales, 219
DMCA (Digital Millennium Copyright
  Act), 153
dock levelers, 223, 225
doctrine of equivalents, 72
  applying, 22
  devices infringing under, 99
  infringing under, 10
  interpretation of, 22
domain names, 155–158
downstream monopoly, 197
duplication, 97, 109
duplicative effort, cost associated with, 18
duplicative recoveries, nonavailability of,
  178
duration, 20, 23
Dutch auction, 188
duty of secrecy, 24

economic loss, measuring, 209
economic models for a patentee-infringer
  competition, 50–55
economic monopolies, 57
economic rent, seeking, 16
economies of scale, 197
effective patent life, 10
efficient infringer, 56
efficient producers, 51
efficient trademarks, 86
e-mail messages, forwarding, 153
EMVR (entire market value rule), 216, 222
  applying, 232
  rendering irrelevant, 233
  restatement of, 223
enablement requirement under patent
  law, 9
English auction, 188

enhanced damages under the Lanham Act, 84
entire market value rule. *See* EMVR
entitlements
    protecting by a liability rule, 39
    protecting by a property rule, 39
entry deterrence, 254
equally efficient infringer, 51, 56
equivalents. *See* doctrine of equivalents
established royalty, 211
ex ante damages versus *ex post*, 230
exceptional circumstances, justifying an
        award of attorney's fees, 234
exceptions
    admitted by copyright law, 29
    to liability for patent infringement, 11
excludable goods, 13
exclude, excercising the right to, 227
exclusive license
    compared to nonexclusive, 203
    conferring standing under patent law, 161
    definition of, 169
    standing under copyright law, 161, 182
exclusive licensee, 168
    as an involuntary plaintiff, 174
    joinder of, 175
    standing, 175, 183
    threatened by infringement, 197
    trademark, 184
    waiver of right to join, 175
exclusive rights
    conferring, 263
    copyright owner assigning, 181
    granting under patents, 165
    under a patent system, 17
    valuable in copyright law, 183
exhaustion doctrine. *See* first-sale doctrine
expectations sense, making infringement
        unprofitable, 45
expected profit versus actual, 73
experience goods, 38
experimental use in patent law, 11, 138

facts, not subject to copyright protection, 27
fair dealing exception, 29
fair use defense, 29
fair use doctrine, 137
    absolving unauthorized use, 75
    in copyright law, 147
    in trademark law, 138
    transaction costs and, 154
famous trademarks, 35, 156

fanciful words, 33
FDA-approved drug, 109
federal antidilution
    law, 35
    protection, 36
Federal Circuit. *See also* Court of Appeals
        for the Federal Circuit
    functionality test, 256
federal registration of trademarks, 33
Federal Rules of Civil Procedure
    complicating standing, 161
    Rule 19, 170–175
    Rule 20 or 24, 175
    Rule 54, 234
Federal Trademark Dilution Act, 36, 95
file-sharing software, 135
firms
    competing by setting quantities, 236
    mutual accommodation of, 241
First Amendment protection, 88
first infringer, 135
first-mover advantage, 15
first-sale doctrine, 11, 29, 133
    not applying to electronic forwarding,
        154
    in patent law compared to copyright, 148
    for trademarks, 33
first-to-file system, 8
fixed costs
    of providing notice, 120
    versus variable, 218
Florentine Art Studio, Inc. v. Vedet K. Corp.,
        82
follow-up inventions, cost of, 17
follow-up inventor, 17
foreseeability of harm, 244
forgone royalty, 56, 59
Fourth Amendment, concerns, 150
fragrances as a source signifier, 32
France, exempting private noncommercial
        use in patent law, 144
Frankenstein example, 160
free speech, copyright doctrines and, 77
freedom, traditional notions of, 149
free-rider problem, 15, 17
free-riding
    curbing, 97
    defining precisely, 97
    permitting various types of, 97
    upon the originator's R&D, 44
Friedman-Landes-Posner theory, 145–147
full search for existing trademarks, 94

functional unit, components constituting, 225
functionality doctrine, 262
functionality test of the Federal Circuit, 256
future damages, awarding, 234
future expected profit flow, 44
future profit
  reduced by free-riding, 44
  stream, 189

Gayler v. Wilder, 163
general baseline rule, 61
generic terms, 33
genericness, invalidating once-trademarked words, 35
Georgia-Pacific Co. v. United States Plywood Co., 228
Gilliam, Terry, 76
good faith, claim of, 88
goods, not functionally related, 257
goodwill, trademarks encouraging firms to create, 38
government funding, competition for, 16
governments, relying on for inventions, 16
Grain Processing Corp. v. American Maize-Products Co., 218
Grokster ruling, 135
Grokster software, 134

Hamilton-Brown Shoe Co. v. Wolf Bros. & Co., 89
harm
  definition of, 245
  foreseeability of, 244
  of the type patent laws intended to prevent, 245
Harrison, George, 91, 103
Hasbro, Inc. v. Internet Entertainment Group, Ltd., 155
He's So Fine, 103
highly distinctive trademarks, 35
hit-and-run infringement, 236–237
holdover franchisees, royalties awarded, 90
home videotaping as noninfringing, 78

ideas, not subject to copyright protection, 27
idle patent. *See also* nonmanufacturing patent owners; patented products
  case of, 246–254
  recovering damages, 102
  reforms centered around, 128

imperfect competition scenario versus monopoly, 57
importation of infringing products, 141
improper means, 24, 105
inadvertent infringement, 114, 264. *See also* innocent infringement
incentive function of trademark law, 66
incentive structure
  damage rules necessary to preserve, 42
  no guarantee of optimality, 45
  preserving by devising damage rules, 45
incentive theory
  additional patent rights theories complementing, 19
  for copyright, 30
incentive-access tradeoff, 146
incentives to invest, 14
incremental income approach to cost estimation, 218
indemnity claim, 141, 142
independent creation as a defense in copyright law, 102
independent discovery
  as a defense of an infringement claim, 106–108
  feigning, 110
  high cost of research and development, 109
  not actionable in copyright, 29
  permitted by trade secret law, 111
  recognizing as a defense, 98
  reducing the incidence of, 12
independent discovery defense
  in both copyright and trade secret law, 107
  exemptions from, 109
  in patent law, 108
independent invention, 12, 108
Independent Wireless Telegraph Co. v. Radio Corp. of America, 169
indirect infringer, 134, 135
indirect liability, 134
indispensable party, 173
indispensable person, 171, 172
indivisibility rule
  in copyright law, 179–180
  in patent law, 182
industrial application requirement, 9
information
  as nonrival and nonexcludable, 13
  spreading of useful, 14
information cost, 187

information paradox, 15
infringement. *See also* law of infringement;
    patent infringement
    amount that would have been earned
        absent, 233
    causing the idle patentee to lose sales, 246
    deterring, 45–47
    economic effect of, 236
    hit-and-run, 236–237
    identifying proper parties, 4
    independent discovery as a defense,
        106–108
    inducing limited amounts of, 64
    intentional, 90
    knowingly induced, 127
    lost profits caused by, 212
    making unprofitable, 243
    measuring the profit attributable to, 47
    multi-period, 237–239
    one-shot, 236–237
    pervasiveness of small-scale, 71
    quantifying the harm caused by, 209
    rendering unprofitable, 45
    resulting in a multiperiod Cournot
        equilibrium, 257
    separating out the effect of, 233
    social cost of, 121
    socially optimal amount of, 114
    standing to sue for, 160
    substantive legal standards applied by
        courts, 60
    taking into account events occurring
        after, 230
infringement revenue function, 47
infringer
    competition with a patentee, 50
    equally efficient, 51
    explicit promise to prosecute all material,
        193
    identifying, 132–159
    less efficient, 52
    more efficient, 54–55
    penalizing for efficiency, 59
    right to sue the customers of, 141
    tolerating because of the risk of
        invalidation, 193
    what it means to an, 97
infringing
    components, 140
    conduct, 3
    product, 120
    return to, 45

inherently distinctive symbols, 33
injunction, 2
    for copyright infringement, 29
    cost of complying with, 46, 125
    substantial costs accompanying, 231
injunctive relief
    allowing nonexclusive licensees to sue for,
        205
    authorized in a suit for patent
        infringement, 12
    in a federal trademark infringement
        action, 36
    incompleteness of, 42
    infringement revenue function under, 47
    for misappropriation of a trade secret, 25
innocent infringement. *See also* inadvertent
    infringement
    in copyright cases, 30
    not a defense under patent law, 99
    of a process patent, 102
    trademark, 138
innocent infringers, leaving vulnerable, 125
innovation patents, 21
inspection goods, 38
intellectual property, compared to real or
    personal, 100
intellectual property law, 1, 263
    assignor-assignee relationship, 186
    mental states in, 96
    standards of liability in, 96
    standing rules, 161
    as strict liability law, 264
intellectual property rights. *See* IPRs
intentional decision to infringe, 101
intentional infringement, 90
intentional tort
    copyright infringement as, 103
    trademark infringement as, 85
intent-to-use (ITU) application for
    trademarks, 33
interdependent demand for licenses, 204
interest, awarding in a patent infringement,
    234
interim infringement, deadweight loss
    during, 63
Intermatic Inc. v. Toeppen, 156
*International Star Class Yacht Racing
    Association v. Tommy Hilfiger, U.S.A.,
    Inc.*, 86, 94
Internet
    applying traditional copyright principles
        to, 153–155

effects on copyright and trademark law, 152

Internet Corporation for Assigned Names and Numbers (ICANN), 157

intrusiveness, necessary to detect violations, 150

invalid patent, 11

invalidation
  rates for patents, 11
  tolerating infringers because of the risk of, 193
  of trademarks compared to patents and copyrights, 185

invalidity argument, 11

invalidity defense, 176

inventions
  cost of follow-up, 17
  creating and marketing new, 42
  incentives for, 17
  later discoveries relating to, 204
  pioneering, 19, 22
  producing through tax revenues, 16
  protectable under the law of utility patents, 7
  qualifying prior, 8

inventive step requirement, 9

inventive success, probability of, 109

involuntary defendants, 174

involuntary plaintiff, 171, 172
  DeForest as an, 169
  licensee joining the patentee as an, 170
  rule, 174

I.P. law. *See* intellectual property law

IPRs (intellectual property rights)
  debating and resolving, 6
  fundamental assumption of, 263
  liability standards for, 96–131
  penalty for infringing, 92
  protecting, 38–41
  protecting through property rules, 40
  simple model of, 47–49, 68, 263
  socially optimal system of, 263
  suboptimal scope and duration of, 4

ISPs, liability as direct or indirect infringers, 153

joinder. *See also* standing
  feasibility of, 171
  of licensee and patentee, 177
  of persons as plaintiffs, 175
  right of, 169

joint marketing, consequences of, 259

Jordan v. Time, Inc., 81

judges
  ability to set patent breadth, 109
  as policy makers, 6

judgment-proof defendant, 140

juries
  determination of statutory damages, 75
  doctrine of presumed damages and, 77
  as more pro-patent owner than judges, 118

Kentucky Fried Chicken recipe, 25

Kewanee Oil Co. v. Bicron Corp., 111

kicker as a means of compensating the patent owner, 231

King Instrument Corp. v. Perego, 225–227

Kitch, Edmund, 19

Klemperer, Paul, 61

Knitwaves Inc. v. Lollytogs Ltd., 82

knowing dilution, 95

knowing infringers
  holding liable for damages accruing prior to receipt of notice, 126
  immunizing from damages liability, 125
  recovering damages from, 128
  remaining immune from damages liability under Section 287, 124

knowledge, dissemination of, 14

KODAK, 157

Kozinski, Alex, 151

Lanham Act
  actual damages authorized by, 84
  enhanced damages under, 37, 84
  recovering damages under, 105
  registration under, 33
  standing under, 161, 183
  statutory damages, 79

law, undermining the rule of, 6

law of defamation. *See* defamation law

law of infringement, regulating patent scope, 22

law of patents. *See* patent law

law of unfair competition. *See* unfair competition

laws of nature, not patentable, 21

"legal" cause. *See* proximate cause

legislative lock-in, 40

less efficient infringer, 52
  awarding patentee's lost profits, 61
  minimal sanction, 56
  modifying the optimal rule for, 58

letters as trademarks, 32
liability
    scope across various bodies of I.P. law, 264
    social costs of imposing, 243
liability exposure of manufacturers, 143
liability rules, 38–41, 251
liability standards, 96–131
Library of Congress, 83
license. *See also* exclusive license;
        nonexclusive license
    versus an assignment in copyright law,
        179–183
    interdependent demand for, 204
    not entailing a transfer of ownership, 196
    requiring the efficient infringer to pay for,
        55
    transfer as a, 168
license agreement between the Watermans,
        165
license fee. *See* royalties
licensee. *See also* exclusive licensee;
        nonexclusive licensees
    versus an assignee of the entire patent,
        163
    better off than independent
        inventors/competitors, 108
    complying with marking requirements,
        119
    disclosing information to potential, 204
    forcing the patentee into litigation, 170
    free to challenge the validity of a patent,
        205
    net profit for, 202
    profit of, 192
    qualifying the right to sue, 176
    relationship to licensor, 176
licensee estoppel, 177
licensing
    failure of the market for, 56
    feasibility of, 111
licensor
    initiating suit without necessarily joining
        the licensee, 161
    relationship to licensee, 175
    retaining greater control than an assignor,
        196
licensor-exclusive licensee relationship,
        196–198
life-plus-seventy term for copyright, 28
likelihood
    of confusion, 85
    of dilution, 36

limited infringement, inducing, 64
literally infringed patent, 10
literary works, 27
litigation
    expected value of, 49
    multiple involving the same patent, 176,
        177
    provoking to declare a patent invalid, 177
    reducing frivolous, 83
lost profits
    awarding the court's best estimate, 243
    awarding under the but-for causation
        principle, 227
    but-for standard of estimating, 220–227
    as a deadweight loss, 52
    defined as, 233
    exceeding a reasonable royalty, 248
    factors for establishing, 217–220
    greater than actual, 219
    mathematical examples, 235–242
    proving the amount of, 231
    recovering on lost sales of
        complementary goods, 254
    as a remedy to an idle patent owner, 248
    requiring from less efficient infringers, 58
    on sales of unpatented goods, 222–227
    when no product is marketed, 225
lost royalties, 233
lost sales, 213
lump-sum fees
    compared to running royalty per unit of
        output, 191
    exclusive licensee in exchange for, 196
    for nonexclusive licenses, 198–199
    patent, trademark, or copyright
        transferred in exchange for, 187–189
    versus a running royalty, 198
lump-sum royalties, 198

magnetism of trademarks, 86
maintenance fees for patents, 21
mandatory joinder provision, 171
marginal deterrence, 60
mark. *See* trademark(s)
market-share
    approach, 221
    basis, 221
    damages, 221–222
marking
    inconsistencies in the current regime, 129
    legibility of, 119
    not required for process patents, 101

patents, 102
trademarked products, 105
mathematical error in *State Industries*, 221
Maurer-Scotchmer thesis, 108–113
maximum profit of a patentee, 235
MDL-55 vehicle restraint, 223
mental states, 96, 98
merger doctrine, 31
minimalist school, 32
misjoinder, 171
mixed recovery, 57
monetary damages. *See* damages
Money Store v. Harriscorp Fin., Inc., 94
monopolistic competition, promoted by
    trademarks, 38
monopolistic nature of patents, 215
monopoly
    causing an allocative welfare loss, 63
    versus imperfect competition, 57
    natural, 197
monopoly leveraging
    claims of, 163
    tying schemes facilitating, 260
monopoly price, patent owners not
    charging, 65
monopoly profit for a patented product, 57
monopoly rights
    cost associated with, 18
    patent conferring, 187
    probability of a patent conferring, 110
moral rights, 28
more efficient infringer
    awarding the profit of, 61
    modifying the optimal rule for, 58
    penalizing, 59
more efficient user, 85
Mor-Flo Industries, 221
Morpheus software, 134
mortgage contract, 190
multiperiod Cournot equilibrium, 257
multiperiod infringement, 237–239
multiple damages under patent law, 12
multiplier
    damages, 71
    optimal, 48
musical performers, 29
musical work, 27
mutual accommodation of firms, 241
My Sweet Lord, 103

NAFTA, article on trade secrets, 23
Napster, 134

narrow patent scope, 21
National Information Infrastructure Task
    Force, 153
natural monopoly, 197. *See also* monopoly
nature. *See* laws of nature
negligence standard, 113–120
neighboring rights, 28, 29
neoclassical school, 32
net present value (NPV), 44
nominal damages, 76
noncommercial use of a trademark, 151
nonexcludable invention, 14
nonexcludable quality of information, 13
nonexclusive license. *See also* license
    conferring no standing, 161
    defining, 168
    distinguishing, 182
nonexclusive licensees, 168. *See also* licensee
    compared to exclusive, 203
    determining expected profit, 205
    effect of infringement on, 198–206
    infringement injuring, 199
    injured by infringement, 201
    lacking standing under copyright law,
        181
    not according standing to, 204
    not harmed by infringement, 203
    potential cost of conferring the right to
        initiate litigation, 205
    standing under trademark law, 183, 185
nonfunctional attributes as source signifiers,
    33
noninfringing substitutes
    assessing the adequacy of, 217
    for a patented invention, 214
noninherently distinctive symbols, 33
noninnocent infringement, 82
nonjoinder, 171
nonmanufacturing infringers, 128
nonmanufacturing patent owners. *See also*
    idle patent
    awarding lost profits to, 248
    nonpreemptive, 254
    recovering a royalty only, 252
    subjecting to a rule of limited damages,
        253
nonmanufacturing patentees, rewarding,
    250
nonobvious invention, 99
nonobviousness
    grounds for declaring patents invalid, 183
    requirement for patent protection, 9

nonrival quality of information, 13
nonrivalrous invention, 13, 14
nonsubstitutability assumption, 57–58
nonwillful dilution, 95
no-restitution rule, 74
normative analysis, 5
notice
  imposing on the patentee, 118
  legibility of, 119
  optimal decision to provide, 119
  of patent infringement, 100
  requirement of a patentee, 118
  rigorousness of standards, 124
  rules, 124
novelty requirement for patent protection, 8
NPV (net present value), 44
numbers as trademarks, 32

object code of computer programs, 27
obscenity, possession of, 149, 150
OCILLA (Online Copyright Infringement Liability Limitation Act), 153
one-shot infringement, 236–237
one-size-fits-all patent term, 21
one-stop shopping, 257
opportunity cost damages, 234
optimal damages rules, 263
optimal multiplier, 48
optimal rules
  application of, 57
  modifying, 58, 61
optimal search, simple model of, 91–93
original works of authorship, 27
originality, 27
overdeterrence
  consequences of, 60
  inducing, 60
  prospect of ruinous liability leading to, 258
  in trademark law, 89
overdeterrent effect, 61
ownership
  of a patent, 161
  of a trademark, 34–36, 183

package, marking on, 119
palming off, 67–68
Panavision Int'l, L.P. v. Toeppen, 157
Panduit Corp. v. Stahlin Bros. Fibre Works, Inc., 217

Panduit factors, 217–220
  factor two, 221
  factor three, 221
Panduit-like standards, rendering irrelevant, 233
Paper Converting Machine Co. v. Magna-Graphics Corp., 223, 225
partial damages thesis of Ayres and Klemperer, 62
partial or probabilistic property right, patents as, 114
party defendant, joining the licensor as, 170
passing off, 67–68
patent
  allowing to lapse, 10
  compulsory licensing of, 39
  conferring monopoly rights in a market, 187
  continuing payments over the life of, 190
  determining the more efficient user of, 60
  duration, 20
  effective life, 10
  enforcing unused pursuant to a liability rule, 251
  extracting the potential value of, 187
  incentive, 123
  incremental gain attributable to, 215
  indivisibility rule, 163
  invalid, 11
  invalidation rates, 11
  lapsing prematurely, 21
  life of, 189
  litigation, 177, 233
  maintenance fees for, 21
  monopolistic nature of, 215
  monopoly, 58
  multiple litigation involving the same, 176
  not conferring monopoly rights, 18
  not enforcing unused, 251
  obtaining a monopoly on unpatented material, 224
  private noncommercial use of, 147
  protecting through property rules, 40
  reasons for not commercializing, 246
  scope, 21–22
  strength, 20
  term, 10, 21
  using to exclude infringing products, 226

Patent Act
  authorizing awards of attorney's fees only
    in exceptional cases, 234
  damages rules, 69
  deletion of restitutionary awards from, 72
  departing from the strict liability model,
    101
  nonuse not equated with misuse, 251
  not requiring inventors to practice their
    patents, 224
  revisions in regard to standing, 162
  Section 287, 124–127
patent breadth, 21, 22
patent cases
  compensatory damages, 211–220
  problem of apportionment in, 73
  restitution as an available remedy in, 72
  simple model of optimal damage rules
    for, 42–69
  standing rules, 206
patent claims, drafting broadly, 22
patent damages model
  extending to the law of trade secrets and
    copyrights, 66
  implications of the basic, 55–57
  refinements to, 57–61
  trademarks and, 66–68
patent infringement, 10. *See also*
    infringement
  absence of a restitutionary remedy in, 70
  compensating monetary damages in,
    266
  defendant in, 11
  extending liability, 139–141
  extending to all sellers and users, 143
  forms of, 10
  isolating the influence of, 264
  notice of, 100
  private acts difficult to detect, 79
  as the proximate cause, 244
  rule, 133, 135, 138–144
  strict liability rule for, 113–115
patent injury requirement, incorporating,
    245
patent invalidity, 176
patent law, 8–13
  compared to trade secret law, 23–26
  complemented by trademark law, 67
  controlling patent scope, 22
  departure from the optimal damages
    model, 264

disclosure requirements imposed upon
    the applicant, 9
factors for establishing lost profits,
    217–220
first-sale doctrine, 133, 148
forms of indirect liability, 134
lack of a fair use doctrine, 148
meaning of a reasonable royalty, 242
public sale disclosing infringer's activities,
    79
remedies contingent upon receipt of
    notice, 99–102
restitution in, 71–74
scope of liability of, 264
standing, 161, 162
standing rules, 182, 265
unauthorized uses of, 132
uncertainty created for sellers and users,
    143
patent owner, 10. *See also* patentee
  additional costs caused by infringement,
    212
  assigning a patent subject to third party
    licenses, 166
  burden of proof, 136
  failing to mark, 102
  interest to choose a forum, 176
  lost profits due to infringement, 212
  right to prevent unauthorized uses and
    sales, 133
"patent pending," marking products with,
    102
patent policy, 13–23
patent protection, 7, 8
patent races, 18
  desirability of, 112
  prompting preemptive patenting, 248
  rent dissipation, 22
patent "rents," 18
patent rights
  cost of processing, enforcing, and
    maintaining, 17
  as indivisible, 162
  optimal scope or duration, 23
  reinforcing the property-like nature of, 59
  theories complementing the standard
    incentive theory, 19
  transfer considered to be a license, 195
  transfer within a single geographic area,
    195
  against unauthorized sales, 136

patent system
  fundamental premise of, 13
  funding invention under, 16
  maximizing social benefits over social
    costs, 20
  premise for, 16
  supplemented by trade secret law, 26,
    145
patentable subject matter, 8, 21
patented component, 216
patented devices, permitting radical
  improvements, 11
patented inventions
  creating a registry for, 130
  maximized profits to a patentee, 50
  nonpatented substitutes for, 19
patented processes
  reforms centered around, 128
  users of, 139
patented products, refusal to sell or license,
  251. *See also* idle patent
patentee. *See also* patent owner
  awarding either lost profits or defendant's
    profits, 61
  awarding the lost profits of, 61
  competing with an infringing entrant
    based on price, 239
  competition with a less efficient infringer,
    52–54
  competition with a more efficient
    infringer, 54
  competition with an equally efficient
    infringer, 51–52
  competition with an infringer, 50
  identifying injury, 49–55
  imposing a notice requirement on, 118
  as an indispensable party, 177
  information available to, 204
  injury risk shifted to under simple
    negligence, 116
  as less risk averse, 49
  maximized profits for a patented
    invention, 50
  maximizing royalty revenue, 191
  optimal to invest no resources in notice,
    120
  recovering either actual damages or
    restitution, 60
  requiring lost profit from the less efficient
    infringer, 58
  rights of, 10
  total royalties received by, 192

pay-per-use, 154
Peer Int'l Corp. v. Luna Records, Inc., 81
perfect complements, 255
performance right, 28
personal property, 100
persuasive advertising, 38
per-unit royalties for nonexclusive licenses,
  199–201
petty patents, 21
pharmaceuticals, 17, 109
pictures as trademarks, 32
pioneering inventions, 19, 22
plant varieties, patentable, 7
pornography. *See* obscenity
positive analysis, 5
positive/normative distinction, 5
pre- and postjudgment interest, 13, 234
precaution model, 114
preemptive nonmanufacturing patent
  owners, 254
preemptive patenting, 248, 250, 252
preinjunction infringement, 124
preinvention search of patented inventions,
  107
presumed damages, 76, 77
pre-use search, 91
price erosion, 212, 237
prior art, 9
prior inventions, 8
privacy
  intrusiveness upon individual, 150
  traditional notions of, 149
private, noncommercial use of patented
  inventions, 132
private acts, disparate treatment of, 150
private consumers. *See* consumers
private noncommercial users. *See*
  consumers
prizes, conferring for patents, 15
probability of detecting an infringer, 48
process
  obtaining a patent on, 139
  patent or trade secret covering, 79
process patent
  infringer of, 125
  recovering damages, 101
procompetitive purpose of a tie, 260
producers, investing in quality control, 38
product packaging, marking, 119
products
  measuring the complementarity of, 255
  as substitutes, 214

products liability
 analogous to patent infringement,
  100
 Landes and Posner analysis of, 141
profit. *See also* actual profit
 attributable to infringement, 47, 210
 expected versus actual, 73
 future stream of, 189
 less-efficient infringer disgorging, 56
 potential for a new invention, 44
profit margins, 213
profit maximizing price, 63
profit recovery for trademark infringement,
  37
profit-sharing, specifying royalties as,
  201–202
proof of demand for a patented invention,
  217
"proper means" of acquisition of trade
  secrets, 146
"propertization" of traditionally
  nonfringing uses, 154
property, duplicating someone else's, 98
property rules, 38–41, 251
prospect theory, 251
 for copyright, 31
 of patent rights, 19–20
protectable expression, selection, or
  arrangement, 27
*Provident Tradesmens Bank & Trust Co. v.
  Patterson*, 172
proximate cause, 243–245
 applying to patent infringement cases,
  244
 doctrine of, 211
 principles of, 62
 in tort law, 243
prudent licensee, 229
prudent patentee, 229
public display
 over the web, 153
 of a work, 137
public distribution right, 136
public goods, 15
public performance, 137, 148
public purpose, taking of intellectual
  property for, 39
public records, patents as, 12
publication, 136
punitive damages. *See also* damages
 compared to statutory damages, 78
 not applicable to copyright, 30

presumed damages more pernicious
 than, 77
 for a trade secret misappropriation, 26
pure strict liability
 model, 99
 rule, 122

R & D
 costs, 43
 process, 249
Radio Corporation of America (RCA),
  169
real property, 100
reasonable commercial interest in
 trademark law, 184
reasonable royalty, 242–243
 awarding, 228–233
 calculating for patent law, 73
 exceeding the infringer's profit, 232
 factors for calculating, 228
 as a more appropriate form of
  compensation, 214
 recovering for failure to commercialize,
  247
 reflecting profit on sales of an entire
  product, 232
records, cost of searching, 91
registrant in trademark law, 183
registration
 acquiring trademark rights through, 33
 conditioning statutory damages upon,
  83–84
 of copyright, 27
 of patents, copyrights, and trademarks,
  90
 purposes served by, 83
 signaling function provided by, 83
 of trademarked products, 105
registries
 for commercialized patented inventions,
  130
 cost of searching, 91
re-making, unlawful, 11
"remote" harms, 62
rent-seeking behavior, 16
repair, lawful, 11
reproduction right, 28, 135
reputation
 free-riding upon the plaintiff's, 105
 statutory or presumed damages for harm
  to, 88
research cost for a new invention, 43

residual demand for the hit-and-run
    infringer, 236
restitution
    in patent law, 71–74
    as a recovery option in patent law, 264
restitutionary awards
    limiting to willful patent infringement,
        72
    in patent law, 128
    rationale for foreclosing, 12
restitutionary damages
    under the Lanham Act, 84
    in trademark law, 84–95
    in utility patent cases, 73
restitutionary recoveries in patent law, 12
reverse confusion, 34–35, 38
reverse doctrine of equivalents, 11
reverse engineering
    an invention, 14
    legality of, 146
    of a trade secret, 111
reverse passing off, 68
reversionary interest, assignor retaining,
    197
right to exclude, 227
risk aversion of a potential infringer, 48–49
risk-averse users, 148
risk-neutral individual, 48
Rite-Hite Corp. v. Kelley Co., 223–225,
    259
rivalrous things, 13
royalties
    awarding reasonable, 210
    for holdover franchises, 90
    levied on total revenue, 193
    for patent infringement, 74
    for patent law, 73
    per-unit for nonexclusive licenses,
        199–201
    profit-sharing, 201–202
    qualifying as established, 212
    range of possible, 233
    received by the patentee, 192
    for trademark cases, 90
royalty-accruing assignor, 194
running royalties. *See also* continuing
    royalties
    for infringement injuring assignor and
        assignee, 193
    license in exchange for, 196
    versus lump-sum fees, 198

sales diversion, 212, 219, 242
sanction for infringement, 46
satisficing behavior, 20
scenes à faire doctrine, 31
Schlicher problem, 244
scope
    of liability across various bodies of I.P.
        law, 264
    patent strength as a function of, 20
    tradeoff with duration, 23
Scotchmer. *See* Maurer-Scotchmer thesis
search cost, minimizing, 114
searching for trademarks, 91
secondary meaning, 33
secrecy
    caused by penalizing patent nonuse, 252
    owing a duty of, 24
secrecy-enhancing character of trade secret
    law, 26
secrets. *See* trade secret(s)
Section 287 of the Patent Act, 124–127
    applicability to products but not
        processes, 127
    suggested reforms of, 128–130
sellers
    possibility of infringement liability, 141
    uncertainty created by patent law, 143
semiconductor industry, complex patents
    in, 116
Shipman, Asa, 165
shop right, 39
signaling function
    provided by registration, 83
    of trademarks, 66
similarity, inferring copying from, 103
Simon, Herbert, 20
simple model
    implications of, 47–49
    of IPRs, 68
simple negligence rule, 115
small-scale infringements, 71
SmithKline Diagnostics, Inc. v. Helena Corp.,
    218
social benefits, maximizing for patents, 13
social costs
    of infringement, 121
    of patent systems, 17
social justice, liability rules implementing,
    41
social wealth, fair use enhancing, 137
social welfare, reduced by a monopoly, 18

socially optimal amount of search, 114
socially optimal duty of care, 116
Sony Corp. of Am. v. Universal City Studios, 134
sound recordings, 27, 29
sounds as a source signifier, 33
source code of computer programs, 27
source signifiers, 33
sponsorship, conveying a false message of, 34
standard royalty. *See* established royalty
standards of liability, 96
standing, 265
  cannot be created by agreement, 175
  conclusions regarding, 265
  conferring by agreement, 194
  to sue for infringement, 160
standing rules
  conclusions with respect to, 206
  in the Copyright Act of 1976, 181
  developed by the Supreme Court, 164
  justifications for, 176
  in patent law, 178
  toward a theory of rational, 186–206
  under trademark law, 183–186
  in U.S. intellectual property law, 161
Stanley v. Georgia, 149
state common-law copyright, 27
State Industries v. Mor-Flo Industries, 221
state of mind
  under patent law, 99
  separating from liability, 105
  in trademark litigation, 105
status symbols, trademarks as, 36
Statute of Anne, 26
statutory damages. *See also* damages
  as applied by U.S. courts, 80–83
  calculated on actual damages, 81
  conditioning on registration, 83–84
  for copyright infringement, 30
  in copyright law, 74–80
  copyright law and, 77
  limited to one award for all infringements, 80
  low awards with no evidence of damages or profits, 82
  permitting in copyright law, 77
  as a response to underenforcement, 78
  for trademark counterfeiting, 76, 79
  under U.S. copyright law, 69, 70

statutory incentive, damages rules preserving, 84
stochastic R & D process, 249
strategic reasons, patenting for, 17
strict liability, 98
  departure from in copyright law, 102
  versus negligence, 113–120
  with notice or knowledge, 120–130
  patent infringement as, 11
  "pure" versus modified, 121
  rule for patent infringement, 113–115
  standard, 98, 99
  tort, 99, 141
strict liability law, I.P. law appearing as, 264
strict liability model, patent law departing from, 101
"strikingly" similar works, 103
substantial portion of likely purchasers, 35
substantially similar works, 29
substantive intellectual property law, 96
substantive patent law, controlling patent scope, 22
substitutability, 214–215, 218, 255
substitute products, 214
substitutionality, degree of, 214
successive monopoly, 197
successor in title, 176
sui generis system, 3
superior technology, leaving idle, 249
suppression of technology, 253
supracompetitive returns, earned by licensees, 206
SURGE trademark, 91

Taney, Chief Justice, 163
tape loaders, 225
Tapematic, 225
tarnishment, dilution by, 36
tax revenues, producing inventions, 16
taxation, solving the public goods problem, 15
technology
  business of licensing, 204
  suppression of, 249, 253
tie, serving a neutral or procompetitive purpose, 260
tied good, 260
Toeppen, Dennis, 156
"token" articles, 125

tort law
  applying in patent law, 232
  proximate cause doctrine, 243
  strict liability in, 98
trade dress as a source signifier, 33
trade secret(s), 23
  accidental disclosure of, 146
  misappropriation of, 105
  public sale disclosing infringer's activities,
    79
  reverse engineering of, 111
trade secret infringement rule, 135
trade secret law
  close conformance to the simple model of
    IPRs, 68
  compared to patent law, 23–26
  discouraging public dissemination of
    information, 26
  discouraging socially wasteful measures,
    26
  extending the patent damages model to,
    66
  independent discovery defense, 107
  infringement rules of, 144–147
  never characterized as a strict liability
    regime, 105–106
  scope of liability, 265
  social benefits of, 26
  supplementing the patent system, 26
trade secret misappropriation
  private acts difficult to detect, 79
  standing to sue for, 160
trade secret owner, independent discovery
    or reverse engineering and, 24
trade secret protection
  based on common law and state statutory
    law, 23
  circumstances for relying on, 145
  compared to patent protection, 7
  easier to obtain than is patent protection,
    23
  indefinite duration of, 25
  independent discovery defense
    encouraging, 111
  less robust and more vulnerable to
    forfeiture, 24
trademark(s), 32
  as "better" or "more efficient," 86
  as components to larger products, 73
  counterfeit, 36
  as domain names, 155

  economic functions of, 38
  extending the patent damages model to,
    66–68
  as a form of commercial speech, 88
  genericness, 35
  invalidation of, 185
  noncommercial uses diluting, 152
  ownership of, 34–36
  promoting monopolistic competition, 38
  as status symbols, 36
  as vehicles for persuasive advertising,
    38
trademark case, award of defendant's profits
    in, 89
trademark counterfeiting, statutory
    damages, 76, 79
trademark dilution
  federal claims for, 184
  right to prevent, 35
trademark infringement. *See also*
    infringement
  cost of detecting, 79
  defendant's profit from, 86
  as an intentional tort, 85
  licensee cannot sue its own licensor for,
    185
  paradigmatic example of, 67–68
  uncertainty of, 93
trademark law, 32–38
  complementing patent law, 67
  contributory infringement, 134
  damages calculation in, 208
  domain name disputes, 155–158
  first-sale doctrine, 133
  liberality of standing rules, 185
  limitations upon restitutionary damages,
    84–95
  of noncommercial uses, 151
  prevailing on a claim of infringement, 79
  scope of liability, 265
  standing rules, 183–186, 207, 266
  standing under, 161
  strict liability regime, 104–105
  substantially similar mark, 107
  unusual things about, 85–87
  use proscription narrower than patent
    law, 138
trademark licensees, exclusive, 184
trademark protection
  for inherently distinctive words, 33
  use as a prerequisite to, 33

trademark rights
  acquiring through registration, 33
  persistence of, 33
transaction costs, 187
  exempting certain uses under copyright
    law, 147
  of requesting permission to reproduce,
    137
transactional complementarity, 257, 259
transfer, determining whether an
    assignment or a license, 167
transferor, retaining significant rights, 196
trespass law, analogous to patent law, 100
TRIPs Agreement, 21, 23, 113
Truk-Stop restraint, 223
12 Monkeys, 76
Twin Peaks Prods. v. Publications Int'l Ltd.,
    82
two-supplier market scenario, 213
Tycom Corp. v. Redactron Corp., 173
tying good, 260
tying sales of patented and complementary
    products, 259–262
Tyler v. Tuel, 162

U. S. Copyright Act. *See* Copyright Act
U. S. Courts. *See* courts
UCC (Uniform Commercial Code), 142,
    143
unauthorized "publication" of a work, 136
unauthorized uses
  narrower in trade secret, copyright, and
    trademark law, 144
  of protected material, 132
uncertainty
  compelling a patentee to prefer
    nonexclusive licenses, 206
  created by seller and user exposure, 142
  discounting the value of a license to
    reflect, 230
  effect on expectations, 204
  risk of incurring an award of enhanced
    damages and, 60
  surrounding the creation of new
    inventions, 42
uncompensable harms, 244
unconscious copying, 91
underdeterrence risk, 72
underenforcement, statutory damages rule
    as a response to, 78
unfair competition, 32

Uniform Commercial Code (UCC), 142,
    143
Uniform Domain Name Resolution Policy,
    156
uniform federal regulations on marking,
    129
Uniform Trade Secret Act. *See* UTSA
unintentional infringement, 114. *See also*
    innocent infringement
United States Patent Act. *See* Patent Act
unlawful manufacture, controlling, 140
unpatented goods
  EMVR applying to, 223
  lost profits on sales of, 222–227
unpatented spare parts. *See* derivative
    goods
unprotectable ideas or facts, 27
unused inventions, creation of, 144
unused patents, 251. *See also* idle patent
unwitting infringer, penalizing, 141
upstream monopoly, 197
U.S. Patent Act. *See* Patent Act
users
  burden of proving fair use, 147
  possibility of infringement liability, 141
  uncertainty created by patent law, 143
utility condition for patent protection, 8
utility models, 21, 145
utility patent cases, 71
utility patents, inventions protectable under,
    7
UTSA (Uniform Trade Secret Act), 23
  awards authorized by, 69
  qualifying right to an injunction, 25

variable costs versus fixed, 218
VCRs, selling, 134
vicarious infringement in copyright law,
    134
*Video Aided Instruction, Inc. v. Y & S Express,
    Inc.*, 81
videocassettes, bootleg, 82
Visual Artists Rights Act, 29

waiver of the assignor's right to sue, 194
Waterman v. Mackenzie, 164–166
  categorical approach to standing, 173
  no overriding need for the rigid standing
    rules exemplified by, 207
  standing rules exemplified by, 266
  transfer as an assignment, 168

webcasting, 29
websites
    addresses for, 155
    authorized versus unauthorized access to, 153
Western Electric Co. v. Pacent Reproducer Corp., 168
"who is liable" question, 97
Wildlife Express Corp. v. Carol Wright Sales, Inc., 81
willful dilution, 95
willful infringement, 87, 128
    in copyright cases, 30
    in trademark cases, 71
    in trademark law, 90
willfulness under patent law, 99

willing licensor/licensee approach, 229
    awarding a reasonable royalty, 229
    estimating a reasonable royalty, 231
Woods v. Universal City Studios, 75
working requirements
    consistently avoided by U.S. law, 254
    countries not imposing, 254
    for patents, 251
works, "strikingly" similar, 103
works made for hire, 27, 28
World Trade Organization (WTO), 21
written description requirement under patent law, 9

Zazu Designs v. L'Oreal, S.A., 86
zero-cost assumption, 58–59